I love you madly

I love you madly

MARIE-ANTOINETTE AND COUNT FERSEN – THE SECRET LETTERS

EVELYN FARR

PETER OWEN
LONDON AND CHICAGO

PETER OWEN PUBLISHERS
81 Ridge Road, London N8 9NP

Peter Owen books are distributed in the USA and Canada by
Independent Publishers Group/Trafalgar Square
814 North Franklin Street, Chicago, IL 60610, USA

First published in English in Great Britain 2016 by
Peter Owen Publishers

HARDBACK ISBN 978-0-7206-1877-8
EPUB ISBN 978-0-7206-1878-5
MOBIPOCKET ISBN 978-0-7206-1879-2
PDF ISBN 978-0-7206-1880-8

Typeset by Octavo Smith Publishing Services

Printed by Printworks Global Ltd, London and Hong Kong

'I love you madly and never, ever can I be
a moment without adoring you.'
Marie-Antoinette to Axel von Fersen, 4 January 1792

'I love you and will love you madly all my life.'
Axel von Fersen to Marie-Antoinette, 29 October 1791

For my friends

ACKNOWLEDGEMENTS

Without the constant encouragement and interest of two dear friends, this book would never have been written, and in consequence the discoveries made during my research would not have seen the light of day. I want to express my deepest gratitude to Jérôme Barbet for his friendship and kindness, his encyclopaedic knowledge of eighteenth-century French history and his boundless enthusiasm for the story of Marie-Antoinette and Fersen. His scientific approach to analysing Fersen's handwriting guided me towards my discoveries in the letters. I am also very grateful for his generous help in verifying the words and passages discovered, for correcting the French manuscript and for his moral support over many months of work during difficult times. Sincere thanks are also due to the charming Nathalie Colas des Francs, author of a key biography of Marie-Antoinette's friend the Duchesse de Polignac, for correcting the French manuscript and for her valued friendship.

I should like to thank the many kind friends at home and across the globe who have helped me in so many ways – by debating ideas, visiting me in hospital and providing online encouragement and support. This book is dedicated to them all.

I am very grateful to Mme Valerie Nachef of the University of Cergy-Pontoise for her interest in my work and for discussing her discoveries in Marie-Antoinette's coded letters to Fersen.[1]

Warmest thanks go to Marie Ohlsén, Annika Karlsson and Morgan Brålin of Löfstad Slott in Sweden, as well as to Olof Hermelin, director of the Östergötland Museum, and the museum team. They thoroughly spoilt me on my visit to Löfstad, where I spent an unforgettable day getting to know Axel von Fersen on his home turf.

The Archives Nationales in Paris and the Swedish Archives in Stockholm and Vadstena were helpful and prompt in providing documents. Thanks are also due to the Kent History and Library Centre in Maidstone for the Duke of Dorset's archive. I am very grateful to His Grace the Duke of Devonshire and the Chatsworth House Trust for a letter from Lafayette to Georgiana, Duchess of Devonshire, mentioned by Fersen and Marie-Antoinette in their correspondence during the French Revolution, as well as for permission to quote the marvellously gossipy letters of the Duke of Dorset and Lady Elizabeth Foster to Georgiana. The assistance of Aidan Haley of the Chatsworth archives was much appreciated.

I enjoyed two delightful meetings in Stockholm with Mme Margareta Reuterskiöld, a descendant of Axel von Fersen's sister Hedda and great-granddaughter of the first editor of Fersen's papers, Baron Rudolf Klinckowström. In explaining the complicated history of the family archives, she gave me some very interesting insights into the conclusions of Swedish historian Alma Söderhjelm on Fersen's relationship with Marie-Antoinette. I am very grateful for her interest in this book, which I hope meets her expectations.

It is hard to find the words to express all that I feel for the dedicated haematology doctors and nurses who saved my life at University College Hospital London – without their superb care and expertise I would have been unable to continue my research. They have my profound respect, admiration and gratitude.

Evelyn Farr
London

CONTENTS

A NOTE ON LANGUAGE

Almost all the documentary sources in this book are in French. It was the language Axel von Fersen and his family used at home and in their correspondence. All translations in this book are mine. I am very grateful to Lisa Almond and Anna-Lena Berg for help with Swedish.

English sources are transcribed from the original, with spelling and punctuation corrected where necessary.

ILLUSTRATIONS

between pages 208 and 209

All photographs are from the author's collection except where marked.

MARIE-ANTOINETTE AND AXEL VON FERSEN CHRONOLOGY

1755

4 September: Birth of Count Hans Axel von Fersen, eldest son of Count Fredrik Axel von Fersen and his wife Hedwig (née de La Gardie), at the Fersen Palace in Stockholm.

2 November: Birth in Vienna of Archduchess Marie-Antoinette (Maria-Antonia), daughter of Holy Roman Emperor Franz I and Empress Maria-Theresa.

1770

16 May: Marriage of Marie-Antoinette to Louis-Auguste, Dauphin of France, celebrated at Versailles.

3 June: Fersen leaves Sweden for his Grand Tour of the Continent.

1773

15 November: Fersen arrives in Paris after completing his studies in Germany and Italy.

19 November: Fersen meets the Dauphine Marie-Antoinette for the first time during his presentation to the Royal Family at Versailles.

November–December: Fersen regularly attends the Dauphine's balls. He visits Versailles on November 18, 19, 24 (ball) and 27, then on December 4, 6 (ball), 10 (ball), 11, 21 (ball) and 28.

1774

January: Fersen visits Versailles on 1 January and again on 10, 17 and 31 to attend the Dauphine's balls.

30 January: Profiting from her mask, Marie-Antoinette talks to Fersen for a long time at the Paris opera ball without his recognizing her. The following day he goes to her ball at Versailles.

February: Carnival; Fersen notes in his diary: 'I attended only Mme la Dauphine's balls.'

10 May: Death of Louis XV. The Dauphin becomes Louis XVI and Marie-Antoinette is now Queen of France. Her husband presents her with the Petit Trianon.

12 May: Fersen leaves Paris for England.

December: Fersen returns to Sweden. He becomes a captain in Gustav III's bodyguard.

1777

August: The marriage of Louis XVI and Marie-Antoinette is finally consummated.

1778

22 August: Fersen returns to Paris after spending several months in London, where he had failed to secure an heiress as his bride. Marie-Antoinette is pregnant with her first child.

25 August: Fersen goes to Court at Versailles. 'The Queen, who is charming, said when she saw me, "Ah! It's an old acquaintance." The rest of the family didn't utter a word to me.'

September–May 1779: Fersen becomes a member of the Queen's intimate circle at Versailles and the Petit Trianon. In a letter to his father on 15 November he describes her 'the most amiable princess I know.'

19 December: Marie-Antoinette gives birth to a daughter, Marie Thérèse Charlotte, known as Madame Royale.

1779

January–June: Fersen and Marie-Antoinette see each other often at Versailles and at opera balls in Paris. She helps him gain a commission in the French army being assembled in Normandy to invade England during the American War of Independence.

April: Marie-Antoinette, ill with measles, scandalizes the Court by spending a month alone at the Petit Trianon with four male friends acting as her nurses.

28 June: Fersen bids farewell to the Queen and on 1 July leaves Paris for his regiment at Le Havre.

July: According to the memoirs of Mme Campan and the abbé de Véri, Marie-Antoinette suffers a miscarriage.

23 December: Fersen returns to Versailles when the invasion of England is abandoned. He is invited to a Christmas Eve dinner hosted by Mme de Lamballe for the Queen and spends several days at Versailles before returning to Paris.

1780

January–March: Fersen resumes his place in the Queen's circle. They are often together at opera balls. Courtiers have started to notice Marie-Antoinette's love for him and are jealous. She helps him to obtain a post as aide-de-camp to General Rochambeau in the French army being sent to America.

23 March: Fersen leaves Versailles for Brest.

16 May: Fersen leaves for America on board the frigate *Jason*.

October: First known letter from Fersen to Marie-Antoinette.

1780–3

Fersen spends three years on active service with the French army during the American War of Independence. He is present at the siege of Yorktown and acts as an interpreter for Rochambeau with American and British generals. Marie-Antoinette obtains a post for him as colonel in the Deux-Ponts regiment. He participates in the Caribbean campaign before returning to France when peace is agreed.

1781

22 October: Marie-Antoinette gives birth to the Dauphin, Louis-Joseph.

1783

23 June: Fersen returns to Paris and Versailles, intending to spend a whole year in France. Marie-Antoinette has proposed that he becomes proprietary colonel of the Royal Suédois regiment.

15 July: Fersen leaves a house party at the château of Dangu to visit Marie-Antoinette in private.

31 July: Fersen writes to his sister Sophie that he will never marry 'because I cannot belong to the only person I want to belong to, the only one who truly loves me'.

25 August: Rumours circulate at Court that the Queen is pregnant. She is not happy about it.

20 September: Fersen leaves Marie-Antoinette to return to Sweden at his father's insistence.

15 October (to June 1784): Fersen accompanies Gustav III on a tour of Italy.

3 November: Marie-Antoinette suffers a miscarriage at Fontainebleau.

7 November: Start of Fersen's letter register, which opens with a letter to Marie-Antoinette under the code name 'Josephine'.

1784

25 May: Last letter from Fersen to Marie-Antoinette before his return to Versailles.

7 June: Fersen arrives at Versailles with Gustav III.

20 June: Fersen feigns an illness to escape the Swedish royal party and spend some time privately at Versailles.

21 June: Marie-Antoinette hosts a party at the Petit Trianon for Gustav III and his entourage.

19 July: Fersen leaves Versailles, arriving back in Sweden on 2 August after an absence of six years.

20 July: A new series of 'Josephine' letters starts.

17 August: Marie-Antoinette confirms that she is pregnant in a letter to her brother Joseph II.

Autumn: Fersen begins to advise Marie-Antoinette on political affairs, writing to her regarding Austria's demands for access to the Scheldt waterway controlled by Holland.

1785

27 March: Marie-Antoinette gives birth to her second son, Louis-Charles, Duc de Normandie (called the 'Chou d'Amour' in his mother's letters to Mme de Polignac).

15 April: Last letter from Fersen to Marie-Antoinette before their reunion.

8 May: Fersen returns to France. His letter register reveals that he has lodgings at Versailles in the Hôtel de Luynes, close to the Queen's apartments in the palace.

22 June: The 'Josephine' correspondence recommences when Fersen goes to his regiment at Landrecies.

25–31 July: Fersen pays a secret visit to Marie-Antoinette.

1 August: Fersen returns to Landrecies. He remains with his regiment until 27 September.

15 August: Cardinal de Rohan is arrested during investigations into the Diamond Necklace Affair.

26 September: Last letter from Fersen to Marie-Antoinette until 2 June 1786.

30 September: Fersen returns to Court, dividing his time between the Hôtel de Luynes at Versailles and a small pied-à-terre in Paris.

4 October: Fersen's 'official' return to Versailles.

13 October–12 November: Fersen and Marie-Antoinette are at Fontainebleau.

November–June 1786: Fersen spends most of his time at Versailles with Marie-Antoinette.

1786

March: Announcement of Marie-Antoinette's pregnancy. The birth is expected at the end of June. Fersen postpones his return to Sweden from May to the end of June.

2–10 June: Fersen is at Valenciennes with his regiment.

11–25 June: Fersen is with Marie-Antoinette at Versailles while Louis XVI visits Cherbourg.

28 June: The 'Josephine' correspondence restarts. Fersen spends some time in England on his way back to Sweden.

9 July: Marie-Antoinette gives birth to her second daughter, Sophie Hélène Béatrice.

26 July: Fersen arrives in Sweden.

1787

30 April: Fersen leaves Sweden to return to France.

15–20 May: Fersen inspects his regiment at Maubeuge.

21 May–21 June: Fersen lodges in secret in the Queen's private apartments at Versailles during the illness and death of little Madame Sophie.

19 June: Death of Madame Sophie.

21 June: Marie-Antoinette shuts herself away at the Petit Trianon with her sister-in-law Madame Elisabeth to mourn her daughter.

23 June: Fersen returns to Maubeuge.

4 July: First letter sent in code in the 'Josephine' correspondence.

5–30 July: Fersen returns to Versailles to comfort Marie-Antoinette.

August: Fersen spends the whole month at Maubeuge with his regiment.

September–5 October: Fersen is at Paris and Versailles.

5–18 October: Fersen moves his regiment to Valenciennes.

6 October: First letter recorded in invisible ink from Fersen to Marie-Antoinette.

19 October–15 April 1788: Fersen divides his time between Paris and his secret lodgings with the Queen at Versailles. She has ordered a Swedish stove to be installed in his apartment in the palace.

1788

18 April: The 'Josephine' correspondence recommences after Fersen's departure for Sweden.

June–24 October: Fersen spends most of his time in Sweden attached to Gustav III's headquarters' staff in Finland during the Russo-Swedish War.

13 October: Last letter to Marie-Antoinette before Fersen leaves Sweden for France.

6 November: Fersen returns to Paris.

November–June 1789: Fersen divides his time between Paris and his secret lodgings with Marie-Antoinette at Versailles.

1789

January–13 June: Fersen's expenses show that he spends most of his time at Versailles.

16–22 March: Fersen inspects his regiment at Valenciennes.

5 May: Opening of the States General at Versailles.

4 June: Death of the Dauphin from tuberculosis. Louis-Charles becomes Dauphin.

13 June: Fersen rejoins his regiment at Valenciennes.

16 June: The 'Josephine' correspondence restarts. Fersen wants his regiment to march to Versailles to protect the Royal Family as unrest in Paris grows.

14 July: Fall of the Bastille.

16 July: Flight of the King's younger brother the Comte d'Artois, Marie-Antoinette's friends the Polignacs and her reader the abbé de Vermond.

28 August: Last letter to Marie-Antoinette in Fersen's register until 1791.

24 September: Fersen leaves Valenciennes to establish himself – this time openly – in the palace of Versailles.

6 October: The palace is stormed by the mob, accompanied by paid assassins who try to kill the Queen. Two of her bodyguards are massacred. Fersen is 'a witness to everything'. Louis XVI agrees to go to Paris. Fersen accompanies the royal cortège. The Royal Family move into the palace of the Tuileries.

27–28 October: Fersen starts visiting the King and Queen in secret at the Tuileries. He takes charge of their secret diplomatic correspondence.

24 December: Intimate reunion of Marie-Antoinette and Fersen for the first time since the Royal Family's arrival in Paris.

29 December: Fersen leaves Paris. He spends a few days at Valenciennes before going to Aix-la-Chapelle.

1790

January: Fersen visits Gustav's chamberlain Baron Taube at Aix-la-Chapelle
and becomes the King of Sweden's secret envoy to Louis XVI and
Marie-Antoinette. He returns to Paris around 18 January.

20 February: Death of Marie-Antoinette's brother, Joseph II. The new
emperor is her brother Leopold, whom she barely knows.

February–June: Fersen sees Marie-Antoinette 'freely' at the Tuileries.

June–October: Fersen lodges at Auteuil, from where he visits Marie-Antoinette
frequently at the château of Saint-Cloud.

November: The Court returns to the Tuileries.

1791

January–June: Fersen organizes the Royal Family's escape from Paris.

18 April: The Royal Family is prevented by a mob from leaving the Tuileries
to spend Easter at Saint-Cloud.

20 June: Fersen drives the Royal Family out of Paris as far as Bondy, where
Louis XVI orders him to leave them.

21 June: The Royal Family is stopped at Varennes. The National Assembly
sends three deputies to bring them back to Paris under armed guard.
Louis XVI is stripped of his powers. They arrive back in Paris on 25 June.

23 June: Fersen learns of the arrest at Arlon, while on his way to join the
Royal Family at Montmédy.

25 June: Fersen arrives in Brussels to discuss measures to save the Royal
Family with the Comte de Mercy, Marie-Antoinette's confidant and
former Austrian Ambassador to France.

27 June: Fersen manages to smuggle a letter through to the Tuileries.

28 June: Marie-Antoinette smuggles a note out of the Tuileries to Fersen.

July: Marie-Antoinette starts negotiations with constitutional deputies to
save the monarchy.

27 July: Having finally received an answer from Louis XVI and
Marie-Antoinette and held discussions with the Austrians, Louis XVI's
brothers and Gustav III, Fersen is sent by the King of Sweden to
negotiate with Leopold II in Vienna.

2 August–26 September: Fersen is left dangling by the Austrians in Vienna
and Prague. They finally refuse to agree to Gustav III's demands for the
assembly of a counter-revolutionary force.

20 August: The private correspondence between Marie-Antoinette and
Fersen, interrupted for seven weeks, finally restarts when he receives a
note from her forwarded by the Comte de Mercy.

13 September: Louis XVI accepts the constitution under duress. The Royal Family is released from imprisonment, but they are still under close surveillance.

October–August 1792: Fersen returns to Brussels, where he is Ambassador for Gustav III for French affairs. At the same time, he corresponds with Marie-Antoinette and directs Louis XVI's secret diplomacy with the Baron de Breteuil. He demands permission to go to Paris.

1792

11 February: Disguised as a diplomatic courier and travelling on a false passport, Fersen leaves Brussels for Paris.

13–14 February: Fersen spends the night and the whole day with Marie-Antoinette at the Tuileries before a meeting with Louis XVI. He fails to persuade the King to undertake another escape, and Marie-Antoinette refuses to save herself and leave her husband.

24 February: Fersen is back in Brussels.

1 March: Sudden death of Leopold II. The new emperor is Marie-Antoinette's nephew, Franz II.

16 March: Gustav III is fatally injured at a masked ball in Stockholm. The assassin, Jakob Anckarström, is a Swedish Jacobin.

29 March: Death of Gustav III. His son Gustav IV Adolf succeeds him under the regency of Gustav's brother, the Duke of Södermanland. Fersen is maintained in his post.

20 April: France declares war on Austria.

20 June: The Tuileries are invaded and the lives of the Royal Family are threatened.

10 August: The Jacobins have brought enough troops to Paris to storm the Tuileries. A dreadful massacre ensues, although the Royal Family has already taken shelter in the Assembly.

13 August: The Royal Family is imprisoned in the Temple.

2–7 September: Massacres of everyone arrested after 10 August take place in Paris and other cities. The Queen's friend, the Princesse de Lamballe, is butchered.

22 September: France is declared a republic.

9 November: Fersen leaves Brussels for Düsseldorf just before the French army moves in.

10–26 December: Louis XVI is tried by the National Convention.

1793

20 January: Louis XVI is condemned to death.

21 January: Execution of Louis XVI.

20 April: Fersen returns to Brussels.

3 July: Louis-Charles, now Louis XVII, is separated from Marie-Antoinette in the Temple.

2 August: Marie-Antoinette is transferred to the Conciergerie.

15–16 October: Marie-Antoinette is tried by the Revolutionary Tribunal. She is condemned to death at 4 a.m. on the morning of her execution.

16 October: Execution of Marie-Antoinette.

I
INTRODUCTION

In preparing this new edition of Marie-Antoinette's correspondence with Axel von Fersen, I examined high-resolution digital images of all the letters to be found in French and Swedish archives. The blacked-out passages, completely indecipherable on microfilm or in print-outs, were much less obscure on a computer screen. This enabled me to read, in some cases for the first time in more than two hundred years, deleted words and passages in Fersen's letters to the Queen as well as a few words in her letters to him, changing the entire tenor of their correspondence.

The destruction and dispersal of Fersen's archives since the nineteenth century has made the task of transcribing the correspondence and comparing it with his letter register even more difficult, but it is the only way to understand its importance. What is absolutely beyond doubt is that today we possess only an infinitesimal amount of the total number of letters exchanged. It would appear that Fersen himself started the process of destruction – the deletion of entire paragraphs, the copies made of certain letters and his editorial marks on others suggest that he intended to follow the example of many of his contemporaries and write his memoirs on the French Revolution. He mentions the idea in a letter on 30 October 1791 to his friend Baron Taube, shortly after Marie-Antoinette's death.

> This dreadful event has made me regret even more the loss of my memoirs since 1780. I used to write them every day. I left them in Paris in 1791; when I left I dared not take them with me, and the person with whom I deposited them burnt them, for fear they would be seized in his possession. They contained precious notes on the Revolution which would have served to write the history of this epoch and make the King and Queen better known. I regret them all the

more because my memory is poor, and I no longer remember every-thing I have done myself. One would have been able to understand how unhappy this princess was, how justly she felt her misfortune, to what degree she was affected by it and how her great soul knew how to forgive and rise above injustice by a consciousness of the good she did and wished to be able to do.[2]

His diary lost, Fersen appears to have gathered together his papers, including what remained of his correspondence with the Queen, with a view to publishing a work explaining his role in the flight to Varennes. It seems unlikely that he would have destroyed any original documents he still possessed, since after Marie-Antoinette's death he wrote to his sister: 'I've sent an order to Paris to buy everything of hers that can be found; everything I already have is sacred to me. They are relics which are and will always be the object of my constant adoration.'[3] Doubtless he kept the original letters after having made copies with the passages containing intimate details omitted. Unfortunately he was assassinated in 1810 before he could complete his work, and the loss of so many of his papers is linked to the terrible circumstances of his death.

Fersen and his sister Countess Sophie Piper were accused quite wrongly of having poisoned the new Crown Prince from Denmark. He had been offered the Swedish crown after Gustav IV Adolf was forced to abdicate in a coup, but he died suddenly of a stroke. On the day of the Prince's funeral, 20 June 1810, Fersen was lynched and murdered by a mob in the heart of Stockholm, with the complicity of the Swedish government who saw him as an obstacle to their plan to replace the Crown Prince with a French republican general, Bernadotte. Sophie, equally implicated in this non-existent 'plot', was arrested after her brother's murder and detained in the island fortress of Vaxholm. Both were eventually cleared of all suspicion, but unfortunately it was too late for Fersen, who had fallen victim to the vengeance of Karl XIII, former Duke of Södermanland. Their relations had always been strained, not only because of their political differences but because of the marked preference of Karl's wife for Fersen.

Sophie could not even organize the funeral of her adored brother. It was their younger brother Fabian who took charge of everything, including Fersen's papers, although he did not receive them until they had been thoroughly examined as part of the investigation into the 'crime' supposedly committed by his siblings. Fabian's letters to Sophie at this dreadful time show that she had asked him for all the souvenirs of Marie-Antoinette that Axel owned, including his correspondence with the Queen. 'Nyblom is bringing you', Fabian wrote, 'a packet containing the late Axel's French correspondence. It's all of it that I could find. The other papers are all diplomatic and relate to the Congress of Rastatt and to his affairs as First Minister of the King's Household.'[4]

This packet clearly failed to meet Sophie's expectations – it contained Marie-Antoinette's correspondence with Barnave as well as other political documents she entrusted to Fersen, since these are all now to be found in the Piper family archives, but not the letters he exchanged with the Queen. Sophie knew everything about their affair and must have hoped for something more personal. Fabian answered her request with further information on the fate of Axel's papers.

> Regarding the history of the portfolios . . . all the portfolios are the same; there are none with hidden locks. They all have normal locks, and I know Nyblom said you wanted to have the secret portfolios. That's why I didn't mind keeping the portfolios from you. I'm keeping them to lock away all my brother's papers which, as I told you last summer, were given to me in a box by the men who had read through them. They had removed all the papers from the drawers and other places where they were secured. Since then no one else has seen these papers, which could be of no interest to anyone. I looked through most of them and took out all those relating to financial affairs . . . For the rest, in the evenings after our small society had retired, Louise and I occupied ourselves in taking extracts from my late brother's letters, which have been printed. These letters were not such as to be left in the hands of editors – they contain expressions that were appropriate at the time they were written but are not so today, and so we had to modify and suppress some sentences.

Is he referring to the Marie-Antoinette correspondence here or to Swedish matters, since the only papers printed at this time were published to clear Fersen of the death of the Crown Prince? Fabian assured Sophie that:

> My brother's manuscripts are already secured, for I sent them to the library at Steninge . . . There was no list made of Axel's papers, and the

examination will be made in two or three days . . . besides, I know positively, because he told me so himself, that after 13 March 1809 he burned a number of papers.[5]

It is clear that he was equivocating in order not to give Fersen's correspondence with Marie-Antoinette to Sophie. He definitely kept those letters that survived, since they passed eventually to his daughter, Louise Gyldenstolpe, who sold the entire Fersen family archive to her cousin Baron Rudolf Klinckowström in order to settle her gambling debts. The baron, like his great-uncle a soldier and diplomat, wasted no time in publishing an edition of Fersen's correspondence with Marie-Antoinette and others, revealing his role during the Revolution but suppressing many details of his career in France prior to 1789. It is from his book *Le Comte de Fersen et la Cour de France* (1877–8) that we derive the image of Axel von Fersen as the devoted, respectful and, above all, purely platonic friend of the Queen of France.

In 1930 the Swedish historian Alma Söderhjelm edited unpublished passages from Fersen's diary as well as letters to his sister Sophie that reveal his true feelings for Marie-Antoinette. She postulated correctly that Marie-Antoinette was the mystery correspondent 'Josephine' in Fersen's letter register. She also published a note suppressed by Klinckowström, in which the Queen addressed Fersen as 'the most loved and most loving of men'; but of the rest of the correspondence she found no trace. Klinckowström's son Axel told her that his father had burnt all the letters for fear that someone would try to read beneath the many redacted passages. The Fersen archive was subsequently deposited in the Swedish national archives by Baron Axel's daughter. It includes only eight letters from Marie-Antoinette to Fersen; all date from 1792 and give news of the Queen but are written by her secretary François Goguelat.

In 1982 the French Archives Nationales nevertheless bought from the Klinckowström family a quantity of letters from the Fersen/Marie-Antoinette correspondence that had supposedly been destroyed. All bar six of these letters date from 1791 and 1792. Letters from the period 1780–8 have never been found, and my recent research has led me to the regrettable conclusion that they may well have been destroyed by Fersen himself in 1792 (see Part IV). It is doubtful that the archive purchased by Baron Rudolf Klinckowström in the nineteenth century contained these letters; if it had, he would have published them after expunging them of any 'delicate' passages, just as he did for the letters from the revolutionary period.

This collection contains all the letters exchanged by Marie-Antoinette and Fersen that it has been possible to trace – including six previously unpublished letters and more than twenty passages discovered by the author under blacked-out lines in the text. Explored in detail and set in context by cross-references to Fersen's letter register, diary and other unpublished documents, they portray one of history's most extraordinary and powerful love stories.

II
ANALYSIS OF THE CORRESPONDENCE

In order to understand the full import of Marie-Antoinette's correspondence with Axel von Fersen, it is essential to place it in its historical context; it then becomes clear that what survives today is but a tiny fraction of a frequent correspondence that continued – with breaks when they were together – for at least twelve years.

The First Meeting

Count Axel von Fersen met Marie-Antoinette for the first time in November 1773. Both had just turned eighteen. She was the Dauphine of France – lively, frivolous, flirtatious and full of mischief. He was the eldest son of the Grand Marshal of Sweden, rounding off his Grand Tour with six months in Paris. The attraction between them was immediate. At a masked opera ball, profiting from her disguise she spoke to him at length without revealing her identity. He became a regular attender at her Court balls at Versailles, and he mentioned her frequently in his diary. But Fersen left France in May 1774 two days after she became queen and did not reappear in her life until August 1778. He then became a member of Marie-Antoinette's inner circle, describing her as 'a charming princess'. In 1779, gossip began to spread about the Queen's liking for the handsome Swedish count; she always danced with him at the opera balls, he used to dine in the private apartments, and young French courtiers were very jealous of him.

In July 1779 Fersen left the amusement of Versailles to join the French army being mustered in Normandy in preparation of an invasion of England; but after months of inaction the idea was abandoned. He returned to Court on 23 December, and on Christmas Eve was invited to a celebration hosted for the Queen by Mme de Lamballe, her friend and superintendent of her household. At the beginning of 1780, as France became more deeply involved in the American War of Independence, Marie-Antoinette helped Fersen obtain a colonel's commission and a post as aide-de-camp to General Rochambeau. He spent his final days before leaving for America with her at Versailles. A letter sent to Gustav III of Sweden on 10 April 1780 by his Ambassador to France, Count Creutz, describes a sad farewell.

> Young Count Fersen has been so well treated by the Queen that several people have taken umbrage at it. I confess that I cannot help believing she has a strong inclination for him; I've seen too many positive indications to doubt it. Young Count Fersen conducted himself admirably in these circumstances by his modesty and reserve, and above all by the decision he took to go to America. In going away he avoided all the dangers, but it evidently required a strength of will above his age to overcome this seduction. The Queen couldn't take her eyes off him during the final days; when she looked at him they were filled with tears.[1]

Baron Evert Taube, who became Fersen's best friend and the lover of his sister Sophie, sent a letter to Gustave III by the same courier, describing in detail just how Marie-Antoinette had succeeded in fixing Fersen in her inner circle of friends.

> The Queen has always distinguished Swedes who have appeared at Court . . . She has particularly noticed young Count Axel. Every time she came to the opera ball this winter, she would walk with him. She even retired to a box with him, where she remained a long time talking to him. Envious people found it astonishing that the Queen should always promenade with young Count Axel, a foreigner, and they were all asking: 'But my God, who is this young Swede then, that the Queen always walks with him?' It was even said: 'But the Queen has never stayed so long at the opera balls as she has done this year!'
>
> I believe that all these jealous remarks finally came to the Queen's ears. It only increased her fancy to see the young count; but in order not to make it too obvious she decided to admit more Swedes to her society. She therefore arranged for M. de Steding, to whom the King has spoken a few times since his return from America, to be ordered to sup in the private apartments. Steding was taken in by it and believed that he owed

this distinction to his fine eyes. There was a great outcry that M. de Steding was shown such favour; one wanted to know if he was a gentleman of sufficiently ancient standing to be allowed to take supper in the private apartments with the King. All this was less than agreeable for our Steding. But in the end the Queen gained by it, because all the clamour fell on him; a week later, and while everyone was still protesting strongly against the favour shown to M. de Steding, young Count Axel was ordered to join the King's suppers. But as these suppers only take place once or twice a week, the Queen's ladies, Mme de Lamballe, the Comtesse de Polignac and the Comtesse d'Ossun hosted little parties and games in their apartments, to which the Queen always came and often the King, too. Count Axel was always present at those suppers as well as all the suppers in the private apartments. He also used to be present at all the Queen's games. These games are blind man's buff and what we call at home: '*war tar sinn, sa tar jag minn, sa far de andra inte*'. Young Count Axel greatly distinguished himself at these games, which greatly pleased the King and the Queen. These games even continued after his departure for Brest. I humbly beg Your Majesty to say nothing of this to his father or mother, nor to anybody, because if word were to get back here it could perhaps do him harm.[2]

The game of blind man's buff in which Fersen so distinguished himself offered the 'blind man', whose eyes were covered, the opportunity to touch the other players. Fragonard, favoured artist of eighteenth-century libertines, depicted a version of this popular game where the potential for caresses is implicit. Naturally, everyone was watching Fersen and Marie-Antoinette. Given the way gossip from Versailles inevitably always found its way back to Stockholm, Fersen talks of walking with the Queen at the opera balls and dining in the private apartments in his letters to his father, but risqué games are certainly never mentioned. She remained 'the most amiable princess I know'. It is clear that he was far from insensible to her charms; had he not been interested, he would have avoided her, just as he always eluded women who did not please him. But Marie-Antoinette was the Queen of France and Fersen a foreign interloper; it was out of the question for him to declare his feelings first. He left France with Rochambeau's army in May 1780. It was to be three years before he returned.

The First Letter

The first known letter in the correspondence between Marie-Antoinette and Axel von Fersen dates from October 1780. Writing to his father from Newport, Rhode Island, Fersen says he is sending a letter to the Queen to ask for her help in obtaining a post in a line regiment. His position as an aide-de-camp bored him extremely and he wanted to become commandant of the Duc de Lauzun's Legion.

> The Duc de Lauzun is writing about it to the Queen, who has a great deal of kindness for him. She has a little for me, too, and I am also writing to her about it.[3]

During the American War of Independence Fersen received letters from Europe very infrequently. A year later he was still Rochambeau's aide-de-camp and had received no letters from home since July 1780. He had to wait two more years for news about his military career; Lauzun, it seems, did not have the influence he boasted of, as Fersen explained to his father on 22 May 1782.

> You know that in September 1780 M. de Lauzun offered me the post of colonel commandant of his corps, which he afterwards proposed to cede to me . . . He said he would arrange this business. It failed owing to Court intrigues which it would be too long and futile to detail here. After the siege of Yorktown [September 1781], M. de Lauzun repeated his offer. I hesitated for a moment. I had written to you the first time, my dear father, but I never received a reply to my letter. I also wrote to the King [Gustav III] by the same post. I don't know if my letters arrived; in this uncertainty I acted as I had the first time, and I accepted Lauzun's offer. He took responsibility for arranging this affair. I notified Staël of it so he could discuss it with the Queen [Marie-Antoinette] . . . Lauzun and Staël write to tell me that it cannot be done at the moment for reasons which Lauzun will explain to me on his arrival, but that the Queen, who still has a great deal of kindness for me and takes an interest in me, has arranged something else for me. Lauzun tells me that she has arranged with M. de Castries that I shall be a colonel attached to his legion with a commission and a salary of 6000 *livres*, and Staël says that she has asked for the post of lieutenant-colonel in the Deux-Ponts regiment

and that I'm going to get it. Their letters bear the same date. I don't know which to believe.[4]

Staël proved to be better informed. Fersen wrote again to his father on 3 October 1782. 'I am in full possession and exercise of my post as lieutenant-colonel in the Royal Deux-Ponts regiment, and I'm delighted to be an aide-de-camp no longer.'[5] Had he received a reply to the letter he wrote to Marie-Antoinette in October 1780? He certainly must have received confirmation of his posting and his new commission from someone well placed at Court.

'Happiness'

On his return to France in June 1783 Fersen made his way straight to Versailles. In the letters he then started to send to his family in Sweden, he talks about his great 'happiness' – a happiness that depended above all on the acquisition of a post that would guarantee his presence in France for several months each year. His relationship with Marie-Antoinette had become intimate, and she did everything in her power to establish him in France. Fersen became proprietary colonel of the Royal Suédois (Royal Swedish) regiment in the French army, despite his father's desire that he pursue a career in Sweden.

The 'Josephine' Correspondence

From the summer of 1783 Fersen's love affair with the Queen of France obliged him to begin a double life that would continue until her death. Their secret liaison required trusted means of communication and gave rise to a double correspondence. On matters regarding his regiment or diplomatic affairs Fersen could write openly to 'the Queen of France'. But the overwhelming majority of his letters to Marie-Antoinette are recorded in his letter register under the name 'Josephine'. Why 'Josephine'? Possibly because Marie-Antoinette's third name was Josèphe, although within her family she had always been called Antoinette (and even 'Antoine' in her childhood in Austria).

The 'Josephine' letters are completely anonymous; in them, Marie-Antoinette is never addressed by name, and there is no signature. They can be identified by Fersen's notes in the margin (date received and date of his reply), corroborated by entries in his letter register.[6] Fersen started keeping this register, listing letters sent to all his correspondents, in November 1783. He also noted letters addressed to the 'Queen of France', but there are only six between 1783 and 1791. By contrast, the correspondence with Marie-Antoinette under the code name 'Josephine' was very regular. It actually started before Fersen began his register. The first recorded letter to 'Josephine' is No. 11, dated 7 November 1783. The numbering would recommence every time the correspondents separated, which means that he sent at least ten letters to Marie-Antoinette between 20 September (when he left Versailles) and 7 November; he wrote to her as often as possible for a man who was obliged to accompany Gustav III on his meanderings through Italy.

Fersen and Marie-Antoinette wrote to each other frequently; they used false names, intermediaries and sometimes invisible ink or a code. They got their servants to write the addresses and used double envelopes ... extra precautions were always required when writing to 'Josephine'. In 1930, the Swedish historian Alma Söderhjelm was the first person to suggest that the 'Josephine' correspondent in Fersen's letter register was Marie-Antoinette.[7] But her theory was not supported by conclusive evidence. She simply remarks that this correspondence began every time Fersen left Paris and stopped every time he returned. She also notes that in his diary he refers to 'Josephine's diamonds', which he sent to the Comte de Mercy for Marie-Antoinette in 1791, and highlights an entry in the register: '23 August 1788, Josephine – in the letter to Est[erhazy], where I begin: "My dear count, it's for Elle."'[8] To make the connection, however, one has to be aware that to their friends, Marie-Antoinette was always Elle ('She') while Fersen was Lui ('Him').[9]

Alma Söderhjelm thought that the entire 'Josephine' correspondence had been destroyed. In fact the French Archives Nationales owns a number of letters addressed to Marie-Antoinette under the code name 'Josephine' that have never been recognized as such – until now. Fersen's letter register confirms their provenance. These letters, duly authenticated by entries in the register, confirm unambiguously Marie-Antoinette's identity as 'Josephine'. Fersen himself provides the proof. Here is an extract of a letter from the Queen deciphered by Fersen, which he has annotated: '8 reçu par M. Lasserez, **chiffre de Joséphine** du 3 juillet 1792, rép le 10 par Lasserez' ('8, received by M. Lasserez, cipher from Josephine of 3 July 1792, replied the 10th by Lasserez').[10]

3 reçu par m.
Lasserez. Chiffre de Josephine du 3 Juil. 1792.
3/7 1792. rep le 10 par Lasserez.
J'ai reçu votre lettre du vingt
cinq

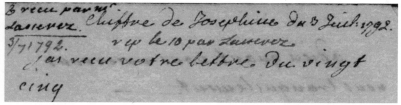

Figure 1a: 'Cipher from Josephine'; letter from Marie-Antoinette dated 3 July 1792 – Fersen's decrypt

In his letter register Fersen notes his reply to the 'cipher from Josephine' under the heading 'Queen of France' on 10 July. '*Reine de France – rép à celles par Lasserez et Leonard, en bl[anc] par Lasserez*' ('Queen of France: rep. to those by Lasserez and Leonard, in invisible ink by Lasserez').[11]

Juil. 1. Roi de Suede chiffre
2. [illegible] rep a celle du 29 que je serai bien aise qu'il m'informe de ce qui se passe que je vais par le chiffre de 1791.
8 Roi de Suede [illegible] clair et chiffre
10 Reine de France rep. a celles par Lasserez et Leonard, en bl. par Lasserez

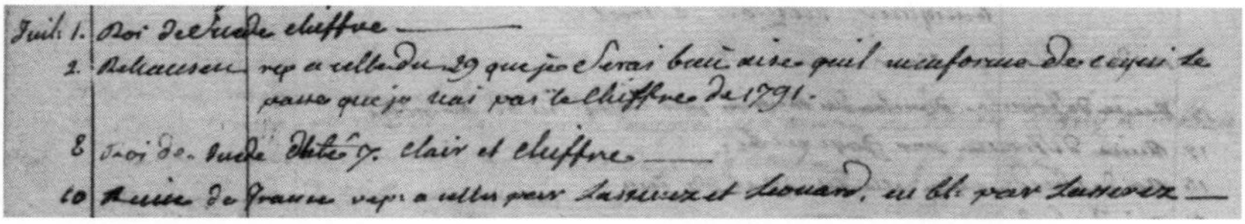

Figure 1b: Reply to the 'cipher from Josephine' sent to the 'Queen of France', 10 July 1792 – Fersen's letter register

Klinckowström must have been aware of Josephine's identity, since he published Marie-Antoinette's letter of 3 July 1792 as 'in code from the Queen' rather than 'code from Josephine'. A cross-check of surviving letters with Fersen's letter register for the period from June 1791 to August 1792 reveals that a high percentage have been lost or destroyed. Letters also exist that were not recorded in the register, and in those that remain other letters are mentioned that are now lost. It is therefore reasonable to assume that Fersen's 'Josephine' correspondence with Marie-Antoinette was considerably more extensive than has been previously supposed.

The 'Queen of France' Correspondence

Fersen's official correspondence with Marie-Antoinette is recorded in his register under the heading the 'Queen of France'. There are only six letters in this category from 1783 to 1789, including five from 1788 and 1789 that are published here for the first time. Another, dating from 1783, is lost. A number of letters for the period 1791–2 come under the 'Queen of France' classification; they are noted as such in Part IV.

Code

The first letter recorded as being sent in code in Fersen's register was addressed to 'Josephine' on 4 July 1787, shortly after the death of the Queen's youngest daughter, Madame Sophie. Fersen recorded other letters sent in code that summer as well as letters sent in invisible ink and noted 'en bl.' – *en blanc*. However, he does not always indicate in the register when a letter was sent in code.

It is clear that some time before the Revolution, Marie-Antoinette had gained experience of encrypting her letters. This is evident not only from the 'Josephine' correspondence but also from a letter she wrote to Comte Valentin d'Esterhazy on 11 August 1791.

> Write to me sometimes in our code; when you were with army headquarters I was used to decoding your letters – in happier days, I always used to undertake the task. Number your letters, too, to make sure none are lost.[12]

Marie-Antoinette was so closely watched at the Tuileries after the return from Varennes that writing any kind of letter was extremely dangerous. She mentions 'our code' and the fact that she was used to decoding Esterhazy's letters from army headquarters, which suggests she was accustomed to decoding his military dispatches to Fersen. On 3 September 1791 she sent precise instructions to Esterhazy on selecting a code word. 'When you encrypt, always use the first word on the page, making sure that it has no less than four letters.'[13] Each correspondent had to have the same edition of the same book to find the code word, which was indicated to the addressee by writing the page number on the coded letter. According to Mme Campan, Marie-Antoinette's code book was the novel *Paul et Virginie* by Bernardin de Saint-Pierre. The Duc de Choiseul mentions another book employed for encrypting his correspondence with Fersen regarding the Royal Family's ill-fated escape from Paris in 1791; the same code words are to be found in the Fersen/Marie-Antoinette correspondence, so it may also have been the book they used. It lacks the romantic connotations of the novel suggested by Mme Campan. 'This code was the small volume *De la grandeur et de la décadence des Romains*,' according to Choiseul, accusing Fersen of having negligently encrypted a crucial letter. It was not deciphered for seven hours, supposedly because

Fersen 'had forgotten to include the mark to indicate the page of the code book'.[14] Fersen's papers, however, attest to his great attention to detail, and he was, in fact, the only member of the escape committee who executed his part of the operation flawlessly. It is difficult to identify the exact edition of Montesquieu's *De la grandeur et de la décadence des Romains* that was used, since several editions had already been published by 1791.

Since Marie-Antoinette sometimes also sent coded letters to Louis XVI's brothers, Emperor Leopold II and the Comte de Mercy, it is likely that she used a different book for each correspondent. A letter from Fersen indicates that the book changed from time to time. He informed the Queen that her secretary, François Goguelat, had used a code book he could not identify. 'I have received a [letter] from Gog. that I haven't been able to read. I certainly do not possess the book he has used.'[15] For those who would like to try to identify the code book used by Marie-Antoinette and Fersen – *Paul et Virginie* or *De la grandeur et de la décadence des Romains* – here is a table that gives the first word on several of its pages. It has been compiled using the page numbers and code words from their letters.

Page Number	First word	Page Number	First word
15	*Neuf*	49	*Adroit*
17	*Courage*	60	*Subvenir*
19	*Raison*	100	*Vertu*
20	*Autres*	111	*Servires*
27	*Contraire*	141	*Paroîtra*
36	*Depuis*	166	*Froid*

Code book used by Marie-Antoinette and Fersen

The code book and code word, however, are utterly useless without the code table. The Swedish National Archives possess an interesting box, little known because it is kept not with Axel von Fersen's papers but among the rest of his family's archive. It is simply labelled 'Codes' and contains the Swedish and French diplomatic ciphers (all numeric) used by Fersen, his father and Baron Taube, as well as a tattered little packet labelled '1790–94: Ciphers used by Count Axel von Fersen for Queen Marie-Antoinette and the French correspondence.'[16] Inside this forgotten packet are to be found not only the actual code table used by Fersen to encrypt and decipher his correspondence with Marie-Antoinette but also a list of code names (never used in the letters which have survived), details of two very important intermediaries for the correspondence of 1791–2 and documents that show that Fersen had tried to persuade the Queen to adopt a code that was considerably more complex than the one they normally used. This code 'No. 2', has never been published before. (Figure 2)

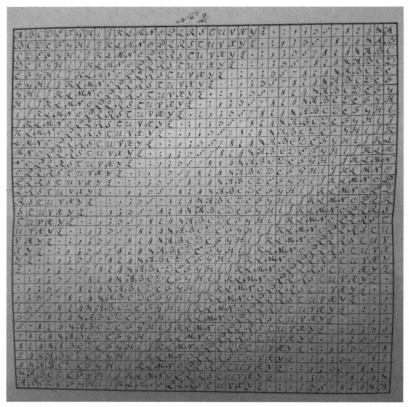

Figure 2: Code 'No. 2', which was rejected by Marie-Antoinette

It is easy to see why Marie-Antoinette rejected it; it was far too complex for her voluminous correspondence and carried a greater risk of basic transcription errors than the code she preferred. This did not prevent Fersen from writing her a letter in which he explained how to use it (see Part IV, letter of 1 February 1790). None of their letters in the archives uses code 'No. 2'. At first glance it would appear that the list of code names in this packet was also never used. There is no evidence of them in the Queen's poly-alphabetic code, where proper names are encrypted in full; on the list they are represented by a single letter of the alphabet. But a letter from Marie-Antoinette to Fersen on 30 March 1792 provides a clue as to the purpose of this list. 'Mr Craufurd will have told you of a way of writing to me in Italian without a code. Don't forget to send me the list of names.'[17] Below is the translated list and the original in Fersen's handwriting[18] (Figure 3a)

NAME	CODE	
The Emperor [Leopold II]	C	
The Empress of Russia	B	
The King of Spain	f	
The King of Prussia	A	
England	i	
The King of Sweden	D	
The King of Naples	L	
The King of Sardinia	M	
The Elector of Bavaria	V	
The Landgrave of Hesse	S	
Denmark	K	
The King [Louis XVI]	N	
The Queen [Marie-Antoinette]	O	
Monsieur	g	
Comte d'Artois	E	
Count Fersen	R	
Baron de Breteuil	Q	
M. de Merci [Mercy]	P	
M. de Calonne	h	
M. de La Vauguyon	y	
M. de Bombelles	X	
The Bishop of Pamiers	g ^{2}	

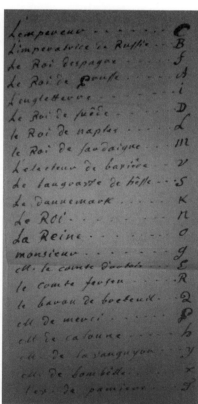

Figure 3a: List of code names to be used for letters written in Italian

It is impossible to confirm that Fersen ever used this method to write to Marie-Antoinette. More interesting is the back of the list of code names (Figure 3b), on which we find the names and addresses of M. Goguelat and M. Gougenot, faithful servants of the Queen whose names appear regularly in her correspondence with Fersen (see below).

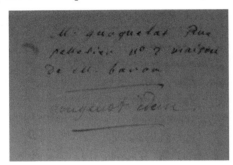

Figure 3b: Reverse of the list of code names, giving the address of Goguelat and Gougenot

Finally, this neglected packet reveals its last treasure: the table for the poly-alphabetic code used by Fersen to encrypt and decrypt the letters he exchanged with Marie-Antoinette in 1791–2.[19] (Figure 4)

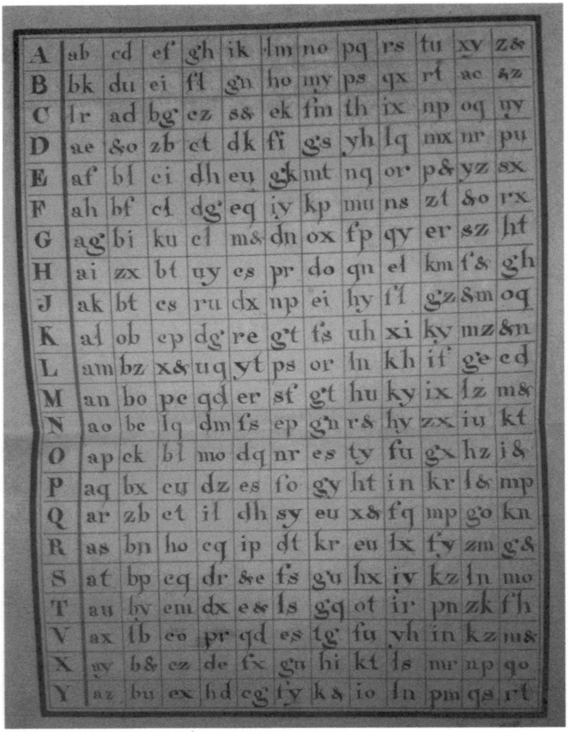

A	ab	cd	ef	gh	ik	lm	no	pq	rs	tu	xy	z&
B	bk	du	ei	fl	gn	ho	my	ps	qx	rt	ac	&z
C	lr	ad	bg	ez	ss	ek	fm	th	ix	np	oq	uy
D	ue	&o	zb	ct	dk	fi	gs	yh	lq	mx	nr	pu
E	af	bl	ci	dh	eu	gk	mt	nq	or	p&	yz	sx
F	ah	bf	cl	dg	eq	iv	kp	mu	ns	zl	&o	rx
G	ag	bi	ku	el	ms	dn	ox	fp	qy	er	sz	ht
H	ai	zx	bt	uy	es	pr	do	qn	el	km	fs	gh
J	ak	bt	es	ru	dx	np	ei	hy	fl	gz	&m	oq
K	al	ob	ep	dg	re	gt	fs	uh	xi	ky	mz	&n
L	am	bz	x&	uq	yt	ps	or	ln	kh	if	ge	ed
M	an	bo	pe	qd	er	st	gt	hu	ky	ix	lz	m&
N	ao	be	lq	dm	fs	ep	gn	rs	hy	zx	iu	kt
O	ap	ck	bl	mo	dq	nr	es	ty	fu	gx	hz	i&
P	aq	bx	cu	dz	es	fo	gy	ht	in	kr	f&	mp
Q	ar	zb	ct	il	dh	sy	eu	x&	fq	mp	go	kn
R	as	bn	ho	cq	ip	dt	kr	eu	lx	ty	zm	g&
S	at	bp	eq	dr	&e	fs	gu	hx	iv	kz	ln	mo
T	au	bv	em	dx	e&	ls	gq	ot	ir	pn	zk	fh
V	ax	lb	eo	pr	qd	es	tg	fu	vh	in	kz	m&
X	xy	b&	ez	de	fx	gn	hi	kt	ls	nr	np	qo
Y	az	bu	ex	hd	eg	fy	k&	io	ln	pm	qs	rt

Figure 4: Code table used by Fersen for his correspondence with Marie-Antoinette

It is relatively easy to decode a letter using this table; for example, using the letter from Marie-Antoinette written by her secretary Goguelat on 1 August 1792.

> P. S. The bale I have sent you by the stage-coach is marked No. 141, and each piece of material carries the following letters. n m f p x a n m g o q [20]

This means that the code word is to be found on page 141 of the book and that every letter is encrypted ('each piece of material'). The code word is *paroître* (Fersen has written it underneath to decode the message).

N	M	F	P	X	A	N	M	G	O	Q	= code
P	A	R	O	I	T	R	A	P	A	R	= code word
I	L	Y	A	D	U	B	L	A	N	C	= decrypt

The message is '*il y a du blanc*', meaning that the rest of the letter is written in invisible ink.

To decode in this case, one looks for the letter N in line P of the table; it is linked to an I, which is the first letter of the decrypt. For the second letter, one looks for M in line A of the table; it is linked to an L, which becomes the second letter of the decrypt, and so on . . . But even this relatively simple code becomes time-consuming when one has to code and decode several letters. There are some coded words in Marie-Antoinette's letters to Fersen that no one has been able to decipher, and Fersen's 'workings' on his decrypts testify to the difficulties he experienced with letters encrypted by the Queen.

In order to speed up the process, often only every other letter was encoded; this is the 'skipped letter' method referred to by Marie-Antoinette in a letter to the Comte de Mercy on 19 October 1791. 'This letter is encrypted using the new method. If you have trouble with it, consult M. de F. [Fersen]. You must skip a letter.' But writing to Fersen himself on 31 October, it would appear that she was not so willing to use the 'skipped letter' method and advised it only for 'occasions', that is, for letters that were carried by trusted intermediaries.

I quite understand everything regarding the code, but we must always write a colon when both words finish at the same time, and leave out the Js and the Vs; that will make it easier for us. Skipping a letter will only serve when we write by occasion.[21]

Fersen replied on 26 November 1791. 'I understand very well what you tell me about the code. We will use it thus; let's put a full-stop . at the beginning, and when a letter is skipped, let's put a colon :'[22] And he actually wrote the punctuation marks in his letter! He observed this method faithfully. For encryption using the 'skipped letter', the page number of the code word is always followed by a colon. Coding and decoding so many letters nevertheless remained a laborious task. Fersen provides some very interesting details in a letter to the Queen dated 6 March 1792. Certain important instructions regarding code and invisible ink were suppressed by Klinckowström and all subsequent editors. The unpublished passage is in bold type.

Goguelat must be notified that every time there is a number and a dash above the code, for example 49–, **that will mean that the letter is for you only, that it is in invisible ink and the code is meaningless. If there is a full-stop or a colon, 49:** that means that there is a code up to the first big full-stop; the rest means nothing and there will be invisible ink. If there is 49, that is, a dash underneath, then the letter will be for him; the code will mean nothing unless there is a full-stop or colon after the number. If there is handwriting after such a number, there will be invisible ink between the lines. It will be necessary to warn him about it. When you write to me in future it would be better to write in invisible ink between the lines of a code which means nothing, because they can find out the code here [in Brussels]. In that case there will have to be a dash after or under the code and no full-stop after to let me know. It will be necessary to number letters exactly to make sure that none are lost.[23]

Despite the headache provoked by this paragraph, one can understand that Fersen far preferred to correspond with Marie-Antoinette in invisible ink ('*en blanc*'). A table clarifies these instructions.

Mark	Meaning
49–	Letter for Marie-Antoinette alone in invisible ink, the code means nothing.
49. or 49:	Letter for Marie-Antoinette but not confidential. Every letter encrypted (49.) or with a skipped letter (49:) up to the first full-stop, followed by a letter in invisible ink.
<u>49</u>	Letter for François Goguelat, the Queen's secretary
<u>49.</u> or <u>49:</u>	Letter for Goguelat. Every letter encrypted (<u>49.</u>) or with a skipped letter (<u>49:</u>).
<u>49.</u> My dear friend, I . . .	Letter for Goguelat in invisible ink between the lines of a code that means nothing.

The use of code and invisible ink by Marie-Antoinette and Fersen over several years underlines the strict secrecy that their correspondence required even before the Revolution; clearly their personal affairs were of a highly compromising nature.

Invisible Ink

In order to save the time required for encryption, Marie-Antoinette and Fersen made far greater use of invisible ink. The letters and Fersen's register refer to it as '*en blanc*' (literally, 'in white') or *en bl*. They adopted invisible ink after the first use of code in 1787, which suggests that code may always have caused them some problems. Fersen records the first letter in code to Marie-Antoinette, under the heading 'Josephine' on 4 July 1787. Four more letters in code followed before the first letter in invisible ink on 6 October 1787. The intermittent use of invisible ink continued until 1791, when once again Fersen began to record letters sent in code.

Given the difficulties encountered with encryption, invisible ink soon made a comeback, but the results were not always successful. There are several reference to it in the correspondence kept at the Archives Nationales. On 19 October 1791, Marie-Antoinette was experiencing difficulties with the invisible ink used by the Baron de Breteuil.

We are finding it impossible to uncover the baron's writing on the papers with the water which the Chevalier de Coigny brought us. Send me word at once by post explaining the method for employing this water and its composition, so that if it is no good we can get some more made.[24]

In the meantime, Fersen continued to send his letters in code, but on 29 October he told the Queen, 'as soon as you receive blank paper or a book with blank leaves or engravings, it [the letter] will be written in invisible ink; when the date is at the end of the letter, the same.'[25] On 31 October she reassured him:

> I received all your papers by M. de Brige yesterday. The writing has come out perfectly with the water I sent for from the apothecary. The one we were sent from there must have evaporated, but that doesn't matter at present.[26]

This message explains why they could not manage without a code – the invisible ink must have been of chemical composition, and the writing could only be revealed by using a water specially prepared by an apothecary. This brought an unpredictable exterior element into the equation; if the water failed, there were no letters. Marie-Antoinette would not agree to such a dependency. On 26 November, after admitting the problems experienced with code, Fersen proposed the use of classic invisible ink: lemon juice.

> There is another method which is not so long and which we should use, that is to squeeze the juice of a lemon into a glass and to write with it. One just needs to write between the lines of a brochure or a newspaper . . . Care should be taken that the printed lines are sufficiently far apart and that the paper is of a good enough quality not to soak up all the ink. You reveal this type in the same way as invisible ink, by heating it.[27]

It would appear that the Queen took the necessary measures to obtain lemons, since letters written in invisible ink became much more frequent than those in code. But the situation was not yet resolved. On 9 December 1791 she informed Fersen that letters in invisible ink were vulnerable and that the King had a supply of water from the apothecary. The lines below in bold are unpublished. They were blacked out by Klinckowström on the original letters but remain on the transcription he made before writing his manuscript.

The bishop must have told you of the inconvenience in writing to me. Yet again today M. de La Porte, who carries everything to the King, had given him your packet. **He has water to reveal the writing, and I find them like that afterwards; luckily he did not have time and I seized the paper** ... [1½ lines blacked out and illegible] **Be careful what you write, especially when discussing business.** As for the *Journal de Brabant*, I will see about it, and it will certainly come straight to me, so you will be able to say what you want.[28]

Does Marie-Antoinette refer to the *Journal de Brabant* in her letter of 22 December 1791, where the ink remained invisible? 'I've already received four printed pages; I've passed them before the fire and rinsed them with the water but found nothing.'[29] Nevertheless she and Fersen continued to use invisible ink, although they changed intermediaries to be sure that his letters were no longer mistakenly delivered to Louis XVI, who was obviously not meant to know the full extent of his wife's correspondence with Fersen. The system worked well for several months until a note came from Marie-Antoinette's secretary Goguelat, on 6 July 1792.

Your last letter in invisible ink was handed to me after the writing had been revealed. It's the second time this has happened. It will be necessary to take other measures so that there are no further mistakes; you will easily understand the importance of this warning.[30]

But in July 1792 the fall of the monarchy was getting ever closer, and soon the correspondence would cease altogether.

Numbered Letters

In Fersen's letter register very often the letters sent to Marie-Antoinette as 'Josephine' are numbered. In fact the very first letter in the register on 7 November 1783 is No. 11. On 14 November 1783, he notes: 'Josephine No. 12 __ No. 4 P.J., replied to her letters numbered 2, 3 and the one from 29 Oct.'[31] There are many reference to this 'P.J.' at the beginning of the correspondence, and the letters are always numbered, but it has not been possible to identify the abbreviation. Does it refer to Marie-Antoinette's letter register, assuming she kept one? To a newspaper used to transmit letters? The initials of an intermediary? The letter register provides no clues at all, but it is worth noting that 'P.J.' is never used with any other correspondent.

At the beginning of their correspondence, not all letters are numbered. Those that were carried by a trustworthy intermediary (that is, those sent by an 'occasion') are not numbered in the register. Only those sent by post were numbered, so Fersen and Marie-Antoinette could be sure that none had gone astray. This was absolutely essential for such a compromising correspondence. The French post was monitored, and any letters deemed to be of interest to the King or his ministers were liable to be opened, read and copied before being sent on to their recipients. The Austrian Ambassador, the Comte de Mercy, wrote to Marie-Antoinette's mother Empress Maria-Theresa on this subject on 7 June 1774, just a month after Louis XVI's accession to the throne.

> The King confided to the Queen that all the letters which reached her during the time of the late king [Louis XV] had been opened, but that he had just given the order to M. d'Ogny, who runs the interception department, not to open in future any letter or packet addressed to the Queen.[32]

This assurance from her husband clearly counted for very little with Marie-Antoinette; in fact, it may well have alerted her to the risk of sending any letter openly by post. In 1778 the Prime Minister, Maurepas, complained to the abbé de Véri that she did not expose her correspondence to surveillance. 'At present the Queen uses only her brother's Ambassador's couriers to take her letters to Vienna. It will not be possible to reform her of this habit, which could easily have been prevented when she arrived to become Dauphine.'[33] Marie-Antoinette therefore had years of experience in hiding her family correspondence from 'the interception department'. But to exchange letters with Fersen the diplomatic bag to Vienna was of no use whatsoever, and they often had to trust to the post, taking care to number their letters and employing an intermediary, a double envelope and a unique seal. The addresses were written by servants, and the intermediary would deliver the inner envelope, probably addressed to the Queen under a code name, directly into her hands.

The letters held in the archives provide some clues regarding the numbering. On 22 December 1791 Marie-Antoinette told Fersen: 'I am worried that you haven't yet received our letters', and informed him that she was going to restart the numbering they had dispensed with for several months. 'Starting with this letter, I shall number all those sent by post, whether in invisible ink or code. Do the same. We must write them all on small paper and check that none are missing.'[34] But the numbering appears to have been somewhat erratic, for on 6 March 1792 Fersen wrote that 'it is will be necessary to number them exactly to find out if any are lost. At Paris I'm sure they do not open them; they don't have a good enough system for that.'[35] It appears that the National Assembly did not have the means to intercept letters with the same ruthless efficiency employed by the Ancien Regime, but the Queen's captivity did not permit her to profit from this relative epistolary freedom.

The Extent of the Correspondence

In his register Fersen often noted the number or date of the letter from Marie-Antoinette to which he was replying. Even if he doesn't mention it expressly, it is very likely (given what we know of the correspondence that survives) that each of his letters to the Queen received a reply. Using the letter register, it has been possible to estimate the approximate number of letters they exchanged before the Revolution. For the period 1791–2 the register, plus the details provided by the letters that survive, enable us to work out how many letters have been destroyed or lost. It is also important to remember that there are letters in the archives Fersen did not record in his register. This study has been undertaken in order to give the reader a clearer idea of the importance of this correspondence, most of which has been lost.

From 1783 to 1790 Fersen records 160 letters sent to Marie-Antoinette (154 to 'Josephine' and six to the 'Queen of France'). From cross-references between the surviving letters, his diary and the register for 1791–2, it is apparent that he did not note down every letter he sent in the register. One also has to account for little notes carried by footmen or friends when he was at Versailles or Paris, which were not recorded in the register; working from the years where more of the correspondence has been preserved, it is possible to estimate that at least ten such letters would have been sent every year, giving a total of 230 letters from Fersen. Allowing for an equal number of replies from Marie-Antoinette, one arrives at a total of 460 letters exchanged for the years 1783–90. Today only five letters from this correspondence are to be found – to whit, copies of official letters from Fersen to the Queen from 1788 and 1789.

The majority of the letters in the archives today cover the period from 28 June 1791 to the beginning of August 1792. During this period, Fersen records forty-nine letters to Marie-Antoinette in his register: twenty-two to 'Josephine' and twenty-seven to the 'Queen of France'. By cross-referencing the letters in the archives with Fersen's diary, it is evident that he has omitted to record at least ten letters sent to the Queen, making a total of fifty-nine letters from him to Marie-Antoinette for this single year. Allowing for an equal number of replies from Marie-Antoinette, we arrive at a figure of 118 letters for the correspondence for this single year. The French and Swedish archives possess only fifty-nine original letters for this period, of which eleven letters presumed to be from Marie-Antoinette are in fact written by her secretary, François Goguelat, and all but four of the rest are minutes or decrypts by Fersen. At least twenty-three letters from Marie-Antoinette for 1791–2 are missing. Just 43 per cent of the correspondence for these years is extant.

For the entire known correspondence from November 1783 to August 1792, Axel von Fersen and the Queen of France exchanged approximately 578 letters; only sixty-eight original letters are to be found in the archives today, roughly 11.8 per cent. It is an enormous loss. The extraordinary continuity of this correspondence for so many years reveals a great deal about the pre-eminent place Fersen occupied in Marie-Antoinette's life.

The Secretaries

Before the Revolution neither Fersen nor Marie-Antoinette required secretarial assistance for a private correspondence that had to be kept strictly secret. But from January 1790 Fersen became Gustave III's representative to Louis XVI and Marie-Antoinette, although he was already closely involved in their secret diplomacy. He had to write political reports and official letters and in 1791, find the money and make all the arrangements for the Royal Family's escape from Paris. It all required a great deal of letter-writing, which had to be done in the greatest secrecy. Fersen did not dare employ a secretary. After the failure of the Royal Family's escape, he spent a summer in fruitless negotiations with Leopold II in Austria before establishing himself in October 1791 in Brussels, where many counter-revolutionary diplomats were based. He maintained an extensive correspondence not only with Marie-Antoinette but with diplomats working for Gustav III and Louis XVI; most of it had to be encrypted. The writing of all these dispatches was an onerous task for a man who for some years had suffered from problems with his eyesight. On the advice of friends, Fersen even had his ears pierced in 1788 to try to improve his sight, as he explained in a letter to his sister Sophie.

> For a week I've had the weakness in my eyes which I get sometimes and everybody has advised me to have my ears pierced. I've decided to do it. It remains to be seen what it will do – at least if it does no good, it cannot do any harm.[36]

Despite this 'treatment', he went on to order his spectacles from Dollond in London, and he certainly had great need of them in the autumn of 1791. 'At present I am drowning in paperwork,' he wrote to Marie-Antoinette on 13 October.[37] It was no exaggeration. He must have been glad to receive a letter from his friend Baron Taube, Gustav III's chamberlain, dated 12 October. 'Franck has just told me that to help you with copying and writing we will be sending you one of the secretaries who is currently posted to the embassy in Copenhagen.'[38] But on 18 October Taube felt that this secretary might be more of a hindrance than a help to Fersen.

> Our Ambassador from Copenhagen is here [in Stockholm] at the moment. He tells me that Brelin is nothing but a busybody who always believes he knows better than his master and that he files reports in consequence. I'm warning you, my friend, so that you only give him the requisite amount of confidence; above all, never let him decipher my private letters.[39]

Given Taube's frank way of expressing himself on people and affairs, it would appear that M. Brelin would not be of much help to Fersen in his correspondence with Sweden. On 31 October, Brelin had not yet arrived, and Marie-Antoinette wanted to ease the burden on Fersen. 'I would very much like the bishop or someone else with legible handwriting to write letters and not you, who already have far too much paperwork.'[40] This certainly excluded the Baron de Breteuil, whose handwriting was atrocious.

The Queen herself suffered from the weight of this extensive diplomatic correspondence, as she remarked in her letter dated 2 and 7 November 1791. 'I am exhausted by all this writing. I've never had such an occupation, and I'm always afraid of forgetting something or of writing something silly.'[41] She was also very concerned about Fersen's safety in Brussels. It appears that in a letter now lost she had asked him to move further away from France, where he was still actively sought for his role in the flight to Varennes. Fersen's reply on 26 November reveals the extent of his responsibilities (previously unpublished words in bold type).

As for my departure from Brussels, however much I would like to satisfy and reassure you on that subject, it's impossible to do so. I am here on the King's orders and I may not absent myself. I'm his chargé d'affaires here. I'm waiting for the secretary he's sending me. He has given orders that all his ministers and ambassadors should correspond with me here and direct their actions according to what I send them. You can see then, **my very tender friend**, that I cannot change places. Besides, you may be quite easy. I run no risk here.[42]

On 25 November Taube wrote to Fersen that 'Brelin ought to be with you with the ciphers by now.' On the same day, Marie-Antoinette, anxious to lighten his workload, sent him a packet with the note: 'The code word is *cause*. I don't know if it's in every letter, because I was obliged to give it to someone to write. There is no [blank] for you inside, so let the b[aron] decipher it.' On 6 December Taube repeated his warning about Fersen's secretary. 'I beg you again not to let M. de Brelin decipher my letters.' But Brelin was still eagerly awaited, and on 7 December 1791 Marie-Antoinette wrote to Fersen: 'I cannot wait to hear that your secretary has arrived.'[43]

There are no further details on Brelin in his correspondence with the Queen, but it appears that Fersen dared not entrust him with the most confidential documents, since among his papers in the Swedish archives are copies of important letters and dispatches in the very legible hand of Fredrik Reutersvärd. A former officer in the Royal Suédois, Reutersvärd was very attached to his colonel and accompanied him on his secret visit to Paris in February 1792. Recalled the following year to Stockholm, he wrote to Fersen: 'I was also told, Monsieur le Comte, that Brelin was sent to spy on you, but I cannot nor do I want to believe him capable of such a role.'[44]

Marie-Antoinette at least had absolutely no reason to doubt her secretary. François Goguelat was a man of exemplary loyalty and discretion. An officer in the engineer corps and much valued by Fersen and the Queen, he was entrusted with secret missions for the escape of the Royal Family in 1791. Marie-Antoinette speaks of him in a letter to the Comte de Mercy on 3 February that year.

> M. Goguelat, who I have mentioned to you several times, will bring you a cipher which he will explain to you. We will only need to use it for things of the greatest importance, which I do not wish to entrust to Blumendorf. M. Gog knows and must know nothing. He is simply a trustworthy man we can make use of; he is an officer at headquarters, very intelligent. You can reply to me by him and say whatever you want, even without a code, so long as you avoid naming me in the letter.[45]

Quite badly wounded at Varennes, Goguelat was arrested and imprisoned and escaped being tried and condemned to death only because Louis XVI's acceptance of the constitution enabled him to benefit from an amnesty. Once free, instead of emigrating like so many others did, he returned to Paris to continue to serve the Queen. His devotion to her was absolute, as his memoirs testify.

> The Queen had no need of a crown to reign over hearts. This princess joined to all the charms of her sex the great qualities of her lineage and all the majesty of her rank. Never has so much grace accompanied so much kindness.[46]

According to a letter of 23 July 1790 from the Russian Ambassador, Baron Simolin, Goguelat had even tried to provoke the Duc d'Orléans to a duel in order to be able to kill him – undoubted proof of his attachment to the Queen, the target for so many years of Orléanist persecutions.

> On the day that M. le Duc d'Orléans went to the Tuileries to pay his court to the King he suffered an insult from an officer named Goguelat from army headquarters, who not only said some very disagreeable things to him but contrived to make him pirouette around him in His Majesty's antechamber, in the presence of the Court. The officer has received orders from His Majesty to return to

the province where he is employed. He took it open himself not to go away without giving the duke notice of his departure, but he has received no answer.[47]

Typically Louis XVI did not know how to profit from this insolence to rid himself of a man who wanted to sit on his throne. Marie-Antoinette's confidence in Goguelat was well placed. His discretion lasted beyond the grave, and he never revealed anything of the delicate and dangerous missions he undertook for the Queen after the flight to Varennes. In her correspondence with Fersen, he is nearly always 'Gog' (it is quicker to encrypt), and his name frequently appears in their letters, as secretary, special envoy and intermediary.

Goguelat, Gougenot, Mme Brown and M. Rignon

In 1791–2 Goguelat appears regularly as an intermediary in Fersen's letter register for his correspondence with Marie-Antoinette – which is perfectly normal, as he was her secretary. But another faithful servant of the Queen had a similar-looking name: Gougenot, or 'Goug' in the correspondence and the register. Klinckowström noted his name correctly, without identifying him, but other editors, thinking he had mistakenly transcribed 'Gog' for Goguelat, have either overlooked him or wrongly 'corrected' his name. This man is nevertheless vital in helping to identify Marie-Antoinette's code name on letters sent through intermediaries, as well as an address in Paris she used to receive letters during the Revolution.

Fersen's family archives in Sweden have finally clarified the identity and role of the mysterious M. Gougenot. His name, published incorrectly as 'M. de Gougens' by Alma Söderhjelm and others, is mentioned in the famous note written by Marie-Antoinette to Fersen after Varennes, in which she calls him 'the most loved and most loving of men'. On the back of the list of code names (Fig 3b above) there is a note by Fersen:

M. Goguelat, rue Pelletier no. 2, maison de M. Baron
Gougenot idem

A letter dated 5 June 1795 for the Swedish chargé d'affaires in Paris, sent by Fersen to try to recover the furniture he left there in 1791, provides more information.

In the closing days of January 1792 furniture belonging to Count Fersen (list attached) was moved by M. Goguelat, in a house on the rue Pelletier, no. 2. The mezzanine floor of the house was at that time occupied by the owner, a receiver general of wines; the first floor by Mme Gougenot and the second by her husband M. Gougenot, the Queen's steward, and by M. Goguelat, who was also in her service. Some of this furniture was placed with M. Gougenot and some with M. Goguelat, and since then there has been no news. M. Goguelat emigrated and is a colonel in the Austrian army, and M. Gougenot having been guillotined, his property would have been sequestrated; but by virtue of decrees by the Convention it was doubtless returned to his wife, and it is from her that the furniture can be obtained by giving her all these details and telling her that they belong to Count Fersen.[48]

The archives of the Revolutionary Tribunal confirm that Louis Georges Gougenot was guillotined on 18 April 1794 'aged 56, born in Paris, living in the rue Lepelletier, former steward of Capet'.[49]

The information required to understand Fersen and Marie-Antoinette's correspondence comes from the note she wrote him after Varennes, telling him to 'write to me by the post: address it to Mme Brown with a double envelope to Mr Gougeno'.[50] This cryptic message tells Fersen that he should address his letters to Gougenot at 2 rue Lepeletier (in today's 9th arrondissement). It also reveals that Marie-Antoinette's code name on the inner envelope was 'Mme Brown'. When he received such a letter Gougenot knew by the name on the inner envelope that it should be handed directly to the Queen. Marie-Antoinette names Gougenot this time because her secretary Goguelat, who normally lived in the same house, was in prison after being arrested at Varennes. Her trust in these two men was amply justified; no one ever knew of the part they played in her correspondence with Fersen, and the unfortunate Gougenot took his secret to the scaffold.

As for the name 'Mme Brown', Marie-Antoinette chose to use the code name that her friend the Duke of Dorset, British Ambassador to France, had given her. Dorset always used to call Louis XVI and Marie-Antoinette 'Mr and Mrs B' in his letters to the Duchess of Devonshire, Quintin Craufurd and Fersen. Sometimes he wrote the name Brown in full and occasionally 'the Browns'. Clearly Marie-Antoinette found this name useful (and doubtless amusing, too). And so, in her correspondence with Fersen, this 'daughter of emperors', the iconic Queen of

France whose elegance and grace captured the imagination of the whole of Europe, became plain, unremarkable *Mme Josephine Brown* . . .

Fersen had a safe address in Brussels and he, too, had a code name for his letters from Marie-Antoinette: 'Rignon'. In his letter of 26 November 1791, when giving instructions on writing with lemon juice, he adds: 'You must write between the lines of a brochure of a gazette, and it can be sent either to Rignon's address or straight to mine.'[51] 'Rignon's address' is probably the one to be found on an envelope kept with the correspondence – 'Abbé de Beauverin, Poste Restante, Brussels'. There is no trace in the records of this abbé, who appears to be as fictitious a personage as 'Mme Brown'.

The Secret Seals

In his diary on 21 January 1794 Fersen copied a message from Marie-Antoinette that she had entrusted to the Chevalier de Jarjayes when she was captive in the Temple in April 1793.

> He sent me only the fragment of a letter from the Queen to him; here's the copy. She wrote it herself.
>
> ' . . . When you are in a safe place, I would very much like you to give news of me to my great friend who came to see me last year. I don't know where he is, but either Mr Gog. [Goguelat] or Mr Crawford, who I believe to be in London, will be able to tell you. I dare not write to him, but here is the stamp of my motto. Tell him when you send it that the person to whom it belongs feels that it has never been more true.'
>
> This motto was a seal with the emblem of a flying pigeon and the motto *Tutto a te mi guida*. Her idea at the time had been to take my arms, and they had mistaken the flying fish for a bird. The stamp was on a scrap of card; unfortunately the heat had completely erased the impression. I will nevertheless guard it preciously in my box with the copy of the note and the design of the seal.[52]

The reason for a special seal becomes obvious as one reads the correspondence. Marie-Antoinette never signed her letters to Fersen and the envelopes were addressed by servants and usually placed inside a second envelope addressed to an intermediary. Sometimes Marie-Antoinette dictated a coded letter to her secretary or maid, as Mme

Campan's memoirs reveal. The seal was therefore the most obvious way for the recipient to be sure of the provenance of a letter. Quintin Craufurd confirms in his memoirs that the Queen used special seals for her correspondence.

> A few days before my departure from Paris, the Queen, noticing an engraved stone I had on my finger, asked me if I were attached to it. I told her no, that I had bought it in Rome. 'In that case, I ask that you give it to me; I may perhaps need to write to you, and if it should happen that I felt unable to do so in my own hand, the seal will serve as an indication.'[53]

Clearly it was for this reason that Marie-Antoinette had a signet ring made with an emblem from Fersen's arms – which the engraver redesigned by taking the flying fish for a pigeon – accompanying the romantic motto in Italian *Tutto a te mi guida* or 'Everything leads me to thee'. The Swedish archives contain letters from Fabian von Fersen to his sister Sophie written after the death of their brother Axel, sealed with the flying fish emblem (Figure 5).[54]

More interesting still, at Fersen's home, Löfstad castle in Sweden, there is a miniature of Marie-Antoinette by Campana in which she wears a large ring. On the copy of this miniature made for her sister the Queen of Naples her hands are bare. If one enlarges the image and adjusts the contrast, it is possible to distinguish the flying pigeon described by Fersen on the ring worn by Marie-Antoinette on the third finger of her left hand (where one would normally wear a wedding ring). The inscription around the edge is visible but illegible. (Figure 6) Fersen, too, had a secret seal for his correspondence with the Queen, as is apparent from a letter written by Fabian to Sophie on 25 December 1810. Sophie wanted to collect all the souvenirs relating to Marie-Antoinette that had belonged to Axel, and Fabian tells her that while his seal with his coat of arms had been destroyed to prevent fraud (he was the Grand Marshal of Sweden), 'the two little seals with the notes of music and the two AA remain intact.'[55] 'The 'two AA' for Axel and Antoinette, as drawn by Fabian in his letter (Figure 7), also trace the M to give Marie-Antoinette and form the Italian word 'AMA' or 's/he loves': *Axel ama Marie-Antoinette* or 'Axel loves Marie-Antoinette'. The discovery of this little seal provides the perfect echo to the Italian inscription on Marie-Antoinette's seal for her correspondence with Fersen – *Tutto a te mi guida*.

Figure 5: The flying fish from Fersen's arms, which Marie-Antoinette took for her own seal with the motto Tutto a te mi guida.

Figures 6 a, b, c: The miniature of Marie-Antoinette at Löfstad (right) with details of the signet ring with a flying pigeon (below).

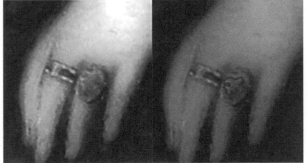

Figure 7: Design for Fersen's AMA seal, forming in three letters the motto Axel ama Marie-Antoinette *('Axel loves Marie-Antoinette').*

III
THE LOST CORRESPONDENCE

Fersen's correspondence with Marie-Antoinette appears to have started in October 1780, when he told his father he was writing to the Queen about his commission in the French army in America. However, his letter register does not start until November 1783, so it is impossible to know if Marie-Antoinette sent him a reply. Given their growing intimacy before he left France, she was probably delighted to have an opportunity to keep in touch with him. All the evidence suggests that she personally took the trouble to find him a post in a line regiment. Patience, however, was required. 'The role of aide-de-camp to M. Rochambeau is very dull and boring,' Fersen told his sister Sophie in March 1782.[1] A month later the courier from Paris still had not brought him the news he so eagerly awaited. 'It seems that I will not get the Legion [Lauzun's] as I requested. It cannot be arranged at the moment, but I will be given something else that will content me, so I am told.'[2] The lack of a source for this information indicates that it came from the Queen, since he always gives the names of his other correspondents on this matter.

Marie-Antoinette had in fact obtained for Fersen Louis XVI's signature on the commission of a '*mestre de camp lieutenant en second*' in the Deux-Ponts regiment on 27 January 1782. (Lieutenant-colonel is the nearest approximate rank in the British army.)[3] But the news did not reach him for many months. The extreme slowness of transatlantic communication during wartime was such that he confessed to Sophie: 'you told me in that letter of the death of one of your daughters. I don't even know how many children you and Hedda have.'[4]

It is highly likely that Fersen started corresponding regularly with Marie-Antoinette during the American War of Independence – at least, as regularly as circumstances permitted. In March 1783 he wrote to Sophie:

If the war continues, I have decided not to quit. If it ends, then it will be necessary, but even in leaving I expect to remain in the French service. I might even be able to stay as the proprietary colonel of a regiment; that means I could own a regiment. It doesn't require my residency and is very agreeable. Don't mention what I have just told you to anyone.[5]

Who had proposed the proprietary regiment and why was Sophie enjoined not to breathe a word about it? The Queen's active intervention in the negotiations for Fersen's purchase of the Royal Suédois – he had to pay 100,000 *livres* for control of the regiment – must certainly have required the exchange of several letters before he returned to Versailles, because everything was almost arranged before he even set foot on French soil, as is clear from his letter to Sophie dated from Paris on 27 June 1783.

I arrived at Brest on the 17th and here on the 23rd. I have been marvellously well received. Count Creutz will tell you what is being proposed for me, my dear friend. If it happens I will be the happiest of men, but if it cannot be arranged the most miserable. My dear friend, persuade my father to consent to it; he will make me happy for life. I've written to him about it, but urge him strongly. It's a question of him giving the money; speak to him for me.[6]

It had taken only four days for Fersen to pay his court, receive the offer to become proprietary colonel of the Royal Suédois regiment with the approval of the War Minister, instruct the Swedish Ambassador to write to Sophie and Gustav III about it and to ask the Baron de Breteuil, an old friend of his father's, to persuade him to consent . . . At Versailles no business was ever conducted with such efficiency. None of it would have been possible without prior communication with the Queen to ensure her support. It was she who wrote to Gustav III and who assumed responsibility for persuading the Sparre brothers to cede the Royal Suédois to Fersen – they promptly demanded the huge sum of 100,000 *livres*. Louis XVI was not involved at all in Fersen's establishment in the French army; on the contrary, he delayed his replies to Gustav III's letters on the subject. The King was in conflict with his wife over her brother Emperor Joseph II's foreign policy. On 28 June 1783 the Marquis de Bombelles notes in his diary that heated arguments between them had been overheard. 'Several people on duty heard the King exclaim very loudly . . . that once one had given birth to a Dauphin, the time was past to seek advantages for the house of Austria which would be to his detriment.' Two days later the Queen refused to speak to him, and the King went to see Mme de Polignac to ask if she were still sulking.[7] It was Marie-Antoinette alone who took an active role in the negotiations for Fersen's regiment; his affairs touched her very closely, because in July 1783 they became lovers.[8]

Fersen was ecstatic on 31 July after learning that his father had agreed to let him buy the regiment – even though he was reluctant to provide the money for the purchase. And despite an absence of five years he was not at all keen to return to Sweden, as he told Sophie.

> Despite all the pleasure it will give me to see you, I cannot leave Paris without regret. You will find it quote natural when you know the reason why . . . I am very happy that Miss Lyell is married. They won't talk to me about her any more and I hope they don't find someone else. I've made up my mind; I never want to tie the conjugal knot, it's against nature . . . I cannot belong to the only person I want to belong to, the only one who truly loves me, so I shall belong to no one.[9]

This 'person' was none other than Marie-Antoinette. He records the first anniversary of her death on 16 October 1794 in exactly the same terms. 'Today was a memorable and terrible day for me. It's the day I lost the person who loved me most in the whole world and who loved me truly.'[10]

Fersen's diary provides an interesting insight into the events of 15 July 1783, which were to change his life for ever. On 15 July 1798 he recalled a special anniversary. 'This was a remarkable day for me; it was the day I returned from Mme de Matignon's at Dangu and when I went after dinner *chez Elle*.'[11] The word *Elle* ('She'), with a capital E, always designated Marie-Antoinette in his diary. Bombelles, who was also present at Mme de Matignon's house party at the Château de Dangu, notes in his diary that Fersen joined them on 12 July and left again on the 15th to go hunting at Versailles with the King.[12] As was to become a habit with him, Fersen (who did not like hunting at all) created an excuse to conceal a private visit to the Queen – a visit that was so significant that he remembered precisely the day and the hour fifteen years later. In view of the fact that at the end of July 1783 he declared how happy he was to Sophie, it seems obvious that it was during their private meeting on the 15th that Marie-Antoinette gave him tangible proof that she loved him 'truly'.

In her memoirs, the Comtesse de Boigne also dates the beginning of Fersen's liaison with Marie-Antoinette to his return from America.

> The Queen only had one great love and, perhaps, one weakness. M. le Comte de Fersen, a Swede, beautiful as an angel and very distinguished for many reasons, came to the court of France. The Queen flirted with him as she did with all foreigners, because they were fashionable. He fell sincerely and passionately in love with her; she was certainly affected but resisted her desire and forced him to go away. He left for America and stayed there for two years, during which time he became so ill that when he returned to Versailles he looked ten years older and had almost lost his fine countenance. It was supposed that this change touched the Queen; whatever the reason, there was no longer any doubt among her intimate friends that she had yielded to M. de Fersen's passion. He merited this sacrifice by a boundless devotion and an affection as sincere as it was respectful and discreet; he breathed only for her, and his whole manner of living was designed to compromise her as little as possible. And so this liaison, although known, never caused any scandal.[13]

The start of their liaison that July led to other clandestine visits to Versailles. They were not too difficult to arrange, for, according to Bombelles, the palace was often empty during the summer. 'Versailles is frequently a desert in the middle of the week when there are no parties.'[14] Discretion was nevertheless an imperative; Fersen could not suddenly start neglecting his old friends. On 6 August he went to dine with Mme de Matignon and Bombelles at Saint-Cloud, while 'the Baron de Breteuil went to Versailles . . . to distract the Queen for a few moments from the boredom which overwhelms her since the summer has reduced the number of courtiers'.[15] On 10 August Fersen was back at Marie-Antoinette's side. He wrote a letter to Sophie from 'Versailles', explaining the content of a letter he had just written to his father dated from 'Paris'. His purchase of a regiment in the French army was evidently meeting with stiff paternal resistance.

> Your letter has been more useful to me that you can imagine, because it told me what the Papa thinks. I have just written to him, but in reply

to another of his letters, from 12 July, which I received three days ago and which says nothing . . . As for a marriage to Mlle Necker, I have already told him to give up the idea, because Staël has hopes. I told him besides that I had heard that her parents did not want to be separated from her and that in such a case it could not suit me. I tell him several times that I am not planning to become an expatriate, and I speak often of the happiness of spending my life near him. I hope this letter is effective; it is eight pages long and very detailed. By the first post I shall reply to the letter which contains neither a refusal nor his consent; he simply says that he wants to see me first, but that cannot happen, because I must have his consent before I leave and the King [Gustav III] must make the request as soon as possible. If my father gives me 5 or 6 *plates* a year, it's all I need, and I would even be content with less. You are now completely aware of everything I have sent him – make whatever use of it you deem suitable.[16]

This letter demonstrates perfectly why it is always necessary to treat the letters which Fersen wrote to his father with considerable caution. Only the letters he wrote to Marie-Antoinette and the officers of his regiment allow one to confirm precisely his comings and goings in France – the colonel could not lie to his adjutant about the date of an inspection, for example, nor to the Queen about when he would arrive '*chez Elle*'. To his other correspondents, and especially to those who had contacts in Sweden, he gave misinformation as to his whereabouts in order to conceal his visits to the Queen.

'The Papa' was very displeased by his son's prolonged absence. 'I have sent him orders for the third time that he must return by mid-October at the latest,' he wrote to Sophie on 15 August 1783.[17] But Fersen did not pack his bags; he stayed with Marie-Antoinette. On 25 August Versailles was buzzing with the news that she was pregnant, when she had 'in the words of her male midwife, M. de Vermond, a shaking of the embryo which has kept her on a chaise-longue or in bed for nine days.'[18] This long-awaited pregnancy caused nothing but worry at Court. Bombelles noted on 29 August 'that the Queen sent word to the Princesse de Chimay that she would not see her, nor her other ladies. As a lady-in-waiting, Mme de Chimay has the right to enter the Queen's apartment whenever she wishes . . . In all, there is a great deal of noticeable ill humour inside the palace'.[19] On 31 August, despite the Queen's condition, Louis XVI left to go hunting at Compiègne for four days with his brothers, leaving his wife behind at Versailles, which became 'a desert the moment the King has left'.[20]

So long as Fersen remained with her, it is highly unlikely that Marie-Antoinette regretted her husband's absence; but in the end he had no choice but to leave, since he needed to obtain money from his father to secure his regiment. He was nevertheless determined to spend no more than six months in Sweden before returning to France, as he explained to Sophie. 'I will come and spend the winter with you, to leave in the spring and finish my business here, only returning to Sweden the following spring.'[21] On 20 September, he told her: 'I'm leaving here in two hours.' It appears that he had spent a few days privately with Marie-Antoinette, because on 24 September Bombelles, who was normally well apprised of Fersen's affairs through the Baron de Breteuil, believed he had left for Stockholm 'eight or ten days ago'.[22]

Gustav III sabotaged Fersen's plans by sending orders that he accompany him on a tour of Italy as captain of his bodyguard. The official reason for this trip was to enable the King to recover from a broken arm, but Fersen's father saw it as a frivolous escapade and accused him in a letter to Sophie of 'despotically employing' his children.[23] But Gustav did not neglect affairs of state, and he would count on Fersen's diplomatic talents when they eventually arrived in France after several months in Italy. At Florence in November 1783 Fersen began to keep his letter register. Two of the very first letters recorded in it were addressed to Marie-Antoinette – one to 'Josephine' and the other to 'the Queen'.

NOVEMBER 1783

7 Josephine No. 11__No. 3 P.J.

7 The Queen, to thank her for the regiment and to request
   Steding for colonel commandant.[24]

Several other letters he sent to Paris that same day – to Breteuil, Steding (a great Swedish friend of Fersen's who served in the French army) and Staël – deal with Fersen's purchase of the Royal Suédois and his wish to have Steding nominated as commandant.[25] In his official letter to the Queen he probably solicited her support with the War Minister, the Maréchal de Ségur. There would be no further letters logged under the heading the 'Queen of France' until 1788, but letters to 'Josephine' were frequent.

'Josephine', however, had far more pressing concerns than the nomination of officers to Fersen's regiment. Marie-Antoinette suffered a miscarriage at Fontainebleau at 3 a.m. on 3 November 1783. The news soon reached Italy. Staël sent word the very same day to Fersen, who noted his reply on 18 November: 'Staël, replied to his letter from Fontainebleau on 3 November which contains details of the miscarriage.'[26] He sent a letter to Marie-Antoinette by post on 18 November (the letter is numbered) and again on 20 November by an 'occasion', that is by the director of the theatre of Naples. Was he as relieved by this miscarriage as the Queen, who reappeared at Court on 11 November in very good humour, according to Bombelles, as though nothing had happened? She was in the third month of her pregnancy when she miscarried, which dates the conception of this 'deformed embryo' – as Bombelles calls it – to shortly after the start of her liaison with Fersen. The Queen should have been very upset at the loss of a potential heir to the throne, but she wrote rather casually to her brother Joseph II that 'although I have a great desire to have a second son, I believe that a few months' rest will put me in a better condition to carry it through'.[27]

Marie-Antoinette's negligence with regard to the fulfilment of her dynastic and conjugal duties was nothing new. As early as 1779, barely two years after the tardy consummation of their marriage, the Austrian Ambassador was complaining of the reluctance of the King and Queen to sleep together. In 1780 the abbé de Véri – a close friend of the abbé de Vermond, Mercy's spy in the Queen's household – remarked of her relations with Louis XVI: 'One could not, in effect, show less regard for one's husband in public. It is known besides that he has very little desire to see her as a woman (despite having no mistresses), and he rarely goes to see her on that footing.' The King was young and had a good constitution, but his sexual apathy was not helped by his gluttony. 'His body grows visibly fatter, and he is approaching the corpulence of his brother, Monsieur, who soon will be no longer able to move. The abundance of food and drink is probably the cause in both one and the other.'[28] In a letter to her mother on 11 October 1780 Marie-Antoinette is quite open about her husband's lack of desire for her.

> We have slept apart for a very long time. I thought my dear mama was aware of it. It is the general custom here between man and wife, and I didn't think I should torment the King on this article, which would greatly interfere with his way of life and personal inclination.[29]

Is she hinting here that Louis XVI had no 'personal inclination' for women at all? It was hardly surprising that the Queen – beautiful, elegant and attractive – preferred to dance the night away at opera balls in Paris rather than stay in bed and risk being joined by her husband, should he perchance remember that they needed to produce more children. They had extremely rare encounters – all fruitless – between her miscarriage in the summer of 1779 and the birth of the Dauphin in October 1781, but nobody at Versailles seemed at all surprised that more children did not arrive to ensure the succession. Yet after two more barren years, and with no change whatsoever in her intimacy with the King, Marie-Antoinette fell pregnant three times: in 1783, 1784 and 1785 – every time that Axel von Fersen returned to Versailles after a long absence.

However, the Queen was not without rivals even at the start of her relationship with Fersen. It was during his voyage in Italy with Gustav III that he met Lady Elizabeth Foster, separated from her husband and children and in exile because of the scandal caused by her relationship with the Duke of Devonshire, husband of her best friend, Duchess Georgiana. Their *ménage à trois* would fuel gossip in England until Georgiana's death; their life together was punctuated by the continental journeys of the two women to give birth in secret to their illegitimate children. Marie-Antoinette's close friend Mme de Polignac was also close to Georgiana and Lady Elizabeth, and she supervised the education of these children, who were placed with families in France under false names. The Queen had received Lady Elizabeth at Versailles, in the process acquiring another fervent English admirer. Lady Elizabeth talks of Marie-Antoinette in her letters to Fersen during the Revolution as 'our unhappy friend' and 'she whom we love'; despite what has been said and surmised, she never shared Fersen's favours with the Queen.

It is worth digressing a little from the correspondence to rectify the entirely false image often presented of Fersen as a libertine who had scores of casual mistresses while he venerated the Queen of France from afar, never daring to touch her for fear of contaminating the royal blood line. This is hardly a credible hypothesis. Royal liaisons were almost *de rigueur* in his family; he was himself descended from the kings of Sweden by just such a liaison. For him, princesses were made of flesh and blood; they were not untouchable idols. The Comte de Bouillé, who passed into the service of Sweden after the French Royal Family's arrest at Varennes in 1791, remarked after seeing the Fersen family at Stockholm that they 'always had to mix grandeur into their love affairs'. He had no doubt about the nature of Axel von Fersen's relationship with the Queen of France.

> It must be said, in praise of this favourite, that the decency and inalterable calmness of his bearing could never give rise to the most active malice. His devotion to the Queen, aided by his phlegmatic nature, guaranteed him from becoming intoxicated by his success, which he justified by unfailing prudence and discretion. He was such indeed as a queen's lover should always be.[30]

To think that Fersen preferred to make love with a string of other women rather than with the one he really loved – Marie-Antoinette – shows a lack of understanding of the character and temperament of them both. Can one really believe that Marie-Antoinette, very loyal in love and friendship, would have offered her heart to such a man when she had already rejected several serial seducers pushed at her by various Court factions who hoped to govern her through her lover? Or that she would have loved him so long, knowing he was a heartless libertine? An unscrupulous egoist thinking of his own pleasure would never have been called 'the most loved and most loving of men', he would not have risked his life more than once to save her, nor would he have loved her to the day he died. It is also illogical to believe that Fersen was an inveterate womanizer yet at the same time afraid to seduce the Queen. Despite these manifest contradictions, many historians continue to repeat – wrongly – that during his Italian voyage of 1783–4 Fersen had two love affairs, with Miss Emily Cowper and Lady Elizabeth Foster; the latter is invariably labelled as his mistress.

As regards Miss Cowper, it is clear that a marriage had been mooted with her; gentlemen did not seduce nubile young ladies, least of all when they were living under the protection of their brothers. Fersen had already evaded two marriages proposed by his father – to heiresses Miss Lyell and Germaine Necker – but despite his vow to his sister Sophie that he would never marry because he could not belong to 'the person who truly loves me' (a vow he kept), he had to continue to appear to be willing to marry to appease his father, who was very displeased by his desire to pursue a career in France. At the same time he had to avoid any serious negotiations; it was a very fine balancing act.

Moreover, Fersen found himself in the delicate position of being a handsome young man in Gustav III's entourage, and the King perhaps admired him too much. It was hardly surprising then that he made a very public show of his fondness for the opposite sex by assiduously paying court to the ladies they met in Italy. Gustav himself refers to it in a letter to Fersen the following year, when it appears that a marriage to Germaine Necker was once more under consideration in certain quarters.

> If I were to believe the gazettes, you are about to contract a grand marriage which poor [Staël] has doubtless failed to secure, I don't know what to believe since you say nothing about it. Besides, I wouldn't be surprised, there are a hundred reasons why M. Necker would prefer to give his daughter to you than to any other, and your great fortune is no small one in the eyes of a banker. But knowing the little desire you have to marry and your predilection for English-women, I still doubt it.[31]

Fersen was quick to quell all speculation. 'Nothing is more false, sire, than what has been said in the papers regarding my marriage.' He claimed that he did not wish to deprive Staël of Mlle Necker's fortune.[32] His tone is firm and resolute; he would not have wanted these rumours to reach Marie-Antoinette. His heart belonged to her, and during her lifetime Fersen never gave marriage a thought. He also despised the mercenary marriages of the eighteenth century, believing instead in the free union of hearts, as he explained in 1797 when he tried to persuade Eléonore Sullivan to leave Quintin Craufurd to live with him.[33] The letters which he wrote to his sister about Eléonore reveal a great deal about his attitude to love, as well as the nature of his past relationship with Marie-Antoinette. He believed in a love freely given, without restraints, but which was no less sacred for him than a union sanctified by marriage.

> I would much rather live with a person who is free in her choice and her desire and be sure there is nothing forced or constrained in our pleasures or in the proofs of love she gives me. I will love her and treat her as I would my wife, but I don't want to start out that way. I would always fear she was with me only for that reason, and then I would no longer be happy.

I've always regarded a relationship that is absolutely free of all restriction, all constraint and all obligation, other than that inspired by sentiment, as the most durable and the kind most designed to render a union happy . . . You talk to me of your sex that wearies of its chains, but ours, my dear Sophie, is the same, and in both a free and voluntary tie which may be broken becomes only stronger and more tender.[34]

Such a romantic man would be anything but a libertine. On his return to Sweden in 1795 Fersen rebuffed the repeated advances of the Duchess of Södermanland, noting in his diary: 'I don't want to betray her and I cannot love her.'[35] A libertine would profit from her weakness for a moment's pleasure, but he always needed more; he wanted to love the woman he desired. It is therefore inconceivable that he would have had a string of mistresses for whom he felt nothing instead of making love with the one woman he loved 'madly': Marie-Antoinette.

It was certainly true that Lady Elizabeth Foster fell for Fersen and that he was drawn to her beauty and sympathized with her predicament; but they were never lovers. Although Lady Elizabeth praised the 'very, very amiable' Fersen in her letters to Georgiana, their physical contact extended to a single kiss on the cheek one evening at a ball when she was in a melancholy mood. The following day he gently let her down in case she had been expecting a declaration of love. 'Today we all went to a party. He drove me; he then expressed himself as fearful of having offended me, but without urging any sentiment but respect & tenderest attachment; he only said he hoped I could do justice to his sentiments; they were such as could never change.' That evening, although they were alone for a few minutes (one feels sure that Lady Elizabeth had contrived it), Fersen did not seize the occasion to kiss her or even take her hands. 'I do not pretend that I shall not regret him,' she wrote to Georgiana. 'He is in every respect amiable & estimable; but you live in my heart, dearest. I confess my weaknesses so you teach me to correct them.' The following year she wrote in her diary that while she was 'attached' to Fersen, she had never even been tempted for a moment to do what she regretted doing with the Duke of Devonshire.[36]

Fersen also wrote about Lady Elizabeth in his letters to Sophie, which he would not have done had she been a casual mistress. On 19 February 1784 he wrote from Naples.

I'm spending my time very agreeably here. I am almost always with the Countess Ruthven and Milady Foster; they live together. We form parties in the morning to go and see what there is to see, and when it's fine we walk or ride in the phaeton. I make Taube come along, as otherwise he gets out very little. Without the company of these women I would not be at all entertained in Naples. I've already mentioned Milady Foster to you; poor woman, she is very unhappy and she so little deserves to be. She has a charming character. Just imagine, a young woman of twenty-four, eaten up with sorrows, alone, far from her family, her children, her friends, abandoned to her servants. This situation is dreadful when one thinks about it, and she feels it keenly. She has a great deal of trust and friendship for me, and I have much for her.[37]

It is perhaps because they were not lovers that their friendship lasted all their lives, although they seldom saw each other. Lady Elizabeth bought souvenirs of Marie-Antoinette for Fersen after the Queen's death; he helped her place her son at the British embassy in Stockholm. As her diary and letters reveal she was well aware of his liaison with Marie-Antoinette. In 1791, learning of his role in the Royal Family's ill-fated escape from Paris, she wrote:

He was considered as the lover and was certainly the intimate friend of the Queen for these last eight years, but he was so unassuming in his great favour, so modest and unpretending in his manners, so brave & loyal in his conduct that he was the only one of the Queen's friends who had escaped the persecutions of malice.[38]

In his letter register Fersen notes a letter sent to Lady Elizabeth on 7 December 1784 in which he 'declared everything'. Had he admitted his relationship with Marie-Antoinette, and was this the reason why she believed their liaison had started in 1783?

Marie-Antoinette doubtless received much comfort from Fersen after her miscarriage in 1783; he owned to having 'a feeling heart'.[39] During the crises that punctuated the Queen's life, if he was not with her the frequency of their letters always increased. Here is a list of all those he sent her during Gustav III's Italian trip, up to their arrival at Versailles on 7 June 1784:

1783

NOVEMBER

7　Josephine No. 11__No. 3 P.J.

14　Josephine No. 12__No. 4 P.J. replied to her letters Nos. 2, 3 and of 29 Oct.

18　Josephine No. 13__No. 5 P.J.

20　Josephine, wrote from Lerici by the director or impresario of the theatre at Naples.

28　Josephine No. 14__No. 6 P.J., replied to No. 4.

DECEMBER

5　Josephine No. 15, acknowledged receipt of No. 5.

17　Josephine, by Fontaine who was returning to Paris.

31　Josephine No. 16.

1784

JANUARY

7　Josephine No. 17.

14　Josephine No. 18__No. 7 P.J., replied to 3 letters.

FEBRUARY

7　Josephine No. 19.

14　Josephine No. 20.

MARCH

6　Josephine No. 21, letter dated 4 March.

17　Josephine No. 22__No. 8 P.J.

24　Josephine No. 23.

31　Josephine No. 24, our itinerary.

APRIL

17　Josephine, with Rosenstein.

28　Josephine, with Rosenstein, wrote about the Count of Albany.

MAY

8　Josephine No. 25__No. 9 P.J.; plan to visit Vienna.

12　Josephine No. 26; that the Vienna visit will no longer happen.

15　Josephine No. 27; news of the King [Gustav, who was ill], that the Vienna visit is no longer happening, that Fontaine has arrived.

18 & 21　Josephine, by Fontaine; that I cannot come before the King & __

25　Josephine No. 28.[40]

The letters carried by messengers – the director of the theatre at Naples, Fontaine and Rosenstein (secretary at the Swedish embassy in Paris) – are not numbered, which suggests that those which had numbers were sent by post. Given the great distance that separated the two correspondents, the regularity of this exchange is impressive. Details on the contents of the letters are rare, but in May 1784 they reveal Marie-Antoinette's desire to see Fersen at Versailles before Gustav III's arrival, which was impossible for a captain of the King's Bodyguard. Fersen mentions the theft of his letter portfolio in a letter to Sophie from Venice on 5 May. 'I have already told you in one of my letters from Rome to send a list to me at Paris of all the commissions you and your husband have for me, because my portfolio was stolen at Rome and it was all inside.'[41] Was an earlier letter register also stolen? This may explain why the register starts in Italy in November 1783. It certainly explains why the letters Fersen exchanged with Marie-Antoinette were never signed and reached her under a code name.

Life at Versailles continued much as normal. On 29 May 1784 the Comte de Mercy informed Joseph II that the Queen 'has been once again worried about the health of M. le Dauphin for a week or ten days; following a cold he fell into a kind of languor and decline for which no cause could be found'. It was the start of the tuberculosis that killed him in 1789, but this time he recovered without treatment. Mercy remarked that 'his existence becomes all the more precious because the regime and habits of the King give hardly any hope at all that he will have a numerous posterity'.[42] This is classic Mercy euphemism and indicates that conjugal relations between Louis XVI and Marie-Antoinette after the birth of their sickly son were almost non-existent. The King had put on even more weight; Bombelles noted that 'the King has never liked to dance, and today he is of such a corpulence that it would deprive him of all means of satisfying this taste had he ever had it'.[43] It is important to note Louis XVI's physique and continued lack of interest in his wife in view of the fact that the Duc de Normandie was conceived only three weeks after the date of Mercy's letter – when Axel von Fersen had returned to Court.

Gustav III was lavished with attentions after he arrived at Versailles on the evening of 7 June, accompanied only by Fersen; but the many fêtes, suppers and entertainments did not make him lose sight of business. He successfully renegotiated his alliance with France and increased the level of subsidies he received. At the same time Fersen completed his purchase of the Royal Suédois. He borrowed the necessary money with a guarantee from Louis XVI (the paperwork is still in his archive in Stockholm) because his father refused to help him. The annual salary of 20,000 *livres* negotiated for him by Gustav enabled him to shake off the paternal yoke and organize his life in France with Marie-Antoinette. During this visit with Gustav, who was an indefatigable tourist, Fersen nevertheless found opportunities to escape to spend time with the Queen, as a letter to his father on 20 June reveals.

> We have already had a grand opera and a dress ball at Versailles, without counting numerous dinners and suppers. Tomorrow there is a fête for us in the Queen's garden at Trianon; it is the last, but we still have many suppers and spectacles in Paris . . . I must close, my dear father. I was obliged to feign an illness to remain in my room to attend to affairs and to write to you. I am going out only this evening, to sup at Versailles.[44]

Precisely forty weeks later the Duc de Normandie was born . . . It's likely that Fersen was actually at Versailles when he wrote his letter, because on 7 June Bombelles records him as staying at the Hôtel des Ambassadeurs in the town. There is not a single letter to Marie-Antoinette recorded in Fersen's register during the whole of his stay in France in 1784, which indicates that they saw each other often. At the fête she hosted for the King of Sweden and his entourage at the Petit Trianon on 21 June Fersen was placed close to the Queen, while Gustav and Louis XVI were seated further away with ladies of the Court. In his journal, Baron Armfelt describes an enchanted evening.

> At six o'clock everyone left for Trianon, where the comic opera *Le dormeur éveillé* was performed at the little theatre – words by Marmontel, music by Piccinni, ballets by Gardel. Taube, Fersen and I were seated behind the Queen, and the kings were at the back, behind the ladies. At the end of the show there was a supper in several pavilions; several of us Swedes were seated at the same table, and the Queen stopped behind each of our chairs to chat for a moment. After that we promenaded in the gardens, which were illuminated in a delightful fashion by Chinese lanterns and looked like a theatre set. The effect was marvellous, and it is hard to imagine the beauty of it all.[45]

A nocturnal promenade in the Trianon gardens, all the ladies wearing white and escorted by Swedish gentlemen . . . For the Queen it was doubtless a chance to steal some precious moments alone with Fersen. But she was very attentive to Gustav III, the real target of this charm offensive. His support and intervention was essential in securing Fersen's purchase of the regiment and in overcoming his father's objections. Gustav, who had known for several years of Marie-Antoinette's penchant for the captain of his bodyguard, always supported Fersen's wish to remain attached to the French service; he thereby ensured the lasting gratitude of a powerful ally at Versailles. But the visit finally came to an end and on the evening of 19 July 1784 Fersen left the woman he loved to return to Stockholm. The separation must have been painful, because their correspondence recommenced the next day in Fersen's letter register and redoubled in frequency. Certain letters deal with a rather unusual present he was trying to obtain for the Queen.

1784
JULY
20   Josephine from Chantilly by Staël.
21   Josephine from Sedan by M. Le Brun, Inspector of Posts.
23   Josephine from Düsseldorf by post.
25   Josephine from Osnabrück by post.
27   Josephine from Lüneburg by post; asked what to call the dog, whether I should make a mystery about it; requested the aria E così fatta il padre &c.
29   Josephine from Warnemünde; asked what to call the dog and if I must be myserious about it. The letter was started at Boizenburg.[46]

Fersen had taken his big dog Polyphemus with him to Paris in 1778, where it had been 'greatly admired'; probably the Queen wanted one of the same breed. The letter register attests to the pains Fersen took to obtain it – and we learn that it was a large Swedish wolfhound.

1784
AUGUST 14   M. de Pollet: begged him to remind Messrs Boye, Thun and Boltinstierna about the wolfhound they have promised me.
OCTOBER 8   M. de Pollet: replied to his of 20 Sept.; that the dog is

for the Queen of France, that she does not want it to be small, on the contrary, but handsome; that I'm leaving in April and as I am not travelling through Germany I would like it before then.

OCTOBER 22   M. de Boye: replied to his of 17 and 28 Sept. That the dog has not arrived, what must I do to get it.

NOVEMBER 9   M. de Boye: begged him to send me a dog which was not little, of the same size as M. de Pollet's, and that it was for the Queen of France.

DECEMBER 16   M. de Pollet: replied to his of 23 Nov; I begged him to send me whichever was the prettier of the two, dog or bitch, it doesn't matter, and to send it to me at my father's.

1785

MARCH 11   M. de Pollet: replied to his of 22 Jan: that I fear it is too late to send me one of the dogs he has for me, but if I pass through Germany I will collect it at Stralsund or Hamburg. I will let him know.

APRIL 1ST   M. de Pollet: that I'm travelling by Copenhagen, that I'll be at Hamburg on the 15th of this month; begged him to send the wolfhound he has promised me to Faxel, telling him that it's for me and asking him to keep it until I arrive.[47]

After so many details about the Swedish wolfhound, the register is very sparing on the content of Fersen's letters to Marie-Antoinette, which nonetheless deal with some important matters. Here is the 'Josephine' register from his arrival in Stockholm up to his return to Paris on 8 May 1785.

1784

AUGUST

3   Josephine No. 1.

9   Josephine No. 2.

14   Josephine No. 3.

24   Josephine by a courier.

31   Josephine by the same courier as the 24th who had not yet passed by.

31   No. 4 by post.

SEPTEMBER

9   Josephine by the courier of the 24th who had not yet passed through Linköping.

24   Josephine: that Cederström had arrived.

OCTOBER

8   Josephine No. 5: begged her to send me a drawing of a woman wearing a riding habit.

NOVEMBER

5   Josephine No. 6: begged her to remind Staël of my commissions.

15   Josephine No. 7.

26   Josephine No. 8_No. 1 P.J.: spoke of the affairs of Holland.

DECEMBER

28   Josephine No. 10.

1785

JANUARY

s.d. Josephine No. 11.

22   Josephine by Baron Cederström: very detailed letter on current affairs.

FEBRUARY

15   Josephine No. 12.

25   Josephine No. 13.

MARCH

15   Josephine No. 14.

24   Josephine No. 15_No.2 P.J. That I am no longer travelling by England.

APRIL

15   Josephine No. 16_No. 3 P.J. That I am leaving on the 18th and expect to arrive on 8 or 9 May, that my arrangement with my father is finished and I am pleased with it.[48]

The letters of 26 November 1784 and 22 January 1785 are particularly interesting. They show that a full five years before the Revolution Marie-Antoinette turned to Fersen for advice on the resolution of a political crisis, that of the navigation of the Scheldt (the Kettle War as it is sometimes called). Her brother Joseph II was demanding that Holland open the waterway to vessels of the Empire and cede Maastricht to the Austrian Netherlands. The Dutch, backed by France, refused. The Austrians put intense pressure on the Queen, who was pregnant with her second son, but her discussions with Louis XVI were fruitless and very unpleasant and the Franco-Austrian alliance had never seemed more fragile. It was hardly surprising that Marie-Antoinette should seek a neutral point of view from her lover, who came from a great Swedish political family and was well versed in diplomacy. Fersen notes in the register that his letter of 22 January was carried by Baron Cederström, an officer in the Royal Suédois who was returning to the regiment in France. Another entry in the register explains how this 'very detailed letter on current affairs' reached the Queen. '22 January: M. de Cohler by Baron Cederström – to send my letters at once to Staël by courier to Paris, to pick a trustworthy man'.[49]

By cross-checking entries in the register it can be seen that Fersen employed no less than three intermediaries to deliver his letter of 22 January 1785 to Marie-Antoinette. Cederström, who took a packet to Cohler, adjutant of the Royal Suédois, would have had no idea of its final recipient. Cohler doubtless thought it contained diplomatic dispatches, since he had to send it on by a trustworthy courier to Staël at the Swedish embassy in Paris. Finally Staël, well known at Versailles, would have given the letter directly to Marie-Antoinette or, more likely, to one of her trusted friends. All these intermediaries show that not only was this letter strictly confidential but that long before the Revolution Fersen and Marie-Antoinette used a variety of methods to keep their correspondence secret. It was customary for them to use a double envelope, code names, several intermediaries and a numbering system for their letters, and it certainly was not the Revolution that necessitated all these precautions.

The more prosaic matters raised in the letters of 1784–5 betray the great degree of familiarity between them. Fersen asks the Queen to send him 'a drawing of a woman wearing a riding habit' or even to 'remind Staël to do my commissions'. Marie-Antoinette replied to the letter of 8 October by sending him a charming drawing of herself in a 'redingote' or riding habit, which is still kept at Löfstad castle in Sweden. Sixteen folds are still clearly visible on this large drawing, where she folded it to fit into the envelope with her letter. One notices the return of 'P.J.' and the double numbering for the letters of 26 November 1784, 24 March and 15 April 1785. In the first, Fersen mentions Dutch affairs, but the last two letters have no political content. It was a question of arranging his return to France and very probably a secret visit to the Queen – and surely they must have mentioned her pregnancy.

Marie-Antoinette gave birth on 27 March 1785 to her second son, Louis-Charles, Duc de Normandie, who was given the nickname *Chou d'Amour* or 'Love's Darling' in his mother's correspondence with the Duchesse de Polignac.[50] It does rather call into question Louis XVI's role in his conception, since at no time can the Queen ever be said to have been passionately in love with her husband. The King in fact recorded this birth very brusquely in his diary, when he should have been overjoyed to welcome a second heir to the throne. He never mentions the words 'my son' once, reserving them for the Dauphin, and focuses on the lack of celebrations for the new prince.

> 27 March 1785. The Queen was delivered of the Duc de Normandie at half-past seven; everything happened exactly as for my son; the baptism and Te Deum were held at eight o'clock; no princes were present except the Duc de Chartres; there were no compliments or curtsies; Monsieur and the Queen of Naples godparents.[51]

There is no letter to the 'Queen of France' in Fersen's register to congratulate her on the birth, which is somewhat surprising. She may have received his compliments in the 'Josephine' letter of 15 April, or perhaps he had no news until he arrived back in France. Several letters in the register indicate his intention to return to the French Court around 8 or 9 May 1785. The register also reveals that he had written to obtain lodgings in Versailles well before his departure from Stockholm. 'February 25, Duc de Luynes . . . I ask him for a room in his hôtel at Versailles.'[52]

The Hôtel de Luynes, largely destroyed in the nineteenth century, was located in the rue de la Surintendance at Versailles (today renamed the rue de l'Indépendance americaine), which backed on to the offices in the left wing of the palace, where the Queen's apartments were situated. From the Hôtel de Luynes, Fersen had a direct view of her apartments and the Cents Suisses. Conveniently, a passage led from the rue de la Surintendance into the *cour d'honneur* of the palace. While his Swedish correspondents believed him to be either in Paris or with his regiment, Fersen's letter register shows that he always maintained a secret pied-à-terre at Versailles. His father was a friend of the Baron de Breteuil, Gustav III had several correspondents at Court and in Paris, and his doings were regularly reported back to Stockholm. To visit Marie-Antoinette in absolute secrecy he made people believe he was with his regiment. His letters to 'Josephine', as well as those he sent to the officers of the Royal Suédois to give them his orders, reveal his actual whereabouts.

From 15 April 1785 up to his arrival at Paris/Versailles around 8 May there are no letters in Fersen's register to Marie-Antoinette. They do not recommence until he was with his regiment at Landrecies on 22 June. He had no need to write to her, because he followed the Queen everywhere, as can be seen from a letter to Gustav III on 26 May. Note her growing unpopularity following the Scheldt affair during her official entry to Paris to celebrate the Duc de Normandie's birth.

> The Queen made her entry the day before yesterday. Your Majesty will see the order of the procession by the Journal de Paris; the carriages were not very fine, and the Queen was received very coldly. There wasn't a single acclamation but perfect silence. The crowd was enormous. In the evening the Queen was much applauded at the opera; the applause lasted for a quarter of an hour. There were some very beautiful illuminations in the evening – those on the Place Louis XV were superb. The Spanish Ambassador, who lodges in one of the pavilions, gave a pretty fireworks display, but it was too small. The Queen was present in the square to watch it, and when she left there was a general cry of 'God save the Queen.' Baron Staël's illuminations were very pretty. The Queen and Madame Elisabeth slept at the Tuileries. Yesterday they went to the Italians, and the Queen received much applause.[53]

It would seem that Fersen spent several weeks with Marie-Antoinette, as there is no record of a Paris lodging for the six weeks he spent in France before going to his regiment. Their correspondence recommenced on 22 June, when he was obliged to go to Landrecies.

1785
JUNE
22   Josephine No. 1.
26   Josephine No. 2.
29   Josephine No. 3.
JULY
4   Josephine No. 4.
8   Josephine No. 5.

20   Josephine No. 6: that I will come on Tuesday evening.

22   Josephine No. 7: that I am leaving on Monday evening.

AUGUST

1   Josephine No. 8.

6   Josephine by the Comte de St Ignon.

13   Josephine by my coachman.

22   Josephine: reply to the letter by Navarre, with Navarre. It was
      from the 12th, 14th, 15th and 16th.

31   Josephine No. 9.

SEPTEMBER

20   Josephine by Navarre.

26   Josephine No. 10.[54]

Almost all the letters above are numbered, except those carried by
trusted messengers – another clue that the numbering was reserved for
letters sent through the post. The couriers, namely the Comte de St
Ignon (or Saintignon) and Navarre, were officers in the Royal Suédois.
One can also see how eager Fersen was to write to Marie-Antoinette
immediately after their separation, before his military duties took
priority. According to a letter he wrote to Gustav III on 20 July he had
gone to visit a detachment of the Austrian army across the border.

> Peace seems more certain than ever . . . I went to Mons a few days ago
> with the Baron de Salis, our inspector, and several other officers.
> General Lillien, the commander there, showed us the garrison, which
> is very fine. They expect orders to return to Austria any day. They are
> as annoyed as we are that there has been no war.[55]

One doubts he was so bellicose in the letter he sent to the Queen the
same day, announcing a lightning visit to Versailles. She was extremely
anxious to avoid a war between her husband and her brother. 'I will
come on Tuesday evening,' wrote Fersen. This dates the visit to 26 July.
He always travelled fast – leaving Landrecies on Monday evening, he
expected to arrive at Versailles the following evening, covering around
230 kilometres at record speed. The letters start once more in the
register on 1 August. Fersen had warned his younger brother Fabian on
17 July that 'I shall be at Landrecies on 5 August, that he mustn't come
before then.' Perhaps he had planned a longer stay at Versailles. Judging
by the Queen's and Mercy's correspondence with Vienna, peace was not

nearly so certain as Fersen appeared to believe. Had Marie-Antoinette turned to him again for advice on the Scheldt affair? The Austrians were harrying her constantly to get Louis XVI to pronounce in favour of his brother-in-law the Emperor, but at the same time the French army was on a war footing against Austria in support of the Dutch. A very interesting and well-argued letter from the Queen to Joseph II, written from the Petit Trianon on 8 August 1785 (just after Fersen's visit), has distinct echoes of her lover's diplomatic prose.

> Trianon, 8 August 1785 . . . I have always thought that the King would do his utmost to avoid a war. Over six months ago, in order to persuade him to adopt a firmer language and conduct with regard to the Dutch, I explained to him that the foolishness and time-wasting of his ministers could drag him into a war against his will. I have shaken him and made him decide more than once; but his minister has always known how to evade the issue, and events have put him in a position of strength from which to persuade the King that there would be more noise than action and that there was nothing to fear. In effect, a deadline of May was announced, just as it has now been for 15 September. You declared that you were sending 80,000 men; it has been said that there weren't even 25,000. You must surely have had good reasons, my dear brother, not to make a display; but if you are determined to act on 15 September, won't the reasons which stopped you in May be the same in September? And since you are persuaded that a firm statement from the King will be sufficient, why not, when you write to him for this purpose, ask him outright to enter into an engagement with you and announce it to the Dutch?[56]

Everyone, it seems, was playing games. Fersen had told Gustav III on 20 July that the French army was selling all its artillery horses: 'out of 6500, only 100 are being kept to provide the essential service and supply munitions to all the positions.'[57] Doubtless he had informed Marie-Antoinette of this as well as the orders the Austrians had received to withdraw. The uncertainty and sabre-rattling nevertheless forced him to spend the whole summer on the northern frontier. In August, when the Diamond Necklace Affair erupted, there was a marked increase in the number of letters sent to Marie-Antoinette; clearly greater secrecy was required, since couriers were used instead of the post.

It would be impossible to cover the Diamond Necklace Affair fully here; suffice to say, the jeweller Boehmer presented himself at Versailles to solicit an interview with the Queen in the early days of August and Cardinal de Rohan was arrested in the Hall of Mirrors on 15 August 1785. At the height of the scandal that followed, Fersen's correspondence with the Queen stopped – from 31 August to 20 September. At least, no letters are recorded in the register. The Queen was at Saint-Cloud for the inoculation of the Dauphin at the end of August; did Fersen spend some days with her there in secret? He was certainly very well informed about the Necklace Affair. His letter to Gustav III dated from Landrecies on 9 September provides details he could only have received from Marie-Antoinette. The key point is the denial of any political motive for the cardinal's arrest. Fersen depicts himself as too far removed from the capital to be aware of all the ins and outs of the affair . . .

I haven't mentioned the cardinal's affair to Your Majesty. M. de Staël, who is at Paris and therefore more likely to know all the details, has doubtless given them to Your Majesty. One would be even less likely to suspect a man who enjoys an income of 120,000 to 150,000 *livres* of such an infamy. It's true that his affairs are very disordered and that he had a very bad business on his hands in the administration of the Quinze Vingts, where there is a deficit of 180,000 to 190,000 francs. All the stories circulating about him, especially in the provinces, are unbelievable. People don't want to believe that the necklace and the forged signature of the Queen are the real causes of his detention. It is supposed there must be a political motive, and there most certainly is not. At Paris, it is even said that it is all a game between the Queen and the cardinal, that he is on very good terms with her, that she had in fact charged him to buy the necklace, and that she used him to pass details to the Emperor of everything which was said in cabinet; that it was to carry news to him that he [the cardinal] had undertaken his journey to Italy and that he had gone to look for him at Venice; that the Queen pretended not to be able to stand him the better to conceal her game; that the King was informed of it, that he had reproached her and she took ill and pretended to be pregnant – I would never end if I were to repeat to Your Majesty all the other absurdities of this nature that are being invented every day and which people never cease to peddle. The sad thing for the cardinal is that no one feels sorry for him.[58]

In a letter to his sister Sophie, Fersen announced his intention to visit some Swedish friends in Brussels on 27 September, leaving there the following day to arrive at Paris on 30 September.[59] The last letter to Marie-Antoinette in his register in 1785 is noted on 26 September. The same day he recorded a letter to Staël: 'that he sends my letter to the Duc de Luynes wherever he may be'. To the duke he wrote: 'that he lets me know to whom I should speak for the lodging at Versailles'.[60] His pied-à-terre in the rue de la Surintendance near Marie-Antoinette secured, Fersen also needed a winter base in Paris. The letter register shows that he rented a small apartment on the third floor of a house in the rue de Caumartin (in the 9th arrondissement today). He certainly liked his carriages – he had to find stabling not only for himself but for his brother Fabian, who spent several months at Paris in 1785 and 1786 with his tutor M. de Bolemany, Fersen's old tutor.

SEPTEMBER 1785

2   Mme La Farre, rue Caumartin No. 14: that my lodging is ready for the 20–26th, that I need stabling for 8 horses and a carriage house for 2 carriages, 2 cabriolets and 2 phaetons, that I suppose I shall find it at her house, that the stables should be close by, that she sends me word of the price.

17   Mme La Farre: for my lodging, asked if I could have the other small lodging opposite.

24   That I will take the little apartment on the 3rd floor; that she procures me stabling and a carriage house at 300 or 400 *livres* for 6 months, that I shall arrive on the 28th.[61]

Fersen, who planned to spend most of his time at Versailles, had no need for a large apartment in Paris. His letters to M. d'Asp at the Swedish embassy clarify the situation.

SEPTEMBER 1785

17   Asp: replied to his of the 10th, begged him to look at a lodging opposite Mme La Farre, stabling and carriage house.

24   Asp: that I'll take the little one on the 3rd floor at Mme La Farre's with the stables that he had the kindness to go and see.

26   Asp: that I shall arrive on the 30th, that he leaves word for me at the barrier about my lodging.[62]

At the beginning of October 1785, Fersen was thus established (at least officially) in the rue de Caumartin in Paris, while maintaining a second, secret lodging at the Hôtel de Luynes at Versailles. He told his father he had given the Paris apartment to Fabian during the Court's sojourn at Fontainebleau in October and November, where he followed the Queen. It would appear in fact that Fabian occupied the apartment almost exclusively while his brother spent his time with Marie-Antoinette. There are no further letters to her in Fersen's register until 2 June 1786. However, they managed to exchange notes by somewhat unorthodox means – a very interesting English correspondence provides details. On 22 September Fersen had written to his friend the Duke of Dorset, British Ambassador to France, asking him 'not to forget my two letters'. Was one of them intended for Marie-Antoinette? Their liaison was no secret for Dorset; his friendship with the Queen went back at least as far as 1777, when Mercy informed Empress Maria-Theresa of their rendezvous at opera balls, saying that Marie-Antoinette always treated Dorset 'particularly well'. Mme Campan also mentions him as a member of the Queen's inner circle of friends.

In his letters to Georgiana, Duchess of Devonshire, Dorset is marvellously indiscreet in reporting the activities of 'Mrs B' and 'the Roman', as he called the Queen and Fersen. Lady Elizabeth Foster had first met Fersen in Rome, which may have suggested his code name. It would appear that Dorset, appointed Ambassador in 1784, was himself a little smitten with Marie-Antoinette. Unfortunately all his letters to Georgiana from the time of Gustav III's visit and the birth of the Duc de Normandie have been destroyed. But in January 1786 a very revealing series of letters on the Queen and her Swedish lover begins.

> Versailles, 11 January 1786
>
> Mrs B is as delightful as ever. I must tell you what I hinted to you in my last, the <u>person</u> you want to see so much, the <u>Roman</u>, I mean, has certainly been jealous of <u>attentions</u> to me. I can account for Mrs B's conduct no other way, and for two or three days I was hardly spoken to. I mentioned this to a friend of mine (who you call <u>beautiful</u> in your letter, Mme H), who guessed the reason, and corroborated her opinion by telling me that she never in her life heard Mrs B so warm in my praise as she was to her the other day. Mrs B knew very well I should hear of that again, and said it, I suppose, in order to prevent my being hurt at her seeming indifference. The surmise proved true, as I

saw Mrs B during the absence of the <u>Roman</u>, and she never was more kind. The ball is tonight, so I dare say I shall be cut again.

I have been interrupted, mia cara Duchessa, by a message from Mrs B to desire to see me. I am just returned and delighted with my visit. An odd thing happened just as I was going out; the <u>Roman</u> called on me and I was obliged to <u>lie most cordially</u>. I told him *que j'allais chez M. de Vergennes par affaire.* I told Mrs B *que je venais de le voir, mais que je lui avais dit que j'allais chez le ministre.* <u>Sotto voce</u> she said, *que c'était bien fait, n'est-ce pas comique?* The <u>Roman</u> and I are the best friends in the world notwithstanding all this, and I believe he only makes her believe he is jealous *pour lui prouver son attachement, <u>car s'il l'était vraiment</u> il ne pourrait pas me souffrir.*[63]

('I told him that I was going to see M. de Vergennes on business. I told Mrs B that I had just seen him, but that I had told him I was going to see the minister. <u>Whispering</u>, she said, 'that was well done, isn't it comic?' The <u>Roman</u> and I are the best friends in the world notwithstanding all this, and I believe he only makes her believe he is jealous to prove his attachment to her, <u>because if he were in truth</u> he could not put up with me.')

Dorset was mistaken, for Fersen had a very jealous temperament and was a past master at hiding his feelings (his diary is especially revealing on the subject). He would feel a violent hatred for Antoine Barnave, who grew close to the Queen during the Revolution. Knowing his temperament very well, she approved of Dorset's subterfuge even though she found it comic. Doubtless it spared her a jealous scene. But Fersen was not the only one who suffered from jealousy. It would appear by Dorset's letter of 8 February that Marie-Antoinette had heard of his friendship with Lady Elizabeth Foster. 'Mrs B enquired about her the other day. I believe she would not wish her to come till the <u>Roman</u> is gone, which will be about the month of April or May. I would not for the world but that you saw him.'[64] Fersen proposed to return to Sweden via England, so Georgiana's curiosity would be gratified. On 15 February Dorset informed her of an unusual method employed by Marie-Antoinette to pass letters to Fersen, even when they were in company. The 'Little Po' is Mme de Polignac and 'Mr B' is Louis XVI.

I have lost the comfort of a friend with whom I could converse about my illness. Mrs B is the only one in this country who knows about my secret, and the opportunities I have of seeing her makes it impossible for me to say a word. I wish she could could <u>unqueen</u> herself for a few months; the Roman goes on as usual, *on en est occupé, vous ne saurez à quel point.* I sometimes tremble *pour elle.* have found out that the dear little Po <u>is in the secret.</u> I saw her give a note out of <u>her muff</u> the other night to the <u>Roman</u>, which Mrs B a moment before had given her. I believe the little Po in her heart will be glad when the <u>Roman</u> is gone. I am sure she is uneasy lest somebody should give some hint to Mr B, who, though not of a suspicious temper, might possibly be tempted to listen. *La grossesse avance toujours, mais on ne l'avoue pas encore.*[65]

('The Roman goes on as usual, you would not believe <u>how occupied one is</u> with him. Sometimes I tremble for her . . . The pregnancy continues, but is not yet acknowledged.')

And so we find Mme de Polignac, governess to the royal children, passing notes between the lovers. The pregnancy of which Dorset speaks – about which Marie-Antoinette seemed to be in denial for several months – resulted in the birth of her younger daughter Madame Sophie on 9 July 1786. In his letter of 2 March Dorset finds the Queen more reserved when her husband and Fersen are together in the same room.

The Comtesse Diane [de Polignac] gave a ball on Tuesday at Versailles. All the beauties and beaux were there; afterwards the company supped at the little Po's and the fête ended with a spectacle given in the Salle du Billiard, when the dancers of the Opera all contrived to appear. A *proverbe* was played by Dugazon and also a *petite pièce* called Les Prunes by the performers of the Italian Theatre. Upon the whole, exceedingly pretty. Mr Brown was there and seemed to enjoy everything vastly. Mrs B as usual charming, tho' somewhat more <u>upon the reserve</u> than common; <u>you know why</u>, *ainsi je n'en dirai pas davantage.* The <u>Roman</u> was there, as you may easily suppose.[66]

('. . . and so I shall say no more about it . . . ')

On 9 March 1786, the Queen's pregnancy was at last made public, and Dorset seemed fairly confident that Fersen was going to be the happy father.

I have written to the ministry today that she [Mrs B] is *grosse de cinq mois*, as she told me I might, so that she will lie in about the end of

June. *L'enfant déjà commence à lui donner des coups terribles dans le ventre* . . . What do you think of your travels? I shall go most certainly to Spa, but I shall not wish to leave Paris (<u>unless you are to be met with somewhere</u>) till the beginning of July. The <u>Roman</u> leaves us in May or April. I shall keep a sharp eye upon the <u>bambino</u>. <u>Without spectacles</u> I can guess who it will most resemble. <u>Take care of your heart</u>, dearest duchess, *<u>vous ne sauriez croire</u> le risque que vous courez.*[67]

('. . . she is five months' pregnant . . . The child is already beginning to give her terrible kicks in the belly . . . I shall keep a sharp eye upon the <u>baby</u> . . . dearest duchess, <u>you would not believe</u> the risk you run.')

Louis XVI was once again very unenthusiastic about this pregnancy. Indeed, he specifically arranged a visit to see the new harbour and fortifications at Cherbourg for the end of June. In a dispatch to Lord Carmarthen Dorset reported: 'The Queen advances happily in her pregnancy, and it is thought possible that Her Majesty may be brought to bed during the King's absence.'[68] Fersen had planned to be long gone before the birth, writing to his father on 10 March 1786 (just after the pregnancy was announced), 'I shall leave here in mid-April and embark from London, Hull or Newcastle.'[69] But he did not leave Versailles until late June; his regimental affairs and his love for Marie-Antoinette explain the delay. On 7 April he told his father 'I shall not return until after the camp.' A letter from Dorset to Georgiana on 18 May reveals that this camp took place from the end of May to early June.

The Roman leaves us in a few days. Poor dear Mrs B begins to look unhappy. She is now bothering herself with her brother and his wife; she wishes them both *dans le fond de l'Italie*. They stay at least three weeks longer.[70]

Neither the demands of the French army nor the prolonged visit of her brother Archduke Ferdinand were going to stop Marie-Antoinette's swift reunion with Fersen. He wrote to her on 7 June to tell her: 'I am coming back on Sunday 11th.' He remained with her at Versailles until his departure for England. It appears that they spent the final few days closeted together at the Petit Trianon. According to the *Correspondance Secrète*, after Louis XVI's departure for Normandy on 20 June 'the Queen stayed in the most absolute seclusion at her Trianon during the whole Cherbourg visit. She was bled there, and Madame, desiring to have news, was refused entry.[71] Fersen's letter register reveals how he concealed this secret stay with the Queen from his family. Here are the register entries for Marie-Antoinette (there is no letter No. 1, which would have been sent at the end of May).

JUNE 1786

2   Josephine No. 2.
4   Josephine by courier.
7   Josephine No. 3, that I am coming back on Sunday 11th.[72]

But to his father Fersen records the following letters, in which he changes the dates to conceal his actual whereabouts.

JUNE 1786

2   My father, dated 20 May, that I'm at Valenciennes.
15   My father, dated from Valenciennes; that I shall leave on the 25th unless I have letters from him, that I shall stay in Paris beforehand.[73]

As the 'Josephine' letters reveal, Fersen had returned to her side on 11 June. It would appear that he spent barely two weeks with his regiment. To ensure a consistent story would get back to Sweden he also records a letter to his brother on 15 June, 'dated from Valenciennes, replied to his of 17 May'. The letter he sent to Steding at Valenciennes that same 15 June confirms the misinformation given to Fabian and his father to conceal this secret stay with the Queen, which would be the last for a very long time. Probably he had planned to be present at the birth of Madame Sophie, had it happened at the end of June as originally predicted; but the new princess had other ideas, and it was in England that Fersen received news of her arrival on 9 July 1786.

Georgiana's wish was granted, for he paid her a visit in London at Devonshire House on Piccadilly, as she informed Lady Elizabeth Foster.

> He is reckoned ugly here, because, from the idea of Mrs B's liking him, a great beauty was expected. He has delightful eyes, the finest countenance that can be, and the most gentlemanlike air. Thank God I an't [am not] in love with him.[74]

Doubtless Fersen also passed on his impressions of Georgiana to 'Mrs B' when he wrote to her. There are twenty-seven letters in his register to Marie-Antoinette during his absence, from 28 June 1786 to May 1787.

1786

JUNE

28   Josephine No. 1.

30   Josephine No. 2.

JULY

7   Josephine by Sheldon.

11   Josephine No. 3.

17   Josephine by my porter Laurent.

25   Josephine No. 4.

AUGUST

9   Josephine No. 5.

23   Josephine No. 6, date erased.

27   Josephine by M. de Pons.

SEPTEMBER

6   Josephine No. 7.

10   Josephine No. 8, numbered 7, dated 1 Sept.

24   Josephine by M. Mouvel.

29   Josephine No. 8.

OCTOBER

8   Josephine No. 9.

27   Josephine No. 10 P.J.

NOVEMBER

6   Josephine No. 11 P.J.

December

5   Josephine No. 13, dated 28 Nov and numbered 13 P.J.

18   Josephine No. 14.

1787

JANUARY

9   Josephine No. 15, dated the 3rd.

25   Josephine No. 16 P.J.: portrait, assembly, Sparre, Esterhazy.

FEBRUARY

9   Josephine No. 17.

22   Josephine No. 18: timing of my voyage, that I will stop at
      Valenciennes. P.J.: spoke of Noirfontaine and the succession.

MARCH

15   Josephine from Ystad, dated 7th and numbered 20 instead of
     19; that I expect to leave between the 15th and 20th.

APRIL

3   Josephine No. 21 dated 17 March.

7   Josephine No. 22 P.J.: garrison, 6000 men, Notables. The
    children, plan to lodge upstairs, that she replies to me at the
    regiment, that I'll be there on 15 May.

20 Josephine No. 24 P.J.: what she needs to get for me to live
    upstairs, that I'm leaving on the 29th or 30th, that I expect to be
    at Maubeuge on 15th and in Paris on the 20th or 21st.

27 Josephine No.25, that I'm leaving on the 30th.[75]

The letters numbered 12 and 23 are missing from the register. The mysterious abbreviation 'P.J.' reappears seven times, and curiously Fersen changes the dates on several letters. One wonders whose portrait is mentioned in the letter of 25 January 1787, his or hers? The most surprising information is to be found in the letters of 7 and 20 April, when he writes of arrangements to 'live upstairs', in a couple of rooms which were to be prepared for him above the Queen's private apartments in the palace of Versailles. He gives his orders quite cavalierly – 'What she must get for me to live upstairs.' Fersen has the assurance of a man who knows he will not be refused.

It is interesting, too, that he writes of 'the children' at the same time as the plan to lodge above the Queen's apartments. The health of little Madame Sophie was beginning to cause concern, and Fersen would be at Versailles to try to comfort Marie-Antoinette during the final illness of her daughter (a child he had not even seen), who died on 19 June 1787. That he lied constantly about his whereabouts in letters to his family to hide the fact that he was staying with the Queen when she was so sadly preoccupied with her baby gives considerable weight to the Duke of Dorset's suspicions about the princess's paternity.

Fersen returned to France on 15 May 1787. He inspected his regiment at Maubeuge and five days later was reunited with the Queen. There are no letters to her in his register between 27 April and 26 June. The letters he sent to officers at his regiment confirm that he spent several weeks at Versailles. He left Marie-Antoinette only after Madame Sophie's death, having written to his adjutant the Comte de Saintignon that he would arrive at the regiment on 23 or 24 June. But the letter he sent to his father on 29 June is 'dated 15th, that I have been at Maubeuge since the 13th'.[76] The deceit is even more apparent in the letter to Sophie dated '5 June', where he tells her: 'I expect to leave here for Maubeuge on the 12th or 13th, if I have completed all my purchases.' In the register, however, this letter is recorded thus: 'Sophie, 15 June, dated the 5th.'[77] He was at Versailles on the 15th when he wrote the letter telling her he would be leaving on the 12th or 13th for Maubeuge . . . Despite Marie-Antoinette's grief on the death of her daughter, Fersen had to leave her for his military duties. Their correspondence recommenced on 26 June, when he had arrived at Maubeuge; and now it seemed to require even more precautions, for the first letter in code is noted on 4 July 1787. During his short absence, Fersen wrote five letters to the Queen, who had shut herself away at the Petit Trianon with her sister-in-law Madame Elisabeth to mourn little Sophie.

1787
JUNE
26   Josephine No. 1.
27   Josephine No. 2 by my waggoner.
30   Josephine No. 3 by Prince Joseph's courier at Valenciennes.
JULY
2   Josephine No. 4 by Gedda.
4   Josephine No. 5 in c. [in code][78]

The letter sent by 'Prince Joseph's courier at Valenciennes' on 30 June seems to indicate Joseph de Lorraine, Prince de Vaudémont, the younger brother of the Prince de Lambesc who also figures as an intermediary in the register for Fersen's correspondence with Marie-Antoinette. He was a paternal cousin of Marie-Antoinette, and his regiment was based at Valenciennes.

Fersen was soon back at Versailles, but as usual he told his father he would not be back until 11 July. He remained with Marie-Antoinette for the rest of the month, writing to his adjutant Saintignon on 19 July. 'I will be at Maubeuge on the 29th or 30th.'[79] His letters to Marie-Antoinette start again on 3 August; two are recorded for the 3rd, the second one in code.

1787

AUGUST

3   Josephine No. 1.

3   Josephine in the evening, No. 2 in c.

7   Josephine by George _____ left the morning of the 8th.

14 Josephine No. 3 and i.c. [in code]

19 Josephine No. 4 and i.c.

28 Josephine No. 5 and i.c.[80]

Fersen returned secretly to Versailles at the beginning of September, although his Swedish correspondents thought he was in Maubeuge until the 15th. He told both his father and Sophie on 8 August 'that I'm returning to Paris on 15 September', but on 7 September he wrote a letter to Baron Taube which he notes in the register as 'dated from Maubeuge'. He never records the place from which his letters to Sweden are sent except when he is giving misinformation. His correspondence with Marie-Antoinette started again on 6 October after he returned to the Royal Suédois. Fersen sent her four letters in five days, with some precise instructions for making his apartment in the palace of Versailles more comfortable for the winter.

OCTOBER 1787

6   Josephine No. 1 invisible ink from Valenciennes.

7   Josephine No. 2 invisible ink.

8   Josephine by M. de Valois: that she gets an alcove made for the stove, that I will be leaving on the 18th to be at Paris on the 19th and with her that evening, that she sends a letter to my address at 3 or 4 o'clock to tell me what I should do.

11 Josephine No. 3 invisible ink.[81]

Just as happened during the Revolution, code had been swiftly abandoned for invisible ink. All these letters in code and invisible ink are numbered, which means they were sent by post. The letter of 8 October carried by M. de Valois (an officer in the Royal Suédois) confirms the existence of Fersen's lodging in the Queen's apartments at Versailles: 'that she gets an alcove made for the stove, that I will be leaving on the 18th to be at Paris on the 19th and with her that evening, that she sends a letter to my address at 3 or 4 o'clock to tell me what I should do'. The style is brief and practical. He does not doubt for an instant that his orders will be executed, as indeed they were. In the archives of the Director General of the King's Buildings, there is a note that shows that Marie-Antoinette issued instructions for the installation of a stove in her private apartments as soon as she received Fersen's letter.

> I have the honour to inform the Director General that the Queen sent for the Swedish stove maker who made the stoves in Madame's apartment, that Her Majesty has ordered one to be installed in one of her inner cabinets with heating pipes to warm a little room at the side. The Queen has also ordered me to arrange for the installation of this stove, which involves the dismantling of two sections of panelling, the demolition of a stretch of the dividing wall, in order to rebuild it in brick, with the removal of the parquet to make a brick hearth.
>
> At Versailles, 10 October 1787.
>
> Loiseleur[82]

A second official in the buildings maintenance department added in the margin that 'the workers have started the small works requested by the Queen, and they will be continued with alacrity'. Fersen's letter would have been in the Queen's hands on the evening of 8 October or the morning of the 9th at the latest: she immediately issued orders to Loiseleur (only a day was required to get to Paris from Maubeuge, as Fersen's register entry for 8 October and his letter to Sophie of 15 June 1787 confirm).[83]

After 11 October 1787 no letters to the Queen are recorded in Fersen's register until 18 April 1788, three days after he left for Sweden. He had notified his family that he would spend only six months there. His father wanted to buy him a Swedish regiment in order to oblige him to spend two years at home, but Fersen's heart was in France. He returned to Marie-Antoinette in November 1788, having spent the summer in Finland attached to Gustav III's headquarters in a disastrous war against Catherine II of Russia. Fersen wrote faithfully to 'Josephine' during this absence, almost always in invisible ink, unless the letter was sent by a trusted intermediary.

1788

APRIL

18 Josephine No. 1 invisible ink.

21 Josephine No. 2 invisible ink.

25 Josephine No. 3.

29 Josephine No. 4 invisible ink.

MAY

2 Josephine No. 5 invisible ink.

9 Josephine No. 6 invisible ink.

13 Josephine No. 7 invisible ink.

16 Josephine, no number, invisible ink.

20 Josephine No. 8 invisible ink.

27 Josephine No. 9 invisible ink.

31 Josephine No. 10 invisible ink.

JUNE

8 Josephine No. 11 invisible ink.

20 Josephine No. 12 invisible ink.

JULY

3 Josephine No. 13 invisible ink.

16 Josephine No. 14 invisible ink.

AUGUST

2 Josephine No. 15 invisible ink; an addition to No. 15 by Asp.

9 Josephine No. 16 invisible ink.

19 Josephine No. 17 invisible ink. Forgot to number it.

23 Josephine, in Esterhazy's letter where I start 'my dear Count, it's for Elle'.

26 Josephine No. 18 invisible ink.

SEPTEMBER

12 Josephine by M. de Pons's courier.

19 Josephine No. 19 invisible ink.

29 Josephine No. 20 invisible ink.

OCTOBER

13 Josephine No. 21 invisible ink.[84]

The letter of 23 August confirms that Esterhazy was a discreet and reliable intermediary between Marie-Antoinette and Fersen, who also wrote two letters addressed to her as the 'Queen of France' during his stay in Sweden in 1788, on 2 and 16 May. One notes that 'Josephine' letters were sent to her on the same dates. The copies of these letters are kept at the French Archives Nationales; they are published in this collection for the first time.

MAY 1788

2   Queen of France, copy attached.

16 Queen of France, copy attached; sent the observations for colonels who have served in America.[85]

The letters that Fersen wrote to his sister Sophie during the summer of 1788 reveal that he had finally confided the secret of his relationship with Marie-Antoinette to her – possibly in order to deflect the pursuit of her close friend the Duchess of Södermanland, who was in love with him. Henceforth, there were to be no more lies to Sophie about his whereabouts in France, and he actually took pleasure in writing about 'Elle'. Owing to the Russo-Swedish war, he did not see as much as he would have liked of his sister on this rare visit home. He wrote to her on 3 July from Finland.

> Ah, how much happier I would be if I could be with you. I would be more at ease both for myself and for others, but their worries increase my pain. I suffer less on my own account than for them, but don't worry. I love them too much and I love you too much not to take good care of myself; to see them again and you, my tender friend, that is my whole happiness. That's all that matters. Everything else is an illusion.[86]

Fersen enclosed his letter to 'Josephine' written the same day in invisible ink, asking Sophie to 'do me the favour of posting this letter'. He was not the only one missing those he loved. In a letter to the Duchess of Devonshire on 12 June 1788 the Duke of Dorset remarked: 'I am exceedingly concerned for Mr and Mrs B – the latter is <u>amazingly</u> out of spirits.' And again on 19 June: 'Mrs B continues amazingly out of spirits.'[87] Political unrest in France and her eldest son's precarious health would have been harder to bear with Fersen absent. He complained about the slowness of the post from France when he wrote to Sophie on 4 July. 'I have not yet received from Staël the packet he was supposed to send me – I'm surprised and impatient. It would give me so much pleasure to receive it at the moment.'[88] Since Staël was the Ambassador at Versailles and had already served as an intermediary in the 'Josephine' correspondence, doubtless it was a letter from the Queen that Fersen was so eager to receive. When peace seemed a little closer, he wrote to Sophie:

> I only have time to tell you that everything that's happening gives me great pleasure, because all will be over here. You will be at ease, *She* too, and I shall see you both again. Ah God, why can't I see you both together![89]

He left Sweden for France on 24 October, and on 6 November 1788 sent Sophie a letter from Paris. 'I only arrived here at two this morning. I am delighted to be here and that my journey has ended. God, if only I could see you there would be nothing <u>at the moment</u> to lessen my joy.'[90]

IV
THE LETTERS

Presentation Notes

This chapter contains all the letters exchanged by Fersen and Marie-Antoinette that it has been possible to locate, published in full. The words discovered under redacted passages (or suppressed in previous editions despite being clearly legible) are shown in bold type. With a single exception, all discoveries in this book have been made by the author. Different formatting has been used to differentiate between the discoveries, as follows.

Text in bold: words discovered under blacked-out lines or words suppressed or altered in published editions of the correspondence.

<u>**Text underlined in bold**</u>: words discovered under blacked-out lines that are harder to read but probable in the context.

[***Text in bold italics in square brackets**†*]: unpublished words that are clearly legible, suppressed by Fersen in his draft letters.

{Normal text in brackets}: passages published by Klinckowström but placed in brackets by Fersen himself, probably with the intention of suppressing them from his memoirs.

Unpublished letter: every complete letter not published in the collections of Klinckowström (1877–8), Alma Söderhjelm (1930) or Evelyne Lever (2009) is marked as such, without being printed in bold font.

The archive catalogue reference for each letter is given as well as any details from Fersen's letter register. All Fersen's decrypts of passages in code have been verified by the author using his code table, and decrypts of unpublished letters in code are also by the author. Spelling and punctuation have been modernized for ease of reading; for the same reason, names of persons and places are spelt out in full.

The correspondence begins with two unpublished letters from Fersen to the 'Queen of France' written from Sweden in 1788, both extremely formal in tone. He wrote many letters to 'Josephine' that summer, but all are lost.[1]

1. FERSEN TO MARIE-ANTOINETTE, UNPUBLISHED LETTER, 2 MAY 1788

AN 440AP/1. Autograph copy of an unpublished letter from Fersen, logged in his register under the heading the 'Queen of France'. He sent a 'Josephine' letter to Marie-Antoinette the same day, which is lost.

Letter to the Queen from Ystad

2 May 1788

Permit me, Madame, to beg at the present time for the kindness which Your Majesty has always condescended to bestow upon Baron Steding.[2] He finds himself forced by an express order from the King of Sweden to go to inspect the regiment of which he is colonel in his service. He tried in vain to prove that he needed to rejoin the Royal Suédois regiment. To remedy the situation, the King[3] has decided to ask for his leave through Baron Staël;[4] he hopes to obtain it through the good offices of Your Majesty. It is with much regret that he has been forced to cede to the King's orders, but he would be desperate if the Queen were to suspect him of a lack of zeal or desire to justify by his conduct the protection with which Your Majesty has always honoured him. I dare to request it for him at the moment and to beg Your Majesty to kindly permit me to lay at Her feet the assurance of my most respectful attachment.

2. FERSEN TO MARIE-ANTOINETTE, UNPUBLISHED LETTER, 16 MAY 1788

AN 440AP/1. Autograph copy of an unpublished letter from Fersen to Marie-Antoinette, logged in his register to the 'Queen of France'. The letter sent to 'Josephine' in invisible ink the same day is lost. Fersen's declaration that he owes his military career to Marie-Antoinette confirms her role in the purchase of the Royal Suédois in 1783.

Copy of the letter written to the Queen

16 May 1788

Madame

The constant interest with which Your Majesty has always condescended to honour me, emboldens me to implore your kindness in a matter which is of the greatest interest for my military advancement. Doubtless Your Majesty has learnt of the decision of the War Council that deprives colonels who have served in America of the advantage of counting those campaigns [towards their promotion], while by virtue of those campaigns some colonels have been made brigadiers and subsequently field marshals. The Comte de Rochambeau[5] has spoken in vain against the manifest injustice of this decision. The Council has persisted, and we see ourselves deprived of an advantage which our comrades have enjoyed without having done any more than we have to earn it.

If Her Majesty would care to cast an eye over the observations I have the honour to give Her,[6] which have been communicated to the Comte de Brienne,[7] She will see the reasons which may be advanced in our favour. The minister seemed to find them good, and if we could flatter ourselves that Your Majesty looked on them in the same light, we would be sure of success. [*It would be very pleasant in my case.*] This anticipated favour would have a new value for me if I owed it to the kindness of the Queen, and it would be very sweet for me to add to the obligation I owe for my military career that of my advancement. I undertook four campaigns in America. If the Council's decision is upheld, I would require another eight to be made field marshal. If it can be changed, I need only four.

I hope the benevolent kindness which characterizes Your Majesty will excuse my importunity [*especially at a time when you must be occupied by more interesting affairs*] and give me the certainty that despite the more important affairs which must occupy Her at present, the Queen will not disdain to cast an eye over the affair I have the honour to speak to her about and that She will condescend to accept the tribute of my respectful attachment. I am &&

These are the only two letters from 1788 to be found in the archives, although there are twenty-six in Fersen's letter register: twenty-four to 'Josephine', as well as the two official letters. After his return to Paris on 6 November 1788 no further letters are logged to Marie-Antoinette until 16 June 1789. His expense book, however, provides a few details on their correspondence and also clarifies how and where he spent his time in France. It confirms that he had lodgings at Versailles.[8]

1789			L.	s.	d.
JANUARY					
	10	Swiss in the Œil de Bœuf	24		
	12	Maid at Versailles	12		
	24	Passage through the yard of the riding school	12		
		Fodder for horses at Versailles in January	53	8	
		Wood at Versailles in January	37	6	
		Small expenses at Versailles in January	10	16	
FEBRUARY					
		Fodder for horses at Versailles in February	35	18	
		Small expenses at Versailles in February	5	1	
		Decorator at Versailles for wallpaper	126		
		Several dinners at Versailles	72		
MARCH					
	16	Journey to Valenciennes	192		
	22	Journey from Valenciennes to Paris	213		
		Dinners on the road to Versailles	72		
		Fodder for horses at Versailles in March	30	19	
		Wood at Versailles in March	15	1	
		Small expenses at Versailles in March	8	18	
APRIL					
	29	Tip for the maid at the Hôtel de Luynes	24		
	29	Tip for the Queen's courier	24		

MAY

3	3 post horses to Versailles	20		
	Dinners on the road to Versailles	13	12	6
11	For the Queen's courier	24		
12	Dinner at Saint-Cloud	8	2	
	Dinners at Versailles in May	30	10	
	Fodder for horses at Versailles in May	158		
	Wood at Versailles in May	80		
	Small expenses at Versailles in May	30		
31	3 post horses from Versailles	18	15	

JUNE

6	Post horses to and from Versailles, 3 horses	39	10
7	The carriage house at Versailles	27	
11	Tip for the Queen's postilion	24	
13	Journey to Valenciennes	200	5

On 29 April and 11 May 1789 Fersen notes tips for the Queen's courier, and on 11 June a 'tip for the Queen's postilion'. It is quite likely he sent replies to her letters by the same messengers, since he did not always record his letters to her in the register. The tip on 11 January to the 'Swiss in the Oeil de Bœuf (a 'Swiss' servant at the palace) is noteworthy. A door from the Salon de l'Œil de Bœuf gave direct access to a staircase leading to the Queen's private apartments. In using this route to gain access to his lodging above her apartments, Fersen was evidently seen by the Swiss on duty – did he have to buy his silence? Normally he did not record tips paid to servants at the palace (they come under the heading 'small expenses at Versailles'), but it would appear that 24 *livres* was the going rate for exceptional services provided by members of the Queen's staff. It was an enormous sum. John, the highest paid of Fersen's servants, received only 100 *livres* per month. The tip given to the Swiss in the Oeil de Bœuf was therefore the equivalent of a week's wages.

This expense book shows that Fersen spent most of his time at Versailles. On 16 March 1789 he records 192 *livres* for a journey to Valenciennes, where he spent only six days. He told his father that he went 'to see if it's possible to establish my regiment in the citadel there; it would be much better than in the town and I will have much more control'.[9] On 29 April there is a 'tip for the maid at the Hôtel de Luynes'. It would appear that he had to return to his lodging in the rue de la Surintendance rather than remain in Marie-Antoinette's private apartments. The great influx of people to Versailles for the assembly of the States General, which opened on 5 May, doubtless caused this move. But Fersen never missed a meeting with Marie-Antoinette; after receiving a message from her courier on 11 May he records a meal at Saint-Cloud the following day.

The increased sums spent on fodder for his horses and heating at Versailles in May indicate that Fersen passed virtually the entire month there. Marie-Antoinette was going through a very distressing time; her eldest son was dying, and each day the States General openly challenged the King's authority. She had real need of comfort. But Fersen himself had suffered a great shock when his father was arrested by Gustav III in a coup against the leaders of the opposition in Sweden. In the Archives Nationales there is a copy in Marie-Antoinette's handwriting of a letter from Fersen's father to his son in which he rails against absolute power. Fersen wanted to resign his post as captain of Gustav's bodyguard, but his father would not permit it, ordering him not to cede to his desire for vengeance and to remain in France.

The Dauphin, who had endured a long, slow decline, died on 4 June 1789. Fersen travelled post-haste to Versailles on 6 June to see the Queen before leaving for his regiment at Valenciennes on 13th, the day the Dauphin was buried. His letter register shows that he corresponded regularly with Marie-Antoinette during that turbulent summer, contrary to the impression given by Alma Söderhjelm, who declared that 'between 13 June, when he left for Valenciennes and 24 September, when he returned to Paris, he sent only two letters to Josephine'.[10] In fact *fifteen* letters to Marie-Antoinette are recorded in Fersen's register between 16 June and 28 August 1789. Twelve are addressed to 'Josephine' and three to the 'Queen of France'. The 'Josephine' correspondence is untraceable, but the three official letters are published here for the first time.

1789

JUNE

16   Josephine No. 1.

19   Josephine No. 2.

20   Josephine by an occasion.

23   Josephine by an occasion.

27   Josephine, her courier.

28   Josephine No. 3, invisible ink.

30   Josephine by the Prince de Lambesc's secretary.

JULY

2 Josephine by the Comte de Saintignon.

6 Josephine by ~~the Prince de Lambesc~~ my lancer Frédéric.

8 Josephine No. 4, invisible ink: sent to the abbé, letters for the
Q__, Broglie and Puységur.

8 The Queen, copy attached.

10 Josephine by Mme d'Esterhazy.

11 Josephine No. 5, invisible ink. I wrote the letter myself.

AUGUST

11 The Queen, copy attached.

28 The Queen, copy attached, by Balthasar.[11]

The two letters sent via the 'the abbé' (de Vermond?) on 8 July illustrate Fersen's double correspondence with Marie-Antoinette – she is both the Queen and 'Josephine'. Interestingly the letter sent on 11 July is annotated: 'I wrote the letter myself', which suggests that he normally wrote his letters in invisible ink between the lines of a letter written by one of his servants. This time he writes the open letter as well as the concealed one between the lines. Fersen did not intend to spend long at Valenciennes. He was very well informed of events in Paris, as his letters to his father show, and since he wrote every two days to Marie-Antoinette after his arrival at the regiment, it is quite likely that it was she who informed him of a plan to summon troops to protect the Court. On 26 June he wrote about it to his father.

> The King seems to determined to support what he said, and approximately 12,000 to 15,000 men are being brought to the areas surrounding Versailles, at La Muette and Meudon && My regiment is not yet among those which march, but we are expecting the order at any moment. What is most troubling is that one cannot rely on French soldiers and so it's necessary to employ foreigners as much as possible. Forty pieces of artillery are also on the move. It's impossible to see how it will end.[12]

Fersen ardently desired to be part of this force, but orders for the Royal Suédois never arrived. He wrote an official letter on the subject to Marie-Antoinette on 8 July, accompanied by a 'Josephine' letter and letters for the War Minister. The Duc de Broglie replaced the Comte de Puységur in this post on 13 July 1789; Fersen, not knowing which one would be minister when his letter reached Versailles, wrote to them both.[13]

3. Fersen to Marie-Antoinette, unpublished letter, 8 July 1789

AN 440AP/1. Autograph copy of an unpublished letter from Fersen to Marie-Antoinette, logged in his register to the 'Queen of France'. The 'Josephine' letter sent the same day is lost. The intermediary for both letters to Marie-Antoinette as well as those to the Duc de Broglie and the Comte de Puységur is the 'abbé', which seems to suggest the abbé de Vermond. The message for 'M. le Comte' at the end of the letter is probably an early draft for Fersen's letter to Puységur.

To the Queen from Valenciennes

8 July 1789

Madame

I dare to flatter myself that Your Majesty is too persuaded of my zeal and devotion to the person of the King and to that of Your Majesty to doubt all that I am feeling in the present circumstances, and that you will receive with kindness the assurances and expression of the keen desire I have to give you proofs of it. The assembly of troops near Paris will furnish me with the opportunity. All my wishes would be granted if the regiment I have the honour to command were there, and the day that I become happy enough [*to be the instrument of the King's wishes*] to serve the King would be the most beautiful day of my life. (My whole regiment shares this desire.) Condescend then, Madame, to grant me the favour I request as an effect of the favours it has pleased you to honour me with, and put me in the position of meriting them by giving the King proofs of my zeal to serve him and showing my respectful attachment to his person and not to Your Majesty's.

I am &&

M. le Comte, please excuse the details I have entered into to explain the motives which guide me. I beg you will accept the assurance of my profound respects. I begged him also to give my letter to the Queen.

Expecting to be recalled to Versailles with his regiment, Fersen wrote to a M. Crignon to ensure that he had lodgings close to the palace.

14 JULY Crignon: that he reserves my aunt's lodging for me at 100
livres. I would prefer something smaller, or could he take a
different one for me at the same price near the palace; that he
fetches my things, mattress &&

27 JULY Crignon: to let me know if I have lodgings at the Écuries
d'Orléans so I can stay there.[14]

Despite the fall of the Bastille on 14 July and the flight of Louis XVI's
brother the Comte d'Artois, the Queen's friends the Polignacs, the abbé
de Vermond and the Baron the Breteuil, Fersen planned to return to her
side. He received news of her when Lady Elizabeth Foster and the Duke
and Duchess of Devonshire passed through Valenciennes on their way
to Brussels, having just visited Versailles. Lady Elizabeth describes
meeting a depressed Marie-Antoinette.

She took me by the hand and said how low her spirits were & how
terrible the times. I told her if she had courage I hoped all would go
well. She shook her head . . . The Queen showed us the Dauphin . . .
[who] . . . is a beautiful boy. The Duke of Dorset told the Queen she
ought to have another son. 'And why?' she replied, 'so the Duc
d'Orléans can have him killed?'[15]

Fersen spent 144 *livres* on a courier from the Swedish Ambassador
Staël on 16 July. News was certainly expensive in 1789, and it was far
from reassuring. Louis XVI had yielded to the demands of the Third
Estate, who had declared itself a National Assembly and was busy
tearing up French law and dismantling the King's apparatus of power,
starting with the army. The project to assemble loyal troops at Versailles
had been abandoned. It is likely that Marie-Antoinette herself dis-
suaded Fersen from returning to Court at this critical time, when her
friends had to flee a murderous mob inspired by the propaganda
spewing out of the Duc d'Orléans' Palais Royal. Fersen's expense book
shows that he spent the entire summer at Valenciennes. On 16 August
he wrote to his father: 'I had planned to make a trip to Paris between my
two reviews, but everything happening there made me change my
mind, and I shall not go back until after the second review, which will
probably take place around 10 to 15 September.'[16]

There are only two letters to Marie-Antoinette recorded in his
register between 11 July and 28 August, both official. It would appear

I LOVE YOU MADLY

that she had decided to suspend their private correspondence during a period that became known as the 'Great Fear'. Fersen told his father of the difficulty in maintaining contact with friends in Paris. 'The epistolary inquisition there has been extreme. The King's and Queen's letters are not exempt. I think it's stopped now, but nevertheless it's more prudent to remain cautious.'[17]

Marie-Antoinette to Fersen and Valentin d'Esterhazy, 8 August 1789, letter missing

In his letter of 11 August Fersen acknowledges receipt of a letter from the Queen dated 8 August.

4. FERSEN TO MARIE-ANTOINETTE, UNPUBLISHED LETTER, 11 AUGUST 1789

AN 440AP/1. Autograph copy of an unpublished letter from Fersen to Marie-Antoinette, logged in his register to the 'Queen of France'. Despite the very formal tone of this letter. Fersen betrays his deep anxiety for the Queen's safety. The last paragraph reveals that they corresponded through their mutual friend Comte Valentin d'Esterhazy, the governor of Valenciennes.[18] *Once again, Fersen asks for a favour for his friend Steding, who was serving in Finland with the Swedish army and could not fulfil his role as commandant of the Royal Suédois. The crucial information, however, is to be found in the final paragraph, where he informs Marie-Antoinette of the expected date of their reunion.*

To the Queen

11 August 1789

Madame

The interest and protection with which Your Majesty has always condescended to honour Baron Steding lead me to hope that you will be kind enough once again to trouble yourself about his future. He is retained in Sweden by his command there and cannot leave while the war continues, and as he cannot perform his duties as colonel commandant [of the Royal Suédois] he solicits the good offices of the King to nominate someone [*to his post*] and to be granted the favour of keeping his salary as colonel commandant and his rank in the army, so that he may in turn be made field marshal. If he obtains this grace, I would beg Your Majesty to consider the Comte de Saintignon to replace Baron Steding as colonel commandant and Baron Staël, nephew of the Swedish Ambassador, as second major. Comte d'Esterhazy has promised me that he will inform Your Majesty of the way the Comte de Saintignon has always served, and I dare to assure Your Majesty that Baron Stael will merit the interest Your Majesty deigns to take on his behalf.

Allow me, Madame to express to Your Majesty all my feelings regarding the letter the King wrote to M. le Comte d'Esterhazy, in which he was so kind as to express his satisfaction with the corps commanders at the garrison of Valenciennes. It's another reason to redouble our zeal and attachment, of which we have no need; we were quite sure we were following the King's and Your Majesty's benevolent views in assuring the peace and happiness of the citizens. It seems at present very established in this province.

The Maréchal de Jaucourt[19] is returning for his final inspection on the 20th or 25th of this month. After that, I hope to be able to return to Paris to lay at Your Majesty's feet the tribute of my zeal, my attachment and my respectful devotion.

Yours &&

News which reached us from Paris gave us the greatest concern about the Queen's [*Your Majesty's*] health, but Your Majesty's letter of 31st to Comte d'Esterhazy, and the one dated 8th and received yesterday, have greatly reassured us and relieved us of the anxiety we were suffering. Your Majesty can never doubt our wishes for the preservation of your days. All is quiet here, and there's no reason for you to be troubled. We are in perfect agreement with the bourgeoisie and we work with them to keep good order.

Marie-Antoinette to Fersen, August 1789, letter missing

The following letter shows that the Queen replied to Fersen's letter of 11 August.

5. FERSEN TO MARIE-ANTOINETTE, UNPUBLISHED LETTER, 28 AUGUST 1789

AN 440AP/1. Autograph copy of an unpublished letter from Fersen to Marie-Antoinette recorded in his register to the 'Queen of France'. The content seems decidedly out of place when France was descending into anarchy. There is now no mention of a swift return to Versailles; according to a letter from Fersen to his father, Jaucourt was not expected at Valenciennes until 20 September.[20]

To the Queen

28 August 1789

Madame

Permit me to lay at Your Majesty's feet my respectful gratitude for the letter you have so kindly honoured to write to me and for the very gracious manner in which Your Majesty is pleased to undertake Baron Steding's affair. [*The interest you are so kind as to show makes me hope for success, but*] I appreciate the reasons for delaying his request in the present circumstances, and beg Your Majesty's permission to call this matter to your attention at another time.

Your Majesty has no doubt been informed of the troubles we have had here. Order has now been restored and I hope that from now on all will be calm. It would appear from letters I have received from Sweden that it is far from peaceful there. An officer embarked with the fleet tells me that the battle they had was not decisive. The fleets were scarcely within firing range, and despite receiving a signal from the duke[21] the vice-admiral failed to give the order to fire to the squadron he commanded. This admiral is called Lilliehorn, and he was also vice-marshal of the Diet. The duke had him arrested and put in prison in the port. The whole squadron came back, several vessels were damaged, but sickness has made terrible ravages; over 3000 men were sick, and it will be very difficult to replace them. The duke was expecting to make another sortie, but everyone doubted it was possible without greatly exposing himself.

A general officer has been arrested in Finland for failing to defend the position he occupied and the King must be very displeased with the admiral commanding the coastal fleet [*for having permitted entry to ? into Fredrikshamn, to which the King wished to lay siege but which he has been obliged to abandon*]. I have also been told that when the fleet returned to port, people wanted to set upon M. de Lilliehorn and that M. de Munck had arrived with the intention of joining the duke at sea to warn him that there was an extremist plot not to fire on the Russians. This news will undoubtedly spread, but I feel able to assure Your Majesty that it is quite untrue and that there is no plot; it will be like those of last summer.

I thought these details might interest Your Majesty, that's what led me to trouble you with them at the moment. If I was mistaken, I beg you will excuse me on account of my motive.

I am with the most &

No letters to Marie-Antoinette are recorded in Fersen's register for two years after 28 August 1789, but it is inconceivable that he did not write to let her know the date of his return as well as his plan to leave Paris and settle 'officially' at Versailles. He even mentions it in letters to his father, claiming that he would save money by this move – possibly the only time in history of Versailles that anyone ever proposed living at Court as a means of reducing their expenditure. Fersen had to appeal to his father's thriftiness to persuade him of the necessity of this move, which would most certainly fuel rumours about his liaison with the Queen.

Valenciennes, 14 September 1789

I still don't know when I shall leave here. I've been told that my inspector will arrive on the 20th, so I imagine I shall be free between the 20th and 30th; but my plan is not to go to Paris. There's hardly anyone there; everyone who has not left the kingdom or gone to the provinces has settled at Versailles. As I have a lodging there, I may perhaps move there myself. I will give up the lease on my house, reduce my horses and staff, which I shall no longer need, and await events . . . My plan is not yet decided, it depends on circumstances.

Versailles, 30 September 1789

I've been here for five days, and I'm going to put into place the economies I spoke of in my last letter. The Comte d'Esterhazy, who isn't coming back this winter, is lending me his apartment and I shall settle here for the winter. In consequence I shall give up my house in Paris and instead rent a very small apartment there as a pied-à-terre.[22]

Fersen was finally admitting to his father the arrangement that had actually been in place since 1785 – renting a very small apartment in Paris while he had another secret lodging at Versailles. One notices that he corrects himself; in the letter of 14 September he says that he already has a lodging at Versailles, but on 30 September he says he is moving into Esterhazy's apartment. Esterhazy in fact had an apartment within the palace of Versailles, giving Fersen the perfect 'official' address to conceal his secret lodging in the attic above Marie-Antoinette's private apartments. His expense book confirms that he left Valenciennes on 24 September.

According to the memoirs of the Comte de Saint-Priest, Minister of the King's Household, the Queen no longer bothered to hide her relationship with Fersen from Louis XVI.

> She had found a way to make him accept her liaison with the Comte de Fersen: by repeating to her husband all the gossip that was being spread in public about this intrigue, she offered to stop seeing him, which the King refused. Doubtless she insinuated to him that, in the explosion of malice there was against her, this foreigner was the only one who could be counted on, and we will see later that the King shared this sentiment entirely.[23]

All her friends having emigrated, Marie-Antoinette 'was more isolated than ever. All she had left was the Comte de Fersen, who continued to enjoy free access to her and to have frequent rendezvous with her at the Petit Trianon.'[24] The events of 5 and 6 October 1789 put a brutal end to these rendezvous. Fersen was indeed inside the palace of Versailles when a group of hired assassins (said to have been paid by the Duc d'Orléans) forced the doors of the Queen's apartments with the aim of killing her. Two of her bodyguards were massacred, their heads cut off. As usual, instead of making a stand, Louis XVI ceded to force and allowed himself to be dragged to Paris, accompanied by his entire Court and government. On 9 October Fersen wrote to his father.

> All the public papers will tell you, my dear father, what happened on Monday and on Tuesday 6th and of the arrival of the King with the whole Royal Family in Paris. I was a witness to everything and I returned to Paris in one of the coaches which followed the King's. We were 6½ hours on the road. God preserve me from ever seeing another spectacle

as distressing as that of those two days. The people seem enchanted to see the King and his family. The Queen is greatly applauded, and she cannot fail to be so when they get to know her and give her credit for her desire to do good and for the kindness of her heart.[25]

According to his letter register, he wrote to Esterhazy on 7 October with details 'of everything that happened' and to Sophie on the 8th – 'what happened at Versailles'. It is inconceivable that Fersen did not stay with Marie-Antoinette that fatal night to protect her, despite the assurance of his erstwhile comrade-in-arms the Marquis de Lafayette, at the head of the Parisian National Guard, that everything was calm and that the Royal Family and courtiers could retire. Nineteenth-century memoirs convey the false impression that everyone waited up in expectation of catastrophe, but contemporary documents speak of a semi-clad Queen fleeing for her life. According to Madame Elisabeth, she was 'obliged to flee in her shift to the King's apartments'. The American envoy Gouverneur Morris noted in his diary on 6 October: 'Capellis gives us a recital of what has passed. Many circumstances of insult to the royal personages. The Queen obliged to fly from her bed in her shift and petticoat with her stockings in her hand to the King's chamber for protection, being pursued by the *poissardes*.'[26] Marie-Antoinette clearly felt sufficiently safe to undress and go to bed, most probably because Fersen's presence reassured her.

Fersen told his father on 22 October: 'My sword is always ready to serve the state, but I take no part in government affairs and live very quietly, in great seclusion . . . I go to Court two or three times a week.'[27] As usual, this was a greatly edited version of the truth. Three days later Gouverneur Morris ran across him in the salon of Finance Minister Jacques Necker. 'See for the first time since I arrived in Europe Count Fersen, whose merit consists in being the Queen's lover. He has the air of a man exhausted.'[28] This exhaustion is entirely understandable when one considers the dangers he faced and his deep anxiety about the Queen. But Lafayette's strict surveillance of the Royal Family at the Tuileries did not in the least impede the activities of this devoted Swede, a man of quite extraordinary sang-froid. He immediately found a means to reach Louis XVI and Marie-Antoinette in their palatial prison in order to discuss a way to liberate them. An extremely interesting letter written in August 1791 to British Prime Minister William Pitt by Quintin Craufurd, a rich Scot who lived in Paris and who would take part in the Royal Family's escape from Paris, reveals how Fersen was smuggled into their apartments at the Tuileries.

> It was hinted to me some months ago, that the Count de Fersen frequently saw the King and Queen of France in private, both at the Tuileries and Saint-Cloud; but the difficulty and danger seemed so great, that I scarcely gave credit to it. I have since understood from him, that, from towards the end of October 1789, about three weeks after Their Majesties were brought from Versailles to Paris, he generally saw them once or twice a week, and sometimes oftener, according as he had business with the King. The place where he constantly saw Their Majesties was the King's Closet. He went to the Palace after it was dark, dressed in a frock [coat], with a round hat, and was admitted into the apartment by means of one of those passes which were given to persons of the Household ... The confidential correspondence of Their Majesties, both within and without the kingdom, was carried on by means of M. de Fersen. The infidelity of some, and the indiscretion of almost all, made them now extremely cautious whom they trusted: but they were under the necessity of employing some one on whom they could depend; and he seems to have enjoyed and to have merited their entire confidence. I know him intimately ... He is calm, resolute, and uncommonly discreet, without being reserved.

Craufurd added a note in the margin which is of considerable interest. 'This gentleman was Colonel of the Royal Suédois; was Her Most Christian Majesty's prime favourite; and is generally supposed to be the father of the present Dauphin.'[29] Craufurd knew Fersen very well, and he would not have made such a revelation in an official letter to the Prime Minister had he not believed it to be true.

The autumn of 1789 was a difficult period for both Marie-Antoinette and Fersen. They saw each other regularly, but they were never alone. However, in a letter to Mme de Polignac on 29 December, the Queen mentions her happiness after a meeting with a 'person' she is careful not to name.

> Your brother at Valenciennes was prompt in sending on your letter ... I have seen him: for after three months of grief and separation, although we were in the same place, the person and I managed to see

each other safely once. You know us both, so you can imagine our happiness. He's going to make a trip to see your brother.[30]

It is absolutely certain that the 'person' Marie-Antoinette refers to is Fersen, since he says virtually the same thing in a letter written on 27 December to his sister Sophie.

Finally on the 24th I spent a whole day with her; it was the first. Imagine my joy – only you would be able to feel it. I'm leaving on the 29th to go to see our friend. I'll be there on the 3rd and am greatly looking forward to seeing him . . . I'm telling my sister Hedda that I'm going to Valenciennes.[31]

It was the Queen's bad leg that provided this opportunity for this intimate reunion. In her letter to Mme de Polignac, Marie-Antoinette wrote: 'I've just sprained my bad leg again, which has obliged me to keep to my room for twelve days . . . ' Just over a month later, on 9 February 1790, Louis XVI informed Mme de Polignac that the Queen had been confined to her apartments 'for almost three weeks'.[32] Despite the romantic opportunities offered by this unromantic sprain, Fersen and Marie-Antoinette no doubt found time to talk about the very discreet visit he was about to make to Gustav III's chamberlain Baron Evert Taube at Aix-la-Chapelle. It would place Fersen at the heart of the counter-revolution being planned by the Swedish king. His letter to Gustav on 7 January gives some insight into his new role.

Only a domestic or external war can re-establish France and royal authority, but how can it be done so long as the King is a prisoner in Paris? He made a mistake in allowing himself to be taken there. Now it is necessary to try to get him out, and the King's declaration in October that he was free, and that to prove it he would go and visit the provinces in the spring, this declaration is a good pretext for getting him out. But beforehand he must let the Assembly carry on with all their nonsense. Once he leaves Paris, a new order will come into being; if he's stopped, his captivity will be well demonstrated to the provinces and even in this case there would have to be a big change . . .

The noble, feeling and generous manner in which Your Majesty has expressed yourself on the situation of the King and Queen of France is worthy of you . . . The letters Your Majesty has written to them cannot fail to touch them; when one is unhappy one is always more sensible. The commission with which Your Majesty has kindly charged me is too agreeable for me not to try to deliver them myself; besides, I wouldn't know who to trust and I will be only too happy to be the bearer of Your Majesty's tender and generous sentiments. I arrived here to see Baron Taube two days ago from Valenciennes, where I spent a week.[33]

From that moment on, Fersen's correspondence became much more extensive and more political in nature; even more precautions were required to keep it confidential, since he was obliged to hide Gustav III's plans from the Swedish Ambassador Staël, whose wife was a fervent revolutionary. Fersen also drafted dispatches and memoranda for Louis XVI and Marie-Antoinette; the extreme secrecy required led him to propose the adoption of code No. 2.

6. FERSEN TO MARIE-ANTOINETTE, UNPUBLISHED LETTER, 1 FEBRUARY 1790

Stafsund, SE/RA/720807/10/20. This letter entitled 'Example' is not logged in Fersen's register. It was found in the packet containing the codes for his correspondence with Marie-Antoinette and is a guide on how to use code No. 2, contained in the same envelope.[34] None of their letters employ this code, which is much more complex than the poly-alphabetic cipher adopted by the Queen.

Example
Stockholm, 1 Feb. 1790

1. J'ai reçu ma chère amie la vôtre du . . .
2. l un dilu nd ilund ilun di lundi lu . . . . .
3. 4q7 08,a &2 58ueb . . . .
4. lun dilu nd ilund . . . .
5. J'ai reçu ma chère . . . .

In order to use this cipher you need a key, that is, any word. The least easy to guess is the day of the date of the letter; in the example above the key would be *lundi* [*Monday*] because 1 February is a Monday. If it were the 2nd, it would be *Tuesday*, the 3rd *Wednesday* and so on. To change it one could underline the place from where the letter is dated, as in <u>Stockholm</u>: the line underneath will indicate that <u>Stockholm</u> is the key. Each time there is a day in front of the date, that will mean that the day is the key. That would only be necessary if one wanted a different key from the actual day of the date, so: Wednesday 1 February – then *Wednesday* would be the key word.

To encrypt line 1, you write *lundi* underneath, because 1 February is a Monday. If it were the 2nd, one would write *Tuesday*. You must be careful to write the letters exactly underneath, as in line 2. Then in the code table you look on side no. 1 for the letter L. You follow the line horizontally until you reach the letter J. Then you go up to the first line of side no. 2, where you will find a 4, which will be the first letter of the code. You go back to side 1 for the letter U. You follow the line to the letter A, you go up and on the first line of side 2 you find a q, which will be the second line of the code – and so on, as you can see from line 3 of the example.

To decipher, you write *lundi* underneath the code, as in line 4 of the example. You then look in side 1 of the code table for the letter L. Then you look in the first line of side 2 for a 4. The place where these two lines cross in the table will give you the letter J. Then a U in side 1 and a 9 from side 2 will give you an A, and so on. One must be careful to leave enough space between the lines to decode. *Lundi* starts again on each line.

In 1790 Fersen did not record a single letter to Marie-Antoinette in his register. His correspondence with Sophie and his father, however, sheds some light on his activities in France: significantly, the Queen had organized her living quarters in the Tuileries so that it was possible for them to see each other in private. Everything shows that Louis XVI did not wish to leave Paris, despite Fersen's opinion that 'he made a mistake in allowing himself to be taken there'. The King was the most irresolute character, and persuading him of the need to take action was difficult; no escape plan seems even to have been discussed at this point. Fersen took no further interest in his regiment, for the National Assembly had begun extensive army reforms and foreign regiments were among the first to be targeted.

In November 1789, despite his apparent acceptance of the status quo, Louis XVI had written 'to the King of Spain, and sent him a protest against whatever he might publicly be engaged to do or sanction during his detention at Paris, or while under any sort of restraint'.[35] Inactive protests, however, were a far cry from positive action. In a letter to George Washington on 24 January 1790 Gouverneur Morris depicts a king who was at the mercy of events and points out his fatal flaw – that he abandoned anyone who attempted to help him.

> The King is in effect a prisoner at Paris, and obeys entirely the National Assembly . . . If the reigning prince were not the small beer character that he is, there can be but little doubt that watching events and making a tolerable use of them he would regain his authority, but what will you have from a creature, who situated as he is, eats and drinks and sleeps well, and laughs as merry as a grig as lives? The idea that they will give him some money which he can economize contents him entirely. Poor man, he little thinks how unstable is his situation. He is beloved, but it is not with the sort of love which a monarch should inspire. It is the

kind of good natural pity which one feels for a led captive. There is besides no possibility of serving him, for at the slightest show of opposition he gives up everything and every person.[36]

In contrast, the Queen felt the full humiliation of her position. She needed Fersen's comforting presence more than ever after the death of her brother Joseph II on 20 February. The Duke of Dorset told the Duchess of Devonshire:

The poor Queen is if possible more unhappy than ever. Her brother wrote her a very affectionate letter the day before he died, full of tenderness and affection for her and thoroughly sensible of her situation. How shocking for her; *pauvre femme, je la plains du fond de mon âme*. M. de Mercy, who delivered the letter to her, repents very much having given it to her. ('poor woman, I pity her from the depths of my soul')

Dorset went on to paint a grim picture of French politics, and was particularly upset by Georgiana's friendship with Lafayette. It would not be at all surprising had Lafayette tried to get him killed, since he had not raised a finger to stop the attempt on the Queen's life at Versailles, and Dorset was known to be her friend.

The National Assembly seem to be determined to overset everything. I think some explosion must happen soon. Bailly and Lafayette sooner or later will share the fate of Foulon and Berthier. The populace in more instances than one have expressed their dislike to them. I am sorry you correspond with the General, for though chance has made him *un homme célèbre*, I don't think in either principle or action he deserves any distinction, *et puis son antipathie pour tout ce qui est anglais* (excepting you, perhaps) is what I cannot forgive him, but is what attaches you to him. He did all he could to have me massacred at Paris. I have known it since; had I been informed of it at the time from good authority, I should not have risked remaining there, but hearing it only as common report I could not believe it.[37] ('and besides, his antipathy for everything English')

No wonder Marie-Antoinette, shackled to a husband who remained inert while his enemies butchered loyal servants of the crown in public, sought solace in the arms of her lover. Fersen spoke often of her ('*elle*' or '*mon amie*' – 'she' or 'my friend') in letters to his sister Sophie that year. They were most definitely a couple.

> 4 April 1790
>
> Thank you so much for everything you said about my friend. Believe me, my dear Sophie, she deserves all the feelings you can have for her. She is the most perfect creature I know and her conduct, which is perfect, too, has won over everyone and everywhere I hear her praised. Imagine how much I enjoy it.

> 10 April 1790
>
> I'm beginning to be a little happier, because from time to time I see my friend freely *chez elle*, and that consoles us a little for all the miseries she's enduring, poor woman. She's an angel for her conduct, courage and sensibility – no one has ever known how to love like that. She's infinitely sensible of everything you wrote to me about her; she cried a lot over it and charged me to tell you how greatly she was touched by it. She would be so happy to be able to see you sometimes. She believes that if our plan succeeds then you will be able to come here and that makes her very happy. In fact it would be possible then.[38]

Fersen had in fact proposed several times, through Sophie and Taube, that he replace Staël at the Swedish embassy in Paris, clearly in order to ensure he had a reason to stay in France after the disbandment of his regiment.[39] His letter to Sophie on 10 April shows that the idea had probably originated with Marie-Antoinette, who clearly could not bear the thought of his return to Sweden.

> 7 May 1790
>
> We never cease making wishes for your happiness, my dear friend, and her thoughts are very much with you. She was moved to tears by everything you said about her. When one is unhappy one is more easily affected, especially when one has such a beautiful soul.

> 31 May 1790
>
> Everything continues the same here, my dear friend, that is to say badly, and you will read in the newspapers of all the horrors and cruel acts being committed in the provinces and in Paris . . . She is

extremely unhappy but very courageous. I told her everything you
wrote to me for her, and it pleased her. I try to comfort her as much as
I can – I owe it to her, she's so perfect for me.[40]

The National Assembly permitted the Royal Family to spend the
summer at Saint-Cloud, Marie-Antoinette's château on the outskirts of
Paris. Fersen wrote to Sophie from there on 28 June 1790.

She is very sensible of everything you say for her. Never has anyone
more deserved it and never has anyone been more perfect. My only
sorrow is that I cannot comfort her entirely for all her sorrows or
make her as happy as she deserves to be. I'm writing to you from *chez
elle* in the country.[41]

The previous year Fersen had asked his sister 'to be prudent when
talking of this country's affairs and of *Her*.' In order to deflect suspicion
should his letter be intercepted, he adds: 'The King and the Royal
Family are at Saint-Cloud. They are much better off there than at Paris
and have more freedom, because they can go out as much as they like.
Nobody goes there except the staff and I haven't been there.'[42] And so
Fersen continued to spread misinformation to conceal his liaison with
the Queen, this time to fool the revolutionaries; but at the same time he
managed to tell Sophie exactly where he was. However, to keep his
presence at Saint-Cloud secret from his father, he sent a letter on this
same 28 June dated 'from Paris'.

The ceremony on 14 July 1790 to mark the first anniversary of the
fall of the Bastille necessitated the Royal Family's return to Paris.
Naturally, Fersen accompanied them. He wrote to his father that 'the
deputies from the provinces behaved perfectly, and never cease to give
the King and Queen proofs of their respect, love and loyalty.'[43] In the
Swedish archives there is a copy of the speech made to the Queen by
these loyal men (who were only too willing to fight for Louis XVI had he
known how to profit from the occasion), on which Fersen recorded
Marie-Antoinette's reply. She paid tribute to M. Durepaire, one of the
bodyguards who had saved her life on 6 October 1789.

The Queen could not hold back her tears and replied: 'My choked
voice will show you more than any words everything I feel in my soul.
You forestalled me in presenting me with your address to the King – I

was going to ask you for it.' Having then spotted M. Durepaire who happened to be there, she continued: 'You praise my courage – here is someone' – presenting M. Durepaire to them – 'who merits your praise more. He's one of those brave bodyguards who was [nearly] slaughtered at our door.' Everyone fell on his neck and kissed him. There were cries of 'God save the Queen, the bodyguards and M. Durepaire', and people burst into tears.[44]

Fersen followed the Queen back to Saint-Cloud. On 31 July he explained to Sophie: 'for some time now I have been mostly in the country, as I told you, with the Comte d'Esterhazy, and tomorrow I'm going to spend a week with the Duchesse de Fitzjames.' On 8 August, writing of this visit, he said: 'there were only seven of us, but we all got along well and I was happy there. However, *She* was needed to complete my happiness and without that there is no perfect happiness for me.'[45] He spent most of the summer at Auteuil, and his frequent nocturnal rendezvous with Marie-Antoinette led the Comte de Saint-Priest to inform her 'that the presence of the Comte de Fersen and his visits to the château could present some danger. "Tell him then," she replied, "if you feel it necessary. As for me, I'm not concerned." And in effect, his visits continued as usual.'[46] Fersen was well aware of the discussions Louis XVI and Marie-Antoinette were holding with Mirabeau in an attempt to block partisans of Lafayette in the National Assembly. On 5 September 1790 he informed Gustav III that

M. de Lafayette is in a bad position and he is very uneasy. He's a low scoundrel; fortunately he only knows how to be one by halves ... The Comte de Mirabeau, from the 89 Club, is Lafayette's sworn enemy and has approached the Court. It seems that they will make use of him, and that worries Lafayette even more; but it's a good way of keeping them both in check, one by the other.[47]

Lafayette was certainly more than half a scoundrel. He allowed Fersen free access to Marie-Antoinette's apartments with the sole aim of compromising her, for he wanted to get rid of the Queen. Fabian von Fersen wrote in invisible ink to his sister Sophie from Strasbourg on 30 November: 'Today's news is that the National Assembly wants the King to separate from the Queen, they want to prosecute her for adultery, declare the children bastards and punish the Queen very severely.'[48]

Three weeks earlier the Comte de La Marck had written to the former Austrian Ambassador, Mercy, describing how, during a long conversation with the Queen, Lafayette had

> employed the most odious methods to trouble her soul and he even went so far as to say that to obtain the divorce, she would be caught committing adultery. The Queen replied with the dignity, firmness and courage you know her to possess, but it's outrageous to think of such conduct from a man like M. de Lafayette.[49]

Note the total lack of surprise with regard to the accusation of adultery; La Marck is simply shocked by Lafayette's 'odious methods'. No wonder Marie-Antoinette detested Lafayette, who avowed he had 'a republican heart'; she was very well aware that he had failed to protect her during the attempt on her life on 6 October 1789.[50]

One of Fersen's letters to Sophie during his stay at Auteuil in October 1790 clears up a misunderstanding about his private life that has long been relayed by biographers. Marie-Antoinette was always the perfection of womanhood for Fersen – 'what gentleness, what tenderness, what kindness, what solicitude, what a delicate, loving and feeling heart!' he wrote of her after her death.[51] However, his handsome face brought him the unwelcome attentions of women who had none of these qualities, among them the Comtesse de Saint-Priest. Her brother, Charles von Ludolf was the Austrian Ambassador in Stockholm. From the following letter Fersen wrote to Sophie, it would appear that far from being his mistress, as has been claimed, she was in fact stalking him.

> 15 October 1790
> What Taube told you about *Her* [Marie-Antoinette] gave me great pleasure. She deserves it – her conduct is angelic. She astonishes me, and I wish everybody would love her as much as she deserves and do her justice. I'm still based at Auteuil and I'm very content and happy here ... You did well not to reply to Nolcken's question on behalf of M. de Ludolf. Never answer any that come from that quarter. I hardly see his sister [Mme de Saint-Priest] at all now I know that all the courtesies she showed me were due only to love; she became mad about me, and despite everything I told her, it continues still. It's truly a madness. I broke with her as soon as she explained herself. Sometimes I feel sorry for her. The details are incredible; there was no humiliation she would

not suffer or endure, even my refusal to profit from all that a woman can grant to a man. She knows everything and it doesn't trouble her.[52]

Doubtless it was from her husband that she had learnt 'everything' about Fersen's liaison with Marie-Antoinette; she gossiped openly about it when she arrived in Stockholm the following year.

Fersen told Sophie on 30 October that he had been back in Paris – 'this vile cesspit' – for two days.[53] His letters to her give further insights into his intimate relationship with the Queen at a time when their political cooperation was becoming critical; but he never breathes a word of this to Sophie. She was very distressed at the idea of being separated from Taube, who Gustav III wished to send on a mission to Moscow. Fersen reveals his compassionate nature as he tries to console her, while Marie-Antoinette offers her a lock of hair and a ring. They both understood her pain but too well.

19 December 1790

I will undertake your commission for the hair. The idea delights me, and it will be a great pleasure for her to learn of it.

3 January 1791

Here's the hair you asked me for; if there isn't enough I'll send you some more. It is she who gives it to you and she was deeply touched by your wish. She's so good and so perfect, and it seems to me that I love her even more now she loves you. She charged me to tell you how much she feels and shares your sorrows. Ah, I shall never die happy until you have seen her.

17 January 1791

My dear and tender Sophie, I've just this minute received yours of the 28th. Ah, how keenly I feel and share your pains. They increase all of mine. They used to be eased formerly by the certainty of your happiness and tranquillity. I was happy to know that you were happy; at present I don't even have that consolation and your sorrows pierce my soul. My dear friend, speak to me often about them, always let me know about them, tell me everything you're going through and all you feel. It's a need, it's a consolation to pour one's heart out to a friend, and you know you have none truer or more tender than I . . . She says a thousand things to you and keenly shares your sorrows. She often cries about them with me – imagine how I must love her. If you have an easier way to get the ring you want made here, let me know and how you want it made. I'll get it done. It's she who wishes it and wants to give it to you.

6 February 1791

Your health made me worry, my dear friend. She felt it deeply – that eased it a little. Thank God our friend [Taube] tells me that you are better . . . My health is good, hers is too, despite all her troubles.[54]

While assuring Sophie that he was in no danger ('as I have no part in affairs and I'm only a spectator, I'm very quiet and run no risk'), Fersen was working with Marie-Antoinette on a daily basis.[55] It was the Queen who took charge of the correspondence for Louis XVI's secret diplomacy because the King himself remained passive. He wished to regain his authority, but he mistrusted his brothers and the émigrés and possessed neither the courage nor the energy to lead a counter-revolution. The Foreign Minister M. de Montmorin told Gouverneur Morris that 'the King is absolutely good for nothing; that at present he always asks, when he is to work with the King, that the Queen be present.'[56] Mercy says the same thing in a letter to the Austrian Chancellor, Prince Kaunitz. 'I've never had any business directly with the King. All the conversations I've had with this monarch have always taken place in the Queen's presence. Everything came from her and was addressed to her.'[57] It is very important to remember this when reading the Queen's correspondence during the Revolution. According to Quintin Craufurd:

The only person abroad fully authorized to treat for the King with foreign powers was the Baron de Breteuil. Though the King loves the Count d'Artois, he seems to be mistrustful of his prudence; and the King and Queen have shown the most decided disapprobation of his employing M. de Calonne.[58]

The correspondence with Breteuil, then living at Soleure in Switzerland, passed through Fersen; he drafted dispatches, proposed solutions and worked tirelessly to extract the Royal Family from Paris in order to establish a monarchist government at Montmédy. This idea had been proposed by Mirabeau as early as July 1790; he correctly foresaw the annihilation of the Royal Family so long as the King remained a prisoner in the Tuileries. 'The first condition of M's plan is that we get away with the whole family from Paris; not to go abroad but within France,' wrote Marie-Antoinette to her brother the Emperor four days after her first meeting with Mirabeau. 'I will keep you informed of details for the execution of this plan, which is too serious not to require extreme prudence and absolute secrecy.'[59]

The story of the Royal Family's escape from Paris and arrest at Varennes requires a book to itself, so here the reader will find only documents and letters that aid the comprehension of Fersen's correspondence with Marie-Antoinette or clarify their relationship. On 11 January 1791 the Queen mentioned the plan to the Comte de Mercy, Plenipotentiary Minister for Leopold II in the Austrian Netherlands, notifying him of the dispatch of a box containing her diamonds.

> If the replies from the first two powers [Austria and Spain] are as favourable as we have reason to hope, we will immediately send our plan to you to be forwarded to Vienna, and work together on the timing and the means of executing it. The baron [Breteuil] at Soleure knows everything; you can write to him about it. Only four people in total are in the secret; it's the best way to ensure it will be kept. It would be useful to have a prompt reply from Vienna.[60]

In Paris it was the Queen's right-hand man Axel von Fersen who was charged with getting the Royal Family out of the closely guarded Tuileries and past the city barriers. He liaised with foreign governments, raised finance, ordered vehicles and refined all the practical details with the Marquis de Bouillé, a royalist general who commanded on the northern frontier. But before they could execute this audacious plan it was necessary to persuade Louis XVI of the need to leave Paris in order to regain his authority. In the following memorandum addressed to the King and Queen Fersen sums up their situation. He starts by talking to them both, but at the end it is apparent that his remarks are for Marie-Antoinette alone.

7. FERSEN TO MARIE-ANTOINETTE AND LOUIS XVI, 27 MARCH 1791

AN 440AP/1. Autograph copy of a letter from Fersen addressed chiefly to Marie-Antoinette. It is not logged in his register (nor are any of the letters relating to the flight to Varennes). Very probably he handed it personally to the Queen. 'The princes' are the Comte d'Artois and the émigré cousins of the King. They wanted the restoration of an absolute monarchy by force.

27 March 1791

There seems to be no doubt that it is necessary to act and to act vigorously if order and happiness are to be re-established in the kingdom, to save it from total ruin, to impede its partition, place the King back on the throne and grant him his authority. The constant, uniform progress by the Jacobins in their villainy, the disunion among the democrats in the Assembly, the dissatisfaction of the princes – which grows visibly but which cannot find an outlet for want of a common rallying point – the determination of the princes, particularly the Prince de Condé, to act if the King does not: all this seems to indicate that the time has come to take a decision. It appears even to be favourable to do so, and the longer the delay, the harder it will be. But how to act after the news received from the Emperor, coupled with the slowness and indecision of Spain and the difficulty of finding the money?

Two courses of action present themselves. One, to do nothing until alliances have been made with various powers to obtain the necessary help, both in men and money. The other, to leave Paris as soon as assurance of the good disposition of foreign powers has been received and the necessary money has been found – six to eight million *livres* – to pay for the troops for two or three months, by which time a loan from Switzerland will have been obtained.

The first of these options is without question the safest. It presents fewer dangers for Your Majesties and the advantage of a less doubtful outcome, or at the least, one that is less contested. But as it is not possible to predict the timing, is it not to be feared that the ills of the state will have considerably increased during this time, such that it will be more difficult to remedy them? Won't habit or discouragement have gained so much ground that it will no longer be possible to overcome them? Won't the fanatics have calmed down and joined together to create a new order which will still be disadvantageous to the King but where individuals will find their satisfaction in the peace they enjoy and which they will then prefer to the convulsions of a civil war? By that time, won't the princes have made some attempt, and rallied all the nobility to their cause, all of them dissatisfied with the current regime; and will they not be then masters of the kingdom and of Your Majesties?

The second option is more hazardous. Both the Comte de Mercy and the Baron de Breteuil seem to indicate it. Its success is predicated on two great probabilities. The Emperor and Spain are well disposed, but Spain does not wish to act without the Emperor, who, by a policy that is misunderstood and fearful foresight, would like to delay the time at which he will manifest his goodwill. The northern powers have good intentions, but their remoteness and the war against the Turks prevents them from seconding Your Majesties' views in an active manner. Sardinia and Switzerland are sure, and it is more than likely that a pronounced movement by Your Majesties would make these two powers make up their minds; their indecision is due solely to the doubts they have about the strength of Your Majesties' resolve and the fear that they will be compromised to no purpose should it change. M. de Mercy seems to indicate it in his letter.[61] Such a measure would have something grand, noble, imposing and daring about it; its effect throughout the kingdom and the whole of Europe would be incalculable. It could bring back the army and prevent its complete disintegration. It would rip up the constitution and stop the rebels from making the necessary changes to render it sustainable to consolidate the Revolution. Taken now, such a step would make the princes' movements useful, whereas if they were to act alone and suffer setbacks they would no longer be able to serve the King's cause.

Whichever course Your Majesties adopt, it is felt necessary to await the replies from Vienna and Spain on the plan which has been communicated to them in order to be fully assured of their dispositions and what one can hope for from them. If the first course is taken, B's [Bouillé's] preparations must be stopped and negotiations must continue.[62] If the second is preferred, one must continue with all the preparations for its execution, take care of finding the necessary money and select at once a capable and favourably disposed person to be sent to England to sound out subtly the intentions of that power, without compromising himself, who will only receive his instructions at the moment of the King's departure. These will be to negotiate for the perfect neutrality of that Court, whether by some reasonable sacrifices or by forcing agreement with the help of the northern powers, whose dispositions are unequivocal but who will not be able to help the King in a more direct manner because of their remoteness.

In view of the certainty Your Majesties have of the King of Sweden's intentions and his desire to be useful, would they have any objection in authorizing me to communicate to him on their behalf the plan they have adopted and their project, in order to profit from his manifest good intentions by calling on his good offices to contain England should that power decline to listen to any proposal of accommodation and desire to throw up obstacles to vex your projects? This mark of confidence will flatter him and could only interest him more in its success. As this overture would pass through Baron Taube, whose attachment to his master and to Your Majesties is known to me, I would tell him only to make what use of it he felt was necessary and which would be most advantageous for Your Majesties.

I have the honour to send the Queen some reflections on the current state of affairs as well as the translation of a letter I have just received. It will prove even more to the Queen how deeply occupied the King of Sweden is with Your Majesties' **position** and with means of being useful to them. I have the honour to attach . . .

The following letter perfectly illustrates Fersen's political role alongside Marie-Antoinette: he drafts a letter to the Baron de Breteuil, gives it to the Queen for her review, she consults Louis XVI and adds some comments in the margin, and the final letter is then encrypted by Fersen and sent to the baron.

Fersen to the Baron de Breteuil, annotated by Marie-Antoinette, 2 April 1791

AN 440AP/1. Autograph letter from Fersen with comments written by Marie-Antoinette in the margin. It is not logged in the letter register. The Royal Family's departure from Paris is now fixed for 'the last fortnight in May'. The first paragraph illustrates the strict confidentiality of this correspondence.

+ <u>MA</u> followed by italics = Marie-Antoinette's comments

No. 10, 2 April 1791

I received your dispatch of 11 and 16 March by the Vicomte de Vérac,[63] but in being so mysterious you were almost unintelligible and I could barely read you. The ink you used was so weak that nothing could be deciphered without holding it against the light, and I had to copy it all out so the King could read it; as I dare not trust anyone it took a very long time.

The correspondence from Berlin appears to be very interesting and the King will surely be pleased with it; after all the various intrigues by this Court and the way affairs are conducted there, I think like you that it would be neither prudent nor useful to start any negotiations there at the moment, and whether it is due to impotence, goodwill or personal interest we have nothing to fear from the King of Prussia for the execution of the King's great projects. His Majesty thinks so, too, but he is not of the same opinion with regard to England; and although He is quite convinced of the danger of making any overture to the Court of London, and having even expressly forbidden M. Barthélemy[64] to do so, He persists in instructing him to sound out the dispositions of this ministry. You will see by the instruction sent to him, of which a copy is attached, that the commission he is given by the King cannot compromise him at all. Young Champcenetz[65] + , [son of] the governor of the Tuileries is charged with taking it to him – his loyalty and discretion can be counted on.

+<u>MA</u>: *It's perhaps dangerous to choose him because of his parents' connections with the baron. Besides, it isn't certain that he can undertake the journey.*

The King agrees with you on the conclusions to be drawn from the different letters from M. de Mercy, and he remains convinced that his departure from Paris is an essential prerequisite, without which no power will want to engage or involve itself in his affairs or to help him; but His Majesty has no reason to be so convinced as you are of the active dispositions of the Emperor + <u>MA</u>: *towards him.* What this prince said to M. de Bombelles, and which has even found its way back to the King, and which he must have said to other people, bears no relation to what he himself has written to the Queen. After many protestations of friendship, interest and sensibility on Their Majesties' position, the Emperor says quite clearly that the difficulty in which he finds himself and those which his neighbours could yet cause him, prevents him at the moment from favouring in any active manner the

King's projects for re-establishing his authority. He enjoins patience and that execution of the plan communicated to him by the King be postponed to a later date. In my view this difference in the Emperor's language can only be attributed to his natural desire for peace, and his fear of compromising its duration by a definite move in the King's favour, to his indecisive character, and to the embarrassment he suffers in giving a positive answer of this nature to people when they prove to him how dreadful the King's position is and how His Majesty's cause, being common to all sovereigns, should be protected by them.

As regards the show of force, here is an extract of what M. de Bouillé tells me in his last letter. He restricted himself to this request after I sent him M. de Mercy's replies, and the little reliance that can be placed on the King's troops, even on the best disposed of them, makes him wish for a certain number of foreign troops to set them an example and impress them, should that be necessary. The King approves of everything you have written to Prince Kaunitz and M. de Mercy. His Majesty has already written to the latter in conformity with M. de B's [Bouillé's] letter and asks him for a positive reply on the article of the 15 million [*livres*].+

+<u>MA</u>: *The positive request will depend on the answer, will they act, yes or no; but the last letters make no mention of 15 million.*

The King is still decided on leaving during the last fortnight of May. His Majesty feels the necessity for it and hopes to have received replies from Spain by then and to have gathered together the money required to meet initial expenses. M. de Mercy is wrong to complain that he is not kept informed. We write to him as often as the difficulty attendant on a correspondence which must be kept so secret and the dearth of opportunities of getting letters to him will allow. These same difficulties, and the small number of people the King can employ, also render his correspondence less regular, but that cannot harm the whole of such a great enterprise, since the secret and its execution is concentrated in only four persons. As for the new agents you mentioned to me, the King has ordered me to tell you that he does not know them and they have not been sent by him, and I repeat on his behalf that you alone are charged to negotiate with the Court of Vienna. I have already told you that M. de Fonbrune[66] was a schemer, and for that reason it was preferred to leave him at Vienna on the pretext that he might perhaps be needed; but he has no mission and knows nothing at all. +<u>MA</u>: *It might perhaps at present be wise to let the baron know for what purpose M. de Fonbrune*

*was initially employed and why he is being managed. This is my idea only.
I didn't think of it until after I saw the King.*

In November 1789, after his arrival in Paris, he was given to H.M. by the Spanish Ambassador as a reliable man, and he was charged to carry a protest against everything the King might do or sign to the King of Spain; this protest was received by the King of Spain and remains in his hands, which is why M. de Fonbrune has to be managed. The Baron d'Escars has never had any relations with the King and His Majesty didn't even know that President de Grosbois had left. As for the barons de Flacksland,[67] they have never been charged with anything other than to sound out the dispositions of the German princes, a commission in which they badly acquitted themselves and which they probably found beyond their means and capabilities, since the baron, to whom we wrote about it six weeks ago, did not even go there. All these gentlemen are probably agents of the Comte d'Artois or the Prince de Condé,[68] or even volunteers who do more to wreck affairs by their importunate and indiscreet zeal than they do to serve the King's cause. His Majesty orders me to warn you about them and to recommend above all that you are wary of them and don't use them. He also desires that you warn Prince Kaunitz,[69] so that he trusts only those people who are sent to him by you or M. de Mercy. It's what the Queen has already told the Emperor.

Recommend to M. de Bombelles the greatest prudence and great circumspection with regard to the Comte d'Artois. The King fears, and with reason, that the Prince de Condé will get wind of his projects and that this prince, pushed by his ambition and desire to play a principal role, will hasten the execution of his fantastic enterprise, and you can easily imagine what the consequences and inconveniences would be for that which the King wants to undertake.

After the King of Spain said that he only wanted to negotiate directly with the King, with no intermediary other than his Ambassador, His Majesty wished you not to transmit to M. de La Vauguyon the instruction dated 14 February as it was when I sent you the copy, but since it is already done, the King will try to arrange this business with the Court of Spain to their satisfaction. His Majesty approves your idea of making use of Cardinal de Bernis's connection with M. de Florida Blanca.[70] As for the King of Sweden's subsidies, it would be better not to mention them until one is sure that he has demanded them.

The King agrees with you on deferring negotiations regarding the formation of a confederation against Prussia, Holland and England until the favourable or unfavourable dispositions of these powers are better known, as well as the advantages or sacrifices necessary to grant them for services rendered. His Majesty has always resisted the idea, and his plan has been never to grant them unless it were to become absolutely necessary. He even thought of only making such a decision in favour of England.

We are still busy trying to find the money required; given that it's essential to keep it secret, this is a very difficult matter. I hope, however, that it can be found through the Dutch patriots and by amassing several small sums. The calling of a new legislature furnishes us with a useful pretext.

After everything that happened on the 18th, the King feels the necessity to act, and to act promptly, even more strongly.[71] He has decided to sacrifice everything to execute his plans, and in order to be able to do so with greater certainty His Majesty has decided to adopt another system of conduct; to blind the rebels to his real intentions, he will seem to recognize the need to enter fully into the Revolution and to get closer to them. He will be directed only by their advice and will constantly forestall the rabble's wishes in order not to give them the slightest pretext for an insurrection, so that peace is maintained and they are inspired with the trust so essential for his departure from Paris. All means must be used to reach such an objective. It is said that he will be asked to dismiss his entire household; it will be granted, and may even provide a little money.

After a very pressing letter from the Comte d'Artois, in which he seemed inclined to go and join the Prince de Condé, and in which he laid emphasis on the means at his disposal, he has been asked to send a trustworthy man to inform us of these means and to devise a plan on a possible course of action. This was imagined as a way of keeping him in check and in order to gain time. A man named Conti, confidential man of the Prince de Condé, is also being sent to that prince to inform him of the King's position and to stop him from acting, by proving to him the dangers to which he would expose the Royal Family should he attempt something at the present time.

Copy of M. Barthélemy instruction

Copy of M. de B's letter

On 18 April 1791 Louis XVI and his family were compelled by a threatening mob to return to their apartments in the Tuileries when they were about to leave to spend Easter at Saint-Cloud. This event finally persuaded the King of the urgent need to leave his capital. 'We must leave or perish,' the Queen wrote to Mercy. Fersen's encrypted correspondence with the Marquis de Bouillé and the Baron de Breteuil give details on the organization of the escape. Note that Fersen's more northerly route included only five major towns, and excluded Sainte-Menehould (where Louis XVI was recognized) and Varennes (where he was stopped), yet Bouillé picked a route with more stages, claiming it was quicker.

1791

Fersen to Bouillé

6 May, No. 12

An escort needs to be scattered along the route. One shudders at the thought of the horrors which could occur if they were betrayed and arrested. The agreed route is through Meaux, Châlons, Reims, Isle Rethel, Pauvres. Tell me if you want to change it and what precautions you will take. There can be no bodyguards at Châlons – the town has asked not to have them there any more.

Bouillé to Fersen

9 May, No. 15

Send me M. Goguelat, who should be with you. I need him for the necessary reconnaissance of the route from here, in the region of Erheim . . . All things considered, the shortest, safest and easiest route is through Meaux, Montmirail (where one must not forget to take the road to La Ferté-sous-Jarre), Châlons, Sainte Menehould, Varennes, Dun and Stenay. You will no longer go through Reims. Good detachments will be placed from Sainte Menehould to Stenay to provide an escort; it's a distance of twelve leagues. Would it not be a good idea, a few days before, to entrust part of the secret to M. d'Agoult and get him to go to Châlons with thirty or so of the most determined bodyguards, as though they were visiting the horses there, to remove them in accordance with the town's request? At the appointed hour, these thirty guards would be on horseback at the city gate and would provide an escort to Sainte Menehould . . .

Here is the route in detail: from Paris to Meaux, ten leagues by post; from Meaux to La Ferté-sous-Jarre, five leagues; from La Ferté to Montmirail, nine leagues; from Montmirail to Châlons-sur-Marne, fourteen; from Châlons to Sainte Menehould, ten; from Sainte Menehould to Varennes, five; from Varennes to Dun, five; from Dun to Stenay, three; from Stenay to M [Montmédy], two. You can see this route on the departments map. In all it is sixty-one leagues by post; by leaving at night and travelling through the second, you arrive during the second day.

Fersen to Breteuil

Paris, 23 May, No. 14

The King wants to leave in the first week of June because he will receive two million [*livres*] from the Civil List around that time which he can take with him. The King is also in difficulty about the person to accompany him. He had thought of M. de Saint-Priest, but he fears that as he has already been in government it would be contracting some kind of engagement with him, and yet it is necessary that he has someone in the carriage with him who could talk, should that be necessary.

Fersen to Bouillé

26 May, No. 13

I've written to Goguelat to tell him to go to you and to do everything you order him to do; he is a trustworthy man, he only requires moderating. The King approves the route, and it will be fixed as you sent it. We are seeing about the bodyguards. By tomorrow's or Tuesday's stage-coach I'm sending you one million [*livres*] in notes, in white taffeta addressed to M. de Coutades. We have four [million], including one outside the kingdom. No precautions are required between here and Châlons. The best of all is to take none – everything depends on speed and secrecy, and if you are not absolutely sure of your detachments it would be better not to place any, or at least to position them only after Varennes, so as not to draw attention to the area. The King would therefore pass through quite simply. It is in order not to create any unrest at Châlons that we cannot muster any bodyguards.

Fersen to Bouillé

29 May, No. 14

The departure is fixed for the 12th of next month. All was ready and we would have chosen the 6th or 7th, but the two million [*livres*] will not be received until the 7th or 8th, and there is besides a very democratic *femme de chambre* in the Dauphin's service who is not leaving until the 11th. The last route indicated is the one that will be taken. I shall not accompany the King; he did not wish it. I will go through Le Quesnoy and leave by Bavay to get to Mons.

Fersen to Breteuil

30 May

The departure was fixed for the 12th, but M. de Bouillé wants it to be delayed to the 15th or 20th to give the Austrians time to reinforce their sector at Luxembourg. It is required to give him a pretext for assembling his troops. Write to M. de Mercy on the subject.

Fersen to Bouillé

13 June, No. 17

The departure has been fixed for the 20th at midnight, without delay. A bad *femme de chambre* attached to the Dauphin who could not be got rid of until Monday morning forced it back to Monday evening, but you can count on it.

Fersen to Bouillé

14 June, No. 18

Nothing has changed and they are leaving on Monday 20th at midnight, to be at Pont de Somme-Vesle on Tuesday at two-thirty by the latest. You can count on that. Have you considered that Monsieur will be arriving, too, and are you able to lodge him in Montmédy, or put him in Longwy? If you could secure me a room at Montmédy I would be pleased. We have not yet received M. de Mercy's reply. We wrote to him again to get the troops to march. Rest assured the departure is the 20th at midnight. Monsieur will take a different route from the King.[72]

Fersen always intended to accompany the Royal Family all the way to Montmédy, but the King would not allow it, entrusting him solely with getting them out of Paris. Louis XVI, also intended to take Saint-Priest with him, who could negotiate in the event of an arrest. His decision to take neither man proved to be fatal. He had no military experience, he did not have the resolve, energy and iron nerve of Fersen or the diplomatic abilities of Saint-Priest. For once in his life, Louis XVI wanted to be in charge. It was unthinkable for him to be escorted by a foreigner rumoured to be his wife's lover, when the whole of Europe was watching his every move; equally, to be dependent on a minister to extract him from difficulties would be seen as a sign of weakness. But Louis XVI was the last man to execute such a daring plan. He certainly did not lack courage; however, as Quintin Craufurd remarked, it was a passive courage that enabled him to suffer with great dignity, not the active courage required to face down his enemies. In June 1791, even though the escape was a well-kept secret, everyone was expecting an energetic response from the King of France to the chaos wrought by two years of revolution; the King of Sweden was in Aix-la-Chapelle, ostensibly for his health but in reality to show his support for the French King once he got to Montmédy. The émigré princes were burning with impatience to enter France and restore royal authority by force if the King was too slow to take measures himself. The stakes could not have been higher.

Fersen must have been very disappointed by the King's decision, yet he had no choice but to accept it and continue, with his usual efficiency, making all the preparations. He borrowed money from his old friends, Mme de Korff and her mother, Mme Stegelmann (262,000 *livres*); he gave 100,000 *livres* of his own, he obtained false passports, he took delivery of the coach built specially to carry the whole Royal Family (because they refused to travel separately), and the carriage for the *femmes de chambre*; he stocked it with provisions, bought horses for Bouillé, the duc de Choiseul and Goguelat. Finally, he undertook the most dangerous part of the operation in extracting the Royal Family from the Tuileries at midnight on 20 June 1791. Disguised as a hackney coachman, he drove them from Paris as far as Bondy. Several documents in the Fersen archive relate to items purchased for this operation, including the following:[73]

Spent	Livres
Travel necessary set	2853
Tumblers, cutlery and cookers	1414
The carriage	5944
1 horse	2400

3 horses	4350
1 horse	720
A carriage and harness	922
1 carriage horse	800
	19,403

A large part of the money borrowed was sent to Bouillé, and the rest was deposited with Wilkierson's Bank in Amsterdam, to meet immediate expenses once the King was established at Montmédy. Fersen entrusted his diary from 1780 to Eléonore Sullivan's major-domo Franz, who burnt it on learning of the Royal Family's arrest. Mme Sullivan was mistress of wealthy Scotsman Quintin Craufurd. Fersen's diary shows that it was during preparations for the Royal Family's escape that he began a liaison with this *femme fatale*, which continued intermittently for several years. Craufurd had been in England since some time in May, and during the week preceding the Royal Family's escape, Fersen notes in Swedish in his diary that he 'stayed there' three times after going to see Eléonore. In later years he is less cryptic, writing 'slept' (*couché* in French) to indicate the nights he spent with her. They were remarkably infrequent, in fact, since they are only ever noted during Craufurd's rare absences. In June 1791 Fersen also notes his visits '*chez Elle*' – Marie-Antoinette – at the Tuileries, without always recording the time that he left her, which could indicate that he also 'stayed' with her. On 16 June he arrived '*chez Elle*' at 6.30 p.m., and gives no more details; normally he expands on the weather, his meals, when he returned home. The following day starts simply with 'to Bondy and Bourget'.

Alma Söderhjelm, who credited Fersen with several mistresses he never had, states in her book that his affair with Eléonore began at the beginning of the Revolution in 1789 – in other words, that he was unfaithful to Marie-Antoinette quite systematically for more than two years. There is absolutely nothing in Fersen's papers to support this assertion; but then Söderhjelm also declares that he wrote only twice to the Queen during the summer of 1789, when as we have seen he was in touch with her constantly. In 1789 and 1790, despite their extremely difficult circumstances, Fersen and Marie-Antoinette were happy together. He spent his time with her at Saint-Cloud while Eléonore was in Paris or London, and he did not correspond with Eléonore at this time. Since he always wrote regularly to his platonic female friends – Mme de Matignon, Lady Elizabeth Foster and Mme de Korff – he would certainly have written to her had their liaison already begun. The first letter to Eléonore Sullivan in his register is on 13 August 1791, several weeks after he had last seen her in Craufurd's salon in Brussels. It would seem that he had no intention of pursuing an affair with her, or he would most certainly have written to her regularly after they parted, as he did in later years.

Without the need for help in organizing the Royal Family's escape, it is doubtful that Fersen would ever have met Eléonore. She and Quintin Craufurd were both actively involved, at considerable risk to themselves. From Fersen's letters to Sophie and his diary it appears that he got to know Eléonore during the first few months of 1791. On 25 November 1793 he noted in his diary that 'she knows everything that I know and we met during the most interesting period of my life'.[74] All his papers show that he always considered the escape of the Royal Family in June 1791 as 'the most interesting period' of his life. Eléonore Sullivan became more than a passing fancy for Fersen; she became a real friend, devoted like him to the cause of the Royal Family. Since Quintin Craufurd was a friend of both the Comte de Mercy and the Duke of Dorset, it seems probably that one of them introduced Fersen to Craufurd and 'Mme Sullivan'. Beautiful Eléonore was the former mistress not only of the Duke of Württemberg, by whom she had two children, but of Marie-Antoinette's brother Joseph II. She hid the royal coach for the escape, she gave money, and as it was very dangerous to remain in Paris she left to meet Craufurd in Brussels at the same time that everyone else involved left the French capital. After crossing the border, Fersen spent just five hours in Mons on 22 June, where he delivered a message from Louis XVI to Monsieur, before setting off to rejoin the Royal Family in Montmédy; Eléonore and Craufurd, on the other hand, settled for a luxurious exile in Brussels while they awaited the chance to return to Paris.

Fersen's diary for 20 June 1791 is in pencil and written at the time: the first part of the day is missing.

20 June . . . and asked what he wanted to do. Both of them [Louis XVI and Marie-Antoinette] told me there was no need to hesitate and we should still go. We agreed on the time &&, and that if they were arrested, it would be necessary to go to Brussels and take action for them &&. On leaving, the King said to me: 'M. de F, whatever may happen to me, I shall never forget all that you are doing for me.' The Queen cried a lot. I left her at 6 o'clock; as an extra precaution she went for a walk with the children. I returned home to finish my affairs. At 7,

to Sullivan's to see if the carriage had been taken there. Back home. At 8, I wrote to the Queen to change the rendezvous for the *femmes de chambre* and to make sure they sent me word of the exact time by the bodyguards. Carried the letter; Mou[?] wrote at 8.45; the guards joined me; they gave me the letter for Mercy. Instructed them; back home, sent off my chaise; gave them my coach and horses to go. Went to pick up the carriage. Thought I had lost the letter for Mercy. At 10.15, in the Cour des Princes; the children came out at 11.15, arrived without difficulty. Lafayette passed by twice. At 11.45, Mme Elisabeth, then the King, then the Queen. Left at 12 o'clock, joined the carriage at the barrier at St. Martin. At 1.30, joined the post at Bondy; I took the back road; at 3 o'clock at Le Bourget and left.[75]

Fersen described his feelings on watching the royal coach disappear into the night to Quintin Craufurd.

M. de Fersen told me that . . . looking after the carriage as it went away, [he] was strongly tempted to disobey an order that was merely the effect of goodness and to follow it. He arrived at Mons on the 22nd, early in the morning; and, having delivered a message to Monsieur, who came there about the same time, he set out to join the King at Montmédy; but at Arlons he met Monsieur de Bouillé, and being informed by him of what had happened at Varennes he came to Brussels.[76]

All the Queen's friends were in a state of shock at the news of her arrest, fearing that she would be massacred by the mob on her return to Paris, escorted by deputies Barnave and Petion and national guards who had demonstrated their bloodlust by decapitating the Comte de Dampierre who came to present his respects to the King. In a letter to the Duchess of Devonshire on 30 June 1791 the Duke of Dorset betrayed his true opinion of Louis XVI and proposed that Marie-Antoinette's English friends exert their influence to save her.

Poor Queen, to what a pitch of wretchedness is she arrived at. I can conceive nothing equal to what her feelings are. You know I take for granted most of the particulars. I am afraid they will shut her up for life, if the mob will allow her to be removed from where she is. That beast of her husband was the cause of their capture, as he would stop and <u>eat</u> at several places on the road. He was quite drunk when he entered Paris. She, poor soul, showed her usual fortitude and courage . . . I think this country should take some part (at least with the individuals of the National Assembly) to save the Queen at all events from the fury of the people . . . at present I have little hopes of seeing the poor Queen any more. Our King is amazingly hurt; he talked with a very great deal of feeling about them last Wednesday and asked me very earnestly whether I thought the King of France would ever behave like a man. I was blunt enough to say I did not think he ever would, and his past behaviour justified me in that idea.[77]

Three days later he wrote:

I have written to Lafayette about poor Mrs B, painting to him in as few words and as strong colours as possible the disgrace that will fall upon the French nation if any misfortune should happen to her. Perhaps you may have had the same thought and have done the same thing . . . Lafayette is made responsible for the safety of the King and Queen. All the decrees now pass into law without the sanction of the King. It is impossible to guess what will be the fate of the poor Queen, for were the Assembly ever so willing to let her go, the mob would be disposed to tear her to pieces without. Her situation is deplorable and torments me to death.[78]

Georgiana did write to Lafayette. A copy of his reply was sent to Fersen, who forwarded it to Marie-Antoinette to try to persuade her not to trust the *enragés* ('madmen'), as the Jacobins were then called. It is published for the first time in this book. Fersen's friends and family in Sweden were no less anxious about him, for the news took much longer to reach them. He spent ten days criss-crossing the Austrian Netherlands to speak to Gustave III, Archduchess Marie-Christine, Mercy and the princes, finally sending a note to Sophie on 5 July.

5 July, Brussels

This is the first moment of peace I have had, the first I have been able to give you, and my heart has real need of it. Yours must feel all the heartbreak I am suffering at the moment and I need my friends more than ever. However, I won't lose heart and I'm determined to sacrifice myself for them and to serve them so long as any hope remains. This thought alone sustains me and allows me to bear all my sorrows patiently.[79]

Gustave III's sister-in-law the Duchess of Södermanland was not at all reassuring on the subject of Fersen when she wrote to Sophie on 10 July.

> You have the satisfaction of knowing that he conducted himself like a man of honour and as he should in such a situation. A deeper sentiment doubtless played its part, and I'm afraid this feeling may destroy him and that he will want to return to France, which would be an atrocious imprudence. I have received a private letter from Paris, with the following postscript: *It is said that C. Fersen drove the carriage, which was a hackney from the rue St Honoré. The whole of Paris is furious with him.*[80]

Fersen was now under the orders of the King of Sweden, who was a key player in diplomatic manoeuvres to try to rescue the French monarchy. But even before the Royal Family's return to Paris on 25 June, he had gone to Brussels to deliver Louis XVI's letter to Mercy and was 'resolved to make an effort to write' to the Queen. On 27 June 1791 he noted in his diary that his officer Fredrik Reutersvärd had arrived. It was he who would return to Paris to take the following letter (No. 8), drafted by Fersen and Mercy, to the royal prisoners in the Tuileries. Craufurd gives some interesting details on how it was delivered and the responses received (letters 12 and 13).

> The officer was furnished with a passport from the King of Sweden, as a person travelling on his own affairs, and was ordered, on his arrival at Paris, to deliver the packet to the King's *maitre d'hotel*, a man of fidelity and discretion . . . On the 14th the Swedish officer returned from Paris. The Royal Family there was so strictly guarded, that some days were spent before opportunities could be found to deliver the packet he carried, and again to obtain an answer. In the packet he brought back, there was a small scrap of paper, written in the King's hand, and a much larger one in cipher that appeared to be written in the Queen's, both dated the 7th of July. The first was addressed to Monsieur and the Count d'Artois, saying that he trusted to the love he knew they bore him, for taking measures with foreign Powers for the security of himself and his family and for restoring; tranquillity to his kingdom. It is, however, to be observed that it was not a full power, as had been suggested to the King. The paper written in cipher spoke of the situation of the King and Queen, and contained reflections on the manner in which the King

thought the foreign Powers should interfere; which seemed to breathe a considerable share of anxiety for the safety of his family.[81]

The discreet and loyal *maitre d'hôtel* was Gougenot (see Part I), which means that Reutersvärd took the letter to no. 2 rue Lepeletier, where he lived.

8. FERSEN AND THE COMTE DE MERCY TO MARIE-ANTOINETTE, 27 JUNE 1791

Stafsund, SE/RA/5802. The original letter is missing. It was not recorded in Fersen's register. This transcription is taken from Klinckowström's manuscript. He annotated it: 'Letter in code, minute in the hand of the Comte de Fersen.'

Brussels, 27 June [1791]

The dreadful calamity which has just occurred must completely change the conduct of affairs, and if one remains resolved that action must be taken on one's behalf, since one can no longer act for oneself, it is necessary to recommence negotiations and to give full powers to this effect. The mass of countries who will act needs to be sufficiently strong to command respect, and for this reason full powers must be given. Here are the questions which must be answered:

1. Does one want action to be taken in spite of all orders which may be received to the contrary?
2. Does one wish full powers to be given to Monsieur or the Comte d'Artois?
3. Does one wish him to employ the Baron de Breteuil, or allow him to use M. de Calonne, or does one leave the choice to him?
   Here is the form for the full powers:

'Being detained prisoner in Paris and being unable to give the necessary orders to restore order to my kingdom, give peace and contentment to my subjects and recover my legitimate authority, I charge Monsieur and in his default the Comte d'Artois to oversee my interests and those of my crown for me, giving for this purpose unlimited powers. I give my royal word to keep religiously and without restriction all engagements which will be made with the said powers, and promise, as soon as I am at liberty, to ratify all treaties, agreements or other pacts which he may make with the various countries who may be kind enough to come to my aid; the same for all commissions, warrants or posts which Monsieur may feel necessary to give, for which I given my word as King. Signed at Paris, 20 June 1791.'

This power should be written in invisible ink and given as soon as possible to the person who will deliver this letter. As we know the number of each question, a very brief reply will be possible. I'm being very well treated here; your sister is well disposed towards you and towards me.[82]

Fersen gives details of Reutersvärd mission in his diary on 13 July 1791.

At Paris he carried out his mission; the paper was presented as a dinner menu; asked, while pretending to read it, if it would be possible to reply; said that he would have the reply the following day, later postponed to the day after. They are kept in constant sight, all the doors open, with guards in the room next to the bedchamber; the doors only close for a second when she puts on her chemise; as soon as she is in bed, someone comes to see, and again several times a night. Never alone. They can only talk in whispers. Nobody enters the palace except with a pass from Lafayette and the mayor.[83]

At the same time as Fersen made his 'effort to write', the Queen had made one of her own.

9. Marie-Antoinette to the Comte de Mercy and Fersen, 28 June 1791

AN 440AP/1. Note in code sent to Mercy and received on 4 July, to which was appended a letter for Fersen alone. Fersen deciphered this note but suppressed the last two sentences from the minute he had obviously prepared for publication (in bold). The code word is vertu, *in very letter; some letters remain undecipherable. Decrypt by the author.*

28 June [1791]

Don't worry about us. We're alive. The leaders of the Assembly seem to want to be lenient in their conduct. Speak to my relations about measures to take externally *posuie*. If they are afraid, it will be necessary to compromise with them. **Burn everything that is *souolfgero* and send the rest of my letter to M. de Fersen. He is with the King of Sweden.**

10. Marie-Antoinette to Fersen, 29 June 1791

AN 440AP/1. There are two versions of this note; Fersen's autograph minute, edited for publication and the original cipher sent by the Queen. Both versions are published here (decrypt by the author). The note was decoded and published in full for the first time in 2009 by Valérie Nachef and Jacques Patarin. The code word is depuis *(Vol. 2, No. 36 indicates the volume and page of the code book), and the note is encrypted using the 'skipped letter' method. On returning to Brussels on 4 July from a meeting with Gustav III in Aix-la-Chapelle, Fersen noted in his diary: 'At 5 o'clock to Mercy's; letter from her, here's the copy.'[84] Klinckowström reproduced Fersen's minute faithfully, but some later publications contain editorial variations. It is interesting to observe Fersen's revisions. He substituted 'compromise' for 'expose', then crossed it out and returned to the original word.*

4 July 1791
Vol. 2, No. 36

29 June [1791]

I exist, my beloved, and it is to adore you. How worried I have been about you, and how I pity you at having no news of us. May heaven let this reach you. Don't write to me: it would expose us. And, above all, do not return here under any pretext. They know it was you who got us out of here – all would be lost if you were to appear. We are watched day and night. I don't care, because you are not here. Don't worry, nothing will happen to me. The Assembly wants to treat us gently. Farewell, most loved of men. Calm yourself, if you can. Look after yourself for me. I won't be able to write to you any more, but nothing in this world can stop me adoring you until I die.

Fersen's minute

I exist _____. How worried I have been about you, and how I pity you at having no news of us. May heaven let this reach you. Don't write to me: it would [*compromise*] expose us, and above all, do not return here under any pretext. They know it was you who got us out of here – all would be lost if you were to appear. We are watched day and night. I don't care. Don't worry, nothing will

happen to me. The assembly wants to treat us gently. Farewell
_____. I won't be able to write to you any more

_____

11. Fersen to Marie-Antoinette, 30 June 1791

Stafsund, SE/RA/5802. The original note is lost. This transcription comes from Klinckowström's manuscript. Fersen had just had a long meeting with Gustav III on French affairs. Well aware of the princes' hostility towards the Baron de Breteuil and Louis XVI's and Marie-Antoinette's mistrust of Calonne, he suggests that the role of Plenipotentiary Minister be given to the Bishop of Arras.

Aix-la-Chapelle, 30 June [1791]

The King is very well disposed towards you; here is a note from him. I'm leaving for Brussels tomorrow, and from there I go to Vienna, to negotiate and to try to bring all the powers together; I shall return to Brussels after that. Wouldn't the Bishop of Arras[85] do as well as Breteuil or Calonne? I am well and live only to serve you. Tell me if you want us to act for you.

Gustav III of Sweden to Marie-Antoinette, 30 June 1791

AN 440AP/1. Fersen's copy of the note from the King of Sweden attached to the preceding letter.

I beg Your Majesty not to doubt the keen concern we take in your misfortune. Your friends will not abandon you. Bear your present state with steadfastness, just as you have withstood the dangers which surround you. Above all, do not permit anyone to debase royal dignity through your person, and kings will come to your aid. That is the advice of your oldest ally and most faithful friend.

Aix-la-Chapelle, 30 June 1791

Fersen had held meetings with the émigré princes as well as with Gustav. He tried to restrain the Comte d'Artois, who was in a very bellicose mood, but had a poor opinion of Monsieur, who promptly dismissed the Baron de Breteuil. He wanted to declare himself regent. 'Mercy has spoken to Monsieur,' Fersen noted in his diary on 26 June; 'he is not up to this task.'[86] Gustav III gave Fersen orders to go to Vienna to persuade Leopold II to open the port of Ostend to the Swedish navy who would bring an army in support of an 'armed congress' of foreign powers to be convened to discuss French affairs and save the monarchy.

Craufurd was dispatched to England to obtain confirmation of British neutrality.

Fersen's mission was in direct conflict with the negotiations initiated by the Queen on her return to the Tuileries with the '*enragés*' or Constitutionals, led by Antoine Barnave[87] and Lafayette. Barnave's manners during the return journey to Paris had made a good impression on Marie-Antoinette. She immediately decided to win him over, to save the monarchy and her family, and would subsequently be accused of having seduced the former president of the Assembly.

The following encrypted letters of 8 and 9 July 1791 were in the packet brought back by Reutersvärd on 13 July. Note that it is the Queen, not the King, who draws up Louis XVI's memorandum. Everything indeed came from her, as Mercy justly observed.

12. MARIE-ANTOINETTE TO FERSEN, 8 JULY 1791

AN 440AP/1. Encrypted memorandum by Marie-Antoinette. The code word courage *is on page 17 of the code book. The Queen's private letter of 9 July begins: 'Here is a long memorandum I have drawn up on the King's ideas . . .' Fersen began decoding this second letter on the same page as his decrypt of the memorandum, since the words 'Here is a long memorandum' are crossed out on his minute. There were letters he could show to Breteuil or Craufurd and others which were strictly confidential.*

17

8 July [1791]

The King thinks that the close confinement in which he is kept and the total state of degradation to which the National Assembly has brought the monarchy, not permitting him to exercise any function whatsoever, is sufficiently well known to foreign powers for there to be any need to explain it here.

The King thinks that their aid can be of use to him and his kingdom by means of negotiations only, that a show of force must be secondary only, and if all offers of negotiation are refused here.

The King thinks that outright force, even after a preliminary declaration, would bring incalculable danger not only to himself and his family but to all French people within the kingdom who do not agree with the Revolution. There is no doubt that a foreign army could enter France, but with the population now armed as it is, fleeing the frontiers and the troops beyond, they would turn their weapons against those of their fellow citizens they have been taught for two years to regard as their enemies. We witnessed this during our journey, and particularly since our return; there are sad examples every day.

The King thinks that an unlimited full power such as the one proposed, even if dated from 20 June, would be dangerous for him in his current position. It would be impossible not to communicate it, and not all cabinets are equally secret. It has been announced that within the next fortnight the articles deemed to be constitutional will be presented to the King, that he will then be given his freedom, leaving him the master, to go where he wants to make up his mind whether to accept them or not, but detaining his son, which would make such freedom illusory. Everything which has been done in the last two years must be regarded as invalid in so far as the King's wishes are concerned, but it's impossible to change so long as the vast majority of the nation favours novelty. We must devote all our efforts to changing this state of mind.

Résumé

The King's captivity is quite evident and well known to foreign powers. He desires that the goodwill of his relatives, friends, allies and the other sovereigns who wish to take part, manifests itself in the form of a congress which follows the path of negotiations; of course there should be an impressive force to support them but always in the background so as not to provoke crimes and massacres. It will be important for the Baron de Breteuil to join forces with the King's brothers and those whom they choose for this important negotiation.

The King does not believe he should nor that he can give an unlimited power, but he sends this paper in invisible ink to be delivered to his brothers. We dare not reply to the King of Sweden. Be our emissary and express our gratitude and attachment to him.

[*here is a long*]

Power given by Louis XVI, 7 July 1791

AN 440AP/1. Autograph copy by Fersen of the power attached to the preceding letter. Its ambiguous wording and the failure to nominate a regent would drive a deep wedge between Louis XVI and his brothers.

Copy of the paper sent to Monsieur by the King

I trust absolutely to my brothers' tenderness for me, to their love and affection for their country and to the friendship of the sovereign princes, my relatives and allies, and to the honour and generosity of other sovereigns, to agree together the ways and means to employ in negotiations whose aim must be to re-establish order and tranquillity in the kingdom; but I think that any use of force [must be] placed after the negotiations. I give full power to my brothers to negotiate in this sense with whomsoever they wish and to choose the persons to be employed for these political purposes.

Paris, 7 July 1791

Louis

13. MARIE-ANTOINETTE TO FERSEN, 9 JULY 1791

AN 440AP/1. Letter in code from Marie-Antoinette, attached to the 'long memorandum' of 8 July. Fersen's decrypt is missing, and the letter – in which the Queen expresses her love for him – did not appear in Klinckowström's edition of their correspondence. It was forgotten until it was rediscovered, decoded and published for the first time by Valérie Nachef and Jacques Patarin in 2009.

It is apparent from this letter that Marie-Antoinette did not want Fersen involved in any activities to save the Royal Family; the National Assembly had just ordered his arrest and gossip about their liaison was circulating in the capitals of Europe. She begs him to stand aside while she pursues a strategy of lulling the Constitutionals into a false sense of security and simultaneously asking her brother, Emperor Leopold II, to convene a congress of foreign powers to resolve the political crisis in France. One can well imagine Fersen's dismay as he decoded this letter: he had risked everything to save her, but he no longer possessed the Queen's absolute confidence. She had decided to deal with her sworn enemies.

She was very well aware that he would be horrified 'by everything you see me doing' and begs him to reserve judgement until she can explain her reasons. Fersen could only have viewed negotiations with the Constitutionals as a betrayal. The Queen reassures him of her love, but he was a jealous man and he needed to be persuaded. 'Our happiness depends on it, because there would be no more for us if we were separated for ever.' He would write to her in almost the same terms when their separation was prolonged. But Marie-Antoinette failed in this plea to keep Fersen out of affairs – he was soon on his way to Vienna armed with Gustav III's full authority to make whatever agreements were necessary to form an army that would restore the French monarchy by force (since Gustav had few expectations of a congress). In addition to the pain caused by their separation, Fersen would suffer pangs of jealousy as he heard of his tender friend's dangerous political manoeuvres with the Constitutionals, even to the point of doubting her love for him. It is interesting to note that in all her letters to Fersen on the subject the Queen never once mentions Barnave and always names only the Lameths or Duport as her main contacts.

The code word is depuis *on page 36 of the code book. Decrypt by the author.*

No. 36

9 July [1791]

Here's a long memorandum I have drawn up on the King's ideas. It is certain that force would only do harm at the moment. We must yield to the storm. We would not have time to be rescued. Give this memorandum to M. de Mercy, let him take charge of it, get the opinion of my brothers and all those who need to be told about it. I do not wish you to go to Vienna. I want you to stay with the King and that throughout you appear as little as possible.[88] In all this believe me, my tender friend, that I, who would like to owe everything to you, I have a strong reason for making this plea. Our happiness depends on it, because there would be no more for us if we were separated for ever. Farewell. Pity me, love me, and above all don't judge me by everything you see me doing until you have listened to me. I would die if for one moment I were condemned by the being I adore and whom I shall never cease to adore. The Lameths and their associates have the appearance of wanting to serve us in good faith. I am profiting by it but will trust them only so far as is necessary. Farewell.

Did she receive a reply to this letter? None is mentioned in Fersen's letter register or his diary. Their correspondence stopped for two months, despite Marie-Antoinette's efforts to reach him. She was deeply affected by their separation after Varennes. They had been almost constantly together from October 1788 to June 1791, and now she no longer even knew where to send her letters to him. She wrote to Valentin d'Esterhazy on 11 August with a message for Fersen: 'If you write to HIM, please tell HIM that no amount of miles and no amount of countries can ever separate hearts.' On 5 September she sent Esterhazy a royalist ring, enclosing a second for Fersen.

I'm delighted to have this opportunity to send you a little ring that will surely please you. They have been selling in prodigious quantities here for the past three days, and it takes all the trouble in the world to find any. The one wrapped in paper is for HIM; make sure he gets it. It is just his size. I wore it for two days before wrapping it. Tell HIM that it's from me. I don't know where he is. It is dreadful torture to have no news and not even to know where the people one loves are living.[89]

Esterhazy, who had seen Fersen in both Brussels and Vienna, was on a mission in St Petersburg for the princes by the time he received this letter. He wrote to his wife about it on 21 October 1791: Marie-Antoinette has the codename *d'Avillart* while Fersen is *le Chou* ('the Darling'). Their liaison was no secret for the Esterhazys.

> I have received a letter from d'Avillart . . . with a little gold and enamel ring bearing the inscription: *Domine salvum fac regem et reginam.* Perhaps you have seen it? He also sent me a ring for the Chou, but I don't know where to find him. Her letter is touching; she asks me not to believe the calumny [about her] and never to doubt either the nobility of her way of thinking or her courage.[90]

The Queen wrote to Fersen that summer through the Comte de Mercy, who knew he had been in Vienna since 2 August. But the indirect route letters had to take via the Netherlands and Germany was so slow that she asked him on 12 September if he had sent Fersen a note she had written to him at the beginning of August. Mercy had in fact done so, writing to Fersen on 12 August:

> The letter you honoured me with, Monsieur le Comte, dated 26 July, has been delivered to me; I was waiting for a safe occasion to reply to it and it has presented itself today with the dispatch of this courier. I'm making use of it to send you a note to which I was instructed to add the address.[91]

On 20 August 1791 Fersen noted in his diary: 'a courier from Mercy had arrived . . . there was also a note from her in code; I was very glad to have a means of writing to her.'[92] He must surely be referring to the following undated letter in which the Queen gives details of how he can write to her by the post, using Gougenot's address.

14. MARIE-ANTOINETTE TO FERSEN, UNDATED
[EARLY AUGUST 1791]

AN 440AP/1. Transcription by Baron Klinckowström of a fragment of a letter 'to the Comte de Fersen from Queen Marie-Antoinette in code'. It is undated but is probably the note received by Fersen in Vienna on 20 August 1791. The original is missing. Klinckowström did not publish it but gave it a 'probable' date of September 1791, which seems rather too late for the content. Various altered versions of this note have led to the creation of a 'M. de Gougens' in some texts. In the transcript, it is definitely 'Mr Gougeno', Marie-Antoinette's spelling for Gougenot, the King's steward (see Part I), who features regularly as an intermediary in her correspondence with Fersen and who lived in the same house as her secretary, François Goguelat.

She asks Fersen to write to her using her code name 'Mme Brown', in a double envelope to Gougenot at 2 rue Lepeletier in Paris. Goguelat, wounded and arrested at Varennes, was still in prison and therefore unable to act as an intermediary at this time.

[no date, probably early August 1791]

. . . I can tell you that I love you and that's even all I have time for. I am well, don't worry about me. I wish I could know that you are, too. Write to me by post in code: **address it** to Mme Browne; **a double envelope to Mr Gougeno. Get your valet de chambre to write the addresses.** Tell me to whom I should address those I may be able to write to you, because I can't go on living without that. Farewell, most loved and most loving of men. I kiss you with all my heart.

The Austrians kept Fersen dangling in fruitless talks in Vienna in order to prevent the Swedish fleet being deployed before winter ice confined them to port; he was eventually obliged to follow Leopold II to Prague to receive a definitive refusal to all Gustave III's proposals. It was decidedly against his wishes that he followed the emperor on 25 August; and it was in Prague three days later that he resumed his correspondence with the Queen.

Fersen to Marie-Antoinette, 28 August 1791, letter missing

Marie-Antoinette acknowledges receipt of this letter in her reply of 26 September. It is not logged in Fersen's register.

In 1791, Fersen recorded eleven letters to Marie-Antoinette, between 5 September and 26 December. All except two are addressed to 'Josephine'. The Archives Nationales hold other letters to the Queen which are not recorded in the register, as well as several listed in the 'Josephine' correspondence, proving beyond doubt that 'Josephine' was Marie-Antoinette.

1791
SEPTEMBER
5 Josephine.
OCTOBER
25 Josephine post.
29 Josephine by Pcsse Lamballe.
NOVEMBER
11 Josephine in code by post.
26 Josephine, detailed memorandum by the bishop
[of Pamiers].
DECEMBER
4 Josephine, invisible ink by Mr_____.
12 Josephine by post in code.
23 Queen of France by post, invisible ink.
24 idem by Craufurd, invisible ink.
24 Josephine by post in code.
26 Josephine by post in code: that the letters had arrived.[93]

Fersen to Marie-Antoinette, 5 September 1791, letter missing

Fersen recorded a letter to 'Josephine' in his register for this date. He sent it from Prague. In his diary, he notes: 'returned home to write to her.'

Made to waste yet more time by the Austrians, Fersen required all his tact to conceal his disappointment in Leopold II, who was playing a deep double game; while pretending to take an interest in his sister's fate, the Emperor did his utmost to prevent other countries from helping her. He even told Archduchess Marie-Christine, Governor of the Austrian Netherlands, to ignore all French requests for assistance. Marie-Antoinette had never liked her elder sister, and a comment in Fersen's diary on 25 September 1791 appears to show that the feeling was mutual.

> News that the King has approved [the Constitution] . . . All sorts of tales are being told about the French. The archduchess in Brussels writes against them (it is all known, because the Emperor repeats everything). They say that the Queen is sleeping with Barnave and being guided by him, that she is holding back the Emperor, that she is against the princes and doesn't want them to do anything &&. It's all going badly.[94]

It was Marie-Antoinette's own sister who accused her of sleeping with Barnave. Fersen is always neutral and reserved when recording comments made about 'the Queen' in his diary, but the tone of his letters to her that autumn would seem to indicate that he feared this rumour might be true. He constantly pleaded with her not to 'go over to the *enragés*', and all his papers reveal a violent hatred of Barnave – a man who never tried to destroy her – while Lafayette, who mounted serious attacks against her, never attracts such acrimony. Exhausted, unhappy and unwell, and with no positive news to send to Gustav III, he left Prague on 26 September and arrived in Brussels on 6 October 1791.

> Arrived in Brussels at six o'clock in the morning . . . Saw the Comte de Mercy. The Queen writes to tell him that it's necessary to go along with the Constitution, to stop the princes. She asks for the convening of a congress and the pretext would be Avignon. The Comte de Mercy considered a congress to be useless at the moment, since he did not know what it would concern itself with and one could not refute the King. I proved its usefulness to him.[95]

Gallons of ink were to flow on the subject of this congress, which never took place: the Austrians made sure of that. But the correspondence of Marie-Antoinette and Fersen was concerned with little else for several months. Once he was Brussels, they could write to each other frequently. On 7 October he received a letter from Lady Elizabeth which talks of 'our unfortunate friend' the Queen of France and of

Fersen's unhappiness. She also mentions the letters sent by the Queen's English friends to Barnave and Lafayette after the Royal Family's arrest at Varennes; Lafayette's reply to the Duchess of Devonshire, mentioned by Lady Elizabeth Foster, is published in this book (after letter No. 25).

Lady Elizabeth Foster to Fersen, 16 September 1791

16 September [1791]

It gave me great pleasure to receive your letter, because although I knew you were safe I feared for your health, which must have been affected by the harsh trials you have been through. I still shudder when I think of the danger you escaped – for a whole day our dreadful gazettes announced that you had been arrested. I didn't know who to turn to for news of you, when fortunately the papers the following day reassured me by saying you had left the kingdom. Yes, you must be wretched indeed. I can't think of a more cruel situation, except that of our unfortunate friend [a]. I really can't express all I suffered during the horrible uncertainty as to whether her life would be spared – and I swear to you, in London nobody seemed to have but that one idea, that interest. Nobody talked to us of anything else, people were thinking only of her. It is therefore cruel to think that her fate depends on the frigid soul of our minister [b] – I am outraged by his hesitation.

Was it I who talked to you about the letters that were written to the leaders of the faction? Or did you learn of it elsewhere? My friend [c] wrote a charming letter – the reply, apart from the just tribute he [d] paid to my friend's merit, seemed little likely to me to uphold his reputation as a hero. He even said that She (our friend) had never been in any danger – as for the rest, don't mention that I've spoken to you about his reply.

19th

We have just heard, almost at the same time, about the coalition signed between nine countries and the King's letter in which he accepts the Constitution. It is said that the Spanish Ambassador has left Paris at last; what is to be expected from all this, and how unfortunate for brave royalists to have such a weak king. My friend [c] and I take the keenest interest in your cause, and our interest in you is even greater; friendship guides and deepens it. Farewell then, my dear friend. Accept her wishes and mine for your happiness and success, and when you can send me your news.[96]

[a] Marie-Antoinette [b] William Pitt [c] Georgiana Devonshire [d] Lafayette

This letter should put paid to the romantic fables woven about Fersen and Lady Elizabeth, who sympathized with him on his cruel separation from Marie-Antoinette. In addition to this stress, his stay in Vienna had not improved his spirits or his health. He told his sister Sophie on 18 October:

> I'm overwhelmed with business and paperwork. I had a little fit of bile or humour . . . I had a touch of fever, but that has passed and I only have the problem with my haemorrhoids, which with all the treatment is not dangerous. I wrote to my father today, but I dated my letter the 12th and I'm telling him I only arrived here on the 10th.[97]

He was indeed 'overwhelmed with business and paperwork'. He corresponded with all Gustav III's ambassadors, he wrote letters for Louis XVI and Marie-Antoinette, he held almost daily meetings with Breteuil and Mercy, he sounded out the opinions of members of the diplomatic corps who spent their evenings in Craufurd's salon, presided over by Eléonore Sullivan – but he was never too busy to write to Marie-Antoinette. Most of the letters he sent her in September and October 1791 are not logged in his letter register.

Marie-Antoinette to Fersen, 25 September 1791, letter missing

In his letter of the 10/12 October, Fersen tells the Queen: 'I have not yet had time to decipher yours of the 25th.' Since he refers to her letter of 26 September in his reply on 10 October, it is clear she had written to him twice in two days.

15. MARIE-ANTOINETTE TO FERSEN, 26 SEPTEMBER 1791

AN 440AP/1. Fersen's autograph decrypt of a coded letter from Marie-Antoinette. He received it on 8 October after his return to Brussels; Mercy was doubtless the intermediary. The original code is missing. Fersen crossed out several sentences in his decrypt, which were subsequently crossed out again in much darker ink. Without the separation of words and letters in the copies of letters that were sent encrypted, it is virtually impossible to read these heavily redacted passages. The 'safe route' Marie-Antoinette speaks of to send letters was the diplomatic courier from Blumendorf, Austrian Ambassador at Paris, to the Comte de Mercy; she soon learnt that she could not trust it.

Received 8 October 1791

26 September [1791]

Your letter of the 28th reached me [*1½ lines deleted*] For two months I had no news of you; nobody could tell me where you were. If I had known her address, I was on the point of writing to Sophie, **she** [*words deleted*] she [*words deleted*] **and** would have told me where you were. [*7½ lines deleted*]

Here we are in a new position since the King's acceptance [of the Constitution]; to refuse would have been nobler, but that was impossible in our circumstances. I would have preferred the acceptance to be simple and shorter, but that's the misfortune of being surrounded only by scoundrels. Still, I assure you that it is the least bad act to have passed. You will judge them one day, because I'm keeping for you *tourdquace&* [*½ line blank*] *ystrcuil ighu* which I had the happiness to find since there are papers belonging to you.

The follies of the princes and emigrants also forced our hand. It was essential in accepting it to allay all fears that it was not in good faith. I believe that the best way to disgust people with all this is to seem to be completely in favour of it – that will soon make it clear that nothing will work. Besides, despite the letter my brothers wrote to the King – and which, by the way, has not produced the effect here which they hoped for at all – I certainly don't see, particularly by the declaration of Pillnitz, that foreign help will be that prompt.[98] Perhaps it is fortunate, because the more we go forward the more these people here will feel their misfortunes and perhaps they themselves will come to want the foreigners. I fear that some ill-disposed people will drag your king into doing something that compromises him, and you as a consequence. Much wisdom is required. I'm writing **in detail** about it to M. de Mercy.

Let me know as soon as you reach Brussels. I will write to you quite easily as I have a safe route always at my disposal. You would not believe how much everything I'm doing at the moment costs me; and that vile race of men, who say they are attached to us but have never done us anything but harm, are still *enragés* at the moment. It appears that one has been brought sufficiently low to do with pleasure whatever one is asked to do. Yet it's their **cowardice** and their conduct which has brought us to the state we are in. I've had only one happiness – that was seeing again all those gentlemen who were locked up on our account, especially M. Goguelat. He is perfectly reasonable, and his ideas have calmed down during his imprisonment. Adieu. [*3 lines deleted*]

The following letter shows the complete freedom with which Marie-Antoinette and Fersen discussed political matters. The remark about the Russian Empress Catherine II reveals that Blumendorf and Simolin, Austrian and Russian ambassadors at Paris respectively, were also part of the secret diplomatic network trying to help the French monarchy. Simolin was a great friend of Craufurd and Eléonore Sullivan and would be invited to private meetings with the King and Queen at the Tuileries.

16. Fersen to Marie-Antoinette, 10 and 12 October 1791

AN 440AP/1. Fersen's autograph copy of a letter sent in code. It is not logged in his register. With the aid of high-resolution photographs and the separation of words and letters required for encryption, I have been able to read the text beneath several deleted lines in this letter to reveal for the first time Fersen's declarations of love for Marie-Antoinette.

The code word autres *is on page 20 of the code book.*

12 Oct 1791. 20 autres

Brussels, 10 October [1791]

I am back at last **and I can tell you, my dearest and most tender friend, how much I love you. It's my only pleasure since that horrible adventure. I'm <u>even more miserable</u>.** Your situation must be horrible, and _ _ _ _ _ _ _ / _ _ _ _ / _ _ _ _ _ _ _ / my tender friend / _ _ _ _ _ _ _ _ / without you there is no happiness for me. / _ _ _ _ _ _ _ _ / <u>is nothing</u> / _ _ _ _ / _ _ _ _. The King of Sweden wanted to give me the post of Grand Equerry and a regiment of hussars. I refused everything. I don't want to be tied. / _ _ _ _ / <u>see</u> / _ _ _ _ / _ _ _ _ _ / and / _ _ _ _ / _ _ _ _ _ _ _ _ _ / is all that I desire.

How I pity you for being forced to accept, but I understand your position; it's dreadful and there was no other choice. At least I have the consolation of knowing some sensible people who are of the same opinion. But what are you going to do? Is all hope lost? If there is any at all, do not be downcast, and if you want to be helped I hope that you can be, but I need to know your wishes and plans in order to moderate or encourage the goodwill of the King of Sweden and the other powers, because in any event, the princes must only be auxiliaries.

The Empress, the kings of Prussia, Naples, Sardinia and Spain are very well disposed, especially the first three. Sweden will sacrifice herself for you. England has given assurances of her neutrality. The Emperor is the least willing. He is weak and indiscreet; he promises everything, but his cabinet, which is afraid of committing itself and wants to avoid getting involved, holds him back on everything. Hence the contradiction you have seen between his letters and his actions. I was sent there by the King with unlimited full powers to agree and propose everything which could be of service to you. All I was able to do was to stop some mad proposals made by the princes and persuade him that nothing should be done by them.

I prepared a detailed memorandum for him in which I proposed the recall of ambassadors and their meeting in congress [*at Aix-la-Chapelle*]; never to insist on your liberty except under the terms of the declaration of Pillnitz; to demand, as proof of your freedom, that you went to the château de l'Hermitage[99] [*on the frontier at Valenciennes*] or to Montmédy, and that you summoned there the bodyguards and troops you wanted; to move the vanguard of the armies on all sides towards the frontier; to request and receive troops from Sweden and Russia at Ostend. I asked for this proposal to be made at once, since all the powers had replied that they would do whatever he did. He agreed with me on all of that, but nothing was done and he dragged matters out until you were forced to accept [the Constitution]. {At present I don't know what he will do; if he considers that you are free then he may no longer wish to do anything}, but if you have a project, he can be pushed by the other powers; and as I'm charged by the King to correspond with all his ministers, I will act in accordance with what you send me. Here are some questions which require answers; so that it takes less time, I'll keep the numbers and you can just indicate them by: one, two, three.

1. Do you plan to take part seriously in the Revolution and do you believe there is no other option?
2. Do you wish to be helped or should we cease all negotiations with other courts?
3. [*Do you approve of the idea in my memorandum and would you like it to be carried forward?*][100]
3. Do you have [*another*] a plan and what is it?

Forgive all these questions. I flatter myself they will only make you see my desire to serve you and proof of an attachment and devotion without limits.

12th

M. de Mercy showed me your letter and I shall write in consequence.[101] He was against the congress at the present time, but I persuaded him to press Vienna for it by proving to him that definite action was needed to stop the princes and the gathering of people they have [*at Coblentz*]. It's frightening, and without it soon they will no longer be in charge. The Avignon business is a good pretext for a congress and I will write to the King of Spain's minister so that court engages the Pope to demand the intervention of the powers. It will be necessary for you to press the Emperor on the formation of this congress, at least, to announce it at once, indicating the place and nominating the members. Exaggerate your fears about the princes and say that it will calm them. Insist that this congress be supported by a show of force.

What the Baron de Breteuil is sending you by the Chevalier de Coigny[102] on Spain and Russia is very good. It would be good to write a letter to the Empress or arrange for something to be told her. Blumendorf would show it to Simolin, who would copy it out and send it in code; he's an honest man, you can trust him. As for the plan for a congress, I will let the King [Gustav III] know, and he will inform the Empress. Mr Craufurd went to England this summer to [*sound out*] get assurances of that court's intentions, and whatever M. de Mercy may say, they wish to observe a perfect neutrality. As Mr Craufurd undertook this **delicate** mission with much grace, wouldn't you like to send me some obliging words for him, which you know how to say better than anyone? He deserves them for his attachment to you. Reply to me as soon as possible.

Farewell, my dear and tender friend, I shall never cease to adore you.

I have not yet had time to decipher your letter of the 25th. The Chevalier de Coigny will tell you what I think about your affairs. He means well, but he likes Calonne a little.

17. FERSEN TO MARIE-ANTOINETTE, 13 OCTOBER 1791

AN 440AP/1. Autograph copy of a note sent in code by Fersen to the Queen. It is not logged in his letter register. Klinckowström published it, omitting the redacted passages but without indicating the gaps in the text. The code word subvenir comes from page 60 of the code book. This note is a reply to Marie-Antoinette's missing letter of 25 September, in which it appears she asked Fersen to return to Sweden. His response shows he had absolutely no intention of obeying her. 'Farewell, I love you madly . . . ' he tells her; but this does not prevent him from issuing a stinging reprimand: 'don't let your craven heart be swayed by the enragés.' Although the word craven (lâche in the original) is perfectly legible, it was suppressed by Klinckowström and all subsequent editors. It is an extraordinary word in this context; why talk of her heart when she is dealing with political matters? And a 'craven heart' suggests that he doubted her ability to withstand gentler treatment from the Constitutionals. Clearly Fersen was jealous of Marie-Antoinette's meetings and discussions with Barnave. She seemed to be in no hurry to see him again; in fact she wanted him to return to Sweden, which could only have exacerbated his concerns and suspicions. The rumours that had reached him in Prague must have hurt, for there is none of the tact Fersen ought to have employed when chastising his 'tender friend'.

No. 60

13 October 1791

My tender friend, I have nothing to add to my letter of yesterday. Keep insisting on the congress to the Emperor and press him; ask that he tells you frankly if [*he has the intention*] he wants to do what you ask. I will try to make the other courts push him. Don't let your **craven** heart be swayed by the *enragés* – they are scoundrels who will never do anything for you. You must be wary of them and make use of them. I have entrusted a part of my negotiations to the Chevalier de Coigny; I don't know any fault in him other than his liking for Calonne. I've only had time to decipher the beginning of your letter. **It moved me to tears**. It was the fear of compromising us which always stopped me from writing to you. At the moment I'm drowning in paperwork. **Farewell, you _ _ _ _ _ _ _ _ and who I will adore all my life** [*½ line crossed out and illegible*]. I cannot return to Sweden because I'm charged with the King's correspondence. **Farewell, I love you madly** [*7 words crossed out and illegible*]. The rest of the code means nothing; it's just to fill up the paper.

As soon as he was back in Brussels, Fersen's role in the Royal Family's escape from Paris and his liaison with Marie-Antoinette were frequent topics of conversation. According to the following letter from his sister Sophie, even Stockholm was buzzing with rumours after Mme de Saint-Priest had arrived there and promptly tried to claim she was a serious rival to the Queen of France.

Sophie Piper to Fersen, 16 October 1791

Engsö, 16 October [1791]

You cannot doubt, my good friend, the deep pleasure your letters give me. But my friend, at a time when I know you are busy with so much business, especially paperwork, I suffer knowing that you're giving me a moment you could use to rest. My dear Axel, you must be exhausted by so many troubles and cares. I hope you'll find a little peace at Brussels; your health needs it when both mind and body have suffered for so long.

I read the King of France's acceptance [of the Constitution] in the newspaper, and above all the manner of it, with real pain. My first thought was how much it would afflict you, my friend. The only reflection that consoles me is that his position must partly excuse his action, which is otherwise humiliating indeed. Poor prince, poor Queen – for *She* undoubtedly feels her condition more than he does. A propos of that, I have heard from my correspondents at Drottningholm that on the day news of the King of France's acceptance arrived, La Saint-Priest indulged herself with plenty of remarks against the Queen – particularly accusing her of being responsible for the King's actions, assuring our King [Gustav III] that it was certainly by the Queen's pleas and counsels that he had acted; that she was terrible. In a word, she tried to persuade the King that it was the Queen who had wrongly encouraged the King to commit acts of weakness.

... The Duchess [of Södermanland] very swiftly countered this remark by La Saint-Priest and even made her see how improper her comment was in a country where, as a foreigner and a Frenchwoman, she ought rather to make excuses for her princes. She succeeded in getting everyone to see that everything La Saint-Priest said was the result of feminine jealousy, and people laughed at it . . . Her chatter amuses the King and the princesses; the latter, however, are somewhat reserved with her, because by her tone and her manners one can imagine she is something of a nuisance. She told them about a great number of passions she has had in France, then she told them that _She_ was also very jealous of her over you, and hinted that it was not without cause . . . I will stem the volubility of her tongue if she spins any stories about you in my presence. They say that Jacob de La Gardie is on very good terms with her, even the best.[103]

And, indeed, having failed to seduce both Axel and Fabian von Fersen, Mme de Saint-Priest consoled herself in the arms of their cousin, Jacob de La Gardie. More light is shed on this affair by letters seized at Fersen's address in Paris after the Royal Family's arrest at Varennes; among them were numerous ardent epistles with which Mme de Saint-Priest had bombarded him (and to which he never replied). On 17 June 1791 she assured him she had at last come to her senses . . .

You should be pleased with me: I am now arrived at that state you desired, that you wished for; you must be able to see it and be persuaded by my letters, which will now have no other tone for you. I desire your happiness above all else, and I shall trouble myself about that alone . . . Before God and men I'm the same as I always was, but I no longer wish to feel anything but friendship for you. I should never have had any other sentiment, or at least I should have kept it locked in my heart; it would have made me much happier. It was past time, and I beg you will believe that it is the greatest sacrifice I could offer you. My resolve will be unshakeable. It has cost me a great deal to take this course, and I didn't want to talk of it until I was sure of myself. You can now believe me, without fear; you will no longer have cause to complain about me. I am at least certain that I shall never say anything to you again which could offend you.[104]

None of these assurances, however, stopped Mme de Saint-Priest from claiming a conquest she had never made once she found herself with an audience avid for gossip in Stockholm.

18. MARIE-ANTOINETTE TO FERSEN, 19 OCTOBER 1791

AN 440AP/1. Autograph decrypt by Fersen of a letter from Marie-Antoinette. There are several lines that have been blacked out twice and remain illegible. On 23 October Fersen noted in his diary: 'Mercy gave me a letter from the Queen: he had already decoded 4 or 5 lines.' She had in fact concluded her letter of the same date to Mercy with: 'the other letter is for M. de F'.[105] This is Marie-Antoinette's reply to Fersen's letter of 13 October. She reassures him that she will not be swayed by the enragés, *and informs him of a new escape plan. This paragraph, as well as the one containing her message for Quintin Craufurd, was crossed through by Fersen to be suppressed from his memoirs. One can understand why he wished to suppress the thanks to Craufurd, since Eléonore Sullivan eventually refused to leave Craufurd for him, but his reasons for not wishing to mention the escape plan are harder to fathom. It shows, at the very least, that the Queen was not exclusively guided by Fersen's advice and that she actively negotiated with others.*

Received 23 Oct 1791

19 October 1791

We have found it impossible to expose the baron's writing on the papers with the water the Chevalier de Coigny brought us. Send me word at once by post on the method for using this water and its composition, so that if this one is no good we may get another made. I am writing to M. de Mercy to press for the congress. I'm telling him to communicate my letter to you and so I will not enter into details about it with you. I have seen M. du Moutier, who also wants this congress very much.[106] He even gave me some ideas for the initial stages which I find reasonable. He is refusing to join the cabinet, and I even made him promise not to; he's a man to keep for better times, and he would have been wasted there.

Rest assured, I'm not going over to the *enragés*, and if I see them or have connections with some of them it's only to make use of them; I loathe them all too much to let myself ever go over to them. I believe the Comte de Ségur is going to be nominated to M. de Montmorin's post.[107] I would like him to accept it; he knows how to talk, and that is all that's required at the moment when we cannot have good ministers of our own, and it will be his undoing. Perhaps that would even be no bad thing.

The bodyguards are causing me much concern. It's clear that they will be entirely lost to us if they are formed into a corps, as is happening now. I have been assured even by the *enragés* that nothing could be easier than taking them back in a little while, but if they appear to want to do something about it, then it will be impossible. The King and I have written to his brothers about it by the *senaubr=* to see if there are any means to do anything about it. It is a question of not seeing them gathered together, and that if we attempt nothing this winter, that a few of them return and show themselves here. {Their return, however, should not be hurried, as we have a plan rather like the one of June. It is not yet firmly decided; I will send it to you in a week to ten days. If it can take place it will be between 15 and 20 November, but if we cannot go then we will do nothing over the winter and carry on while waiting for the congress, which I shall press for strongly.

I cannot tell you how touched I am by what that kind Mr Craufurd did for us, the King is, too. I will write to you in a few days telling you what to say to him on our behalf. We would be so happy to be able to do something for him; there are so few people who give proof of a real attachment to us. It is [**suspected**] known here that he was involved in our affairs, and I was very anxious about his house. Everything appears to be quiet at the moment, but peace hangs by a thread and the people are as they were, ever ready to commit atrocities. We are told they support us. I don't believe it at all, at least not as far as I'm concerned. I know the price to be put on all of that. Most of the time they are paid, and they only like us so long as we do what they want. It's impossible to carry on like that for long. There is no more safety for us in Paris now than there was before and perhaps even less, because people are accustomed to seeing us degraded.}

You tell me nothing about your health. Mine is good [*1½ lines deleted*]. The French are atrocious on all sides. One has to be very careful that if those here have the advantage and we have to live with them, they should be able to reproach us with nothing. But one also has to consider that if those outside become masters again one must not displease them.

[*4½ lines deleted*]

{**bensaahe I love**}

In his reply to this letter, Fersen repeated the unwelcome news he had received from Baron Simolin, Russian Ambassador to Paris, in a letter to Eléonore Sullivan. Doubtless he sought reassurance from Marie-Antoinette that she had not spoken against him. Fersen was wounded by the accusations being made against him, tormented perhaps by the idea that she was drifting away from him and following the advice of the *enragés* who had tried to destroy her. In his diary he blames the failure of the escape to Varennes for all his woes.

18 October: Simolin writes to Mme Sullivan that he [Stael] is saying awful things about me, that he says I did nothing but scheme to get him removed from his post; he has even shown letters, he says, from the King of Sweden &. All those gentlemen, especially Spain, Simolin etc. are all against me, saying that I did everything out of ambition, that I caused the downfall of the King and Queen for this reason and to be [*illegible word*]. Spain says that the King and Queen said that they could see we had deceived them and they are very discontented &&. That's what happens when something fails.[108]

19. Fersen to Marie-Antoinette, 25 October 1791

AN 440AP/1. Autograph copy of a 'Josephine' letter from Fersen to Marie-Antoinette, sent in code. The code word is contraire *on page 27 of the code book. I have succeeded in reading beneath several deleted lines. Fersen logged this letter in his register to 'Josephine by post'. There is no farewell, so it is possible that the last page is missing.*

27 contraire

25 October 1791 by post

My dear and very kind friend, my God how cruel it is to be so close and not be able to see each other, and how <u>we would be probably even more</u>/ _ _ _ _ / _ _ _ _ _ / _ _ _ _ / _ _ _ _ / <u>to say how much we love each other.</u> No, I live and exist only to love you; **adoring you is my only consolation, and apart from you / _ _ _ _ _ _ _ / there is no / _ _ _ _ / but the sentiment and / _ _ _ _ / _ _ _ _ / _ _ _ / _ff _ _ _ _ _ /.**

Continue to press [*your brother*] the Emperor for this congress. Without a prompt and very definite action I fear everything from the follies of the princes and emigrants. They are very fired up and believe they have been abandoned; I will no longer answer for anything on their part. I've written along these lines to all my King's ambassadors in various courts, so that they press the Emperor about it. He needs to be pushed; without that he will do nothing. Don't fear any rash action by the King [of Sweden], I'll be able to restrain him. His conduct in all your affairs deserves your gratitude; if they had all behaved like him you wouldn't be in the state you are in now.

Staël is saying awful things about me. He has even poached my coachman and taken him into his service, which upsets me. He has turned many people against me, who criticize my conduct and say that I acted only out of ambition and that I have brought about your downfall and the King's. The Spanish Ambassador and others are of this opinion. He's at Louvain and has seen no one here. They are right. My ambition was to serve you and I will regret my whole life that I did not succeed. {I was jealous of this happiness.} I wanted to repay you for some of those obligations which it's so sweet for me to owe you, and I wanted to show that one can be attached to people like you for no other reason. The rest of my conduct should have proved to them that that was my sole ambition, and that the glory of having served you was my most precious recompense.

My horses have arrived. I know that you have seen my valet de chambre's wife – what kindness![109] But I ought to be used to it **for there has never been a being more perfect than you** _ _ _ _ _ / _ _ / _ _ _ / **never** / _ _ _ /t_ _ t / _ _ _é/ **that** / **I love you**. It is being said a great deal that you would prefer to remain as you are rather than make use of the princes. That's very true, but take good care – it mustn't be talked about, it's dangerous for you.

My father was absolutely determined that I return, but I hope to reconcile him to my ideas. It's the article of money which frightens him most. Let me know what you want me to do with the money I sent to Holland for you – if it should be placed somewhere or left on deposit where it is. Although I told M. de Bouillé to return to me what was left of the one million, he had the weakness to give it to the princes. That was seven hundred thousand *livres* it would have been very useful for you to have. If the princes can be contained, the big emigration of the moment is not perhaps an evil for you and may serve to enlighten the people and bring them round through want and misery.

Fersen to Marie-Antoinette, 26 October 1791, letter missing

On 26 October, Fersen noted in his diary: 'de Brige left this morning for Paris, wrote by him.' Marie-Antoinette acknowledged receipt of this letter in her reply on 31 October.

20. Fersen to Marie-Antoinette, 29 October 1791

*AN 440AP/1. Autograph copy of a letter from Fersen to Marie-Antoinette
sent partly in code. It is logged in the register: 'Josephine by Pcsse
Lamballe'. Fersen had known Mme de Lamballe since his first visit to
Paris in 1774; she would have provided what the Queen called 'a secure
occasion' to write. The code word is* depuis *on page 36 of the code book.
There is a magnificent declaration of love from Fersen to Marie-
Antoinette at the end of the letter, discovered by the author under blacked-
out lines. Fersen also proposes a visit to Paris, in which several details
are crossed out; this passage is not encrypted so may well have been
written in invisible ink on the actual letter received by Marie-Antoinette.
Klinckowström suppressed this passage from his edition, and in Lever's*
Correspondance *it appears in a footnote.*

By the Princesse de Lamballe
36 depuis

29 October [1791]

I have received letters from Sweden which are perfect. The King is
strongly pushing the Empress, who is very well disposed. She wishes
to have a meeting with him, which will take place as soon as the
borders are finally agreed. It is a great mystery, so it's important not to
mention it to anyone. It would be useful if your letter to the Empress
reached her before this meeting; it would produce a good effect. I have
told the King what you wish to be done, and I shall reiterate it to him
once again. Baron Taube has already come round to my idea of a
congress, and I am sure that the King will insist on that point. All
envoys and ambassadors must also depart on leave and Chère
Clotilde must be done as soon as possible. But it will be necessary also
to insist with the Emperor so that there is a demonstration of force to
support the congress – at least to make preparations to deploy troops
(without that it will have neither the force nor the consideration it
must have). The Emperor, Spain and the King of Sardinia could order
their troops to be ready to march; the King of Prussia could order
those at Vesel to prepare their equipment and stand by; Sweden and
Russia the same. Insist on that. I will write the same everywhere.

There is disunity in the cabinet at Coblentz. The Bishop of Arras
has left; they are tired of the Maréchal de Broglie; Calonne and

Jaucourt have fallen out. The former does not want to stay if the latter remains. It is even said that he's returning to England. The Maréchal de Castries is here.[110] He has a fancy to go to Coblentz but he's very reasonable and would like to engage the Baron de Breteuil to go there, which he will not do; but I hope he will have sufficient contact with the princes to impede their follies. The two princes have even fallen out, and I hope there is nothing to fear from them. However, one should always use this threat to push the Emperor, who needs it, or otherwise he will do nothing. If the émigrés were to return at the moment it would be a great misfortune. It would have been better had they not left, but since they have, their return would be a great triumph for the *enragés* and you would lose much of your power to contain them. I think therefore that you should appear to desire the return of the émigrés but do nothing to provoke it. They must simply be contained and the congress will have that effect.

It could be very {necessary for me to <u>see</u> you [*1 line deleted*] **of pleasure. That might even be possible.** I would leave here alone with the [*same*] officer who brought you my letter in July.[111] The pretext would be to go and see a gentleman of the country who has looked after my saddle horses all summer. I would arrive in the evening. I would go [*1½ lines deleted*] and then I would leave again. They are no longer asking for passports, besides I have one as a courier. It would be stamped as though I were coming from Spain. That seems feasible to me – it will be in December.}

As soon as you receive blank paper or a book with blank pages, the letter will be in invisible ink; the same if the date is written at the end.

Farewell, my tender friend. I love you and will love you madly all my life.

Fersen's visit to Marie-Antoinette in the Tuileries is presented by Klinckowström and others as a mission for Gustav III to propose a new escape for the French Royal Family. And indeed, when he finally undertook the trip in February 1792 he was armed with dispatches from the King of Sweden for this purpose; but it is clear from his papers that the idea to go to Paris was Fersen's alone. On 30 October 1791, the day after proposing the visit to the Queen, he wrote to Taube to get him to persuade Gustav to authorize this dangerous mission. Note that he asks Taube for a courier's passport, although he had told Marie-Antoinette he already had one . . .

It could be necessary for me to see the King of France and the Queen and if it's possible I will go. It will be a matter of 6 or 7 days, but I don't want to be seen; to this end the King [Gustav] would need to send me 4 couriers' passports for Spain, authorized from Stockholm and leaving the date blank. One would be in my name and the other in Reutersvärd's. We will go alone; and to come back I'll get Baron Ehrensverd to give us a passport as if we were coming from Spain. If the King wanted to write to them [Louis XVI and Marie-Antoinette], the address must be to the King of Spain. This packet could be sent by post to me at Hamburg and from there by courier. In this way I could at least explain to them their true position, inform them of everything and organize something with them.[112]

Fersen gives political reasons for wanting to risk his life by returning to France, where he was still a wanted man for his part in the flight to Varennes. Naturally, he would never mention a private visit to the Queen in official letters, but he had very personal motives for wanting to go to Paris. The notes in his letter register and diary about this visit confirm that he told Marie-Antoinette he intended to arrive 'chez Elle' in the evening in order to spend the night with her. In this context, the word 'pleasure' may have special significance. Marie-Antoinette kept promising him in her letters that she was not being influenced by the enragés; he wanted her to confirm it to him face to face. And doubtless he also wished to know why she kept urging him to return to Sweden – was it really because she was fearful for his safety that she begged him to put even more distance between them, or was there another reason: Barnave? She did not even reply to Fersen about this visit. He repeated his proposal a month later on 26 November 1791, in response to a fresh demand from Marie-Antoinette that he leave Brussels. This time he tried to persuade her that it was Gustav III's idea.

As for my departure from Brussels, despite my desire to satisfy you about it and set your mind at rest, it is impossible. I am here on the King's orders, and cannot leave . . . Besides, you must not worry; I run no risk here. Let me know about the possibility of coming to see you completely alone and without a servant, in case I receive the order from the King. He has already hinted something to me of his wish for it.[113]

The Queen replied on 7 December: 'It is impossible for you to come here at the moment. It would risk our happiness and when I say it you can believe me, because I have an extreme desire to see you.'[114] Fersen would have to wait until 21 January 1792 to receive permission to visit her, and even then she kept prevaricating. He finally arrived '*chez Elle*' on 13 February 1792.

21. Marie-Antoinette to Fersen, 31 October and 7 November 1791

AN 440AP/1. Autograph letter from Marie-Antoinette to Fersen. He did not receive it from Mercy until 24 November; it seems that Mercy did not give the Queen's letters to Fersen until after he had read them. There are no redacted passages in this letter, which is purely political in nature. It is likely that Marie-Antoinette showed it to Louis XVI before adding the last paragraph in code. The code word is neuf followed by the letter i.

The style of this letter is interesting. Marie-Antoinette writes as a sovereign, with authority and assurance. The use of 'we' indicates that she is also speaking for the King, but why did he burden his wife with the full weight of this diplomatic correspondence? The rift between Louis XVI and his brothers was widening. The Queen says that she and the King are revolted by the letter Monsieur wrote after Varennes, dismissing the Baron de Breteuil[115] – and now Monsieur is trying to justify his presumption in sacking the only man authorized by Louis XVI to negotiate on his behalf, by blaming Fersen . . .

Marie-Antoinette indicates an opportunity for Fersen to write to her privately: 'The person who is leaving tomorrow and who will deliver a letter in code is coming back soon. I think it is a secure occasion.'

24 Nov 1791 by M. de Mercy

31 October [1791]

I received all your papers by M. de Brige yesterday.[116] The writing came out perfectly with the water which I had fetched from the apothecary. The water we were sent from over there [Brussels] must have evaporated, but that doesn't matter at present. I shall try to answer everything succinctly, and I'll take it up again whenever I have time until Thursday, when the man who is charged with this letter will leave. I was so rushed the last time I wrote to you that I couldn't speak of M. Craufurd. Please tell him that we know how perfect his behaviour is for us; that I have always been pleased to believe in his attachment, but that, in the dreadful position we are in, every new proof of interest is another very sweet claim on our gratitude.

Monsieur's letter to the baron [de Breteuil] surprised and appalled us; but patience is required at the moment and one mustn't allow one's anger to show too much. Nevertheless I shall copy it out and show it to my sister [Mme Elisabeth]. I'm curious to know how she will justify it with all that's happening. Our domestic life is a hell; there is no way to say anything, even with the best will in the world. My sister is so indiscreet, surrounded by intriguers and, above all, dominated by her brothers abroad, that we cannot find a way to talk to one another, or we should quarrel all day long. I see that the ambition of the people surrounding Monsieur will ruin him entirely. In the first moment, he believed that he was everything; but try though he may, he will never play a role. His brother will always have the confidence and advantage over him with all parties, by the constancy and immutability of his conduct. It is very unfortunate that Monsieur did not return at once when we were arrested. He would then have followed the course he had always proclaimed, that of never wanting to leave us, and he would have spared us many worries and troubles which will perhaps result from the summons we are going to be forced to issue for his return – and with which we are well aware that he will not be able to comply, especially when made in such a manner.

For a long time now we have lamented the number of émigrés; we are aware of the harm it does within the kingdom as well as for the princes themselves. What is dreadful is the manner in which these honest people are being deceived and have been deceived; soon there will be nothing left to them but to resort to rage and despair. Those who have had enough confidence in us to consult us have been stopped; or, at least, if they thought their honour demanded they go, we have told them the truth. But what do you expect? In order not to follow our wishes, it's the fashion and the craze to say that we are not free (which is indeed true) and that consequently we cannot say what we think and that it's necessary to do the opposite. That was the fate of the memorandum we sent to my brothers, which you saw and approved. The answer is that we were forced to write that memorandum, that those could not be our sentiments and that consequently one would take no account of it. And after that they expect us to trust them, that we speak frankly – which is tantamount to saying: 'Do everything we want, and then we will serve you, but, otherwise, nothing.'

As it is possible, however, that they may at this very moment be committing follies that could ruin everything, I believe it necessary to stop them at all costs; and as I hope – from what your papers and M. de Mercy's letter say – that the congress will take place, I think we should send them someone trustworthy from here who could show them the danger and the extravagance of their project and at the same time show them our true position and our wishes, proving to them that the only course for us to follow at the moment is to gain the confidence of the people here; that it is necessary and useful for any project at all, that to achieve this we should all march together, and that as the powers cannot come to the help of France with great forces during the winter only a congress can rally and bring together the possible means for the spring. But, in making this confidence we must beware of their extreme indiscretion; for that reason, the person to be sent from here must be told only precisely what we want to be made known there.

M. Grimm has arrived here.[117] He desired to see me, but I replied that it was impossible for me to receive him, and that is true to a certain extent; I am too closely watched. But I have had him told my reasons by a person who will, at the same time, speak in appropriate terms of our feelings for the Empress. It is essential that she is brought to adopt the idea of a congress; by her character she will get all the powers to agree on it, and she will also contain the princes. I only fear M. de Calonne's flippancy and M. de Nassau's petulance.

There is nothing to be gained from the current Assembly; it is a gaggle of scoundrels, madmen and fools. The few people there who want order, and a little less evil than the rest, are not listened to and dare not speak. On top of that it is in disrepute, even with the people, who they constantly try to stir up by every means possible. But that no longer works. Nothing concerns them but the high cost of bread, and the decrees and the papers do not even give it any attention. There has been a visible change on that in Paris, where the vast majority, without knowing whether they want this regime or another, is weary of the troubles and wants tranquillity. I speak of Paris alone, for I believe the provincial cities are much worse than here at the moment; and yet at Coblentz they never cease to tell us that there is great accord throughout the kingdom, but the affair at Lyon makes us wary and little likely to believe such statements.

In returning to the King his letter of notification on his acceptance [of the Constitution] without reading it, the King of Sweden did something which I wish had been done everywhere else in the same way; but [*if he is*] alone I fear this action might be imprudent. However, it is impossible to be more touched than we are by the frankness, loyalty and nobility of his conduct towards us, and I hope that one day we will at last benefit from all that he is so kindly doing for us. I've just read two dispatches from Spain, one from 13 October, the other from the 20th. They are fine, and I do not think Spain will make any difficulty about the congress. The idea even enters into part of her plan, but she first wants the King to be free and able to go where he pleases. That idea is impossible, because they will always say here that he is the master and can go wherever he deems fit, when in fact he cannot; for besides getting out of here, which would be dangerous, and where he might perhaps be obliged to leave his wife and son, his personal safety would never be greater anywhere than it is here, since there is not a town or a troop that can be relied on. On the contrary, it seems to me that it is only by seeking to gain more popularity and trust every day that we will be able to join the congress once it is established – or at least go to the frontier to be in some way responsible ourselves for representing the interests of this country. If we were ever to gain this point, it would be everything, and we must aim for this single goal, but to reach it all our daily actions must be focused on inspiring confidence.

The misfortune is that we are seconded here by no one except ourselves, and that whatever efforts I make alone I cannot do all that I would wish and which I also feel is so necessary for the general good. Spain had yet another idea, which I find detestable, which is to let the princes enter with all the French, supported only by the King of Sweden as our ally, and declare by a manifesto that they are coming not to wage war but to rally all good Frenchmen to their party and declare themselves protectors of true French liberty. The big powers would provide all the necessary money for this operation and remain outside the country with enough troops to impress, but they would do nothing that could be viewed as a pretext for an invasion and partition. But none of that is practicable, and I believe that if the Emperor hurries up and announces the congress it is the only suitable and useful way to end all this.

I really do not understand why you desire the immediate withdrawal of all the ministers and ambassadors. It seems to me that as this congress is supposedly being convened, at least at the outset, as much to discuss affairs which interest all the European powers as for those of France, there is no reason for this prompt withdrawal. Besides, can one be sure that all the powers will do the same, or believe that England and Holland (which is guided by her) and even Prussia would not perhaps leave their ministers in order to thwart all the others? Then there would be a division in the opinions of Europe that could only harm our affairs. I may be mistaken, but I believe that only a great accord (at least in appearance) will be able to inspire respect here. Do not trust Denmark; from the dispatches it appears to be detestable, above all, for Russia and Sweden.

Apparently I didn't explain myself clearly about the bodyguards. It is not our intention to recall them, only to stop them becoming a corps, and that if we do nothing this winter, the officers, or the richest among them, come back here and show themselves. It is the same thing for the émigrés. I know perfectly well that once they have left, and especially in such a manner, it is impossible that they should return; but it is a great misfortune, even greater for the rest of France than for Paris, because the provinces are left entirely to their own devices or to a horde of villains and rebels. In our position, with the dreadful mistrust they constantly try to keep up against us, it is impossible for us not to do publicly everything necessary to make everyone come home. The decree for the *parlements* proposed in the princes' council is mad. I am not surprised it was rejected. It seems to me that the wisest heads of the *parlement* of Paris oppose all extravagance and don't even wish to leave.

I quite understand about the code, but it will still be necessary to put a colon when the two words finish at the same time and leave the Js and the Vs; that will make it easier for us. Skipping a letter will only serve when we write by occasions. We read everything in invisible ink, but from now on the King dispenses with ceremony; it will be simpler if you simply put 'you'. I also desire that either the bishop or someone else with a legible hand writes the letters and not you, who are already so overwhelmed with paperwork. By the next secure occasion you must tell us exactly how much money we have abroad, both at Brussels and in Holland, and the name of the bankers. Let me know too how much [money] we owe Mme de Korff, from what time and how to get it to her. Since the Maréchal de Castries is well disposed, the baron could confer with him on everything concerning us and our ideas. He could go to Coblentz to talk to our brothers. We will look for someone to send him to authorize him on our behalf, but he should be taught the code and found a book. I will entrust it to the person we send. I would like it to be the Baron de Vioménil, but I do not know if he will want to go.[118] I believe that M. Puisignieux and the Comte Etienne are coming back; find out if that would be a secure occasion to write. Messieurs Odun and Okelie have been suggested for foreign affairs; I do not know them at all, but the safest thing to do is never to negotiate through him. Do not mention these two men as it is not certain they will be chosen.

7 November

I hope this letter will finally go tomorrow. It should have left on the 3rd, but the person was delayed by his business affairs, and I preferred to wait to ensure it was safely delivered. The person leaving tomorrow, who will deliver a letter in code, is supposed to return soon – I believe it's a safe occasion. Is it true that the King of Sweden is sending a minister to the princes at Coblentz? I very much fear that the King [Louis XVI] will be asked to write in his own hand to the King of Sweden on current affairs, but should that happen it will be simply another proof of his lack of freedom. Still no minister; Mme de Staël is exerting herself a great deal on behalf of M. de Narbonne.[119] I have never seen such a deep and involved intrigue. The Emperor's response to the King's acceptance contains, I have been told (since I have not yet seen it) a very good sentence which could prepare the ground for the congress, provided he sustains it and hurries to announce it; because despite the apparent calm in Coblentz minds there are very agitated, and it is to be feared that soon the princes will be able to restrain them no longer. I must give my letter tomorrow morning, so I shall close. Adieu.

No. 15 [*in code*]

My sister showed me a letter from M [Monsieur], dated while he was still in Brussels, to justify the one he had written to the **b** [baron], in which he says that you had told him that the King wanted to put him in charge of everything during his imprisonment. I am warning you about it in case it is talked about where you are; as for us, we know very well what it is about. Farewell, **my beloved**.

22. Marie-Antoinette to Fersen, 2 and 7 November 1791

AN 440AP/1. Fersen's autograph minute of a letter from the Queen. It would appear to be all that he judged prudent to keep of the coded letter she spoke of in her letter of 31 October and 7 November: 'The person leaving tomorrow, who will deliver a letter in code . . . ' Note that he received this letter on 11 November, while the long political letter sent through Mercy did not reach him until the 24th. Marie-Antoinette reassures Fersen again that she is not yielding to the enragés, *and, interestingly, she expresses concern about his close links to Breteuil, fearing that the clamour from Coblentz against the baron will also engulf him. The dotted lines in this letter are from the original.*

Fragments of a letter from the Queen

Received 11 November

2 and 7 November [1791]

——————————————————————————————————————

————————————————————————————————— be quite easy, I shall never go over to the *enragés*. They need to be used to prevent even greater evils, but as for doing good I am well aware that they are incapable of it. Farewell, I am tired because of all this paperwork. I have never performed such a role, and I am always afraid of forgetting something or making silly mistakes—————

——————————- I see that all the aristocratic and democratic parties are up in arms against the Baron de Breteuil. I am worried that you are with him; once again we owe this cruel persecution to Coblentz and the émigrés. They have repeated so often that we only act on the advice of the baron, that he knew all our secrets, that the government and all the *enragés* are starting to talk about it.

At the beginning of November 1791 Fersen was unwell and even stopped writing his diary for three days. By 12 November he was able to get out again, and that evening he dined at Craufurd's, where he notes that he saw 'a caricature of Lafayette'. In it Lafayette is depicted as a racehorse named '*Le Sans Tort*' ('Blameless'), a nickname that Marie-Antoinette would use in a letter to Fersen. The caricature, reproduced in this book, is to be found with Fersen's archives in Stockholm.

23. FERSEN TO MARIE-ANTOINETTE, 11 NOVEMBER 1791

Stafsund, SE/RA/5802. The original letter is missing. This transcription is taken from Klinckowström's manuscript. Fersen logged it in his register to 'Josephine, in code by post'. He warns the Queen that they need to find other intermediaries for their correspondence: 'never write to me by M. de Mercy; he can decipher all your letters', and asks if she has enough confidence in M. de La Porte 'so that the bishop can forward letters through him, as if they came from the baron'.[120] *Marie-Antoinette agreed to adopt this idea, with unforeseen consequences.*

11 November 1791

The bishop is going to Paris. I shall send you a long summary of your position by him with my ideas on what needs to be done.[121] It is essential that you write to Spain and Russia to ask for their help and to convince them that you do not want to surrender entirely to the Constitution. It will be better for the letter for Russia to go through Simolin, without passing through Blumendorf; the one for Spain could go through the Baron de Breteuil. A note for Sweden would go down well; I will send it on. In this way you will prevent the powers from going over to the princes, by proving to them that you want to act by yourselves. It would be as well to tell them about the congress which you have asked the Emperor to propose and to tell them that you will explain your projects to them in detail, in the hope they will want to participate in them.

Let me know if you have enough confidence in M. de La Porte so that the bishop can forward letters through him, as if they came from the baron.

I cannot tell you enough how important it is for you to write confidentially as soon as possible to Sweden and Russia, to stop them from turning to the princes in the persuasion that you will never want to do anything. This first letter would be only to tell him [Gustav III] that you hope he will not refuse to give you new proofs of the friendship and interest which he has already shown you; that your position imposes many restraints but that you will soon take him into your confidence regarding your projects, and, knowing his noble and generous way of thinking, you have no doubt that he will support them with all his might and that he will use his influence with the Empress to get her to decide in your favour, and that which he has with the princes to prevent them from committing some folly that would upset all your plans. The letter to the Empress would be the same, flattering her a little. In this way they could be very useful to you.

You will need to wait until the bishop has brought you the summary I am preparing for you on your position abroad before writing the second letter. You will then be better able to judge what needs to be done and decide on the course of conduct I am proposing to you. Never write through M. de Mercy; he can decipher all your letters.

Staël will receive three months' leave, with the order to depart at once. Do not forget to write me something amiable from you and the King for Mr Craufurd; he has earned it.

Despite all Fersen's and the Queen's efforts during the autumn of 1791, Leopold II continued to prevaricate on the idea of a congress, while the princes and émigrés at Coblentz spread slanders about the Queen. According to a letter from Quintin Craufurd to the Duke of Dorset from Brussels on 18 November, there was now complete misunderstanding between Coblentz and the Tuileries.

The Princes grow very impatient, and wish to attempt something, which the wiser part of their advisers endeavours to persuade them from, and I hope their counsel will prevail. Calonne and others of that party have endeavoured to make the noblesse believe that the backwardness of the Emperor is to be ascribed to the Queen, who they say is jealous of the influence of the Princes. But the idea is absurd and entirely without foundation. Both the King and Queen are, I believe, apprehensive of their being precipitate and unwise, but there is but little probability of their having much occasion to be jealous either of their influence or power.[122]

More worrying were the letters Fersen received from Sweden: Gustav III was ready to form an alliance with his recent enemy Catherine II of Russia to support the princes in order to overthrow the French Constitution by force, completely ignoring Louis XVI's desire to avoid a war. It is for this reason that Fersen kept insisting that Marie-Antoinette write to the King of Sweden and the Empress to explain her position. Gustav III (who nevertheless correctly analysed the deceitful posturing of Austria) had ideas that were diametrically opposed to those expressed by Louis XVI in a memorandum sent to the Baron de Breteuil by the Queen on 25 November 1791 (see below).

Fersen, who loved the Queen of France but who had to obey the King of Sweden, was caught between a rock and a hard place. Nevertheless he tried to reconcile these apparently irreconcilable positions to rally foreign governments to the idea of a congress that would resolve the political crisis in France through negotiation. A particularly vehement letter he received from Gustav III reveals what an uphill struggle he faced; it appears that Leopold II's duplicity had triumphed, for Gustav makes quite unfounded accusations against Marie-Antoinette, all of which originated in Vienna and which were then embellished and broadcast from Coblentz.

Gustav III to Fersen, 11 November 1791

The equivocal conduct of this prince [Leopold II] and his continual prevarication forewarned us of the course he would take a long time ago, and everything he did was done solely to prevent other powers from taking action, by making them waste time; but it is true that the shameful conduct of the King of France has favoured his projects perfectly, and, although we should have expected acts of weakness, the conduct of the French court has surely surpassed in cowardice and ignominy everything that could have been expected from them and which their past conduct could indicate. But what is much more regrettable is that, having debased himself so much already, he is still trying to hamper efforts which his brothers and the countries who are sincerely interested in the fate of these princes and the French throne can make to help him; and if the Queen prefers to live in her current state of subjection and danger rather than depend upon her brothers, which she seems to fear more, quite wrongly, I have to tell you that the Empress is very dissatisfied with this conduct and, above all, that the Queen of France writes letter after letter to the Emperor to stop him from taking action, while the Empress is exerting all her influence over this prince's mind to engage him to take more active steps . . .

The Queen will not achieve her goal by such conduct; she will only arouse the discontent of her true friends, who, through interest, necessity and even resentment, will encourage the princes further than even they themselves wish or could hope. You must therefore strongly represent to the Queen that it is essential for her to give written assurances which prove the violence which has been and is being used against her since she appeared again [in public] in apparent freedom, so that this paper can be used as a weapon against the excuses employed by the Emperor, and force this prince alone to take the blame for his conduct, which he is now trying to throw on to his sister.

. . . As regards the congress you tell me of, I vow that I scarcely see its usefulness. Arms alone must decide this great quarrel. The congress would have been good before the King of France's acceptance and before the Emperor recognized that he was free; then such a step would have engaged the Emperor and could have, in consequence, committed this prince enough so that he could not have withdrawn without shame (if he is capable of feeling any): but now this congress would be of no use at all.[123]

Marie-Antoinette to Fersen, 20 November 1791, letter missing

In his diary Fersen noted 'Went to Mercy's – he gave me a letter from the Queen. They are very unhappy but want to take action.' Quintin Craufurd gave an idea of this letter's content to the Duke of Dorset on 22 November.

It appears by a letter from the Queen received a few days ago, that she is, notwithstanding what has been said, in a most disconsolate situation 'without any resource but what she finds in her own mind, without any one to aid, or any one to advise her', but notwithstanding this she expresses herself with great fortitude and magnanimity. I know that some have found fault with her for not having used her influence with the King to engage him to reject the Constitution; but when her conduct on this occasion is explained I am persuaded that your Grace, and even Mr Burke, will think her entirely blameless.[124]

24. MARIE-ANTOINETTE TO FERSEN, 25 NOVEMBER 1791

AN 440AP/1. Autograph decrypt by Fersen of a letter from the Queen. A copy of the memorandum from Louis XVI attached to this letter is to be found in the Swedish archives. Fersen annotated it: 'Received 1 Dec. note for the Baron de Breteuil, sent to me by the Queen, extract of a memorandum by the King.'[125] *The whole of Europe accused Louis XVI of weakness and was expecting him to regain his authority by force, but aware of the mood of his people he looked on such force as certain to lead to his downfall. 'The King cannot nor must he, by himself, renege on what has been done. The majority of the nation must wish it.' And so 'the tyrant' was learning the principles of democracy . . .*

25 November 1791

I am waiting for the bishop with great impatience. Here is a note for the baron: it is an extract from a long memorandum the King has written to remind himself of all he has done recently. The paper is very well done, but as well as containing some arguments which are unnecessary it would have been far too long to cipher.

Our position is terrible at the moment. {The rebels are constantly busy, the people are ready at any moment to rise up and commit atrocities,} and the republicans use all their means. However, I still believe that if we are wise, we could even take advantage of all this by the excess of evil, and sooner than people think, but great prudence is required {and without foreign help we will do nothing.} [*four lines deleted and illegible except 'for project'*] but the paper which I told you about at the beginning will not leave until tomorrow by another occasion. I preferred that for fear of making too big a packet. There will be two letters in invisible ink inside: one for Spain and the other for Sweden. We dared not write in any other way. You must expose the writing, and the baron can take responsibility for the letter for Spain. If you deem them to be no good, burn them and write to me to tell me what we must write. The code word is *cause*. I don't know if it is in all letters, as I was obliged to give it to be written. There is no [*blank*] for you inside, therefore let **the b**[aron] decode it.

M. de Staël has not left, and he's still coming to court. Farewell. It is nearly two o'clock.

Extract of a memorandum from Louis XVI for the Baron de Breteuil, sent to Fersen by Marie-Antoinette with her letter of 25 November 1791

All policy must come down to ruling out the ideas of an invasion the émigrés could attempt by themselves; it would be a calamity for France if the interests of the émigrés came first and if they had only the help of a few powers. Who is to say that others like England would not, at least secretly, provide aid to the other side and would not take advantage of the unfortunate situation of a France tearing herself apart? The émigrés must be persuaded that they will do nothing of any value between now and the spring; that their interest, as well as ours, demands that they cease to cause disquiet. One is well aware that if they think they are abandoned they will be carried to excesses which need to be avoided. The hopes of some must be focused on the spring while the needs of others are provided for.

A congress would achieve the desired outcome. It could contain the émigrés and frighten the rebels. The powers should agree together the language which needs to be spoken to all parties. An action devised by them can only impress without harming the King's interests; besides their individual interests, there could perhaps be occasions where these interventions would be necessary – if, for example, it was desired to establish a republic on the ruins of the monarchy. Moreover, it is not possible that they could be unconcerned to see, Monsieur and M. le Comte d'Artois not returning, the Duc d'Orléans next in line to the throne. What a subject for reflection!

A firm and constant language by all the powers of Europe, supported by a formidable army, would have the most favourable consequences. It would moderate the ardour of the émigrés, whose role would only be secondary. The rebels would be confounded, and good citizens who are the friends of order and the monarchy would regain their courage. These ideas are for the future, and for the present the powers have several reasons to desire an understanding among themselves. They are summarized in a memorandum sent to M. de Mercy six weeks ago.

The King cannot nor must he, by himself, renege on what has been done. The majority of the nation must wish it, or he must be forced to it by circumstances; and in that case he needs to gain trust and popularity by acting under the terms of the Constitution. By executing it literally, they will soon get to know all it vices, especially in removing all the worries caused by the émigrés. If they burst in without major forces, they will cause the downfall of France and of the King. We have spoken to the Baron de Vioménil in this respect, and he will be able to develop the general ideas contained in this memorandum.

On 19 November 1791, Fersen wrote in his diary that 'D'Ecquevilly told Mme Sullivan that the King is certainly leaving on the 19th or 20th.' This refers to the escape plan mentioned by Marie-Antoinette in her letter of 19 October and to which Fersen refers in his letter and memorandum to her of 26 November. He had spent several days drafting it when news arrived that Leopold II had refused to convene a congress. Craufurd informed the Duke of Dorset of reactions in Brussels.

I had the honour to write your Grace on Friday last. On Saturday a messenger arrived from Vienna, who brought the Emperor's refusal to the proposal of assembling a congress. It was communicated by M. de Mercy on Sunday to the Baron de Breteuil. The baron was extremely out of humour, and expressed his sentiments to M. de M. on the conduct of the Emperor, with a considerable degree of warmth and freedom. M. de M. heard the baron without being in the least discomposed but concluded by saying that it was not impossible that His Imperial Majesty might be induced to alter his opinion. The baron said he was sorry to observe to him that the Emperor's conduct hitherto gave him but very faint hope of what might be done by him hereafter.[126]

All this only confirmed Fersen's fears about the Austrians' double game; the memorandum he sent to Marie-Antoinette shows that he had already discounted any idea of positive action by the Emperor.

25. FERSEN TO MARIE-ANTOINETTE, 26 NOVEMBER 1791,
POLITICAL MEMORANDUM

AN 440AP/1. Autograph copy of the 'long summary of your position with my ideas on what needs to be done' announced by Fersen in his letter to the Queen on 11 November. This memorandum was written in invisible ink and taken to Paris by the Bishop of Pamiers. It is followed by a private letter that starts on a new page; therefore in this edition of the correspondence the letter is presented separately to distinguish it from the memorandum, which had been read by others. 'Wrote my long letter to the Queen,' Fersen noted in his diary on 17 November. 'Read my letter at Craufurd's at luncheon, then to the baron'.[127] It is logged in his register under 'Josephine, detailed memorandum by the bishop.'

The major part of this letter contains nothing that could not be read by Louis XVI, but at the end, and starting on a fresh page, the tone becomes intimate and there are the usual endearments Fersen employs when writing to Marie-Antoinette. However, it is interesting to observe that he addresses the Queen alone, giving her instructions on what to write in letters to foreign countries and exhorting her to adopt a policy. He treats her as a sovereign. Louis XVI is never consulted on the measures required to save his throne. Indeed, in giving instructions for the letters to be sent to foreign allies, he is relegated to rubber-stamping letters written by the Queen: 'It would be useful for the King to write a line to the King of Spain at the same time. He would refer to what you would have already written.' Fersen operates exactly like Barnave and the Constitutionals, although for a diametrically opposite end. Neither man seemed even to consider speaking to the King about how to restore order to France.

After Leopold II's refusal to support a congress, Fersen tells the Queen to forget any idea of being helped by her brother and to appeal to Spain instead to lead a coalition with Russia, Sweden and Prussia in order to circumvent the Emperor. He is never too critical of Leopold when he writes to Marie-Antoinette, but he is less tactful when writing to Baron Taube, who had correctly summed up the Austrians' game in September. Fersen's disgust with them would reach its peak in 1792 when he realized that they wanted nothing less than to partition France.

Memorandum for the Queen

November 1791, sent in invisible ink by the Bishop

Brussels, 26 November 1791

After everything I have sent you regarding the Emperor's dawdling and his lack of active goodwill for you, of which I am convinced by everything I saw myself in Vienna and by all the means he constantly employs to paralyse the goodwill of other courts and to stop them from acting (and one day I will give you proof positive of it), I believe it is necessary for you to adopt another plan of action; but before I propose it you need to be given an accurate idea of your position abroad.

The powers who sincerely wish to help you, such as Spain, Russia, Sweden and perhaps Prussia, still see in the King's acceptance and in all his conduct nothing but an act of weakness, particularly in his conduct afterwards, for which they see no necessity even while admitting the need for him to sanction [the Constitution]. They fear that your intention is to do nothing and to continue to follow the Constitution through weakness. They are aware of the danger of this example, and, as the re-establishment of the monarchy is in their political interest, they will ally themselves with the princes rather than allow such a monstrous government to take root in France. [*The cabinet of Vienna is insincere and under the pretext of fearing for your personal safety.*] The other powers, like the Empire, Holland and England, for whom the abasement of France could be to some advantage, will seek different excuses to impede the effect of the good intentions of the others and do not want to declare themselves at all. For them, it is useful that disorder and anarchy continue and the kingdom is thereby weakened, without them seeming to contribute to it and without it having cost them a thing.

The King of Spain is very well disposed; all his interests combine to [make him] come to the aid of the King, and he has given positive assurances of them. The Emperor alone wishes to doubt them, even though the King of Spain wrote to him that he 'will nevertheless refer himself in everything to his decision and wait to learn of the intentions and measures his ministers will indicate in order to give the necessary orders'. Those are the terms of his letter. In his letter to the King of Sweden he proposes to await the outcome of the hopes he had that the King of France would be set free to accept or refuse the

Constitution, and he adds: 'If that took place, it would then be appropriate to support him so that his subjects submit to the modifications which their king would make to it, and Your Majesty can count on my assistance, particularly of a pecuniary nature, as far as my means will allow.' The rest of his letter contains specious arguments, which I recognized for those of his Ambassador influenced by M. de Montmorin. Given that he is in disgrace, would it not seem to prove that the King of Spain has recognized their falsity? In a conversation between the minister of Sweden with M. de Florida Blanca, this minister complained that His Catholic Majesty, having at different times made overtures to His Imperial Majesty on the measures that needed to be taken to support the King of France, has never been able to get a reply; that the Emperor had first sought to elude when he could not avoid and had never given anything but evasive answers while posing hypothetical questions; that he had promised to send somebody to Madrid for this purpose, but they had never come. Despite the declarations proposed by the Emperor, the minister cast doubts on his true intentions, in which, he added, no one could have any faith. He finished by promising that if the King of Sweden 'could at the present time establish an agreement with the other powers, Spain would contribute to it financially to the tune of 8 to 10 million *livres*'. Add to that the current conduct of the King of Spain and the assurance I have been told he gave to Vienna, that he will never recognize the King's acceptance, and you will see that his good intentions cannot be doubted. They only need to be directed and coordinated to a common end and in concert with you. The kings of Sardinia and Naples will follow Spain's momentum.

I have positive assurance of the King of Poland's favourable way of thinking, but, whatever his goodwill, his political position does not allow him to take active steps in your favour; but his personal feeling must encourage him rather to cede to the influence of friendly courts and give them more means to determine or impress, should that be necessary, those who are more hesitant or who could be tempted to oppose you.

After everything that happened at the meeting at Pillnitz, after everything that M. de Bischoffswerder[128] told me in Vienna and never ceased to repeat to the Emperor in the most pressing manner – that his master was ready to act in your favour, that 50,000 men were ready to march at his first command and on condition that the Emperor did the same, that he would carry out in conjunction with him all measures he would indicate to him, and that the treaty he had just signed ought to reassure the Emperor as to his intentions; finally, after all he got M. Dumoutier to tell you, you should be able to count on him, at least enough not to fear that he might oppose you or wish to oppose what the other powers would like to do for you.

Sweden's Ambassador to Berlin tells me, in a letter of 27 August, that having had a conversation with M. de Schulembourg, who had succeeded M. de Hertzberg[129] in dealing with French affairs, this minister seemed to him better disposed than formerly and told him that it was necessary first to be assured of the Emperor's cooperation, that 'the first overture that he had just made was much too vague to be able to confirm his real intentions'; that in order to obtain clarification the King of Prussia had just made him aware that although he had decided to take part for the proposed common goal, which seemed to him to be of interest to all sovereigns, he nevertheless believed that the declaration of [*Mantua*] Padua, proposed by the Emperor, could render the King of France's situation even more critical if it were not backed up by imposing forces and that first it was necessary to agree on the serious measures to take in the event of a refusal by the Assembly; that then it would be easy to reach agreement on the declaration. This minister seemed very surprised that the Emperor, who could not be ignorant of the King of Sweden's good dispositions, had not addressed his circular with the draft common declaration to him as he had to the others. The King of Prussia sent word to the King of Sweden 'that he wanted first to be certain that he was not acting contrary to the wishes of the King of France and that this prince should let him know in secret but in an authentic manner.'

The Duke of York[130] told someone, when he passed through here, that he was convinced that the Emperor did not want to do anything and that he could not act without him; that the King of Prussia was in good faith. But despite all that it does not appear to me to be clearly demonstrated that one can firmly rely on the court of Berlin. Intrigues govern business there, it has always been dependent on England, and the treaty they have just signed with the Emperor and the distrust that prevails between the two courts in spite of it are such contradictory factors, which must cast so great an uncertainty over the conduct of this cabinet, that it is impossible to form a precise idea of where it stands. What seems most probable to me from all this information, and especially from the King of Prussia's conversation with M. Dumoutier in the presence of M. de Schulembourg, is that this minister is aware of the advantage of an alliance with France, that he desires it and that this is the price he will put on any help he may be in a position to give you; that a fear of England and uncertainty about the Emperor's true intentions are holding him back but that he would not hesitate to declare himself for you if he were pushed by other great powers, such as Russia and Spain, and if he were sure he would be acting in concert with them and with you.

The Empress's dispositions are not equivocal at all; they are only too pronounced and could be dangerous if they were influenced by others rather than by you and if you do not make them form part of a plan of operations formed in concert with her. The two million she has given to the princes, the letter of authorization she has given to the Comte de Romanzoff[131] to deal with them – for it is not a letter of credit but simply a letter from the cabinet authorizing him to talk to the princes so that they have faith in what he says on her behalf – all proves her desire to assist you. But not being informed in any way of your projects, she is taking the only path that appears to her most likely to do so and the only one which remains to her. The slowness of the Emperor has inspired her with mistrust about his wish to serve you. Her Ambassador explained it at Vienna, and she will never model her conduct on his. She will join in a common cause with the King of Sweden, and you see the proof of it by the way in which she treated the French chargé d'affaires and received the notification of the King's approval of the Constitution. Re-establishment of the French monarchy is the principal aim of the treaty she has just signed with the King of Sweden. She writes to him that she 'persists in the idea of contributing everything in her power to overturn the new Constitution in France, despite the King's acceptance, which must be regarded as null and void and forced'. In a first letter, in reply to the one in which the Emperor had sent her the declaration he made at Mantua, she agreed to do the same and again proposed the recall of ambassadors, their formation in a congress and the cessation of all communication and all relations with France. She even wrote a very pressing letter to the Emperor in which she said: 'The princes must be effectively helped and operations must begin without delay.' She brings extreme warmth to her wish to rescue you. It only needs to be moderated, and to indicate to her the ways and means to serve you. Therefore you should write to her, asking for her help and letting her know your plans so you can work with her.

You have long known the King of Sweden's friendly dispositions and his ardour to serve you, but his lively and restless spirit needs to be pacified. He is occupied solely with the means of helping you and will spare no means to achieve this end. You know the sacrifices he has made for this purpose in his treaty with the Empress, and all his actions tend towards this object. Here are some fragments of his letters:

'There are rumours of some very unjust sentiments of the Court with regard to the princes which are very harmful to the common good and which I cannot believe. Give me weapons to defend the Court, especially to the Empress, for I fear they will have the most pernicious effect on her. If everyone were to listen to me, I would not wait until the spring to take action. It seems to me that it will simply give the rebels time to strengthen their position.'

He finished, in speaking of the King:

'And even were he to abandon the rights of his son, of his family and of his peers, I will not abandon theirs, and I will employ the same ardour in serving his brothers that I am ready to deploy for his service, and the Empress of Russia shares this sentiment.'

The King of Sweden cannot conceive the reasons that prevent you from trusting to the goodwill of the princes. To understand its necessity requires a more intimate and detailed knowledge of your position than he can have. We are applying ourselves to giving it to him, in order to convince him of the need for your conduct, but only a friendly and confidential communication from you on your situation and projects will have the desired effect. It will bring him round to calmer ideas and prevent him from acting with the princes, and engage him to cooperate with you, and in that case his zeal for you and that of the Empress of Russia could be very helpful to you. You could even make use of his influence with the princes without them suspecting it, and use him to direct their conduct and make their actions conform to a common goal concerted with the other powers. Denmark can have no other desire than the one which will be dictated to it by Sweden and Russia.

England views with pleasure the woes that ravage France. The disorder and anarchy that reign there ensure even further the abasement of that power. It is to her advantage that they continue, and whatever the personal sentiments of the King of England may be, and the general horror the English have of the means employed, he will never do anything to stop them. But at the same time there is every reason to think that the English government will never contribute to their fomentation, nor will it impede the goodwill of the powers who would like to help the King. On the contrary, there is every appearance that it is only waiting for the moment when all the other powers are engaged to declare itself also in favour of the King, but without that prerequisite it will remain in a passive state. That at least is the opinion of a man who, by his wit, knowledge and relations with his native county, is better able than anyone else to know its true intentions: it is Mr Craufurd, and during the journey to England he was so kind as to undertake through attachment to you and for your service, he assured himself of these dispositions. The King of England has never wavered in giving the Emperor the most positive assurances of wishing to maintain a perfect and exact neutrality, and the King of Prussia's conduct ought to weigh in favour of the sincerity of these assurances. One could object that the treaty concluded with the Emperor, probably without the knowledge of England, is proof that the influence of the cabinet of London on that of Berlin no longer exists or is weakened; but in that supposition an England without allies would no longer be so formidable and could not, alone with Holland, resist the impetus of the other powers. The King of England replied to the letter from the King of Sweden which M. Craufurd kindly took to him, that

> 'My conduct in relation to the troubles which have so agitated the kingdom of France has been guided by the principles of an exact and perfect neutrality . . . My intention is to take no part in the measures which the other European powers may be disposed to adopt in this matter, neither by seconding them nor by opposing them. The wishes I form in this regard are all

for the happiness of Their Most Christian Majesties and their subjects, etc . . . I would be pleased to see any event which will contribute to such an interesting outcome.'

After a meeting with Lord Grenville, the Foreign Secretary, the Swedish Ambassador wrote to the King: 'After this conversation on French affairs it's clear to see that England has no intention of getting involved.' The Ambassador at Berlin writes that it is believed there that the English government dared not declare in favour of the King for fear of the nation's disapprobation. Everything must therefore lead one to believe that England will remain perfectly neutral. Holland is absolutely dependent on her; however, she must be interested in seeing the stifling of the seeds of democracy which could soon also overcome her and destroy all the Stadtholder's work.[132]

The Emperor is deceiving you. He will do nothing for you, and under the specious pretext of your personal safety and by fulfilling your intentions by not acting with the princes he will abandon you to your fate and allow the total ruin of the kingdom to be completed. He will abandon you to the hatred of the nobility, which he is reducing to despair and which he is pushing by that means to some desperate act, equally dreadful for you should it succeed, by making you absolutely dependent on them, as if it fails, by depriving you of all means of acting and perhaps exposing you even more, You can see the effect already in the decree that has just been issued against the émigrés and by the Vicomte d'Agoult's letter which the Baron de Breteuil is sending you. The Emperor is personally well disposed, but he has neither the strength, the means nor the character needed to take a stand and support it against the advice of his government. He is weak and good and does not know how to withstand his cabinet, which is slow, weak, indecisive and fearful, afraid to commit itself where the humbling of France enters into their calculations, in order to gain themselves a greater supremacy in Europe. Hence the contradiction you have seen so often between the Emperor's letters and his actions. His first thought for you has always been good, but it has always been dampened by his ministers and has never had any effect, and remember you could never obtain, although he had written to you, the assembly of 12,000 men to protect your escape.

I myself have heard M. de Mercy say that if he had received positive orders from the Emperor to assemble an army corps, he would have taken it upon himself to delay executing them, to make representations about the dangers of such an assembly and to await new orders. Remember everything that happened, examine the Emperor's conduct, and you will be convinced yourself of the truth of what I suggest. You asked him in July to convene a congress that could impress the rebels and furnish you with the means to talk or to act. [*He avoided doing it.*] It was a good opportunity and the pretext for recalling the ambassadors. He only did the measure by half, in refusing to receive the French Ambassador at his court, and he avoided proposing the congress with the excuse that he was waiting for replies to the circular he had written to the other powers to propose a common declaration; and he did not make that same communication to the King of Sweden, whose zeal he was aware of and who had already made offers to serve you when he was at Milan, sending him for this purpose his Ambassador at Genoa; and when he received replies from all the courts, who all offered to be guided by him and to take steps together, as you saw by the King of Spain's letter, he interpreted their observations, with as much art as deceit, as proof of their ill will and that they could not be relied on.

I arrived in Vienna on 2 August with the most positive offers from the King of Sweden to provide 16,000 men and ships, with orders to make the liveliest representations on the necessity to rescue you, and to demand that these troops could disembark in Ostend. I had carte blanche from the King to make whatever agreements he would deem appropriate and to save time. I experienced nothing but continual delays. I was told it was necessary to wait for the King of Spain's reply, then the meeting with the King of Prussia, then the replies from Russia; and when all these were favourable I was told it was impossible to take a decision without knowing what the King would do about accepting the constitution. I represented in vain to Prince Kaunitz and the Emperor the difficulty the King must be in by his total ignorance of the dispositions of the European powers towards him and of the Emperor's intentions and that it would be kinder and more generous to inform him of them, thus permitting him to regulate his conduct by the degree of hope he might have of being rescued.

Prince Kaunitz replied that one did not know the King's position sufficiently well to hazard any advice. The Emperor shared my opinion, and, after having told me that the only way to be able to involve himself in the King's affairs would be if he approved the constitution purely and simply without restrictions, he now presents that same acceptance as a reason not to involve himself in French affairs and seeks to inspire the other courts with the same sentiments to dampen their enthusiasm. I could not obtain a definite response to the King of Sweden's offers until 26 September, and that response was negative, on the pretext that it was necessary to wait for replies from various courts on the proposal which had been made to them of a general understanding on measures relative to French affairs.

The conclusions of the Diet of Ratisbon are favourable.[133] The German princes will rely on everything the Emperor indicates in support of their rights. They beg him to take all suitable measures which his wisdom suggests to maintain order and peace in the empire and prevent the French doctrine from spreading. The Emperor has never replied to the positive offers the King of Prussia made him [*nor to the request he made several times to designate the number of troops*]. He has always contented himself with casting doubts on their sincerity, and, despite all that I could say, he has never wanted to concert any plan with him nor make any proposal, for fear that his agreement to it would deny him the means to doubt his good faith. I do not know if a reply was sent to the Empress of Russia's proposals, but I doubt it. They were too pronounced, like Sweden's, for the Emperor not to have tried, by his delays, to make it impossible for these two powers to act.

You have just asked of the Emperor the [*reasonable*] formation of a congress, indicating the pretext to him. M. de Mercy's first instinct was to oppose it, and it was only by proving to him the necessity of a resounding action that could stop the enterprises of the princes and the émigrés, by proving to them that the Emperor wanted to come to your aid, that he decided to present it from this point of view, nevertheless reserving the possibility not to convene it until later or not at all, according to circumstances. Since then, M. de Mercy's language has changed. He told someone that the Emperor would not consent to this congress, for fear of being committed by such a measure, and that once it was assembled it would go no further than he wanted. [*But after the very clear way in which Sweden and Russia have declared themselves, M. de Mercy's language has changed once again.*] For the past week this Ambassador has given some hope that the Emperor will decide to consent to your request. Doubtless Spain's refusal and the frank manner in which Sweden and Russia have spoken will have influenced the Emperor's resolutions. However, I believe it difficult to count on their activity, and I have no doubt that on this occasion he will follow the same system, which is to temporize, to await everything from events, thus avoiding having to act and commit himself, while keeping up the appearance of the greatest interest so he can make it pay according to circumstances.

In all probability, the cabinet of Vienna's policy is to take advantage of France's position, whatever it may be, without having spent anything to fix it. Whatever happens, even events which are most favourable to you, he considers this power as nil in the European political system for at least a half century; but he wants to keep himself in a position to profit from the feigned interest he will show you, should, by some chance that cannot be foreseen or hoped for, and which seems even improbable, matters be set to rights in France. In that case the Emperor would seek an alliance with you and stress everything he pretends to have done for you. In the opposite scenario, his views would turn in a different direction and he would tie himself to England. Everything leads me to believe that is his plan. Prince Kaunitz does not like France at all. The Emperor is personally pro-English, and the snippets of a conversation which the Comte de Mercy had during his voyage to London with someone who relayed it to me confirm me in this opinion. He told him that it was much more natural for the Emperor to be an ally of England than of France; that such an alliance would be more advantageous to both countries; and that the state of nullity in which France would be for a long time, being only able to manage her internal affairs, rendered this alliance even more beneficial. If, as I believe, this is the cabinet of Vienna's plan, continuation of unrest and anarchy must enter into its views, and its entire conduct proves it to me. In this way the kingdom will wreck itself without them taking the blame for having contributed to it; it guarantees the humbling of France, and in rendering her thus useless to these new allies it increases his [the Emperor's] supremacy all the more. That, in my opinion, is the Emperor's cabinet's policy, and you may easily judge by it the help you can expect from him.

The Emperor's indiscretion in announcing to all the world that he was receiving letters from you and the lack of effort he gave to demonstrating his goodwill has made people conclude that you wrote to him only to prevent him taking action. Your enemies have used this to spread the idea that you were against every enterprise, that the desire to dominate and the fear of being so yourself made you prefer to follow the Constitution and make use of the rebels rather than owe to the princes and the émigrés the obligation of the re-establishment of your authority, and a thousand other tales of this kind, each one more absurd than the last. These ideas have spread among the nobility and are given credence; very sensible people who were attached to you are even tempted to adopt them. The Baron de Breteuil is looked on here as your agent to this effect, and when he arrived the great majority of the French here wouldn't go to see him. Like you I feel how little one should take notice of such an injustice, to which you, unfortunately, are more accustomed than any other, but in your current position, with the uncertainty as to what events may give rise to, there should be an effort to quash these rumours, so that the outcome of what you will have done for them will one day prove their inaccuracy to them, as well as to the whole of Europe. To do that it is necessary [*at the least*] to adopt a plan and to follow it up with all possible activity, and here is the one I propose to you.

If it is true, as I believe it is, that you will not be able to count on the Emperor, you must absolutely place your hopes elsewhere, and it can only be to the North and to Spain, who will make Prussia decide and draw in the Emperor. Of all the European powers, these are the ones on whose disinterestedness you may count the most. Their geographical position does not allow for any views of a conquest, and their political stance binds them to the continuation of the French monarchy. You should request of them:

1. Not the recall of their ambassadors but their departure on leave;
2. The prompt assembly of a congress, on the pretexts you have already outlined to the Emperor;
3. The dispatch of troops to support this congress and make its deliberations respectable, or, if the season does not permit such a gathering, at least steps are taken that prove the intention to march as soon as it is possible.

These actions by the European powers, which you would not seem to have provoked and cannot expose you at all, would combine the advantages of not compromising you, of inspiring a great terror whose effect would be to throw oneself on to the King's mercy, and the King, as the sole person with whom the congress would negotiate, would naturally find himself the mediator between his people and the powers and through them would obtain the means to take action, by telling them the steps to follow according to circumstances. At that time the princes and émigrés could be useful, their conduct and actions being regulated by the congress.

But as it would be impossible to achieve any results without some leader [*and one cannot count sufficiently on the effects of imperial goodwill*] and as the King cannot be this leader, not being able to come out into the open, you should engage the King of Spain to take on the role as head of the house of Bourbon. He has more right to it than any other, and as he has just refused to recognize the King's acceptance he shows a great willingness. Russia and Sweden would easily adopt this idea, which has already been presented to them, and by signalling all the necessary steps to take to the cabinet of Madrid in concert with these two courts you would no longer have anything to fear from Spanish indecision and hesitation. The coalition of these three courts would convince the King of Prussia to declare himself, and the Emperor would finally be forced to choose a side.

I do not believe, however, that you should break with the Emperor or upset him. You must manage him and keep in step with him, and, despite the just cause you have to mistrust the sincerity of his interest for you, he must not be allowed to see it, and you must maintain an air of confidence in him. If you adopt this new plan, it would be necessary for you to inform the well-intentioned courts whose help you decide to ask for – Spain, Russia and Sweden. Even a letter to the King of Prussia could perhaps be useful after the message he sent to the King of Sweden.

After having thanked the King of Spain for everything he is doing for you, for the way in which he received your protestation of 1789 and for the resolve he is showing at the moment, you should paint a brief picture for him of your position and of how impossible it is for you to remain in it; communicate to him the plan you have adopted; and, because of the friendship and interest which he had already proved to you and that which you have the right to hope for from your blood ties to him, ask him to assume responsibility for your interests with the foreign powers and to support the demands you will make of them; that no one has more right than he to head the league which must re-establish your authority and repair the insults and outrages made over the last two years to the house of Bourbon and that you would like to owe this entire obligation to him. Inform him that you have asked the Emperor to convene a congress; ask him to propose an armed congress and indicate the pretext for it. Tell him you are making the same communication to Russia and Sweden, whose views are known to you. Beg him to agree with these two powers on the steps to be taken and tell him that you wish to use the influence of these two courts on the princes to direct their conduct. Beg him to encourage the zeal of Prussia, which has given you positive proofs of interest through M. Dumoutier; and if you decide to write to him [the King of Prussia] let him [the King of Spain] know. You should finish by making him realize how essential it is not to waste time and to adopt prompt measures. You will ask him to exert his influence with Portugal, Sardinia and Naples, to engage them to take similar steps or charge the Baron de Breteuil to speak about it to the Neapolitan Ambassador, who is here; and, after a few compliments, add that you have no doubt that he will consent to give you proofs of his friendship, on which you have always counted. It would be good to add that the Baron de Breteuil remains charged with all your correspondence.[134] It would be useful for the King to write a line to the King of Spain at the same time. He would refer to what you would have already written. These two letters could be sent by the bishop, unsealed in a book, and the baron would send them on in code through M. de La Vauguyon; or you could send them sealed by Spain's chargé d'affaires – you could ask him to send a courier to take them. This route is preferable as it is quicker. In that case you should send a copy to the baron.

If the letter to the Empress of Russia which I had the honour to suggest to you is already written, it would simply be a question of saying that you hope she has received your letter, and that by the proofs of interest so worthy of her great soul she has already shown you, you cannot doubt that she will consent to give you fresh proofs and therefore you have no hesitation in entrusting her with your plans. You will tell her briefly the reasons why the King decided to accept [the constitution], which were his total ignorance of foreign powers' dispositions towards him and the extent of the assistance he could expect from them; that seeing no action on their part you felt that there was no other option than to bring people round through the vices of the constitution itself; that, having made the decision to accept it, it was necessary to submit to all the measures which would be demanded of you in order to prove your good faith and to gain the confidence of the public, re-establish a little peace and thus acquire the means to take action more safely, without exposing the faithful people who remain with you and within the kingdom, because you take no notice of your personal dangers; that these are the reasons that [*forced*] led you to take **humiliating** steps, and which must appear, in the eyes of European powers less well informed of the details of your position, as akin to acts of weakness; that it is important to you to destroy the impression she may have of them; that you do not doubt Monsieur's and M. le Comte d'Artois's attachment for you, but that you do not have the same reason to be sure of that of those who surround them, who are more occupied with their personal interests than with yours; but despite this great uncertainty you would not hesitate to employ them, to reach an understanding with them and to communicate your projects to them if the indiscretion which reigns among those they have chosen to counsel them [*and habit*] did not forbid you from confiding anything to them; that they have accustomed the nobility gathered at Coblentz to be informed of everything, that nothing is secret there, and that any plan you communicated to them would soon become public and immediately known at Paris, through the spies who abound at Coblentz [*among this selfsame nobility*]; but that you are asking her to exert the influence which the generosity of her conduct towards the princes has given her over them, in conjunction with the King of Sweden, to relay your desires to them without them being aware of anything and to direct their conduct and their actions towards a common goal.

You will tell her of the demands you have made of the Emperor. You will inform her of your plan and its advantages for you. You will make the same requests to her as to the King of Spain, adding that of her Ambassador's departure on leave, as a step which will make a big impression. You will propose the King of Spain, as head of the house of Bourbon, as the spokesman for the proposals to be made and ask her to guide his actions, to push him and to work with him, as well as with the Emperor and the King of Prussia, to whom you have written about it without entering into the same details. You will tell her that you are informing the King of Sweden of your projects, as you know his dispositions to be similar to hers. You will ask her to persuade Denmark to decide in your favour, and you will indicate the Baron de Breteuil as the person in whom you place your confidence and who will be charged with your correspondence.

To avoid repeating the same things to the King of Sweden, you could send him a copy of your letter to the Empress, adding proofs of your sensibility for that which he has always shown you and for the marks of friendship he never ceases to give you, for the zeal and warmth which he employs in order to serve you, assuring him of all your gratitude when happier times permit you to give him proof of it. You will refer to your letter to the Empress for the different demands to be made of him and for the plan you will adopt; tell him that you hope he will adopt and second it; ask him to work in concert with the Empress in employing his influence to regulate the conduct of the princes and stop them from making some mad attempt which would ruin all your plans, but to make sure they do not see that this comes from you, for the same reasons already explained to the Empress.

The King of Sweden writes to the Baron de Breteuil, when talking of the necessity of informing the King of Prussia of your projects and demanding his cooperation: 'If the King of France fears he will compromise himself, I offer to make known, or to carry his words to the King of Prussia with the greatest possible secrecy &&.' Although this proposal by the King of Sweden is very flattering, it cannot be accepted. The active and restless temperament of this prince inspires distrust, and that distrust could harm your interests at the moment; but without giving a reason you must thank him for his offers and tell him that you would prefer to write to the King of Prussia yourself, as a more certain means of exciting his zeal and goodwill. You will ask him to keep the Empress imbued with the good sentiments she has already shown for you and for which you know you are obliged to him. You will ask him to persuade Denmark, and after having said a word for the Baron de Breteuil you will finish with those amiable things that you know how to say better than anyone. If you forward your letter to me, I will send it all in code. The bishop can send it to me glued inside a book.

Your letter to the King of Prussia would be brief. You will thank him for the message sent you by M. du Moutier. You will tell him that necessity forced you to approve the constitution but that you are determined to change your current position; that the sole means of achieving this is through an armed congress; that you have made the request to the Emperor and the other powers and that you hope, given the goodwill he has shown you, that he will work with them, that he will adopt this measure and that following the example of the other powers he will order his Ambassador at Paris to depart on leave.

You will be able to tell the Emperor that after the doubts he seems to have as to the true intentions of the different powers and on the sincerity of their goodwill, you have decided to write yourself to Spain, Prussia, Russia and Sweden in order to be persuaded of it and to be able to adapt your conduct according to the degree of interest they show you and on the actual help they will promise you; that you are asking them for the recall of their ministers and ambassadors on leave and the immediate convening of a congress, which would be then be supported by armed force to give their deliberations more weight. [*You should not speak in any of your letters of your reasons for mistrusting.*] You must order the baron to hint to Spain, Russia and Sweden the reasons which have put distance between you and the Emperor and make you wish to be obliged to the King of Spain for the re-establishment of your authority.

Every day your position becomes more critical. France is galloping towards ruination. The rebels are working constantly to make you lose the small amount of popularity you were beginning to gain, and the veto the King has just used is an excuse they will not fail to turn to account.[135] You have already seen the rumours constantly circulated about you abroad in order to alienate the nobility. They are also trying to demean you in all the courts, by representing all your actions as so many acts of weakness, and if you cannot extricate yourself promptly from your current position you will be abandoned by all parties and left entirely to the mercy of the rebels and the republicans, who will find no more obstacles to impede the execution of their criminal projects. Only the measures I have just indicated with all the European powers can save you. They will give you abroad the consideration you deserve, by proving to all these courts the falseness of the allegations against you, they will make it easier for you to act by yourselves and to bring round the nobility, led astray by a hundred absurd tales given credence by your current inaction.

Coblentz seems determined, and if you don't act they will. You have already seen the decree of the members of the *parlements* and their aim to assemble. The Vicomte d'Agoult's letter proves to you yet again that they have formed a plan, and, however mad it may be, they will be encouraged by the powers whose political interest lies in the re-establishment of the French monarchy. But, for the same reason, these powers will act for you and in a manner indicated by you as soon as they are convinced that you wish it and have informed them of your intentions.

I have nothing to add to the baron's letter except regarding his view of England. I believe he is entirely mistaken in his opinion and that this power is only awaiting definite measures from other courts and to see them engaged before declaring itself also in your favour.

{It seems that M. de Lafayette will become mayor. That is a great misfortune for you. In this way he will control civil power and military power, and you will be even more **his** prisoners.} In order to give you a better idea of [*this man's*] M. de Lafayette's way of thinking, and of everything you may expect of him, here's a copy of a letter he wrote to one of his acquaintances in London in reply to the letter she wrote to him after your arrest, to represent to him the full horror of his conduct if you were to be placed in the slightest danger (see below). I am obliged to Mr Craufurd for it. He procured it for me, believing that it might be useful to you. [*six lines deleted – three are illegible and the rest repeat Fersen's views on England's position*].

If you adopt this plan, and if the Baron de Breteuil is charged with all this correspondence, he will need secretaries. He will take on young Vérac, who he already made use of in Soleure, and M. de Vibray's son,[136] who is here; but M. de Vérac has no money for his lodgings. He will need to send young Bouillé to Berlin; he is already known there, and the pretext will be that he is going to see his brother who is in their army. Someone also needs to be sent to Russia who won't create a sensation [*and who won't cause umbrage to the princes*]. The baron thinks that Bombelles would do well there. He is amiable in society and his conduct at Venice is in the Empress's style. She has already granted [him] a pension of 12,000 [*livres*] on account of his brother's honourable conduct. It will be necessary to send couriers from time to time, and for all these activities money will be required, and the baron hardly has enough to live on. A credit of 50,000 [*livres*] needs to be forwarded to him at Brussels, which he will account for. At Soleure he spent the sum of 22,000 [*livres*] on your behalf, for which he also needs to be reimbursed, but as 25 per cent is lost on the exchange you must make allowances for the loss.

The Emperor's reply has finally arrived and his rejection of a congress is fresh evidence of how little you can count on his help and how essential it is that you address yourself to the other courts. The baron had a very lively conversation on the subject with M. de Mercy

Axel von Fersen in 1793,
portrait by Pierre Dreuillon

Left: Marie-Antoinette in a riding habit in 1784, miniature by Vincenza Benzi

Right: A young Axel von Fersen in Swedish national dress; Marie-Antoinette asked him to wear it to Versailles in November 1778.

Below: The Palace of Versailles from the Route de Saint-Cyr. In the centre, the Cent Suisses, with the Queen's apartments in the background; to the right, the former Rue de la Surintendance (now Rue de l'Indépendance americaine) where Fersen had lodgings in the Hôtel de Luynes in 1785–6.

Dattes	Noms des Personnes	Contenu des lettres
1787 avrill 20.	Joséphine	N° 24. [...] ce qu'elle doit me rendre pour l'habiter en haut que je pars le 29 ou 30. que je compte être le 15 a Maubeuge et le 20 ou 21 a Paris.
27.	Joséphine	N° 25 que je pars le 30.
Juin. 26.	Joséphine	N° 1.
26	John	Si j'ai les [...] noirs [...] l'anglois [...]
27	Joséphine	N° 2 par mon [...]
30.	Joséphine	N° 3. par le [...] de St Joseph de Valenciennes.
Juillet 2.	Joséphine	N° 4 par Gedda
4	Joséphine	N° 5. En: 6:
4	John	De faire faire une selle pour le cheval bay quelle [...]
6	John	De faire des [...] de [...] pour cette selle, et une couverture [...] blanche.
aout 3	Joséphine	N° 1.
3	Joséphine	le soir N° 2. En: 6.
7	Joséphine	par George [...]
14	Joséphine	N° 3. et E: 6:
parti 19	Joséphine	N° 4. et E: 6:
23	Joséphine	N° 5. et E: 6:
Oct. 6.	Joséphine	N° 1. En: 13: de Valenciennes
7.	Joséphine	N° 2. En: 13:
8.	Joséphine	par Mr de Valois, quelle fasse faire une [...] au Poele, que je partirai le 18. pour être le 19 a Paris elle [...] des elles quelle [...] une lettre chez [...] pour me dire ce que je dois faire.
1788 11.	Joséphine	N° 3. En: 13:
avrill 28.	John	[...] a l'al: le 1er Juin [...] les [...] quelle [...] En 2, 2 fois par semaine [...] quelle [...] payé jusqu'au 25 mars qu'il le paye depuis [...] a 40 [...] la reception de cette lettre.
14	Joséphine	N° 1. En: 13:
21	Joséphine	N° 2. En: 13:
25	Joséphine	N° 3.
29	Joséphine	N° 4. En: 13:
may 2.	Joséphine	N° 5. En: 13:
9	Joséphine	N° 6. En: 13:
13.	Joséphine	N° 7. En: 13:
16.	Joséphine	Sans N° En: 13:

A page from Fersen's letter register for 'Joséphine'; on 8 October 1787 he asks Marie-Antoinette to have a stove installed in his secret lodging above her private apartments.

Marie-Antoinette's son, Louis-Charles (Louis XVII, born 1785), and the Fersen family

I

Louis-Charles in
the Temple 1793

Axel von Fersen

Sophie Piper,
Fersen's sister

Louis-Charles, Dauphin

Charlotte Piper,
Fersen's niece

Sophie Piper,
Fersen's sister

Louis XVI,
Bourbon profile

Marie-Antoinette,
Habsburg profile

A bust of Louis-Charles

Axel von Fersen by
Adolf Ulrik Wertmüller

Axel Piper, Axel von Fersen's
great-nephew

Axel von Fersen in later life

Below: The flying fish emblem from Fersen's coat of arms, used by Marie-Antoinette as the basis for her seal with the motto *Tutto a te mi guida*

Above: This drawing of Marie-Antoinette in a riding habit, requested by Fersen in his letter to her of 8 October 1784, is displayed at Löfstad in Sweden. It can be seen that she had to fold it sixteen times to fit it into an envelope.

LE SANS TORT

Left: Caricature of Lafayette as 'Sans Tort' ('Blameless'), a name by which Marie-Antoinette refers to him in her letter to Fersen of 7 December 1791

Marie-Antoinette in a riding habit at the Petit Trianon, by Antoine Vestier, 1778

Louis XVI, portrait by Antoine Callet, 1778

Baron Evert Taube, Gustav III's Court Chamberlain, was a great friend of Axel von Fersen and the lover of Sophie Piper.

Sophie, Countess Piper, Axel von Fersen's sister and confidante

Marie-Antoinette in 1791, sanguine drawing
by Alexander Kucharski

in which he expressed all his sensibility on the Emperor's lack of interest in your situation and said that he foresaw that the Empress of Russia would have the glory of having achieved what the Emperor did not desire to attempt; that it would be to her and the King of Sweden that the King would owe obligations which it would have been sweeter to owe to the Emperor; and that in this case the Emperor should at least dispense him from showing any gratitude and not be surprised by that which he would show to those who would have rendered him such a great service. M. de Mercy defended himself very badly. He alleged that a congress would serve no purpose, that it would not be impressive and that for want of matters to discuss it would remain inactive, and that, besides, the other powers didn't want it, which is absolutely untrue, since you saw that Russia proposed it in September, Spain desires it, Prussia would consent to it if the Emperor proposed it and the King of Sweden was opposed to it only because he considered it too slow a measure; but as soon as he is assured that you wish it and that it is the only way to procure you means to take action he will consent to it, and I assured the Emperor of this in Vienna, even offering to give him the signed consent in writing.

This reason put forward by the Emperor is one more reason for you to follow the plan I am proposing to you (that is if you consider it a good one) and to write to the other courts. And that must not change your letter to the Emperor, except to show him your feelings about his refusal and to tell him that you regard this congress as the only step that will procure you the means to act, and that it is in this light that you consider it indispensable for you. M. de Mercy has not yet communicated the Emperor's reply to me. [*M. de Mercy has not yet spoken to me of it. If I can procure the Emperor's reply I will send it to you by another occasion with my ideas for the reply to be made to it.*]

I've received the following from Berlin:

'The Empress of Russia has written to the King of Prussia to invite him in a most urgent manner to take part with her in vigorous measures to render unto the King of France his liberty and the prerogatives of his throne. His Prussian Majesty replied that he was ready and that he persisted in the sentiments he declared at Pillnitz provided that all the other powers, but, above all, the Emperor, desired to cooperate to the same end. A message has also been sent to the French princes that one will be guided here strictly by what is done by the court of Vienna, and that if it remains inactive the King of Prussia will do nothing on his own. You see, Monsieur le Comte, that everything depends on the final resolutions adopted by the Emperor. A letter supposedly written by the Queen of France to her brother has been seen here, in which this princess begs him to desist from any enterprise in her favour; one is not certain as to the extent of the Queen's liberty in writing this letter. Prince Hohenlohe's corps is still on a war footing. It comprises ten infantry battalions and some cavalry regiments.'

By this fragment of a dispatch you can see Prussia's dispositions and judge those of the Emperor, and you will feel an even greater necessity to write to the King of Prussia.

Here's a dispatch from M. de L Vauguyon to the baron from 10 October. He writes that M. de Florida Blanca, after having said that the King of Spain would join the Emperor's proposed declaration, added that he foresaw that the King would end up by accepting the constitution and would do it in such haste that it would render the declarations agreed between the different courts too late. He proposed an addition, in the event that the King sanctioned or approved the constitution, that the powers should declare they would not recognize it before this sanction had been renewed by the King in a place where he was perfectly free; and at the same time he sent a plan of operations (it is the one which was communicated to you in the Spanish dispatches of the 13th and 20th). These proposals were sent to the Emperor by special courier at the end of August, and the reply must come at any moment. He writes that M. de Florida Blanca declared to the French chargé d'affaires, in the name of the King his master, that His Catholic Majesty did not believe that the letter addressed to him was written by the King and that as long as he was of that opinion he would not reply to it; that this response was communicated to the ambassadors of the other courts (and it is the Swedish Ambassador who sends it to me). M. de La Vauguyon finishes: 'In addition, as this minister (M. de Florida Blanca) only desires at heart the restoration of France and the re-establishment of the personal power of the King and Queen, he will adopt all measures that could end our woes and will hasten to follow with vigour active plans and to lend himself to conciliatory views, so long as those views and those plans effectively lead to the single objective that guides and fixes his zeal.'

All these dispatches are new proofs of Spain's goodwill towards you and make your proposal to them even more necessary. You must add to your letter your thanks for the interest he's [the King of Spain] showing you and for the way he's occupied with your interests. Tell him that the liberty he desires won't perhaps be possible until the congress you are asking for, and that this congress, by inspiring a great terror, should give you the necessary freedom to act; and it is in this light that you view it as absolutely essential; that the plan he has put to you seems to be good once everything is in place for its execution; that he must besides wait on events which the convening of the congress and its assembly could produce; that this plan presupposes an accord between the powers with armies within reach of the frontiers; that the negotiations which have continued for the past five months have produced nothing and that this essential accord is far from being established; that the powers who have not yet fixed their interest for you and those whose goodwill seems doubtful or at least lukewarm, will always find pretexts to hold back the goodwill of the others by persisting, despite the most positive proofs, in doubting the sincerity of their good intentions; that the congress still appears to you to be the only way to force them to declare themselves and to speed up negotiations; that the plenipotentiaries of the different courts, arriving there armed with sufficient instructions, will observe each other and will be soon in the position of being able to understand the dispositions of their respective courts; that couriers sent from Aix-la-Chapelle or Cologne, which is at the centre of Europe, will be able to bring replies back there much faster than if they have to cross the whole of Europe; that the ministers of the courts whose interest for you has been pronounced in a decided manner will find it easier to agree among themselves once they are together in the same place than if everything had to go to Vienna and it meant awaiting replies on the slightest matters; that the proximity of this congress would make it easier for you to work with it and to adapt your conduct at home to the steps it takes; that all these considerations make you continue to demand the assembly of an armed congress, and that you believe it cannot happen soon enough.

I see no need to send anyone to the princes especially if you adopt the idea of using Sweden and Russia to guide their conduct. Their extreme indiscretion does not allow anything to be confided to them without exposing you, and if it is only to prevent them from acting, you know how little effect preceding envoys have had. I believe, moreover, that one should not multiply one's confidants, and entrusting a mission to the Maréchal de Castries seems to me to be pointless at the moment. One could always return to the idea later if necessary. {If, however, you feel it would be useful to send someone to Coblentz and the Baron de Vioménil would like to go, you must say nothing to them but your express wish: that you don't want them to attempt anything at the moment, and} in giving them details of your position, prove to them the necessity for your current course of action. But I would still fear that the arrival there of someone sent on your behalf would cause a great stir. People would be curious as to his mission. If it were to be found out, as there is no doubt it would be, the certainty that you wish to do nothing will throw them into despair and could lead them to do something rash. If they cannot discover the object of his mission, they will conclude that there is a plan agreed with you. This news will spread and could have dangerous consequences for you. I think it would be better to write to them; it would cause less of a sensation and they would find it easier to keep it secret. You will simply tell them that you believe they should do nothing and that they should wait to know the courts' decisions regarding the congress [*and that whatever happens, it is impossible to act before the spring*].

I think the course of action you are taking is very wise; you simply must, when you are forced into taking some significant step, like the proclamation against the émigrés,[137] order the baron to warn the courts on your behalf, to repeat that it is the result of the constraint you are under, but that you persist as ever in the same ideas. I do not consider Spain's plan to be that bad, but it is not yet the right time for it. Besides, it may vary according to circumstances, and, even were it to be carried out, an accord between the powers must first be established, and, given the Emperor's bad faith and delays, this accord can only be established by a congress. Your personal safety must also be guaranteed, without which this plan cannot happen.

Your view of the King of Sweden's action is correct; however, as he is acting with Russia, and Spain wishes to act, such pronounced steps that cannot be retracted could commit the other powers and be very useful to you. It is true that the King of Sweden is sending Baron Oxenstierna as a minister to the princes, but, as he was formerly at Ratisbon and has just been nominated to the mission in Portugal, his role with the princes should be regarded more as a temporary commission such as the one M. de Romanzoff has from the Empress of Russia. I will pass on to the King what you sent me for him, and I will alert him to the King's letter.

If matters were still in the same state that they were in August, if one were not convinced of the impossibility of counting on the Emperor and if one could hope to obtain by means other than a congress the agreement among the powers that is essential; if it were not absolutely necessary that those who have the best intentions draw in, by decisive actions, those who are doubtful or of bad faith, I would agree with you in seeing no reason to withdraw the ministers and ambassadors. But in the current state of affairs, this manifestation of their sentiments, which doesn't commit them – since these ministers and ambassadors are only going on leave – will be another confirmation of their intention of assisting you. It proves how much they disapprove of everything that is being done and could lead others to make similar gestures and furnish those who need it with a pretext to do the same. For I repeat that England, whatever goodwill she may have, will not declare herself until the other powers are engaged. The English government needs an excuse, and this pretext will be the need to act with the other powers. The ambassadors of the Emperor, Sardinia, Spain, Naples and the Papal nuncio are absent and will not return. By making those from Sweden, Russia and Prussia leave, this will be almost a general movement. It can create a sensation and perhaps be useful to you, by proving the foreign powers' discontent to the people.

You should let Prussia know that the Baron de Breteuil has all your confidence and that he will send your letter and will be charged with your correspondence. You should send him one of the King's seals and one of yours as soon as possible by the stage. All the letters should be forwarded to the bishop in their envelopes with the addresses on them but unsealed, so that it is easier for him to send them to us. We will seal them here.

During a conversation the baron has just had with M. de Mercy, this Ambassador has hinted at the possibility that the Emperor might change his mind and consent to the congress. Doubtless this is due to the way the baron took it and the fear that you will turn to the other powers and be tempted to do without him. You must therefore insist on the congress in your letter to the Emperor.

Marquis de Lafayette to Georgiana, Duchess of Devonshire, unpublished letter attached to the memorandum of 26 November 1791

Quintin Craufurd provided a copy of this unpublished letter which Fersen sent to Marie-Antoinette with his memorandum. The original is at Chatsworth House in England, home of the dukes of Devonshire, but Marie-Antoinette kept a copy in the hand of her secretary François Goguelat (without the opening and closing courtesies, which would have been suppressed in the copy sent to her).[138] This copy is now in the Swedish archives with several other important papers the Queen entrusted to Fersen for safe-keeping. Clearly she attached great importance to this letter by Lafayette, and had she ever regained her freedom doubtless would have settled several scores with the man who vowed he had a republican heart, who had failed to prevent attempts on her life, who had tried to compromise her to obtain her divorce from the King and who had imprisoned her in the most humiliating circumstances. He would make a fresh attempt to get rid of her in March 1792, for Marie-Antoinette was the only member of the Royal Family who ever dared stand up to him. Fersen clearly hoped this letter would persuade her that Barnave, whom she appeared to like, and Lafayette, whom she loathed, were in fact working together and deceiving her. He hoped to discredit Barnave, whose influence over her clearly exasperated him.

This letter is Lafayette's response to the letter Georgiana wrote him after the Royal Family's arrest at Varennes in June 1791, expressing her anxiety for the Queen's safety. Lady Elizabeth Foster mentioned both letters when she wrote to Fersen on 16 September (see above). His prose exhales arrogance. He believes himself to be the master of France; he holds the King prisoner, he lays down the law and he believes he knows better than his fellow citizens what will make them happy. But his arguments are specious. Stripped of his power and having no legal function since his arrest, Louis XVI could not freely consent to the Constitution. An acceptance made under duress could never be valid, but such legal niceties seem to elude 'the General'.

'The thing they call a Constitution which the Assemblée have framed is good for nothing,' wrote the American Gouverneur Morris, who was nonetheless the representative of a republic. He would rally to the royalist cause after seeing the immediate and deplorable effects of this constitution, so fervently supported by his old friend Lafayette.[139] But 'Sans Tort' would never listen to criticism or advice, however well meant. And while showering the Duchess of Devonshire with compliments, he issues thinly veiled threats against England should it be tempted to come to the rescue of the King and Queen of France, who, at the very moment he was writing his letter, were under twenty-four-hour close guard in their own palace, on his orders. The most absolute monarch of all could not have written with more courtly malice.

Paris, 18 July [1791]

I received your kind letter, my dear duchess. Like you, it is angelic, and, although you give me greater importance than I deserve, I relished the justice you attribute to my sentiments, and, above all, to those you expressed for me. You know, my dear duchess, how much I deserve them by my deep and constant affection, and when you promised an unknown portrait and a lock of your hair (which, by the way, you still have not given me), I swore an admiration and attachment to you which will last as long as I live. But let us leave this topic, about which I imagine you have nothing to learn, and turn to the one which has caused your worries.

It is true, my dear duchess, that the national disposition on matters and on persons would not have been reassuring if the French population, and, above all, a people regenerated and free, were not susceptible to those generous urges which immediately succeed a first and less lofty impression. The departure of the Royal Family, about which, between ourselves, I should have some personal complaints to make, brought about a reunion of old friends who should never have fallen out and who for some time burnt with desire to forgive each other their mutual wrongs. It hurts to make war, where there is mutual esteem and former liking, and each of us has felt stronger in no longer having to fight against his heart. You needed to be told of this resumption of the suspended intimacy between Duport, Alex Lameth, Barnarve, my other friends and myself in order to be able to judge our political operations.

A very great movement was declared against hereditary royalty; another against the person of Louis XVI, and a rabble of anarchists, instigators and traitors joined these two similar camps. I have often told you that my heart is republican, that it hates all heredity, but I believe that the circumstances, character and number of my compatriots, their geographical situation and, above all, the intrigues and ambition of the leaders of a popular government, which one such as ours could not fail to produce, required a hereditary presidency in name as the executive power. The flight of one man could not change my opinion. I have therefore defended the constitutional monarchy as it has been decreed.

As for the present King, my friends and I, considering the age of his son, the drawbacks of an abdication, the aristocratic principles of constitutional regents, the justly deserved debasement of M. d'Orléans, did not hesitate to keep a monarch who is weak, in truth, and who has not been sincere with us but who suits us better than anyone else in the family and who we will put in a position, once the constitution is finished, to accept it or freely reject it. The Queen followed her husband, and it is not for us to understand hearts. We know only that she is unhappy, we desire that she be so no longer, and you will observe, my dear duchess, that in a very violent debate of three days at the National Assembly her name was not even mentioned.

I wish you to be aware of the Assembly's decrees since 21 June; except the one on the emigrants, I would wish you were equally satisfied of the state in which the Royal Family currently finds itself, but consider that until the constitutional act is finalized the King cannot exercise any function, consider that he promised that no one in the Royal Family would leave, and consider, above all, that we were on the point of presenting the constitution to him.

You should see, my dear duchess, that at present we are taking every measure to ensure liberty through maintaining public order. Our emigrants should help us by coming back into our outstretched arms, which we gladly open to them. They will have everything from us, except compromise on constitutional principles, and if perchance foreign powers should interfere in our affairs we will defend ourselves by every means, and in no instance would we yield on anything.

That is a great deal of political discussion, my dear duchess. I will not reply to your Shakespeare quotation, but I shall keep one for the portrait, so often promised, so much desired.

> What winning grace, what enchanting sheen
> She moves a Goddess and she looks a Queen.

I mean to call you the queen of all hearts. Farewell, a thousand compliments to Madame your sister.[140]

26. FERSEN TO MARIE-ANTOINETTE, 26 NOVEMBER 1791

AN 440AP/1. This letter, attached to the memorandum above, is for the Queen's eyes only. Fersen speaks here to his 'tender friend', the woman he loves and whom he longs to see. He reassures her about his safety at Brussels – it seems that once again she had asked him to return to Sweden. Fersen repeats his proposal to visit her in Paris, this time claiming it is Gustav III's wish, which is not true. And he begs Marie-Antoinette to take a decision before the political climate in Europe becomes even more unfavourable to the restoration of order to France. It is also necessary for their happiness, he tells her – for as soon as the Royal Family are free again he can rejoin her in Paris. One notes that he addresses her as sovereign in this private letter, just as he did in the memorandum.

Fersen gives interesting instructions for the continuation of the correspondence and notifies the Queen that she has been imprudent enough to send a letter for him through the Comte de Mercy without sealing it in an inner envelope. He gives his code name 'Rignon'. It has not been possible to identify the origin of this name; however, there was a prominent Piedmontese family called 'Rignon' in the eighteenth century, and even today a park and villa in Turin bear the name. Since Fersen spent eighteen months in Turin on his Grand Tour, there may be a connection to that period of his life.

[26 November 1791]

By everything I have sent you, you can see, **my dearest and most tender friend,** how essential it is that you take a decision as soon as possible and inform me of it. [*Every day your position becomes more . . .*] You cannot remain in your current state, and your have everything to fear from Coblentz and the émigrés, where some are of good faith and the others bad. The baron conducts himself very well and is completely devoted to you. As for me, do not worry at all; I am nothing to the French any more. I serve the King of Sweden, and I have no dealings with them, and the only way I can spend time agreeably and safely with them is to do so always as a foreigner. They all treat me wonderfully well and with distinction, because they know I have no need of them and they fear me. I am taking no risks. But for [*several words deleted*] I believe it necessary that you take a course of action and one that cannot be taxed with feebleness in the eyes of Europe and which won't force the other powers to withdraw from France and maintain in future only the most distant relations with her.

As for my departure from Brussels, however much I would like to satisfy and reassure you on that subject, it is impossible to do so. I am here on the King's orders and I may not absent myself. I am his chargé d'affaires here. I am waiting for the secretary he is sending me. He has given orders that all his ministers and ambassadors should correspond with me here and direct their actions according to what I send them. You can see then, **my very tender friend**, that I cannot change places. Besides, you may be quite easy. I run no risk here.

I beg that you reply to me as soon as possible on the course you wish to take. It's absolutely essential to write to the different courts. It must be as soon as possible; there is not a moment to lose. You risk nothing by writing to Prussia, and that is necessary. Except the letter for Spain, which you can send by a courier from the chargé d'affaires, you could send all the other letters here by a trustworthy man, either to me or to the baron, and we will forward them by courier. But it all requires great promptness, because the season advances. I received your long letter yesterday,[141] but **my dear friend**, M. de Mercy, thinking it was for him, had read it before he gave it to me. It would be better not to send any through him in future or at least use a second envelope and write him a note to tell him to whom he should deliver it. What you tell me about your domestic life grieves me but doesn't surprise me. It seems you must suffer every misfortune at the same time. My God [½ *line deleted*]

I understand very well what you tell me about the code. We will use it thus; let us put a full-stop . at the beginning, and when a letter is skipped, let us put a colon : . There is another method which is not so long and which we should use, that is to squeeze the juice of a lemon into a glass and to write with it. One just needs to write between the lines of a brochure or a newspaper that could be sent to me at Rignon's address or directly to mine. I will write to you in the same way and send the brochure to the Comte de Coigny or the Duc de Choiseul or Goguelat: warn them. If you have enough confidence in M. de La Porte, it would be safer and more convenient to forward them through him and not use these three others except occasionally. Reply to me about it. Care should be taken that the printed lines are sufficiently far apart and that the paper is of a good enough quality not to soak up all the ink. You expose this type in the same way as invisible ink by heating it.

You have no money in Brussels. M. de Bouillé gave the princes the 500,000 or 600,000 [*livres*] that were left. I will send details of the money I sent to Holland for you as soon as I have a moment to make enquiries. You will certainly lose a quarter of it, because for 2,000 they only give 1,500 here. {It's an enormous loss. I will find out about Mme de Korff's money and let you know. As I would like to fetch my things from Valenciennes, if possible, and I will need to pay for myself, for **Steding** and for various Swedes the sum of eleven thousand and a few hundred *livres*, would you please, **my dear friend**, forward to me 12,000 *livres* **from the money I have in Paris**, in notes, including two thousand in small bills, in a parcel by the stage? That will avoid having to give silver and stop me losing 25per cent. See **if** I don't love to owe everything to you.}[142]

You can see what to expect from the Emperor by his refusal. I am not pleased with him, nor with M. de Mercy. He is very well disposed towards me and to you in words, but they are without effect, and you must absolutely act by yourself or give up doing anything and resolve to remain as you are. I am doing what I can to restrain the King of Sweden, but that is not easy because he has the Empress with him, and if he is once convinced that you wish to do nothing it will be impossible. Choose a course then, **my tender friend**. It is essential **for our** happiness **as well as** for your glory and your reputation.

On Sunday the news was spread here that you had left and had arrived at Raismes at La Marck's home. All the French were crazy; several had already set off and those who doubted it were looked upon as bad citizens. The Baron de Vioménil gave you and the Dauphin his arm, and the Duc de Choiseul did the same for the King disguised as a woman. No one dared to give me this news, nor speak to me about it, nor ask me if it were true. They never talk to me of affairs, nor do I. I keep them at a great distance from me. It is a horror to have spread this news, and we are trying to find out at the moment from whence it came. M. de Nicolaï and M. de Limon were the first to mention it.[143] It is believed it came from Coblentz and even Paris, to prevent you from leaving if such had been or could be your plan. {The more I see of this nation the more I hate and despise it. Without you, my decision would soon be made.}

Farewell, my dearest friend [*3½ lines in the margin deleted*].

Reply to me about the possibility of coming to see you all alone and without a servant, in case I should receive an order from the King. He has already hinted something to me of his wish for it.

[*The Pope had sent a long memorandum to the different courts, and here is the ending; besides His Holiness declares strongly to the whole of Europe that He will listen to no proposition of? compensation or exchange.*]

Tell me if you approve of what I advise you to write to Spain about the plan I propose, and if I can send the same thing to the King of Sweden, and that you like this plan all the more because it will be one more obligation you owe him, insisting always that the congress is assembled first. This communication would have the advantage of calming the King of Sweden and of engaging him to hold back the princes by the hope he will have that he is serving you, and it commits you to nothing, because circumstances could always give rise to another plan that you will always be able to adopt, especially when supported by the other powers.

Baron Thugut told Mr Craufurd that you begged the Emperor with clasped hands to keep calm and do nothing for you and that therefore he could not act.[144]

Marie-Antoinette to Fersen, 26 November 1791, letter missing

Fersen acknowledges receipt of this letter in his reply on 4 December.

It seems that Fersen was ill again, for his diary remains empty between 20 November and 2 December 1791. On 3 December he started writing it again, very briefly, with the remark that 'Thugut says that Mercy is returning to Paris' – news he sent to the Queen the following day.

27. FERSEN TO MARIE-ANTOINETTE, 4 DECEMBER 1791

AN 440AP/1. Autograph copy of a letter from Fersen to Marie-Antoinette written in invisible ink. There are no gaps, deletions or endearments, which suggests that it was also intended to be read by Louis XVI. In his register it is logged to 'Josephine, invisible ink by M.____' with no further details on the person who took it to the Queen. On 9 December Marie-Antoinette replied: 'I have received this instant your letter which enveloped an image; I am charmed that you received mine.' This indicates that their letters were concealed in the packaging of objects the better to conceal them.

Fersen protests strongly against the inertia of Louis XVI's and Marie-Antoinette's politics, exhorting the Queen once again to choose a course of action and not to trust the Constitutionals. In order to convince her, he quotes some of the most vehement passages from Gustav III's letter of 11 November.

To the Queen in invisible ink
Sent 5 December by an occasion

Brussels, 4 December 1791

I have received your two letters of the 25th and 26th. We will send the ones to the King of Sweden and King of Spain in code. They are excellent. When you decide to write the second letters, we shall send both the originals. The note is perfect; I have given it to the baron.[145] I perfectly understand all the horror of your position, but it will never change without foreign help and by a surfeit of evil alone. The current evil will make way for another, but you will always be wretched and the kingdom will fall to pieces. You will never win over the rebels; they have too much to fear from you and your character. They feel all their wrongs too much not to fear revenge, not to keep you continually in the state of captivity you are in, preventing you even from making use of the authority granted to you by the Constitution. They are making the people used to not respecting you and to no longer liking you.

The nobility, believing that you have abandoned it, feels that it owes you nothing. It will act for itself, by itself or with the princes. It will reproach you with its ruin and you will lose even its attachment, as well as that of all the parties, some of which accuse you of betraying them and the others of having abandoned them. You will be vilified in the eyes of Europe, who will accuse you of cowardice, and the weakness which they will charge you with will stop them from allying themselves with [*you*] a ruined country, which will no longer be of any use to them. The King of Sweden [*is persuaded*] fears that you want to do nothing and await everything from time and events which you cannot foresee, not being able to create any, and that you do not wish to make use of the princes. He writes to me: 'The Empress is very dissatisfied with this conduct and above all, that the Queen of France writes letter after letter to the Emperor to stop him from taking action, while the Empress is exerting all her influence over this prince's mind to engage him to take more active steps. The Empress herself has written to me about it.' In speaking of the discontent which such a conduct inspires, he says: 'I count among this number not only the emigrants but all the powers who, in order to show her their zeal and friendship in these dangerous times, have advanced too far to be able to retreat; and with the Empress I rank myself among those princes who could find themselves forced to carry the princes further than even they themselves wish for or could hope for.'

Then, in speaking of you, he says: 'Judge for yourself what the Queen's position would be if the King were to die and she should find herself at the mercy of her brothers-in-law and of a nobility who would reproach her for sacrificing them to petty female jealousies and being the sole cause of their ruin and their proscription.'

The King gives me positive assurances of the good dispositions of Russia and Spain, hopes on those of Prussia and of England's neutrality.

After all that, you see that through interest and honour it is necessary, it is indispensable that you choose a course of action. Forgive me if the zeal and attachment I have vowed to you have made me expose some hard truths; but I know you are capable of hearing them, and nothing will stop me when it is essential to serve you. Besides, I thought it was my duty to hide nothing from you. I believe it is certain that M. de Mercy is returning to Paris. It is very unfortunate for you. That should prove to you even more everything I told you regarding the Emperor and how little you can count on him. Perhaps when he hears of the steps you are taking with the other courts he will change his mind, particularly since one of the reasons for M. de Mercy's journey is doubtless to influence your conduct and direct it according to the wishes of the court of Vienna.

28. Marie-Antoinette to Fersen, 7 and 9 December 1791

AN 440AP/1 and Stafsund, SE/RA/5802. Autograph letter from Marie-Antoinette to Fersen, with twelve lines and several words deleted at least twice. The original letter as well as the transcription Baron Klinckow-ström made for his edition are in the French Archives Nationales, while the baron's manuscript is in Sweden. After examining the original, the transcription and the manuscript, it became apparent that initially Fersen had deleted some words and phrases before Klinckowström transcribed the redacted letter. Later, however, he had scruples when Marie-Antoinette talks about Fersen's letters being carried to Louis XVI, and he crossed these lines out both on the original letter and in his manuscript; but he forgot to do the same to his transcription. It has therefore been possible to restore three lines to the letter (in bold). I have also found 'my tender and dear friend' beneath the deletions on page 4. Certain sentences in which Marie-Antoinette is scathing about the French were placed in brackets by Fersen and surely would have been suppressed from his memoirs, but Klinckowström published those in full.

Marie-Antoinette is replying to Fersen's letter of 26 November received by the Bishop of Pamiers. She at last answers him about his planned visit to Paris, refusing him permission to come despite her 'extreme desire' to see him; to soften the blow she talks of 'the happy time when we'll see each other again'. It would appear from her comments that she had changed her mind about the Baron de Vioménil's mission to the princes, and in the blacked-out lines she cautions Fersen when writing about politics. Clearly Louis XVI was not informed of all his wife's political negotiations, and while the royal couple had complementary strategies, their efforts were not well coordinated. Once again the Queen justifies her dealings with the Constitutionals, assuring Fersen that 'we would be much worse off than we are if I hadn't taken this course straight away'. One can also see how she used to manage him. She flatters him about the letters for Spain and Sweden, hoping he will be satisfied with them. 'I tried to include every-thing you indicated to us, but it's very difficult for someone unaccustomed to affairs.' And yet her correspondence with Mercy, Barnave and with Fersen himself reveals a woman with keen political insight who expresses herself with great lucidity and punctures specious arguments with incisive prose. She pretends to have 'forgotten' to include certain things in the letters to the foreign powers, but, given her dislike of waffle and obsequiousness, it was probably an excuse not to include everything Fersen had instructed her to say.

Marie-Antoinette also refers to the copy of Lafayette's letter to the Duchess of Devonshire – 'I didn't need Sans Tort's letter to loathe him' – and talks about the projected return to Paris of Quintin Craufurd and Eléonore Sullivan. 'I am waiting impatiently for Mr Craufurd, but I am annoyed for you that he is leaving you. I hope they will not spend the winter here and he returns to Brussels, because you have need of distraction.' This does rather seem to contradict an 'extreme desire' to see Fersen again, and it seems very surprising that she should wish him to seek distraction with Craufurd and Eléonore Sullivan. One can only assume that she knew nothing of his fling in June with Eléonore. Rumours about Fersen and Eléonore Sullivan/Craufurd had nevertheless reached Stockholm, and Sophie warned him about it on 15 December 1791, in a letter clarifying the nature of his relationship with the Queen – 'Her'.

C. Strömfelt, who knows everything as you know, came to tell me a day or so ago: 'By the way, you must know that Axel is very much in love with an Englishwoman in Brussels called Krabert (perhaps he said another name, but it was something in that style). I've received a letter,' he added, 'which talks of it, and they say that Axel follows her about everywhere, sits in her box at the theatre, that she is pretty.'

'That may be,' I replied, 'but I doubt he has a passion for her and people often make suppositions about the truth by exaggerating the facts.'

I said no more about it and I'm warning you, my dear Axel, for the love of Her. If this news is sent elsewhere it could cause her mortal grief. Everyone watches you and talks about you. Think of the unhappy Her, spare her the most mortal of all pains.[146]

Fersen saw Eléonore almost every day when he dined with her and Craufurd but records no moments of intimacy; there is not a single 'stayed there' or 'slept' in his diary after his return to Brussels on 6 October 1791. He was staying at the Hotel Bellevue while Craufurd and Eléonore had rented a house; and Craufurd was omnipresent. In the diary at this period Eléonore is always 'Mme Sullivan' or simply 'Sullivan'. Later, when he was in love with her, she became 'El.' or 'Eléonore'. Marie-Antoinette knew Fersen well – he could not bear to be alone. His diary and letters demonstrate a horror of solitude from his earliest youth, and he would slide into depression when he was left alone. He needed company, friends. Craufurd's salon was full every evening, there was much conversation – very political in tone, naturally, but that would have suited Fersen. In the autumn of 1791 he was thinking only of arranging a reunion with the Queen, whom he loved madly, but she kept refusing him permission to come – and her permission was crucial if he was going to spend the night with her Tuileries.

The idea of sending letters in boxes of chocolate, mentioned by Marie-Antoinette, clearly comes from a missing letter in Fersen which also talks of Craufurd's return to Paris.

Received 26 Dec, rep. 3 Jan by M. Lasserez

7 December [1791]

Here are our last two letters; I do not know if you will be pleased with them. I tried to include everything you indicated to us, but it is very difficult to someone unaccustomed to affairs. On re-reading your papers I realized that we forgot plenty of things in our two long letters – fortunately they are not the most essential. You cannot imagine the pleasure it gave me to see the bishop.[147] I could not leave him. I would dearly have liked to write to you by him, even just a line [*1¼ line in brackets deleted*], but I could not find the time. He will tell you plenty of things for me and, above all, about my new acquaintances and relations. I found him very severe; I thought I had already done plenty, and that he would admire me – not at all. Instead he told me that I could never do too much. {But, joking aside, I'm keeping for you, for the happy time when we see each other again, a very curious volume of correspondence; and all the more curious, because one must be just to those concerned in it – no one at all even suspects it, and if it has been mentioned, it is in such vague terms that it is just another of the thousand and one absurdities repeated every day.}

I did not need *Sans Tort's* letter to loathe him. The bishop can tell you how entitled I am to detest him. He is the most dangerous and perhaps the only one really to fear. {It is absolutely impossible for you to come here at the moment; it would jeopardize our happiness, and when I say it I can be believed, because I have an extreme desire to see you.}

I've received this instant a letter from M. de Mercy, who complains bitterly of the conduct at Coblentz towards the Emperor. He says: 'that they are trying to excite the whole of Germany against its leader; that they are inciting Sweden and especially Russia.' He proposes to me that he write himself to the latter to enlighten her and strengthen her good intentions by regulating them. I will reply to him that we have already written to thank her, without entering into any further details with him. The bishop must have told you that because of the Emperor's extreme indiscretion I felt that he should not be informed of our other correspondences. M. de Mercy seems to want to come here; I believe he is being pushed to it by my friends the *enragés* here. But he would be very wrong to do so at the moment. He could do no good; on the contrary it would lead to a thousand remarks about me; besides, such a step would only aggravate the émigrés' rage against the Emperor and me.

You must have seen the Baron de Vioménil; I do not know what the baron [Breteuil] will have told him, but it is becoming rather embarrassing. I believe one should seize on the Emperor's refusal or delays, which mean that we can say nothing positive. The indiscretion at Coblentz is too great, nothing can be confided to them, and I was astounded to receive a letter from fat d'Agoult a few days ago that said baldly: 'We await with impatience the fat baron from Lorraine so there is perfect accord between here and where you are.'[148] Can you conceive anything like it? {Oh, the cursed nation, how unfortunate it is to be obliged to live with them and to have to serve them.}

Our position is a little better since the bishop's departure. It appears that everything that calls itself constitutional is rallying to form a big force against the republicans and Jacobins. They have got a large part of the militia on their side, especially the paid militia, which will be organized into regiments in a few days. They are very well disposed and burn to make an example of the Jacobins; those who are here commit all the atrocities which they are capable of, but at the moment they have only brigands and villains on their side. I say at the moment, because everything changes from one day to the next in this country and you no longer know where you are.

The department is supposed to bring its address opposing the decree against the priests to the King today or tomorrow. I am delighted by it, because even if it does no good at least it declares war between the parties and forces that one, by the act itself, to support the King and rally to him. The address is from a M. Garnier and drafted by Duport and Barnave, but that is a secret. Comte Louis de Narbonne is finally Minister of War, since yesterday; what glory for Mme de Staël, and what pleasure for her to see the entire army . . . hers! He could be useful if he wants to be, having enough wit to rally the Constitutionals and the right tone to use with the present army. Moreover, he seems to me to want to attach himself to M. Bertrand in cabinet, and he is right, because he's the only one of any worth.[149]

But, **my tender and <u>dear</u> friend**, can you understand my position and the role I am obliged to play all day long? Sometimes I do not even understand myself and I am obliged to reflect to see if it is really me speaking. But what do you expect? It is all necessary, and, believe me, we would be much worse off than we are if I hadn't taken this course straight away. At least we are gaining time that way, and that is all that is needed. What joy if one day I may recover enough to prove to all these wretches that I was not their dupe. The baron must press Russia and Spain for us. How unfortunate if the Emperor has let us down; if he had served us well, even from September when I sent him the details, the congress could have been fixed for next month, and that would have been very fortunate because a crisis is fast approaching here and may perhaps arrive before the congress – and then what protection will we have?

Beware of Prussia: M. de Schulembourg writes constantly to M. Dumoutier and if M. Heymann finds out something he will send it to M. de Gillier. In other words, everyone will know it. The department's address has arrived; it is perfectly fine for the discussion on the decree on the priests, but the wretches are scared and have added a heap of impertinences. On his entry to the Assembly, M. de Narbonne made a speech of scarcely credible banality for a man of wit. I am waiting impatiently for Mr Craufurd, {but I am annoyed for you that he is leaving you. I hope they will not spend the winter here and he returns to Brussels, because you have need of distraction.} I cannot wait to hear that your secretary has arrived.

How is your health? I wager you aren't looking after yourself, and you are wrong [*2¾ lines deleted*] As for me, I am bearing up better than I ought to, given the prodigious weariness of spirit I constantly feel in going out so little. I have barely a moment to myself between the people I need to see, paperwork and the time I spend with my children. This last occupation, which is not the least, is my sole happiness [*three words deleted*] and when I am really sad I take my little boy in my arms, I kiss him with all my heart and that comforts me for a moment. Farewell – the idea of the chocolate is doubly useful, and I shall use it with prudence but occasionally this winter. Farewell once again. [*1¼ lines deleted*]

Friday 9th

I have received this instant your letter which enveloped an image.[150] I am delighted that you have received mine. I hope our letters to the powers will calm them, and show them our true characters. What is being said about my letters to the Emperor is incomprehensible. For some time now I have suspected that my handwriting has been imitated to write to him; I will clarify this fact. M. de Mercy would be very wrong to come, but I believe I must write him a line about our letters to the powers. Let me know at once when you have received this packet. I could not manage to finish the letter to the King of Sweden any better; I rewrote it in all sorts of ways over 24 hours.

I agree with you that evil alone cannot produce any good, but that is why there is need of a foreign and external force. But if you believe that the French {reflect and that they're capable of following a system, you give them too much credit, and I assure you that for the simple desire for change they will return as quickly as they turned so violently in favour of the new order. Meanwhile, I believe that we are going to declare war – not on some power who would have arms against us, we are too cowardly for that – but against the electors and some German princes, in the hope that they cannot defend themselves. The imbeciles do not see that if they do such a thing they will help us, because, if we start, at last all the powers will have to get involved, each in defence of their rights. But they must be entirely convinced that we will do nothing here but carry out others' wishes, and in that case the best way to serve us is indeed to set upon us}.

The bishop must have told you of the inconvenience in writing to me. Yet again today M. de La Porte, who carries everything to the King, had given him your packet. **He has water to expose the writing, and I find them like that afterwards; luckily he didn't have time and I seized the paper.** [*1½ lines deleted*] **Be careful what you write, especially when discussing affairs.** As for the *Journal de Brabant*, I will see about it, and it will certainly come straight to me, so you will be able to say what you want. Farewell [*several words deleted*].

Fersen noted in his diary on 8 December 1791 that the Bishop of Pamiers had returned and was very satisfied with his meeting with the Queen. On 10 December he was busy with the Baron de Vioménil, who had arrived in Brussels, charged with a mission from Louis XVI to the princes. Once again, every effort to restore harmony between the King and the princes would be thwarted by the personal interests and egoism of those who surrounded them. The hatred of Monsieur and the Comte d'Artois for Breteuil (fuelled by their minister, Calonne) had caused a rift between Louis XVI and his brothers that would never be bridged. Fersen wanted the King to negotiate with Spain, Sweden and Russia through the Baron de Breteuil to establish the congress, with the utmost discretion. Nothing of these secret negotiations should reach Coblentz, where members of the princes' council plotted between the salons of their various mistresses and hangers-on, and everything was discussed with the greatest indiscretion. In her letter of 7 and 9 December Marie-Antoinette talks of Vioménil's mission as 'becoming quite embarrassing', but Fersen did not receive it until 26 December. However, it would appear from his diary that he received another letter from the Queen before Vioménil's arrival in Brussels – otherwise how could he have known that she was 'very vexed at having sent him'?

> 10 December. Baron de Vioménil a poor negotiator. He's going to Cologne and to Coblentz to charge the Maréchal de Castries to be the King's man in the princes' council. It is a wrong move by the Queen, who is very vexed at having sent him; my letter arrived too late to prevent it. He came to see me in the morning. I was tempted to stop him from going, but I dared not because it would have been believed it was with the agreement of the Baron de Breteuil and he would have been accused of wanting to get rid of everybody and take sole control of affairs; and in the meeting we had in the evening at the baron's with the Baron de Vioménil, I proposed changes to what he had to say, to weaken his commission and make it as least influential as possible. Besides, it is to be hoped that Castries will refuse to go.[151]

29. FERSEN TO MARIE-ANTOINETTE, 12 DECEMBER 1791

AN 440AP/1. Autograph copy of a letter from Fersen to the Queen that was sent in code. He logged it in his register to 'Josephine, by post in code'. There are two sentences, without code, crossed out by Fersen but which remain quite legible. One-and-a-half lines at the end of the letter contain a declaration of love. The margin note 'by post Gougenot' indicates that the letter was addressed to 'Mme Brown' and placed inside another envelope sent to M. Gougenot at 2 rue Lepeletier in Paris. The code word adroit *is from page 49 of the code book. In his diary on 11 December Fersen notes: 'letters arrived from the Queen for Russia, from the King for Spain, quite good'; but to Marie-Antoinette he writes that they are 'perfect'.*

By post Gougenot
49 adroit

Brussels, 12 December [1791]

The letters for Spain and Russia have arrived. They are perfect. I await those for Sweden and Prussia. There is another step which is very necessary, which is to write yourself a confidential courtesy letter to the Queen of Spain, referring to the King's letter, and making her understand the need for the greatest secrecy [*so that it does not get back*] because of Paris. You know what influence she has, and this step [*is very important*] cannot be prompt enough. You could send it to me by the stage in a box of Boue [*sic*] tea, addressed to Messrs Daniel Danoot fils, bankers.

M. de Vioménil passed through here. [*His mission will greatly embarrass us, but we will try to remedy it as much as possible. If it had not been for the Baron de Breteuil I would have taken it upon myself to keep him here until I had taken your orders on the matter.*] The Emperor is seeking a close alliance with Prussia, Holland and England. It is believed that England will refuse.

Farewell, my most tender friend, never will I cease to love you madly.

There is a gap in Fersen's diary between 16 December 1791 and 1 January 1792 and a similar gap in his correspondence with Marie-Antoinette until the letter of 22 December. It seems from the diary in

January that he fell ill again, but there may also have been another reason for this silence, since it seems that their political strategies were diverging. And of course there could have been unrecorded letters which are missing.

30. FERSEN TO MARIE-ANTOINETTE, 22 DECEMBER 1791

Stafsund, SE/RA/5802. The original letter is missing, and this transcription is taken from Klinckowström's manuscript. Fersen logged this letter in his register to 'the Queen of France, by post'. He repeats almost verbatim his deleted warnings about the Baron de Vioménil's mission from his letter of 12 December, which seems to indicate that he had indeed been out of action for ten days. She had not replied to that letter – he asks if she had received it.

Fersen makes a direct appeal to Marie-Antoinette in this letter. He clearly fears he has lost her confidence, that she has indeed 'gone over to the enragés', despite all her assurances to the contrary. He is 'appalled and deeply grieved' by Louis XVI's demand on 14 December to his uncle, the Elector of Trèves, to expel French émigrés from his territory by 15 January 1792. This threat of war against the princes could completely negate the negotiations to convene a congress of friendly countries, who had already shown their marked disapproval of the King's flirtation with democracy and his mistrust of his brothers. It was all the more unwelcome because Fersen had received news from Taube that Gustav III was 'going to agree on a congress and he's writing to the Empress about it'.[152] Fersen considered it insupportable only to learn of such an important step from the newspapers and believed that his place had been usurped by Barnave and the Constitutionals. He cannot understand the Queen's reticence towards him. 'I know that there is no trust,' he complains. Finally, letters arrive from the King and Queen explaining how they simply could not warn him and Breteuil in time (the declaration was in fact drawn up one day and voted on the next). Louis XVI wrote a long justification of his conduct to Breteuil, explaining the difficulties of his position and his reasons for wishing to disperse the princes' army. Fersen sent a copy to Gustav III to try to mitigate the extremely bad impression the declaration had made on him. On 17 January 1792 Taube replied that Gustav 'strongly approves of the King of France's current conduct with the rebels; one cannot deceive them enough'; but he warned Fersen that Stockholm and St Petersburg took a very dim view of Louis XVI's actions. 'With his friends he must never speak or propose anything other than the total re-establishment of the monarchy as it was before the Revolution.'[153] Both Louis XVI and Marie-Antoinette had long seen the impossibility of such an outcome: the chasm between monarchists within France and those without was growing ever wider.

Note by Klinckowström: 'From a minute by the Comte de Fersen, who wrote in the margin: sent to the Queen by post in invisible ink on 23 Dec. The letter of 23 Dec was taken by Craufurd on 24 Dec.'

22 December 1791

I hope you have received the letter in which I propose that you write to the Queen of Spain. I believe this is an important measure. It will also be important later to write to the King of England and to the Stadtholder, but now is not the time. Let me know when you decide to do it. The Baron de Breteuil has engaged M. de Brantzen,[154] who is very well disposed towards you and who it would be good to treat kindly, to write to the Stadtholder, with whom he is reconciled, so that he gets the King of Prussia to declare himself and makes a positive proposal to the Emperor, to prove still further to the whole of Europe how wrong he is to doubt his goodwill and that the lack of action comes only from the Emperor. These proposals cannot commit him, since he is still able only to take action to match that the Emperor will take.

It is very important that you put your papers in a safe place where they cannot be found, because you must always be prepared for anything.

The Baron de Vioménil's mission will cause us the greatest difficulties now you have adopted the plan I proposed to you. I would have taken it upon myself, had it not been for the Baron de Breteuil, to keep him here until I had taken your orders on the matter; but his departure and his arrival being known already at Coblentz, such a change would have been badly interpreted for him. We made some changes to what he must say, and we will do all we can to contain the damage. You are right not to write to the Emperor until you have received answers from all the other courts. As for your guard, the bishop's idea seems good to me, to forbid them to show themselves off duty in uniform in Paris until the day they must mount guard. Without that there will be quarrels; there would be plots against them and you would find it impossible to make use of them.

The M. de Toulongeon who came from Franche-Comte was pained by the cool reception his good intentions received.[155] Do you not think that, without distinguishing them too much, reasonable people of goodwill should be shown marks of kindness? No one knows better than you how to make use of such currency.

The Duke of Brunswick is a man of wit, talent and great

ambition.[156] He has influence in Berlin. Do you not think it would be interesting to win him over? He has always loved France, and it was the army he preferred for his son, whom he loves very much. A move towards him could do much good and advance your affairs in Prussia. One would make him hope for something for his son. If you think it would be useful, a man of some distinction who can please him needs to be sent. M. le Maréchal de Castries would be a good choice or M. de Bouillé. Let me know if you adopt this idea. I have not yet spoken about it with the baron, but I am sure he will approve of it. Comte Etienne Durfort would very much like a place in your new guard.[157] He has mentioned it to the baron, who charged me to write to you about it. M. de Mercy is no longer going to Paris; he has, however, the freedom to go there whenever and how he likes. The conduct of Sweden and Russia is certainly the reason for this change. Your letters for Sweden and Prussia have not yet arrived. That worries me. It's safer and quicker to use the stage coaches. The letter for Spain has gone by the Comte de Seuil, who is travelling through England. Bombelles, who is going to take the one for Russia, has not yet arrived.

Monday

We learnt of the King's action yesterday. As I'm ignorant both of the reasons for it and its aim, I vow to you that it has appalled and deeply grieved me. I fear that you have been given dangerous advice. I fear that you have taken this step, which is good in itself, too soon, and which would have been helpful to you at another time, when made in agreement with the other powers once they were ready to act for you by seeming to support the German princes. I believe you should have been forced to it by the Assembly, and in ceding to their wish you could have demonstrated to them how many drawbacks such a step has at a time when peace is needed to establish the constitution, to restore finances, to secure the national debt and to avoid increasing taxes on the population. Now I see only a source of embarrassments and dangers for you and the bad effect it will have in Europe. It will be attributed once again to your perceived weakness, and friendly powers will become discouraged.

Indeed, what must be the impression of those to whom you have written and in whom you wish to trust when they learn of such an important step only from public papers, without knowing the motives behind it and without having been warned about it by the Baron de

Breteuil? They will be tempted to believe that you have only partial confidence in him, and this belief will make his negotiations more difficult. They will even suspect your intention, and with some cause, and the confidence you will seem to show in them will appear doubtful. Having adopted the proposed plan, no important step must be taken unless in concert with them or at least not without consulting the Baron de Breteuil, who, being more aware of these powers' attitudes, could inform you of the effect your action would have and would then be in a position to inform them of the reasons that could engage you to do it and prevent the bad impression it could make. I am aware there are circumstances where you may be obliged to take decisions and act promptly, but as you can always expect that possibility you must let us know and delay things so our letters have sufficient time to arrive before the newspapers, to shape the first reaction more favourably for you.

I know there is no trust, and I am far from asking for more than you wish to grant me. Your interest alone guides and will always guide me, and, if you may suspect the views or projects of the Baron de Breteuil, I have the vanity to believe that my past conduct must remove the possibility in my case and convince you of the purity of mine and of the zeal, attachment and devotion I have vowed to you. My sole desire is to serve you, and my sweetest recompense, the only one I strive for, is the glory of having succeeded; I shall never wish for any other. I will be only too well rewarded if I knew you were happy and if I could think that I had done enough to make you so. I hope to receive a note from you which may guide what I have to write to the King of Sweden, giving me the possibility to justify in his and the Empress's view the step that has just been taken.

Everything I've just written is useless, as the letters for the baron and M. de Mercy have just arrived, However, I must remark to you that it would have been useful to receive them sooner, so that the powers could have been forewarned by you before learning of your action from the gazettes.

31. MARIE-ANTOINETTE TO FERSEN, 22 DECEMBER 1791

AN 440AP/1. Autograph decrypt by Fersen of a letter from the Queen. As it is numbered, it was sent by post. Marie-Antoinette has just received a 'little letter' from Fersen, probably the one in code from 12 December (despite the 'impossible' date of the 19th). She still hopes that her brother Leopold II will come to her aid – even though Fersen told her in his letter of 26 November that she could not count on him and it would be better to establish a congress without him, with the help of other allies. The Queen also informs Fersen not to tell Goguelat about her negotiations with the Constitutionals, which is rather curious. Why was her loyal secretary not permitted to know that she corresponded with Barnave? It would appear that in a letter now missing Fersen had suggested she send someone to Vienna. She finishes her letter with a tender farewell; Fersen had started to decipher 'adieu, le plus', then realizing the nature of the sentence doubtless finished decoding it on another page.

Received 27 Dec. 1791
Rep. 3 Jan
No. 1 from the Queen

22 December 1791

I received your little letter yesterday. I would be worried that you still had not received our letters[158] if the date on yours was possible; it is the 19th and I received it on the 21st. No post can go that fast. I've already received four printed pages; I passed them in front of the fire and washed them with water, but I found nothing.

I am very anxious to have the replies to the last letters. It was impossible for me to send someone to Vienna; I have not found anyone strong enough to make the journey or reliable and discreet enough. I'm vexed about it. It is very important at present that the Emperor should know our true intentions, so that at last I may know what to count on from him, because without that I shall be constantly led into making false steps; for my language and manner towards people here must be adapted to what one can expect from abroad. I am strongly tempted to send M. Goguelat to you, if only for three days, so that he can talk in depth with you. I have not yet mentioned this idea to him. Let me know what you think of it. He knows nothing of my correspondence with the persons the bishop mentioned to you; he must not be told of it.

There is talk here of a loan for forty million which the émigré nobles wish to raise on their assets. It is madness and the rest of their lands will end up being plundered. If the baron has the means, he must make my brothers see (and we authorize him to do so) that we cannot approve of this idea, which will be the ruin of all honest people.

I will wait for your replies to all my letters to write to you and to the Queen of Spain. Tell me when the secretary that you [*blank line*] nffkkue. I am worried about you because of his tardiness.

Farewell **the most** [*2 lines blank*]. I missed the occasion to send my letter. Beginning with this one, I shall number all that go by post, whether in invisible ink or in code. Do the same. Keep small paper to write them all on, and see that none are lost. Farewell.

Fersen to Marie-Antoinette, 23 December 1791, letter missing

On 23 December Fersen logged a letter to Marie-Antoinette as 'the Queen of France'. It was taken to her by Quintin Craufurd, who left Brussels for Paris with Eléonore Sullivan on 24 December 1791.

32. FERSEN TO MARIE-ANTOINETTE, 24 DECEMBER 1791

AN 440AP/1. Autograph copy of a letter from Fersen sent in code. The code word is raison, *from page 9 of the code book. It is logged in his register to 'Josephine, by post in code'. There are some deletions of intimate words. This note is simply to alert the Queen to the letter sent by Craufurd dated 23 December, which is missing.*

19 raison

24 December 1791

Mr Craufurd left this morning. He will be in Paris on Tuesday [*afternoon*]. Goguelat must be sent there at ten o'clock on Wednesday morning. He should ask to speak to him without giving his name and present him with the enclosed paper in code. He will give him what he has for you. It would be good for you to talk to Craufurd, **my tender friend**, as soon as possible. Your man will leave from here on Tuesday or Wednesday. Your letters for Prussia and Sweden have still not arrived. I received one from Goguelat that I could not read. I certainly do not have the book he used.

You were wrong, **my tender friend**, not to warn us that the Comte de Ségur was being sent to Berlin. We will have trouble trying to prevent the bad effect it will have. Ill send a courier there tomorrow. **Farewell [my God]**

Fersen to Marie-Antoinette, 26 December 1791, letter missing

In his register, Fersen logs a letter to 'Josephine, in code by the post: that the letters have arrived'. These are the letters for Sweden and Prussia he mentioned on 24 December.

Marie-Antoinette to Fersen, 22–28 December 1791, letter missing

Letter No. 2 in the series that started on 22 December 1791 is missing.

33. MARIE-ANTOINETTE TO FERSEN, 28 DECEMBER 1791

AN 440AP/1. Autograph note from Marie-Antoinette to Fersen written in invisible ink. The envelope, in another hand, is addressed to the abbé de Beauverin, Poste Restante at Brussels. This may possibly be 'Rignon's address' used by Fersen. A clearer facsimile of this letter is kept in Stockholm with Klinckowström's manuscript – made in 1877, the ink is much less faded than it is today. The numbering shows that this is the third letter from Marie-Antoinette to Fersen in six days. She lets him see that the tone of his recent missives has been rather high-handed: 'I'm warning you about all this to avoid being scolded.'

Received 3 Jan 1792; rep. 3 Jan

No. 3, 28 December 1791

M. de Narbonne has had a mad idea which I thought had been dropped, to engage the Duke of Brunswick to come to take command of the army. This idea is so nonsensical that I thought it would not be spoken of again. Yesterday I learnt that young De Custine is being sent to negotiate this business.[159] The Comte de Ségur could well be charged to speak about it, too, without our knowledge. I am warning you about all this to avoid being scolded and so you and the baron may take your precautions. I do not doubt that the duke will refuse and that will even help us. Farewell. I have not yet got Mr Craufurd's packet. [*At least one line deleted and torn off*]

Fersen's correspondence with Marie-Antoinette increased noticeably in January 1792. He had at last received orders from Gustav III to go to Paris to propose a new escape plan to the King and Queen and devise measures to take with their allies. But Marie-Antoinette continually refused him permission to undertake this journey, which he had first proposed back in October 1791. Was her reluctance solely motivated by her concerns for his safety, or was there another reason – Barnave? Fersen was aching to see her, and she sent him words of love, yet she wanted him to withdraw completely from affairs and return to Sweden. Doubtless he was very disappointed to receive yet another refusal after actually fixing his arrival '*chez Elle*' for 3 February 1792. On 30 January he issued her with an ultimatum: 'that I will postpone, but after a fortnight it can no longer happen' (see below, 'The Reunion').

Here is a list of all the letters to Marie-Antoinette in Fersen's register for 1792. The one on 11 August was the last he ever sent her, although it was not the last he wrote.[160] Note that with the exception of the letters on 24 February and 15 May, all those sent after his return from Paris are logged to 'the Queen of France'. Letters sent through Gougenot or Goguelat were sent in a double envelope to 'Mme Brown' at 2 rue Lepeletier in Paris.

1792

JANUARY

- 3 Josephine by M. Lasserez
- 3 Queen by M. Lasserez: replied to those of 7 Dec., 22 Dec. No. 1 and 28th No. 3
- 6 Josephine by La P[orte]: for the purchase of the baron's bookcases
- s.d. Queen by Gog [Goguelat]
- 12 Josephine by La P[orte]: the trip, the 12,000 *livres* and the bookcases
- 17 Josephine by Hodges: replied to No. 5
- 24 Josephine by post
- 24 Queen by Vibray and Craufurd
- 26 Josephine: all the means to come
- 30 Josephine: that I will postpone, but after a fortnight it can no longer happen

FEBRUARY

- 1 Josephine by Goug[enot]: that I shall come Friday or Monday
- 6 Josephine by Goug[enot]: according to the minute
- 9 Josephine by Gog[uelat]: that I will be with her on Monday evening
- 10 Josephine
- 24 Josephine by Hodges

MARCH

- 4 Queen of France, invisible ink
- 6 Queen of France, invisible ink, replied to the one of the 2nd
- 9 Queen of France: on the death of the Emperor
- 15 Queen of France: despatch from Russia by Craufurd in invisible ink, biscuits
- 17 Queen of France by Gog[uelat], invisible ink
- 27 Queen of France by Gog[uelat] in code: that I have received No. 1

APRIL

1   Hierta in Paris by a Spanish courier: to communicate to the King and Queen news of the King of Sweden's assassination

9   Queen of France: No. 2 replied to No. 2 by Gog[uelat]

9   idem: account of the King's assassination by Goug[enot]

19   Queen of France: Nos. 3 and 4. No. 3 dated the 17th

24   Queen of France, invisible ink in biscuits addressed to Mme Tosc [Toscani]

MAY

15   Josephine: No. 6 by Goug[enot]

JUNE

2   Queen of France, invisible ink by Tosc[ani]

10   Queen of France in code by Tosc[ani]

21   Queen of France, replied to the one of the 7th, in code and invisible ink by Tosc[ani] and Gog[uelat]. No. 10

27   Queen of France: dated 25th, No. 11 in code by Goug[enot]. *Above all try not to leave Paris and use every means; that must be your sole aim, then it will be easy to come to your rescue and help will come.*

30   Queen of France: No. 12, invisible ink by Tosc[ani], replied to the one of the 23rd

JULY

10   Queen of France: replied to those by Lasserez and Leonard, invisible ink by Lasserez

18   Queen of France: No. 12 invisible ink by Tosc[ani]

26   Queen of France, invisible ink by Tosc[ani] No. 14

28   Queen of France, invisible ink by Tosc[ani] No. 15

AUGUST

3   Queen of France, invisible ink by Tosc[ani] No. 16 replied to No.5

7   Queen of France, invisible ink by Tosc[ani] No. 17 replied to No.7

11   Queen of France, invisible ink by Tosc[ani] No. 18[161]

Fersen to Marie-Antoinette, 3 January 1792, two letters missing

On 3 January Fersen sent two letters to Marie-Antoinette – one addressed to 'Josephine' and the other to 'the Queen'. Both were taken to Paris by a M. Lasserez. In the letter to 'the Queen', Fersen replies to all her letters, as she had requested on 28 December.

34. MARIE-ANTOINETTE TO FERSEN, 4 JANUARY 1792

AN 440AP/1. Autograph letter from Marie-Antoinette to Fersen with 5½ lines deleted. There is also a facsimile with Baron Klinckowström's manuscript in Stockholm. I have been able to read the deleted words in the first two lines. In November 2015 the Fondation des Sciences du Patrimoine (Foundation for Heritage Sciences) in France announced that the Centre de Recherche sur la Conservation des Collections (Research Centre for the Conservation of Collections) had succeeded in revealing the deleted words in the last 4½ lines, with the aid of new imaging techniques that differentiate between the original ink and the ink used in the deletions.[162] We therefore have a complete autograph letter from the Queen in which she declares her love for Fersen.

The 'bearer of all these papers' is the Queen's secretary François Goguelat. According to Fersen, he was carrying 'a detestable memorandum from the Queen, written by Barnave, Lameth, Duport: wanting to scare the Emperor, prove to him that his interest lies in not going to war but in maintaining the constitution for fear that the French will spread their doctrine and subvert his soldiers'.[163] Marie-Antoinette undoubtedly hoped that Goguelat would be able to convince her brother that she and Louis XVI were not free and still wished for a congress, but she had been trapped by the Constitutionals. Leopold sought every excuse to avoid having to help his sister, and he would use this memorandum against her.

Received 8 January by Goguelat

4 January [1792]

I am only writing you a line, **my adorable and tender friend**. The person who is bringing you this letter will tell you and make you aware of our actual position; I have total confidence in him, and he deserves it because of his attachment and his reason. He carries an absurd memorandum but one I am obliged to send. It is essential that the Emperor is quite convinced that there is not a word in it of ours nor of our way of looking at things, but that he nevertheless sends me a reply as though he believed that is my point of view, and which I may show, because they are so mistrustful here they will demand the reply.

The bearer of all these papers does not know how they reached me, and he must not be told. The memorandum is very badly done, and one sees that the wretches are afraid, but for our personal safety they still need to be managed, and, above all, our conduct here must inspire them with confidence. All that will be explained to you, as well as the reasons why often I cannot warn you in advance of what we are going to do. My man has not yet returned; yet I would very much like news from where you are.

What does this sudden declaration by the Emperor mean? Why this profound silence from Vienna, and even from Brussels, towards me? I'm at a loss, but this I know well – if I am being told nothing through prudence or policy, then it is very wrong and I am being greatly exposed, since nobody will believe I could be in such ignorance; and yet it it is necessary to regulate my speech and actions according to what is happening. This is what I have charged the person to tell M. de Mercy. I am going to close **but not without telling you, my dear and most tender friend, that I love you madly and never, ever can I be a moment without adoring you.**

35. FERSEN TO MARIE-ANTOINETTE, 6 JANUARY 1792

AN 440AP/1. Autograph copy of a letter from Fersen. He logged it in his register to 'Josephine' for 'the purchase of the baron's bookcases'. However, there is no mention of this in the pages that survive, nor are there any intimacies. Fersen gives his opinion on the response to Louis XVI's demand to the Elector of Trèves to disperse the émigrés assembled on his territory.

6 January 1792 by La P[orte] to the Queen

Brussels, 6 January 1792

An aide-de-camp from M. de Jaucourt has taken an order to the encampment at Ath to move to the frontiers of the electorate of Trèves. You will easily understand how many drawbacks there are to this operation and how disadvantageous it is.

1. It increases the difficulties faced by the electors and forces you to into sabre-rattling which it would be useful to delay until there is something organized abroad.
2. It is one less way to make the Emperor commit; and
3. It allows the Assembly to present this departure as the effect of the King's threats.

It will perhaps demand the same action from the electors. They will no longer be able to reply that they are acting at home in accordance with what is being done in the Low Countries, and from what I know of the Emperor's intentions I would not be surprised if he did not support this demand. I know he is determined not to supply more than the quota he is obliged to as a fellow-state in support of the electors and princes of the Empire. He is afraid of a war, he is afraid to get involved in your affairs, and no longer having assemblies [of troops] on his lands he could demand that there are none on anyone else's.

The Baron de Breteuil has written to the Maréchal de Castries to stop the assemblies' departure. I have written the same to Baron Oxenstierna.[164] The King's reply to the Emperor's mediation seems to me to be too strong. Do you not think it better to remain in a position where you are ready to go to war but withdraw at the moment it is about to start until agreement has been reached and there is some sort of force which could serve as a rallying point? Do you not think it would have been preferable to say that if, at the due date, the Elector of Trèves has not dispersed the assemblies, the King expects the Emperor's friendship to persuade him to use his good offices to oblige him to do so? I believe it would be useful to grant the Elector of Trèves a second deadline, up to 1 or 15 February if possible. This delay would give us time to receive the replies. Could not the King emphasize his desire to keep the peace and avoid a ruinous war, above all, at a time when finances require such great care?

Marie-Antoinette to Fersen, [9] January 1792, letter missing

In his diary on 11 January Fersen notes the arrival of several letters from Paris, including one from Marie-Antoinette. Note that he refers to a letter from '*elle*' ('her'), but, when he moves on to political matters, in the next sentence she becomes 'the Queen'. 'Letter from Sullivan written by Simolin, news. One from *her*, brought by Hodges, one from Craufurd. He has seen the Queen and talked with her.'[165]

Fersen to Marie-Antoinette, 12 January 1792, letter missing

'Josephine by La P[orte], the trip, the 12,000 *livres* and the bookcases.' This letter logged in Fersen's register was clearly a reply to Marie-Antoinette's letter received the previous day. He is still talking about the 12,000 *livres* he needed in November 1791 to pay debts for his officers at Valenciennes.

Marie-Antoinette to Fersen, January 1792, letters numbered 4 and 5 missing

Only letters sent by post were numbered, therefore the letter delivered by Mr Hodges on 11 January would not have had a number. The Queen wrote letter No. 3 on 28 December 1791; letters 4 and 5, sent between 28 December and 17 January 1792, are missing.

Fersen to Marie-Antoinette, 17 January 1792, letter missing

Fersen notes a letter to Josephine in his register on this date, in reply to her letter No. 5.

36. MARIE-ANTOINETTE TO FERSEN, UNPUBLISHED NOTE, JANUARY 1792

Stafsund, SE/RA/720807/02/6/V/17. Fragment in code on behalf of the Queen, received by Fersen on 23 January, regarding his request to reimburse the Baron de Breteuil, made in his letter of 26 November. The code word is adroit *on page 49 of the code book. It is interesting to note that Fersen alone was entrusted with financial affairs for Louis XVI's secret diplomacy and that former government minister Breteuil, a Frenchman, had to apply to him for payment.*

49. Received 23 January [1792]
It is desired that the payment due to the Baron de Breteuil is taken from the money on deposit in Holland. You may give authorization to that effect.

Marie-Antoinette to Fersen, [18] January 1792, letter missing

In his diary on 21 January Fersen notes that he has received a letter in which 'the Queen consents to my going to Paris'.[166]

Marie-Antoinette to Fersen [22] January 1792, letter missing

On 25 January 1792 Fersen noted in his diary that he 'received 12,000 [*livres*] in assignats', which he had reminded Marie-Antoinette about in his letter of 12 January.

37. FERSEN TO MARIE-ANTOINETTE, 24 JANUARY 1792

AN 440AP/1. Autograph copy of a letter from Fersen to Marie-Antoinette, logged in his register to 'the Queen of France, by Vibray[167] and Craufurd'. There is no code. He mentions a new escape plan for the Royal Family proposed by Gustav III, as well as his 'official' visit to Louis XVI and the Queen in Paris. All the arrangements for his secret reunion with Marie-Antoinette are reserved for 'Josephine' letters. On 24 January Fersen notes in his diary: 'Wrote to Paris by young Vibray. My journey to Paris is fixed for 3 February.'

To the Queen by Vibray and Craufurd

24 January [1792]

You will see by the King of Prussia's letter that his dispositions are good, but that he does not want to do anything without the Emperor: therefore it is now only a question of encouraging the King of Prussia to make positive proposals to this prince. I have received a perfect letter from Spain, and I will tell you the details. Those from Russia are the same. The Empress writes to the King of Sweden: 'Perhaps the Queen of France herself will find it necessary to claim her brother's assistance. Your Majesty must know better than I how difficult that will be to achieve.' The Empress will be completely convinced on that point by your letter. She goes on to say: 'The more this cause is worthy of all our attentions, the more we must neglect nothing to make it triumph; and we shall have, my dear brother, among our contemporaries and in posterity, the credit for not having turned away from such a fine enterprise without having made every possible effort to surmount the difficulties we have encountered.'

But the King and the Empress still insist on a new escape, and I am bringing you a memorandum about it with letters from the King. His plan is that it should be executed by sea and by the English; only two should be in the secret. I am bringing you new evidence on the Emperor's conduct. It's said that the Queen of Portugal is very well disposed; she has plenty of money and they say she would give some. I think it would be good to write to her – that would help her make up her mind.

Madame de Vaudémont is in Paris to prevent her house being taken or to demand an indemnity, but as she is bringing M. de

Lambesc's and M. de Vaudémont's resignations at the same time[168] doubtless you will believe that you are not obliged to give them anything; nor to grant them the pensions they are asking for at the moment, especially to M. de Vaudémont. And if M. de Lambesc has 20,000 or 30,000 [*livres*], that is all he can hope for. You will therefore think that he should not be allowed to sell his appointment. He came to propose it to the Baron de Breteuil for his son-in-law, for the sum of 300,000 [*livres*]. He refused it, saying that he believed the King should no longer be so fettered and should not tolerate the [*sale*] the market in places [at Court]. But the baron asks for the King's indulgence to be allowed to give this place to his son-in-law one day, and he added to me: 'He thinks favourably, he is too rich to demand anything from the King and has enough to maintain a great position. Besides, he is too stupid ever to be a nuisance to him or to interfere in affairs.'[169]

I will pay the baron the 22,000 [*livres*] due to him, but you need to authorize me to give him 20,000 or 30,000 more, for which he will render accounts, for the cost of couriers and other expenses that must be incurred. The loss on money is terrible: it is 40 per cent, which means that of the [ ] you have in Holland, you really only have [ ]. I will give you an exact account and I am choosing to raise it all at once and to place it on deposit, for fear the loss will increase yet more. I suffer the same loss on all the money I draw,

I will make all my arrangements to arrive on the 3rd at six o'clock in the evening.

Fersen to Marie-Antoinette, 24 January 1792, letter missing

In his register this day Fersen records a letter to 'Josephine by post'.

Fersen to Marie-Antoinette, 26 January 1792, letter missing

Fersen notes a letter to organize his secret visit to the Tuileries: 'Josephine, all the means to come'.

Marie-Antoinette to Fersen, [26] January 1792, letter missing

The Queen wants to postpone Fersen's visit yet again. In his diary on 29 January he wrote: 'Letter from *Her* which begs me to postpone my

LOVE YOU MADLY

journey until the decree on passports is pronounced and Paris is a little
calmer again.'[170]

Fersen to Marie-Antoinette, 30 January 1792, letter missing

Fersen replied the next day to Marie-Antoinette's letter regarding his
visit to Paris. In his register on 30 January he notes his reply to
'Josephine, that I will postpone, but after a fortnight it can no longer
happen'.

There was certainly unrest in Paris. Quintin Craufurd told the Duke of
Dorset on 27 January 1792: 'Paris has for some days past been in a state
of great fermentation ... Among many other idle stories, they have been
circulating with great industry that the Royal Family have again in
contemplation to make their escape.' He passed on a message from
Marie-Antoinette regarding the mission of Talleyrand, the Bishop of
Autun (known as the 'Diable Boiteux' or 'Lame Devil'), who had been
sent to London by the Constitutionals. 'Mrs B. is sorry that you are
obliged to leave London at the debut of the *Diable Boiteux*. She desires
me to say many obliging things and to thank you for your attentions,
which she hopes you will continue.'[171]

While Fersen was waiting in Brussels, the Queen held private
discussions with Craufurd in the Tuileries and with the Russian
Ambassador Baron Simolin in her apartments. On 31 January Simolin
sent Catherine II an account of a meeting with Marie-Antoinette in her
bedchamber with the door locked – thus proving that she was quite able
to receive visitors in private without fear of discovery. Like Gustav III,
the Empress had given her Ambassador to France an extended leave,
publicizing her refusal to recognize the French constitution. Marie-
Antoinette took the opportunity to entrust Simolin with a private
mission to Vienna. Once again she was trying to stir some fraternal
feeling in Leopold II to persuade him to promote the idea of a congress:
a formal commitment from him would rally everyone else to the idea.
The following extract from Simolin's letter to the Empress – with details
on how he was smuggled into the Tuileries – also clearly demonstrates
that Fersen's mission was doomed to failure, since Louis XVI, passive as
always, did not wish to attempt another escape. The secretary
mentioned by Simolin was doubtless Goguelat.

Baron Simolin to Catherine II, 31 January 1792

That same Sunday evening the Queen sent me, by one of the secretaries in her confidence, word that the following evening at six o'clock she would get this same confidant to fetch me to introduce me into her apartment in a frock coat and overcoat. Her Majesty received me in her bedchamber, and, after having herself locked the outer door, she told me that . . . I found her occupied in drafting the letters she proposed to write to Your Imperial Majesty and to her brother the Emperor. She herself gave them to me to read, asking me if I thought she could add anything to them. She did it having sat down, asking me to be seated near her.

She entered into the details of their position, telling me that Your Imperial Majesty was already informed of their real thoughts on their situation, by the letter she had addressed to you around the Christmas holidays through the Baron de Breteuil, who was charged in their name to correspond with foreign powers. She did me the honour of recounting their escape from the Tuileries, which according to her was discovered through one of her women of the Wardrobe, and told me what has happened to her since 21 June, and there were moments during her recital when her eyes were swimming in tears in spite of herself.

After an hour's conversation the King entered and did me the honour to say that he wished to see me alone before my departure and to confirm what the Queen had told me . . . he added that in St Petersburg and Stockholm they seemed to wish that he could leave Paris, but he did not see any possibility of doing so, nor what would become of him, except to play the role of a pretender.[172]

Simolin arrived in Brussels on 9 February, with a letter from Marie-Antoinette to Mercy, in which she is quite bitter about the Emperor's treatment of her. In the space of a month, she sent both Goguelat and Simolin to Vienna and still seemed to hope for help from Leopold II despite letters from Fersen for four months telling her to abandon all hope of any action from him and to organize the congress without him. This loyalty to her family would prove to be fatal.

Marie-Antoinette to the Comte de Mercy, January 1792

M. de S[imolin] who will be joining you, Monsieur, is kind enough to carry my messages . . . I have begged him to take a letter from me directly to my brother. My total ignorance of the views of the cabinet of Vienna makes my situation more distressing and more critical every day. I do not know what countenance I should have nor what tone to adopt. Everybody accuses me of dissimulation, of deceit, and no one can believe (with reason) that a brother could take so little interest in the dreadful position of his sister and expose her constantly to danger while saying nothing to her. Yes, he is putting me in danger, and a thousand times more than if he were to act . . . The trip that M. de Laborde has just made has made me reflect on my money in his bank. I would very much like him to place it in England. See if you would care to write to him about it, or let me know what you think about it.[173]

The last sentence seems to indicate that the Queen at least approved of Gustav's escape plan, since he wanted the Royal Family to leave France for England. Fersen would carry dispatches with full details to Paris; he most certainly would have given some indication about them to Marie-Antoinette in the letters that are now lost. There is very little left of their correspondence for January and February 1792, most of which dealt with their long-delayed reunion (see below).

Fersen to Marie-Antoinette, 1 February 1792, letter missing

After his letter of 30 January in which he agreed to postpone his visit, Fersen wrote to say that it would take place as arranged (on 3 February).

Marie-Antoinette to Fersen, [1] February 1792, letter missing

On 3 February Fersen mentions the arrival of a letter from the Queen.

Marie-Antoinette to Fersen, [3] February 1792, letter missing

Fersen received another letter from the Queen on 6 February. He decides to go ahead with the visit to Paris.

38. FERSEN TO MARIE-ANTOINETTE, 6 FEBRUARY 1792

AN 440AP/1. Autograph minute of a letter from Fersen to Marie-Antoinette, logged in his letter register: 'Josephine by Goug[enot], according to the minute'. His editorial processes can be clearly seen on this minute, where he has marked sentences he has suppressed with a dotted line. It is another indication that one day he intended to publish the correspondence and his memoirs. He is replying to the letter received the same day from Marie-Antoinette. The redacted passages certainly concerned the visit to Paris, since in his diary he notes that he 'wrote to warn her' of it, yet there is no mention of it in this minute.

To the Queen

6 February 1792

_____ It is essential to extract you from the state you're in and only violent means will get you out. _____ The young archduke said, about the order to the officers, that they were going to receive them so that everything was ready here for 1 March; that 6,000 men had already left and 14,000 others would follow them, that a war against France seemed certain.[174]

M. de Metternich said that at last there would be a change of language, that he was only waiting for the decision of the council of Brabant on the people who were recently arrested in order to deliver a very strong note on the subject to M. de La Gravière. He added that one would soon have more interesting news from Prussia than M. de Ségur's suicide. Despite that, I will believe nothing said on behalf of the Emperor without seeing some effects.[175]

It is said that they want the King to veto the decree on passports. Those who advise this action will afterwards want to present it as a sign of his freedom, and I believe that the King should approve it. The rebels would present his refusal as proof that he wants to leave and keep the means to do so; and as this decree is a vexatious thing which weighs on the people, especially because of the stamp duty, they should be allowed to feel the full burden of it. Besides, despite the King's veto the Jacobins will use their influence to disrupt travellers. The veto will serve no purpose and people will still be obliged to have passports. To counter the arguments for the veto, the King could claim that he needs to prove that he does not want to go away.

Fersen to Marie-Antoinette, 10 February 1792, letter missing

In his register Fersen records a 'Josephine' letter on this date without giving more details.

The Reunion

To understand how Fersen succeeded in sneaking into the Tuileries under the very noses of Lafayette's guards, it is helpful to build up a timeline from his diary and letter register. The very first time he mentioned this visit to Taube, on 30 October 1791, Fersen said that he did not want to be seen. He was still being sought for his role in the Royal Family's escape, and too many people knew him in Paris. He would have to disguise himself and hide. But while proposing to spend the night in Marie-Antoinette's arms – and his letters reveal a great desire to see her again – it appears that he did not entirely trust her. Bizarrely, he organized their reunion with the help of Eléonore Sullivan.

By cross-checking information from his diary with the letter register, it is clear that he always intended to arrive at Marie-Antoinette's apartment in the evening to spend the whole night and the following day with her, before leaving the following evening after having seen the King. In the autumn of 1791 Fersen would have found another trustworthy friend who would hide him before his return to Brussels; but, as Craufurd and Eléonore had returned to Paris on 24 December, he succeeded in getting Eléonore to conceal him in the attic of their house, unbeknownst to Craufurd and Marie-Antoinette, who had regular meetings at the Tuileries. Instead of making a detour as a supposed diplomatic courier towards Spain, Fersen spent a week holed up in Craufurd's house in Paris. The dates of his trip changed, but so did his letters to Marie-Antoinette and Eléonore: he tells the Queen he will arrive at the Tuileries on 3 February and Eléonore that he will see her on the 4th; or the 13th with the Queen and the 14th at Craufurd's house. And since he had to spend the whole time there in hiding, afraid to make a sound, Eléonore had to know he had come expressly to Paris for a private reunion with Marie-Antoinette. He would not have undertaken a very dangerous journey to Paris for the sole pleasure of reading four or five novels hidden in Craufurd's garret.

Why was Marie-Antoinette kept in ignorance of this secret stay in Craufurd's house? Did Fersen keep it from her for fear of betrayal by a spy in her household or fear that she might guess at a liaison with Eléonore? Or was he more afraid and suspicious of the Queen's contacts with the Constitutionals? Clearly Craufurd could not know he was in Paris because he would have told Marie-Antoinette, and Fersen was in fact annoyed when she alerted Craufurd of his supposed 'return' from his journey to the south. It would seem that Fersen's jealousy of Barnave, coupled with Marie-Antoinette's continual refusals to grant him permission to come, had given rise to a certain mistrust. He would realize – far too late – how ill-founded his suspicions were

.

Letters from Sweden to Fersen about an Escape Plan for the Royal Family and His Visit to Paris in February 1792

Baron Evert Taube to Fersen

16 December 1791

He [Gustav III] wants the King of France and the Queen to leave France. He believes that if they do not succeed in getting out of France it will perhaps be impossible to free them from the hands of their assassins. His idea is that they go by sea, that there is a little English ship at [*illegible*] or some other port ready to take them aboard, which would transport them to Ostend or the first port in Flanders . . . The secret must be confided to only two people at the most: to the man who will drive them from Paris to the sea and to the one who takes them aboard. Do not trust a single native in this matter. Only the English must be employed; they have the necessary daring and generosity for this action.

20 December 1791

The courier I told you about is ready to leave in five days with every-thing you asked for – recall of the Swedish and Russian ambassadors, the two passports and credentials for Lisbon in case you should need them.

30 December 1791

In God's name, be careful. I dream of you at night, I'm so worried. Take no one into your confidence.[176]

Gustav III to Fersen, 22 December 1791

I regard it as absolutely essential for the success of all our plans that the Royal Family escapes from Paris as soon as possible. I therefore recommend that, above all, you exert your influence to persuade the King of France to take this course, on which everything else depends . . . You will develop better than can be done in writing, the expedient of a disguise, which I have simply indicated as the safest way, in telling the King and Queen of the necessity of sacrificing on this occasion, for such a vital interest, comforts whose momentary privation cannot be compared to the object of this exercise, on which depends the fate of the kingdom and the Royal Family. But for that reason it is essential that the King takes a different route from the Queen with the Dauphin and Madame Elisabeth; and if the King wishes, as I believe would be most helpful, to travel through England, while the rest of the Royal Family finds it better to take an entirely opposite direction, their reunion must not be fixed until the place where they embark for England. Without this precaution the scenes of Varennes could easily recur.[177]

Fersen's diary and letter register: visit to Marie-Antoinette, February 1792

(D)	Fersen's Diary
(LR)	Fersen's Letter Register
Her (Diary) and Josephine (Letter Register)	Marie-Antoinette
El.	Eléonore Sullivan
Lui	Quintin Craufurd
Gog	François Goguelat

JANUARY 1792

21 The Queen consents that I go to Paris. (D)

24 My journey to Paris fixed for 3 February. (D) [*Friday 3 February*]

24 Josephine by post. (LR)

26 Josephine: all the manner of coming. (LR)

29 Eléonore: that it's the 4th at 9.30 p.m. (LR) [*Saturday 4 February*]

29 Letter from *Her* which begs me to postpone my journey until the decree on passports is pronounced and Paris is a little calmer again. (D)

30 Josephine: that I will postpone, but after a fortnight it can no longer happen. (LR)

30 Eléonore: that I'm no longer coming. (LR)

31 Received letters: that I can come, but I must wait for Simolin's arrival. (D)

31 Eléonore: that I'm coming.

FEBRUARY 1792

1 Josephine: that I'll come Friday or Monday. (LR) [*3 or 6 February*]

2 Eléonore: that I'll come ~~Fri~~ Saturday or ~~Mon~~ Tuesday. (LR) [*4 or 5 February*]

3 Letter from *Her*, that because of individual passports it's impossible to come and I must give it up. That's bad for me and for affairs. They pretended to suspect the King was leaving, created a stir in Paris, and all to stop the new guard assuming its functions, which is fixed for the 10th; and they have introduced passports to prevent the King's departure had it been going to take place. (D)

4 Eléonore: that I'm no longer coming at all. (LR)

6 Decided to go to Paris after receiving a letter from the Queen, who tells me the decree on passports won't be approved and some French people have travelled successfully; wrote to notify her. (D)

6 Josephine by Goug[enot]: according to the minute. (D)

9 Simolin arrived at 11 o'clock without difficulty. (D)

9 Josephine by Gog[uelat]: that I'll be with her on Monday evening. (LR) [*13 February*]

9 Eléonore: that I'll be with her on Tuesday evening. (LR) [*14 February*]

10 Josephine. (LR)

10 Made all my preparations to depart. (D)

10 Eléonore: that I'll come on Tuesday. (LR)

Extracts from Fersen's diary, February 1792

Monday 13. Arrived without incident at Paris at 5.30 in the evening without anyone saying anything to us. Left my officer [Reutersvärd] at the Hôtel des Princes, rue de Richelieu. Took a fiacre to go to Gog's house, rue Pelletier. The driver did not know the street. Afraid he would not find it. Another driver pointed it out to us. Gog wasn't there; waited in the street until 6.30 p.m. He didn't come; that worried me. Wanted to go and pick up Reutersvärd. He had not found a room at the Hôtel des Princes. Nobody knew where he had gone. Returned to Gog's. He had not come in. Decided to wait in the street. At last he came at 7 p.m. My letter didn't arrive until midday today, and they couldn't find him before. Went to see _Her_, passed through my usual way. Afraid of the Nat. Guard. [Got to] her lodging perfectly. Did not see the King. Stayed there.

T[uesday] 14. Very fine and mild. Saw the King at six in the evening. He does not want to leave, and he cannot because of the extreme surveillance; but in truth he has scruples about it, having so often promised to stay, because he is an honourable man. He has nevertheless consented that when the armies arrive he will go with smugglers through the forests to meet a squadron of light troops. He wants the congress at first to make only demands and, if they are granted, to insist then that he is allowed out of Paris to go to a specified place for the ratification . . . The Queen told me she was seeing Alex Lameth and Duport, that they constantly told her there was no other remedy but foreign troops; without them all would be lost . . . They speak like aristocrats, but she believes it is the effect of their hatred for the current Assembly, where they are nothing and have no influence . . . she believes they are bad and does not trust them but makes use of them. That's useful . . .

[_Marie-Antoinette on the Royal Family's return from Varennes_] . . . Latour-Maubourg and Barnave behaved very well, Pétion was indecent . . . Pétion said he knew everything, that they had seized a hackney carriage near the palace driven by a Swede named . . . he pretended not to know my name and asked the Queen for it. She replied: 'I'm not in the habit of knowing the names of hackney coachmen.' . . . For six weeks, there were always officers in the antechamber. They wanted to sleep in the Queen's room. All she could obtain was that stayed between the two doors; two or three times they came in the night to see if she were in her bed. One night when she could not sleep and she lit her lantern, the officer came in and settled down and struck up a conversation. There was a camp outside her windows which made an infernal racket all night. The officers in her room were relieved every two hours.

[_Half page blank_]

I said that for the sake of appearances I would make a trip towards Spain as far as Orléans or Tours and that I would be back on Monday or Tuesday. At 9.30 p.m. I left her. I found Reutersvärd at the Pont Royal. We took a hackney to El.'s. I took the same route as with the King; that brought it back to me vividly. At 10 o'clock Frantz let me in. I lodged with Jos. [Josephine, chambermaid], who had two rooms. *Lui* had gone out. We took tea together. At 12.30 I went to bed.

15–18 February [hiding in Craufurd's house] . . . They brought me a little dinner that had been taken from the table on the pretext of giving it to Joseph: When they were alone I had very little, when they had company I had more. I had a good fire and I used to read after dinner. It was necessary to keep very quiet, because the salon was below . . . I had to go to bed very quietly so as not to make a noise . . .

Sunday 19 . . . While they were at the theatre I sent for Reutersvärd; told him to go to the chargé d'affaires Bergstedt with a letter in which I told him everything and asked for a courier's passport.

Monday 20 . . . Bergstedt was very afraid. All was arranged; it would be a courier's passport for Reutersvärd and one for me as his lackey. We agreed on everything in case I was arrested . . . El. had warned me in the morning that Gog. had written to *Lui* to see him. I imagined that having said I would be returning on Monday or Tuesday *She* wanted to let him know so he would be at home. Useless precaution which vexed me. Gog came at 6 o'clock. El. went to the theatre, but *Lui* stayed at the house with Gog waiting for me. They left at 8.30 . . .

Tuesday 21 . . . At 6 I went out. I found Reutersvärd, with whom I made all the arrangements to leave at midnight . . . He took a note to El. in which I had the air of announcing my arrival, asking to see *Lui*. I was smuggled in. We played our parts well. He believed it. I wrote a note to *Her* that I had arrived. Gog came. She told me that the reply to the bad memorandum she had sent to the Emperor written by Barnave, Duport and Lameth had just arrived and it was detestable. I took tea and supper with them [Eléonore and Craufurd]. I told *Lui* the same story I had told *Her* about my supposed journey. At midnight I left them. Frantz let me out by the front door. We could not find Reutersvärd, which troubled me. He came after half an hour. We went to his inn, the Prince Royal, rue Croix des Petits Champs . . . I found my little dog Odin there, which he had fetched for me . . . At one o'clock we got into the carriage. I had nothing in my pockets thatcould betray me, nor did he; however, I was not very reassured, and as it was Mardi Gras there were many drunk national guards everywhere. It was because of that I didn't leave the day before as I wished.

Thursday 23 . . . At 4 o'clock we were at Tournai; we dined well there and in the same room we had slept in on going out – what a difference! I wrote a line to Paris and at 5.30 we left . . . we went to Brussels, where we arrived at three o'clock in the morning. My joy was great to have succeeded so well and to find myself back home.[179]

The Cruel Separation

Fersen's official mission, to persuade Louis XVI to attempt a fresh escape, had been a resounding failure. As regards his private visit to Marie-Antoinette, he indeed wrote the words 'stayed there' after his arrival *chez Elle* on 13 February 1792 (they were crossed out in a manner reminiscent of Baron Klinckowström's deletions on the letters). He spent the whole night and the following day with the Queen before his meeting with Louis XVI, who was as reluctant as ever to take any daring measures. It seems that Fersen then tried to persuade Marie-Antoinette to escape alone, which she refused to do. And when he left her, he made her believe he was travelling to Tours or Orléans, when in fact he was holed up in Craufurd's attic in Paris. Why did he lie to Marie-Antoinette about it? It also seems very strange that after a separation of eight months she did not ask to see him again when he sent her a note on 21 February announcing his 'return' to Paris, even though she had showered him with words of love in her letter of 4 January.

On 14 February 1792 there is a good half-page blank in Fersen's diary, at the end of the report of his conversation with 'the Queen'. He starts again at the bottom of the page with 'I said that for the sake of appearances . . . ' so it appears that he had been going to add more details and then thought better of it. 'What a difference!' he remarked nine days later, finding himself in the same room of the same inn at Tournai as on the outward journey to Paris. These words deserve some attention, given the marked chilliness in the tone of the letters he wrote to Marie-Antoinette after his return to Brussels. His letters for March 1792, particularly on 4 March, are written in such a formal style, so alien to the easy and familiar tone of their exchanges before the Paris visit, that they betray the resentment of a spurned lover. Various other factors support this hypothesis.

'There would be no more happiness for us if we were separated for ever,' an imprisoned Marie-Antoinette wrote to Fersen after Varennes. This dreaded separation had nevertheless finally arrived. Both Fersen's diary and letter register confirm that in his opinion a profound change occurred in their relationship in February 1792. In the diary, written up on his return to Brussels, he is remarkably mute on intimate details about the Queen. There is absolutely nothing about *Her* in fact: not on her health, or her looks (Gouverneur Morris and Mme Campan both mention Marie-Antoinette's hair turning white in the summer of 1791), nor any of those little details which enliven a journal and which Fersen, despite a very dry style, sometimes liked to record. It is even very sparing on politics, her dealings with the Constitutionals, the reasons for her strategy. And yet she was the woman he loved madly, the woman he had longed to see for months. In 1793 he would scour newspapers for every little mention of her, he interrogated émigrés who arrived in Brussels who had seen her, and every last detail about Marie-Antoinette is recorded in his diary. But on 13 and 14 February 1792, seeing her again after a long absence during which both had suffered terribly, Fersen's diary is as uninformative as Louis XVI's on the subject of the Queen of France.

Turning to the letter register, after 24 February 1792 Fersen only logs a single letter to Marie-Antoinette under the heading 'Josephine' on 15 May 1792. From 4 March all his letters to her are recorded to 'the Queen of France'. This is a crucial distinction. It suggests that for him, at least, there had been a major change in the nature of their relationship. Where is the intimacy of yore? The frequency and tenor of their correspondence before the visit to Paris did not presage a break-up (despite the Queen's great reluctance to give him permission to come), so something clearly happened during their reunion. It would seem that after having made love – for the last time – on 13 February Marie-Antoinette told Fersen she would not leave Louis XVI and her children to flee with him. Quintin Craufurd's memoirs are quite interesting on this subject.

In March and April 1792 I had the means and the certainty of taking her to Brussels; but she always said that she would never separate from the King or her children. History presents no example of a more sublime devotion. She refused to save her life by a feeling of duty to her spouse; the feeling of maternal love made her brave a death she could regard as certain.[180]

Doubtless Fersen would have tried in vain to make her change her mind, for he was a persistent man. It may well be that they had a lively discussion, and things were said in the heat of the moment he later regretted. Perhaps his jealousy got the better of him and he scolded her once too often about Barnave. Did she express suspicions with regard to Eléonore Sullivan? It would be most unlike Fersen to give up any plan on which he had set his heart; he would have tried his utmost to persuade her to save herself. If the King did not wish to leave, that did not mean the Queen could not leave him. Her sister Archduchess Marie-Christine was governor of the Austrian Netherlands; it would be easy to join her there. On 28 February, four days after his return to Brussels, Fersen logged a letter to Craufurd in his register: 'sent the route'.[181] It was doubtless the route for Marie-Antoinette's escape escorted by Craufurd. But she remained inflexible, and Fersen noted bleakly in his diary on 22 March: 'I don't think she will ever separate from the King.'[182]

He was devastated. He had been rejected by the woman he had loved for over a decade ... in favour of Louis XVI, a man he had never for a single moment considered a rival. The glacial tone of his letters to the Queen in March 1792 betrays his hurt and resentment. But how could she forget she was both a queen and a mother? According to Craufurd, it was duty alone that led her to stay with her husband. But that had not stopped her giving herself body and soul to Fersen long before February 1792; on 4 January she was still telling him that she loved him madly, and when he arrived in Paris on his extremely hazardous mission he was still madly in love with her. Had he perhaps asked for too much? He had given her an ultimatum about his visit ('I shall postpone, but after another fortnight it will not be possible'), which could also relate to an escape plan. And so he went, brimful of hope that he could take her back to Brussels with him ... but she then refused to leave. Her role as queen brought with it heavy responsibilities, and her maternal heart would have revolted at the thought of leaving her children – even for a short while. To flee at this juncture with Fersen would not only have created the most enormous scandal it would also have granted the dearest wish of her enemy Lafayette, who was still plotting to get rid of her by forcing the King to divorce her and having her locked up in a convent. It would have meant abandoning a hapless Louis XVI to his inertia, the end of the monarchy and the start of the civil war she had so long tried to avoid.

One cannot exclude the possibility either that as Sophie had feared, Marie-Antoinette had got wind of Fersen's liaison with Eléonore Sullivan. Sophie had warned him that 'everyone is watching you and talking about you – think of the unhappy _Her_, spare her the most mortal of all pains'.[183] Leopold II, who wanted to exclude Sweden from European politics, would not have hesitated to discredit Fersen by spreading rumours among courtiers at the Tuileries on his life in Brussels. It is worth noting that a month after her last meeting with Fersen Marie-Antoinette admits to having a broken heart in a letter to Mme de Polignac. 'Your two letters, both as amiable as you are, reached me a long time ago, my tender friend; I shed tears of affection over them as I do with all your letters, and my poor broken heart really needed to reply to you.'[184] Who else would she want to pour out her sorrows to but Mme de Polignac, her closest friend, who knew everything about her liaison with Fersen? The expression 'my poor broken heart', rather than conjuring up the image of a sovereign strengthened by the knowledge she has done the right thing, evokes a woman who is deeply wounded. How else would she have felt, if, surrounded by danger and bearing the full burden of diplomatic negotiations to rescue the monarchy, she discovered that Fersen had been unfaithful to her at such a critical moment as the Royal Family's escape in June 1791? And yet she loved him too much to break with him completely.

Fersen, too, was deeply affected by his final meeting with Marie-Antoinette. They would have both known that her refusal to escape was fatal. On his return to Brussels, the effect on his health was immediate. He could not eat, he felt weak, he stopped writing his diary for two days. He displayed classic symptoms that follow an emotional shock. On 25 February he noted: 'My stomach not good, malaise, extreme weakness', and on 26th and 29th, 'I wasn't well.'[185] On 17 March he writes a deplorable summary of his physical condition: he still had difficulty eating, was very thin, suffered from bouts of weakness and intestinal problems. On 24 February he had logged his penultimate letter to 'Josephine', in which he perhaps tried to get Marie-Antoinette to change her mind. On the 28th he sent the route for the escape to Craufurd. She replied on 2 March – but the woman had to sacrifice herself for the queen.

Fersen had no choice other than to accept Marie-Antoinette's decision; but he did so with profound bitterness. As his old friend Mme de Korff, who had known him since he was eighteen, justly remarked, he had 'a burning soul inside a shell of ice'.[186] Great self-control and reserve always dominated his character and gave him a dignified manner, but it cost him enormously not to be able to express his feelings, and so his health suffered. His papers, however, reveal that he, too, had a 'poor broken heart'. Marie-Antoinette still had absolute confidence in Fersen and insisted that he continued to work with Breteuil to negotiate with foreign powers; moreover he was Gustav III's special envoy to the King and Queen of France, so he could not suddenly abandon them. He would continue to fulfil his duties – to the letter. Marie-Antoinette was no longer 'Josephine' in his letter register but 'the Queen of France'. He began to write to her in an extremely cold and formal style. All his dispatches – for it is impossible to call them letters – betray his acute disappointment.

Fersen's letter register for that painful month of March 1792 contains some very curious annotations. He records a letter to Quintin Craufurd in Paris on 9 March: 'on the death of the Emperor, referred him to the letter to Rozina', and on 11th, again to Craufurd, 'a note for Rozine on M. de Bounay's journey'. He had also written to 'the Queen of France on the death of the Emperor' on 9 March. On 2 March Marie-Antoinette, who saw Craufurd regularly at the Tuileries, wrote to Fersen: 'I see from a letter of Mr Craufurd's that you refer him to me for details.' (See below.) If all that was being discussed was politics, it made sense to refer Craufurd to the Queen for news, since it saved writing two letters on the same topic. However, there is no correspondent named 'Rozina' or 'Rozine' in the letter register, and all letters sent to Eléonore Sullivan are logged under 'Eléonore' or 'Mme Sullivan'. To what other woman could Fersen refer Craufurd, to save himself the trouble of copying out a letter on the Emperor's death, if not to Marie-Antoinette?

His use of the code name 'Rozina' for Marie-Antoinette in the letter register, just after their meeting in February, is highly significant. 'Rozina' refers to a very specific character. Fersen adored opera and the theatre, he played music and he knew many opera scores and plays; he had also attended many performances with the Queen. He would not have forgotten that in happier days at the Petit Trianon she herself had played the part of Rosina in Mozart's *The Marriage of Figaro*, based on Beaumarchais's wildly successful play of the same name (in which the character is 'Rosine') – the very same Rosina who gives up Cherubino, who is madly in love with her, to reconcile with her husband. Fersen would certainly not have chosen this code name for the Queen unless he found it particularly appropriate.

It may well be that this rupture caused Fersen to burn all his private correspondence with Marie-Antoinette for the period 1780–91. This explains better than any other theory why there is no trace of the 'Josephine' letters prior to 1791. From Baron Klinckowström's notes and manuscript it appears that he never saw them and that he had only the correspondence from June 1791 with the exception of five official letters from 1788 and 1789 that Fersen had kept with his letter register. We know that Klinckowström or his son burnt a considerable number of letters for the period 1791–2; but the earlier 'Josephine' letters may well have met a similar fate immediately after Fersen returned to Brussels in February 1792, feeling rejected and bitter.

However, the story does not end there. The assassination of Gustav III on 29 March 1792 seemed to reignite Fersen's feelings – or rather hopes, since his feelings for Marie-Antoinette never died. After they had both exchanged very business-like letters for several weeks, without a single word of tenderness, there are once more deleted lines in two letters from April 1792 after Gustav's brutal death. On 24 April Fersen writes again to his 'dear and tender friend', and on 15 May he records a letter to her under the heading 'Josephine' – the very last, as it happened. But from June 1792, with war making communication extremely difficult, almost all their letters passed through the Queen's secretary François Goguelat. For the most part her letters are also written by Goguelat, and Fersen's replies are logged under the 'Queen of France' in the register. It is impossible to say, therefore, if Marie-Antoinette had relented. Certainly they appear to have got closer again, but, as long as Louis XVI lived and she remained in such a delicate and dangerous position, how could she have gone back on such a painful decision? Her letters to Fersen in May 1792 have not survived, and at the end of May, finally recovered from his malaise, he profited from Quintin Craufurd's brief absence from Brussels to resume his affair with Eléonore Sullivan. The great joy he had known with the Queen of France was now nothing but a memory.

Marie-Antoinette to Fersen, 21 February 1792, letter missing

In his diary Fersen mentions receiving a note from the Queen delivered by Goguelat while he was staying at Craufurd's house in Paris.

Fersen to Marie-Antoinette, 23 February, letter missing

At Tournai Fersen noted in his diary: 'I wrote a note to Paris' – presumably to let Marie-Antoinette know he had left France safely.[187]

Fersen to Marie-Antoinette, 24 February, letter missing

On his return to Brussels Fersen recorded a penultimate letter to 'Josephine' in his register – 'Josephine by Hodges'.

On 26 February 1792 Fersen sent Taube an 'official' account of his mission to Paris.

I left here on the 11th, and I arrived in Paris with no difficulty at all at six on the evening of the 13th. I saw their Majesties that evening and again the following evening at midnight. I left again, and to avert suspicion I was obliged to go as far as Tours and came back by Fontainebleau. I returned to Paris on the 19th at six o'clock in the evening. I did not dare risk going to the palace. I wrote to see if they had any orders to give me, and I left at midnight on the 21st. As I had been warned that there would be difficulties in leaving because the municipalities were demanding passports even though the King had not approved the decree, and that many people had been stopped, I took the decision to inform the chargé d'affaires of my journey, and I obtained a courier's passport from him and one from M. de Lessart. This is what delayed my departure, and I remained hidden during that time. I was stopped several times but not recognized, although closely examined, and in a little village of about ten or twelve houses they wanted to arrest us because there was no stamp on the passport, and it was only by telling them we were foreign couriers that they let us through, after detaining us there an hour. But it is impossible that my journey will ever be discovered. I am fairly content with my trip, even though I could not bring about what the King [of Sweden] wished. An escape is physically impossible at the moment because of the extreme surveillance.[188]

However, the Swedish chargé d'affaires Bergstedt had felt it necessary to inform Stockholm of his fears on the very day of his meeting with Fersen in the snow outside Craufurd's house. It is clear that Fersen had disobeyed a direct order from Gustav III to give up his mission because of the need for passports. Taube sent him a severe reprimand on 13 March before receiving word of his safe return to Brussels.

> I cannot describe to you, my friend, the state of panic the King [Gustav] and I have been in since yesterday morning, when Silversparre came to read the King a letter from Bergstedt. You have committed there, my friend, more than an imprudence in taking such a risk in going to Paris since the decree on passports. Even if the Good Lord should bring you back, which can only happen by a miracle, you have struck death into the hearts of your friend and the King by the dreadful fears and worry the letter from Paris on the 19th has caused us. I am moreover certain that should some misfortune befall you it will be blamed on Vårman ['Our man' – Gustav] and me, and S. [Sophie] will reproach me with it eternally . . . I strongly disapprove of what you have just done. You have endangered Their Majesties and your master and all that you hold dear in the world.[189]

At Stockholm the following year there was still talk about Fersen's visit to Paris. On 8 February 1793 Reutersvärd assured him that the secret was safe: 'Rest assured that I will speak of the journey to Paris as we agreed . . . that we arrived at Paris in the evening, left the following day, and that on our return we stayed for two days to get passports from Bergstedt.'[190] Given that the diary for the trip was written up on Fersen's return to Brussels, a question mark does rather hang over what exactly he did during his week in Paris and why such secrecy was essential.

Marie-Antoinette's decision to stand by the King to the bitter end had repercussions on Fersen's health for several weeks. 'I wasn't well,' he noted, even at the beginning of April.[191] But he was always very professional, and he continued to draft his dispatches with his customary rigour. On 29 February he reported to Gustav III that Marie-Antoinette had seemed favourable to the proposed escape. 'The Queen, above all, feels keenly all its advantages and assured me that the failure of their first attempt of this kind would never deter them from a second.' But Louis XVI had flatly refused to consider flight when he spoke to Fersen on 14 February, telling him that the counter-revolutionaries should 'put me completely to one side' in their plans and 'leave me alone'.[192] In other words, he had no intention whatsoever of helping himself or allowing his allies to help him. In such circumstances, Marie-Antoinette's decision to stay with him was suicide; it is no wonder Fersen was so upset.

The Queen alone now seemed to be responsible for trying to salvage the monarchy. Madame Elisabeth confirms her key role in politics after the Royal Family's return from Varennes in a letter to her brother the Comte d'Artois on 23 February 1792, just after Fersen's visit.

> I find that the son [Artois] is too severe towards the mother-in-law [the Queen]. She does not have the faults she is accused of. I believe she may have listened to questionable advice, but she supports the troubles which beset her with great courage and she must be pitied rather than blamed, for her intentions are good. She seeks to settle the doubts of the father [Louis XVI], who, to his family's misfortune, is no longer the master, and, God willing I am mistaken, but I greatly fear that she will be one of the first victims of everything that's happening, and my heart is too full at this foreboding to cast any blame . . . You know the difference in habits and society there has always been between your sister and the mother-in-law; despite that, one feels closer to her when one sees her unjustly accused and when one looks to the future. It is very unfortunate that the son did not wish or try to win over the intimate friend of the mother-in-law's brother [Mercy]. That old fox is misleading her, and it would have been wise to take it upon oneself, if possible, and make the sacrifice of coming to an understanding with him to thwart him and prevent the damage which has now become frightening.[193]

Madame Elisabeth, who certainly had never approved of Fersen (he mentions it in his diary), nevertheless shared his view about Mercy's role and the Austrians' duplicity. Leopold II, who was in perfect agreement with Mercy, never stopped sowing discord between his sister, the princes and the countries that were in favour of the armed congress Marie-Antoinette had been asking for since the summer of 1791. On the very day that Fersen returned to Brussels Leopold launched a smear campaign against him, writing to the Archduchess Marie-Christine: 'French affairs continue the same, as do my dispositions. I am warning you to beware of all of them but, above all, of Count Fersen, whose falseness and animosity against you and me and even the Queen is known to me.'[194] Seeing that diplomatic efforts to convene a congress without his participation were beginning to bear fruit, the Emperor – with the deviousness at which he excelled – hoped to discredit the man who had done the most to promote it on Marie-Antoinette's behalf. Fersen suspected that Mercy had slandered him, and the confidentiality of his correspondence with the Queen was called into question.

> 27 February. Breteuil . . . warned me that Mercy has complained of the discontent the Queen has shown with the Emperor, that he believes I am the cause of it, and gave to understand that he had found it out. That could only be by my letters, and I do.not think he could have decoded them. The Swedish cipher is too difficult, and my letters sent to Paris in invisible ink would not have arrived if they had been read . . . M. de Mercy let it be known that I was highly suspect and very inconvenient.[195]

A letter from Marie-Antoinette to Mercy on 2 March completely refutes her brother's accusations. 'You know that the King and I have complete confidence in the Baron de Breteuil and the Comte de Fersen . . . they know how to discuss affairs better than I do. Deal with them: they know our intentions and our position perfectly.'[196]

Her correspondence with Fersen had restarted the moment she knew he was back in Brussels.

Marie-Antoinette to Fersen, February 1792, letter missing

This letter is No. 1 in the series that started after Fersen left Paris.

39. MARIE-ANTOINETTE TO FERSEN, 2 MARCH 1792

AN 440AP/1. Autograph decrypt by Fersen of a coded letter from the Queen. It is numbered 2, so therefore went by post. The first letter in the series is missing. There are deletions at the beginning and end of this letter, where one normally finds intimate words, but the words are illegible to the naked eye.

Received 5 March, rep. 6th
No. 2

2 March [1792]

[½ *line deleted*] M. de La Porte hasn't received any newspapers for a month. I am worried that you may have written that way, the more so as I saw in a letter of Mr Craufurd's that you refer him to me for details. I have received nothing from you since your return. We must not use newspapers any more; it is likely that they are being stopped. The dispatch from Vienna has caused a great stir here; as for me, I do not understand it. I greatly fear it is yet more ill will. It is clear that he wants to gain time in order to do nothing.[197] M. Goguelat has sent you all the papers about that. Adieu [2½ *lines deleted*]

During March 1792, Fersen sent only six letters to Marie-Antoinette, all of them logged in his register under the heading 'the Queen of France'. They are more like dispatches. One can picture her dismay, reading that he hoped 'to continue to merit the very flattering confidence with which you have so graciously honoured me'. He would have been more amiable to an old friend with whom he had never had a romantic liaison; from regularly punctuating his letters with 'my tender friend' and writing the most ardent declarations of love, he changed to the turgid diplomatic prose and polite formulations to be found in the correspondence of two diplomats who scarcely knew each other – 'what a difference' indeed!

40. FERSEN TO MARIE-ANTOINETTE, 4 MARCH 1792

AN 440AP/1. Autograph copy of a letter from Fersen to Marie-Antoinette sent in invisible ink. It comprises a note from the Baron de Breteuil with Fersen's letter written in the margins. He informs the Queen of Mercy's complaints against him, adding: 'I don't doubt they will use all possible means to give me a bad name with you, even by making up stories.' This letter is logged to the 'Queen of France' in his register and it is all business.

4 March, invisible ink by Goguelat

Brussels, 4 March [1792]

I am sending you a note the Baron de Breteuil has given me. He is in most pressing need, and I hope you will grant his request. This is what he says:

'I am obliged to return to the pressing need for money I face in order to meet the daily expenses of the persons employed in the service, in to-ing and fro-ing. I have already advanced a great deal for this, and I cannot carry on much longer without getting into serious difficulties, which will harm both affairs and my personal standing. I request that 300,000 [*livres*] is transferred and placed at my disposal, to remove all worries regarding current measures and those which circumstances may subsequently require. Besides, I must tell you frankly, and with the confidence I owe to your kindness, that I no longer have the means to subsist without help from the King. In the three years since his benefits and my rents have been seized, I have lived off the little I could draw on from my estate and the successive sales of my finest possessions. The sequestration depriving me of the yield from my estate, my silverware exhausted, I cannot prevent myself, however much it pains me, from becoming a charge on the King, and I beg His Majesty to grant me 6,000 *livres* a month for my current expenses; that makes 72,000 for the year. I have reduced my expenditure to this sum, restricting myself to simple necessity and what is decent. I only request this help from the King in begging that I be permitted to repay it the day I can obtain the arrears of my sequestered income once I regain my assets.'

The baron's request is very fair. He has no resources and is about to lose everything he owns on St Dominique. He could be sent 150,000 *livres* for current expenses and 30,000 *livres* for his expenses. That would be for six months; if you like, remit this money to Perregaux as though to me, asking him to transfer it to me. But he should be given much more, because it is necessary to have the whole sum here, and, for the rest, if you wish I will see if you can borrow some in Holland. It would only cost you 5 per cent instead of 60 or 70. As for the money I have for you, I will send you an account in a few days. It is however insufficient for this expense and it would be better to keep it; it will be useful to find it again one day. See if you can find someone in Paris who can obtain a loan of 200,000 *livres* for you in Holland or elsewhere – but outside the kingdom – and take it. You would gain greatly by it, and if you would like to remit it to me here at the bank of Mssrs Danoot, fils and Co., I would give it to the baron only on your authorization.

M. de Mercy has complained to the baron about the dissatisfaction you have expressed regarding the Emperor's conduct. He suspects me of being the cause and has given to understand that he found it out. I believe it is only a suspicion, because all my letters have reached you and if he had revealed the handwriting he could not have forwarded them. It is also impossible that he could have deciphered my letters to the King, but the baron has warned me that they consider me very suspect and very inconvenient and that often M. de Mercy recommends that he does not tell me what he has confided to him. After all that I do not doubt that they will use all possible means to give me a bad name with you, even by making up stories. Although I ought to hope that my zeal and my devotion are too well known to you to fear that you would believe them, I nonetheless dare to request that you do not leave me in ignorance of them, so that I may rebut them and continue to merit the very flattering confidence with which you have so graciously honoured me.

The news from Prussia is still good. Mr Craufurd is charged to communicate it to you. The King of Prussia wants to lead his army himself. M. de Mercy is delighted by the Emperor's response. He boasted to the baron that he was the author of it.

Fersen's letter of 6 March 1792 contains important instructions on the precautions to be taken to ensure the confidentiality of his correspondence with the Queen. But they both had vast experience of all the required techniques for a secret correspondence – code, invisible ink, intermediaries and so on. If he felt it necessary on his return from Paris to provide so many fresh instructions, it seems to be because henceforth their correspondence would all pass through the Queen's secretary, François Goguelat. In this context, letters for Marie-Antoinette alone deal with political matters (we know that Goguelat knew nothing of her correspondence with the Constitutionals; see letter of 4 January 1792).

41. FERSEN TO MARIE-ANTOINETTE, 6 MARCH 1792

AN 440AP/1. Autograph copy of a letter from Fersen, recorded in his register to 'the Queen of France, invisible ink, replied to hers of the 2nd.' Note that there are deletions in Marie-Antoinette's letter of the 2nd. Note, too, that the '49 –' at the beginning of this letter means that it was for her eyes only; but there is no intimacy, nor are there deletions or gaps. Fersen simply issues orders that put his correspondence with Marie-Antoinette on an entirely different footing, making her aware that henceforth it would be strictly official. One cannot wonder that she wrote shortly after receiving this letter that she had a 'poor broken heart'.

Fersen remains very much in his dignity, very aloof. He tells her that he referred Quintin Craufurd to papers sent to her by the Baron de Breteuil, confirming that he tended to refer Marie-Antoinette and Craufurd to letters he wrote to both of them, and above all that 'Rozina' was the pseudonym he employed for the Queen in his letter register immediately after his return from Paris. His response to the Queen's enquiry about newspapers is designed to show her that there will be no need for them since he will be sending her nothing private – one recalls that they started using the Journal de Brabant *so he could 'say what he liked' in his letters.*

6 March, invisible ink

49 – by Gog.

No. 2, 6 March [1792]

I received your No. 2 yesterday. The details to which I referred Mr Craufurd are contained in the baron's papers, which he sent to you. As newspapers are no longer being used, they have not been sent for the past two months and will not be sent except when there is a need for them. Tell M. de La Porte to give them to you when he receives any.

The Emperor's response is political gibberish, an appeal that says nothing, and that is the only favourable way of looking at it. One cannot reconcile it with what he proposed to Berlin except by supposing that he reserves the right, if he is eventually forced to take action, to make the subtle distinction between his conduct as head of the house of Austria and as head of the Empire; and in this case it is clear that he only wanted to gain time to spare himself an invasion and have the time to put himself in readiness. If he is still acting in bad faith, which is more likely, his reply serves him perfectly. I believe both suppositions. I believe that he still wants to avoid having to act, but that he is afraid of being forced to do so by the other powers and that he only consented to the King of Prussia's proposal to bring their forces up to 50,000 men each in the hope that he would thereby exclude the northern courts, by representing to them that this force is more than sufficient and that it would be futile to employ any more. And if he cannot achieve that, to be so superior [in numbers] that they will find themselves subordinated to the course he wishes to prescribe, and then he can create a government in France according to his wishes which will make the kingdom dependant on him, deprive it of its strength and prevent it from ever regaining the consideration in Europe it had. But he does not feel that with the influence of the Empress, Prussia's goodwill and the Duke of Brunswick's ambition it will be easy to thwart this plan; and it is then that the princes can be useful to you, because the friendly powers will seem to yield to the demands of the princes, which will have been dictated secretly by you.

It is essential to agree on the arrival of troops from the different countries on the frontiers, and I have written to the King of Sweden and to Russia and Spain that I believed it would be necessary to sacrifice everything to obtain this agreement, and while they were on the march one could discuss the issue of the King's lack of liberty and of the location of the congress, whose convocation becomes daily less important and perhaps futile. It is from this view of the Emperor's plans that I counselled the baron not to hurry and to make sure he specified in the promise of the reimbursement of costs demanded by M. de Mercy that it would only be once the King was re-established in the fullness of the authority he had before the Revolution. M. de Mercy boasted that he had written the Emperor's reply.

Goguelat must be notified that every time there is a number and a dash above the code, for example 49–, **that will mean that the letter is for you only, that it is in invisible ink and the code is meaningless. If there is a full-stop or a colon, 49:** that means that there is a code up to the first big full-stop; the rest means nothing and there will be invisible ink. If there is 49, that is, a dash underneath, then the letter will be for him; the code will mean nothing unless there is a full-stop or colon after the number. If there is handwriting after such a number, there will be invisible ink between the lines. It will be necessary to warn him about it. When you write to me in future it would be better to write in invisible ink between the lines of a code which means

I LOVE YOU MADLY

nothing, because they can find out the code here. In that case there will have to be a dash after or under the code and no full-stop after, to let me know. It will be necessary to number letters exactly to make sure that none are lost. I am sure they do not open them in Paris; they do not have a good enough system for that.

Leopold II's sudden death on 1 March 1792 at the age of forty-four was considered by Fersen to be favourable for France. His son Archduke Franz, who became King of Hungry and then Emperor on 5 July 1792, had been educated by his uncle Joseph and Fersen expected a much more active policy in favour of Marie-Antoinette from her young nephew.

42. Fersen to Marie-Antoinette, 9 March 1792

The original letter is missing. Fersen noted it in his register to 'the Queen of France on the death of the Emperor'. This transcription is taken from Klinckowström's edition of Fersen's papers.[198] *In his diary on 8 March Fersen records how the news was being received in Brussels:*

> The Vicomte de Vérac, who came to see me in the evening, told me that people in the street fear that it will change and slow down everything, cause delays. I was not of that opinion; I proved it to them and I feel that the baron shared my view. I therefore took my decision to write to the Queen with my opinion on it, which I sent her the next day by post.[199]

Why bother to record that he took a decision to write to the Queen unless to indicate that it was now the exception rather than the rule for him to write unless in reply to a letter from her? His remarks on the Comte de Mercy confirm the Austrian Ambassador's habitual inscrutability. Fersen's tone is less glacial than in his letter of 4 March. He informs the Queen that he has not received the papers she is going to send him: is this her correspondence with Barnave, now kept in the Fersen family archives? He would never have dared to take such a compromising and voluminous correspondence with him when returning to Brussels, given that he was in fact stopped and detained more than once. Marie-Antoinette entrusted this correspondence to Fersen not only for safe-keeping but also to prove to him that it was entirely political in nature – 'I would die if for one moment I were condemned by the being I adore,' she had told him on 9 July 1791. He would indeed be hard put to find a single sign of affection in her letters to Barnave.

Fersen also recorded a letter to Quintin Craufurd in his register on 9 March 'on the death of the Emperor, referred him to the letter to Rozina'.

To the Queen in invisible ink by Gog.

No. 3, 9 March 1792

We heard of the Emperor's death yesterday. This news pleases some and troubles others, by the delay they fear this event will cause in affairs. I believe that it is more of an advantage for you. The Emperor is dead, but the Archduke of Austria is not; his power and his interest remain the same, and in this state he can do everything he would have done as emperor and, in accordance with the King of Prussia, grant the same protection to his fellow states as if he were emperor. Both have no other right than that of their influence, founded on their strength, and reasons other than those of general and common interest. Besides, Archduke Franz has always had favourable dispositions, and I know he often criticized his father's slow, half-hearted and indecisive conduct. He has the soul of a soldier, he resembles Joseph more than he does Leopold. This event must increase the King of Prussia's influence still more at the moment; the court of Vienna's interest lies in pleasing him to retain imperial dignity, and from the good intentions of this prince towards you this circumstance must be very favourable for you.

I believe that a letter from you and the King to Archduke Franz would be very useful at the moment. This attention will flatter him and inspire his zeal for you. After having shared his grief on his loss of a father and yours of a brother, you could say to him that you have not been left in ignorance of all the sensibility and interest he has expressed on your fate and that you hope that in light of these sentiments he will give even more activity to the hopes his father had given you; that you are not hesitating to give him the same marks of confidence and repeat your request for the sending of imposing forces on the frontiers and the formation of a congress at Aix-la-Chapelle or Cologne; that you have reason to be assured of the King of Prussia's goodwill, who should already have made proposals similar to your wishes; and that for a long time you have had unequivocal proof of the interest of the courts of St Petersburg, Stockholm and Madrid. You could finish by making him realize how your position imposes the greatest secrecy and particularly with regard to the princes, owing to the indiscretion of their entourage, and by requesting his kindness for the Baron de Breteuil, who has all your confidence. This letter cannot be written too soon. It must be sent to me by the diligence, straight to my address in a box that contains some material for a frock-coat, some waistcoats and new cravats, to make it look more likely and to avoid all suspicion.

I have not yet received the papers from Goguelat, the papers you told me about or the letter for the Queen of Portugal; it will, however, be necessary. Don't forget the question of money. To avoid all suspicion it will be necessary also to write a simple letter of compliments to the Archduke, which you will forward through M. de Lessart, in which you will add something along the lines of those gentleman [the Constitutionals], reminding him briefly of what you already told his father, and how much you hope that he will follow in his father's footsteps and that he will be desirous of maintaining peace with France which is equally advantageous to both countries. But these letters must both arrive at the same time so that the Archduke is not uncertain as to your true intentions.

You could inform M. de Mercy of this step, so that he writes about it. In a conversation he had with the baron, he was fine, and he said: 'It is no longer declarations that are required; the Emperor has finally changed his system.' Then, standing up with warmth and pointing to his sword: 'That's what is needed. The Emperor has made up his mind, and soon we shall have it.' I would have very much liked to witness M. de Mercy's vivacity – it must have presented a quite extraordinary contrast.

Send me the papers and the letter for the Archduke as soon as possible; it is urgent. The baron wants to send M. de Choiseul d'Aillecourt, the deputy, to the Archduke.[200] Let me know what you think of it.

Fersen to Marie-Antoinette, 11 March 1792, letter missing

On 11 March Fersen recorded a letter to Craufurd in his register accompanied by 'a note for Rozine on M. de Bounay's journey'. The previous day in his diary, he wrote: 'M. de Bounay has gone to Paris, no doubt sent by the princes and the Maréchal de Castries to complain about the Baron de Breteuil.'[201] Rozina was indeed Marie-Antoinette. This is the last time Fersen uses this code name in his letter register.

Fersen to Marie-Antoinette, 15 March 1792, letter missing

Fersen recorded a letter in his register on this day to 'the Queen of France, dispatch from Russia, by Craufurd in invisible ink, biscuits', which means the letter was sent via Craufurd in a box of biscuits. 'A dispatch from Russia' does not indicate a private letter.

43. Fersen to Marie-Antoinette, 17 March 1792

AN 440AP/1. Autograph copy of a letter from Fersen to Marie-Antoinette, logged in his register to 'the Queen of France by Gog[uelat], invisible ink'. In his transcription of this letter, Klinckowström put 'half a million' instead of one-and-half million livres *given by Spain to the princes. Once again, Fersen is all business. He outlines the terms of a letter he wants Louis XVI to write to the new Spanish prime minister and presses Marie-Antoinette to send him the letter he asked her to write to her nephew, the King of Hungary. 'I beg you to see nothing in my importunities and solicitations but the good of your service,' he pleads, in stark contrast to his private letter of 26 November 1791, where the highly political content did not prevent him expressing his love at the same time. It is no longer necessary for the Queen to act promptly 'for our happiness' but 'for the good of your service'.*

To the Queen in invisible ink by Goguelat

Brussels, 17 March 1792

I do not consider the change of government in Spain as an evil, and the Comte d'Aranda's known character should be reassuring as to his dispositions towards you. However, one cannot know how far he may be carried by his aversion towards his predecessor and the desire he has to undo everything done by him. In his dispatch to the baron, M. de La Vauguyon regrets the loss of M. de Florida Blanca, without, however, having much notion of his successor's ideas.[202] In this situation I believe a letter from the King to the Comte d'Aranda would be absolutely essential and would have greater effect on a haughty man whose vanity is one of his first passions. It would persuade him in favour of your interests, if he is not so already, and if he is, it can only make him more active and more zealous. In either case, I think it therefore very important to write to him, and, if the King decided to do so, I believe there is not a moment to be lost and it cannot be sent fast enough. I spoke about it to the baron, who thinks as I do and plans to write to him as well.

In this letter the King, after having expressed to the Comte d'Aranda how delighted he is to see the King's [of Spain] choice fall upon a man whose renowned qualities so amply justify the confidence his master shows in him, will remind him of the time he spent in

France and how many reasons the King has to count on his attachment by that which he has always shown to the house of Bourbon. The King would express his desire to be helped by the King of Spain and would speak of his letter to the King of Spain and the measures he has taken with the other courts, whose success must depend on the interest taken by the King of Spain in encouraging their zeal; and that he hopes the Comte d'Aranda will support and strengthen the King of Spain in the goodwill he has already shown and on which he likes to rely. The King would renew the request for the congress or would simply refer him to the letter he has already written to the King of Spain on this subject. He would nominate the Baron de Breteuil as his man of confidence charged with his full powers and would demand that he receives the Comte d'Aranda's trust. He would make him appreciate the necessity for the greatest secrecy and would finish with a compliment that would flatter him and prove to him how important the King thinks he is. It is of interest that this letter be written as soon as possible. The baron will send it by courier.

Spain is giving 4 million [*livres*] to Sweden and 1½ million to the princes. They have sent a plan of operations to the Empress which we shall receive shortly. They consent to the congress, and the Comte d'Ouis has been designated to attend, but this choice will probably be changed by the Comte d'Aranda.

Prussia is still good and the Comte de Schulemberg has said that he considers the Emperor's death as advantageous for French affairs, that it will hasten matters; but the letter I have asked of you for the new king is absolutely essential. The baron will attach one of his own. This step is very urgent, as it the one with regard to the Comte d'Aranda. The last article in my letter to M. Goguelat is the safest, simplest and easiest way to get it to me, but I cannot repeat too often how essential it is that it be done promptly. I beg you to see nothing in my importunities and solicitations but the good of your service. I dare to remind you of the question of money, the baron being without resource in this matter.

In Paris, Marie-Antoinette had far too many worries to reply to all these demands. On 10 March 1792 the Foreign Minister M. de Lessart was denounced in the Assembly. Fersen records it in his diary on the 13th: 'M. de Lessart has been arrested, with his papers, on the orders of the Assembly, and indicted. It's a triumph for the Jacobins.' On 18 March the news was yet more troubling: 'The Chevalier de Coigny had sent the Jacobins' scheme, to put the Queen in a convent or take her to Orléans to be confronted with M. de Lessart.'[203] The Jacobins feared the martial temperament of Franz II, and they wanted to be rid of the Queen before she had a chance to appeal to her nephew for help. Quintin Craufurd sent a letter to the Duke of Dorset with poignant details on this fresh attempt to depose and imprison Marie-Antoinette – a plan devised, as one might have expected, by her long-standing enemies Lafayette and the Duc d'Orléans.

Quintin Craufurd to the Duke of Dorset, 16 March 1792

Paris has for some time been in a state of uncommon fermentation, and the cry against the Queen, since the news of the death of the Emperor, has been renewed and propagated with great industry and zeal. It was evident that something still more serious than the imprisonment of M. de Lessart was intended; indeed, that act of violence was only a prelude to what was proposed, for it has been discovered that a plan has been forming to impeach the Queen, under a variety of articles, which was to have been immediately followed by a decree to arrest her, seize her papers and keep her entirely separate from the King and her children. M. de Lafayette and M. de Narbonne are supposed to have taken part in this conspiracy, but the principal ostensible actors are Condorcet and Pétion. It is to be observed that Lafayette is the lover of Madame Condorcet, who entirely governs her husband. Your Grace may remember what Lafayette said of the Duke of Orléans, yet in one of their secret meetings they affected to be reconciled and embraced; but as they are equally false I dare say they most cordially hate each other.

When the Queen received information of the plot (and from undoubted authority), the blow that was meditated against her was thought inevitable, and perhaps, she observed to me, it is only suspended: yet she never, even for an instant, lost either her fortitude or presence of mind. She sent for Mme Elisabeth and, after informing her of what was carrying on, conjured her never to quit the King and the children, as long as it should be possible for them to remain together. Mme Elisabeth was so violently affected (and probably the more so as she lately had some altercation with the Queen about her brothers) that the Queen was obliged to ring for one of her women.

The children came in, and seeing their mother and aunt in tears burst out crying, and, as if they had known what they were threatened with, clung about their mother and said they hoped <u>they were not going to take them away from her</u>. The Queen, who had hitherto spoken to me with great composure, here burst out into a flood of tears.

The accusation was to have been produced yesterday, but whether they were afraid to risk it, or that they are satisfied with the nominations of the Jacobin minister Mr Dumouriez, it has at least been deferred.[204]

Marie-Antoinette certainly had every reason to loathe Lafayette; this was not the first time he had threatened to take her children from her. Indeed, it had been his plan in November 1790 when he wanted to force the King to divorce her. It is difficult to understand, even more so to forgive this repeated cruelty to a woman and her children, but such was the courage of heroic '*Sans Tort*'. Fersen's pleas to the Queen in July 1792 not to let herself be taken out of Paris under Lafayette's 'protection' were very well founded.

On 29 March, having received Craufurd's letter, the Duke of Dorset spoke of his fears for 'Mrs B' in a letter to the Duchess of Devonshire. More intriguing are his comments on Fersen ('the Roman').

I have been somewhat uneasy for the safety of Mrs B, but *grâce à Dieu* my fears have not been realized. I had a letter the other day from the <u>Roman</u> who is at Bruxelles. His hopes are faint but still he has some; poor fellow, he has enough to think of. He has as yet no particular object in view, although he has a good opinion of the sentiments of the young emperor for his aunt.[205]

44. MARIE-ANTOINETTE TO FERSEN, [15] MARCH,
LETTER MISSING

According to Fersen's diary, on 18 March he received a letter from Craufurd containing details from the Queen herself on this Jacobin plot against her. 'Letter from Craufurd written by Josephine which worried me.'[206] *Note that now his concern for her is heightened Marie-Antoinette is once again 'Josephine'.*

Extracts from Fersen's diary

21 March Worried about Goguelat's arrival, which was [announced] in Craufurd's letter written by Josephine.

22 March The abbé de St Albin arrived from Paris. Letter from Mme de Lamballe to the baron which says they want to denounce the Queen in M. de Lessart's affair and thus separate her from the King and put her in a convent. That matches my letter from Craufurd. I believe in the plan, but I doubt its execution. The abbé de St Albin says that it was believed the Queen would go away. I do not believe she will ever separate from the King, and where would she go; it would be difficult because of Coblentz.

23 March Found Goguelat at home when I returned. He had travelled through Calais, Dover and Ostend. He left six days ago. Their situation is horrifying. I am writing the details in my dispatch to the King of the 24th, with the events that led up to it all. The deputies were heard saying, 'Lessart will get off, but the Queen will not get away with it.'[207]

Marie-Antoinette had entrusted Goguelat with a mission to Vienna to speak directly to her nephew Franz. A letter could be misinterpreted, like all those she had sent to Leopold II. On 21 March 1792, having received 'the letter from Craufurd written by Josephine', Fersen wrote to Taube defending Marie-Antoinette's negotiations with the Constitutionals. She had at last convinced him of the necessity for her political strategy, forced on her by the impossible position in which she found herself.

The Queen is not the dupe of the scoundrels she is forced to deal with; she knows them for what they are ... If like me, my friend, you knew all the details of her relations [with them] far from blaming her you would be forced to admire her courage and to feel sorry for her overwhelming misfortunes and the continual efforts she is forced to make on herself to support their insolence and the ceaseless degradation to which she is exposed.[208]

Marie-Antoinette to Fersen [23] March 1792, No. 1, letter missing

It appears from Fersen's diary that he received a packet from Paris on 27 March. 'Received by the diligence copies of the Emperor's reply to that bad memorandum sent by the Queen and written by Barnave, and a private letter from the Emperor, both equally bad.'[209] These copies are in Goguelat's handwriting and are to be found in the Swedish archives. Interestingly, in January Fersen believed the memorandum had been written by Duport, Lameth and Barnave. After his visit to Paris he attributed it to Barnave alone.

On 30 March 1792 Craufurd and Eléonore Sullivan returned to Brussels. The following day Craufurd told Fersen that 'everything is going badly at Paris. The Queen sent word that they have decided to attack and that warnings should be sent. He found his route covered with very good recruits and artillery.'[210]

Fersen to Marie-Antoinette, 27 March 1792, letter missing

Fersen recorded a letter in his register this day to 'the Queen of France by Gog., in code – that I have received No. 1'.

45. MARIE-ANTOINETTE TO FERSEN, 30 MARCH 1792

*AN 440AP/1. Autograph decrypt by Fersen of a 'cipher from the Queen'.
He clearly had some difficulty in deciphering it, as words in code and
blanks remain in the decrypt. There are no deleted passages in this letter,
in contrast to the letter of 2 March. Marie-Antoinette seems to have
adopted the same tone as Fersen since his return to Brussels. 'I'm very
worried at the moment about the governor for my son,' she wrote – and
with reason, for, the Lessart plot having failed, the Jacobins were now
trying to remove the 'Chou d'Amour' from his governess and usurp the
right to nominate his governor. In giving instructions for the code, Marie-
Antoinette indicates that there may be letters for Fersen alone: was the
'Josephine' correspondence about to start again? 'When my letters have a
second number after one has already been written . . . it will be things that
no longer concern the Baron de Breteuil.'*

Received 3 April
Cipher from the Queen

30 March 1792

I received [*tughkbigygillje*] your letter of the 27th yesterday. This is a
very safe way, and you can always write to me either at that address or
at M. Broune's,[211] but you must number all your letters and number
the first one number 2; that will be even safer. Talk to Mme Sullivan
about a means she discussed with Jarjayes to get **papers** to me . . .
[*paphupaers*] box of biscuits. We need to know the name of the woman
to ask for them at her house, but take care that Mr Craufurd knows
nothing about it; he didn't even want her to see Jarjayes the last time.

What does the new letter from Vienna mean in reply to M. de
Lessart's? It seems to me to be as bad as the last; as for here, everyone
thinks it is superb and an excellent policy. It is certain that it will make
us really decide to attack. Only the reply to M. Dumouriez's letter is
awaited first.[212] I have sent word to M. de Mercy. The plan is to attack
by Savoy and the countryside around Liège. It is to be hoped that,
there still being insufficient troops on those two fronts, something
may be achieved. Turin was warned [*epartoi*] three weeks ago. It is
essential to take precautions around Liège. A M. de Naillac who used
to live in Vienna with Cardinal de Rohan is being sent to
Zweibrücken, and M. Chauvelin goes as Ambassador to London.[213]

I'm very worried at the moment about the governor for my son. We have decided on M. de Fleurieu, but we don't know yet when we will tell him.[214]

Mr Craufurd will have told you about a way to write to me in Italian without code. Don't forget to send me the list of names.[215] When my letters have a second number after one had already been written, it will be from the first volume of [*ectiuhepletyrx*] in all letters. It will be things that no longer concern the Baron de Breteuil. Our situation is still dreadful, however, less dangerous if it is we who attack. The ministers have just got approval for the decree on passports.

Craufurd and Eléonore Sullivan had agreed to rent a house with Fersen when they returned to Brussels. But, despite this proximity, Fersen, who was still suffering from intestinal problems and weakness, was in no condition to forget his problems in Eléonore's arms. And he was completely devastated when he received news on 1 April 1792 that his friend and protector Gustav III had been grievously wounded after being shot in the back at an opera ball in Stockholm on 16 March. He immediately sent word to Paris, not knowing that Gustav had died two days earlier: 'April 1st. Hierta at Paris by a Spanish courier – to communicate to the King and Queen news of the attempt on the King of Sweden's life.'[216]

Marie-Antoinette to Fersen, No. 2, April 1792, letter missing

In his letter to the Queen on 9 April Fersen says he has received her letter 'number 2' in which it is clear she mentioned Gustav's assassination.

46. FERSEN TO MARIE-ANTOINETTE, 9 APRIL 1792

Minute of a letter from Fersen to Marie-Antoinette 'sent in code'. The original is missing and this transcription comes from Baron Klinckowström's edition of Fersen's papers.[217] *It is logged in Fersen's letter register to the 'Queen of France, No. 2 – replied to No. 2 by Goguelat'. It would appear that the beginning of this letter has been suppressed. The tone is now much more normal. Fersen raises the question again of the costs associated with Louis XVI's secret diplomacy, in which Quintin Craufurd was involved to a hitherto unsuspected degree. He had received letters from Sweden indicating that Gustav would recover from his wounds, hence the more optimistic news about him.*

9 April 1792

As for the money, M. de Septeuil[218] should give a draft on his correspondent at London in favour of MM. Danoot fils, either in my name ot Mr Craufurd's. Nothing is simpler, but it needs to be as soon as possible, and that I am warned about it. The sum will be 100,000 écus for current expenses and 36,000 francs for the baron.

I received your No. 2; yes, it is a dreadful event, but one must hope the attempt has failed. The King continues to do well. I am sending you a little account I prepared for you; I am sending it to M. Broune. I will write to you tomorrow by M. d'Agoult, who is going to Paris. I was very sad, but I am a little calmer now.

As M. d'Agoult is leaving this evening, I cannot write to you by him. Besides, without having confirmation of the Comte d'Aranda's intentions, there is nothing interesting to send you. A letter from the King to him would have a good effect.

Fersen to Marie-Antoinette, 9 April 1792, letter missing

Fersen logged a second letter to Marie-Antoinette in his register on 9 April, to 'the Queen of France, relation of the assassination attempt on the King, by Goug[enot]'. In his diary on 8 April he wrote: 'Prepared an account of the assassination attempt on the King which I sent to Paris.' In the preceding letter he says he is addressing it to 'M. Broune', or 'Mr Brown' – in other words, to Louis XVI at Gougenot's address at 2 rue Lepeletier.

A copy of this account is to be found in the Duke of Dorset's papers. Gustav had absolutely no chance, being shot with the eighteenth-century equivalent of an exploding bullet. 'The shot entered the flesh on the left side at the commencement of the hip bone. The pistol was loaded with two balls, one of them square, 12 pieces of lead and 7 small nails.'[219]

Marie-Antoinette to Fersen, No. 3, early April 1792, letter missing

The next surviving letter from the Queen on 15 April is No. 4, which means that No. 3 in the series is missing.

47. MARIE-ANTOINETTE TO FERSEN, 15 APRIL 1792

AN 440AP/1. Autograph decrypt by Fersen of a note from the Queen. Marie-Antoinette is fearful that Goguelat will be followed when returning from his secret mission to Vienna and asks Fersen to warn him. It is interesting to observe that after ten months during which she had tried to avoid a war at all costs she now believes it to be the only way to precipitate a crisis that could save the monarchy. Her first instinct – to avoid war – proved to be correct, for she was surrounded by cowards who could not turn any fresh circumstances to their advantage. One by one, even the enragés would flee, including her arch-enemy Lafayette.

Received 18 April
From the Queen

No. 4, 15 April 1792

M. de Maulde is leaving for Vienna tomorrow.[221] It seems that it is the last [mission] to the King [of Hungary]. They absolutely want war here; so much the better if it makes everyone make up their minds, because our position is no longer bearable. I have received your letter of the 9th. It was not numbered, but I am counting it as number 2. I am worried about M. Goguelat's return. I fear he will be watched. He must take plenty of precautions. Farewell.

It is no longer certain that M. de Maulde will go. I cannot say more about it. I must give my letter. Farewell.

48. FERSEN TO MARIE-ANTOINETTE, 17 APRIL 1792

AN 440AP/1. Autograph letter from Fersen to Marie-Antoinette sent in code. It is logged in his register to the 'Queen of France'. The code word servires *comes from page 111 of the code book.*[222] *There are no endearments, but his tone is friendlier than it was in March. He confirms that Gustav III has died and then passes on to business.*

111 *servires* No. 3
19 Apr. 1792, dated 17th
Cipher to the Queen

17 April [1792]

You will have received the sad and overwhelming news of the King's death. You lose in him a firm support, a good ally and I, a protector and [*good*] friend. This loss is cruel. The account M. de Simolin gave the baron of his talks in Vienna promises little more in the way of activity from that court than in the past. It seems that the same system will be followed there, and since the death of the King of Sweden one cannot be sure of the course the Empress will take; but in this uncertainty the most sure method is to try to force an attack. A hostile action on your part is the only thing that may [*finally*] make them all make up their minds. If it could be delayed by a month that would be better. I will explain it all to you in greater detail by a tin of biscuits.

I have spoken to Mme Sullivan. She has told J. [Jarjayes] that she would leave orders so that, despite her absence, I might send you papers as in the past and you could send them to me. The woman to talk to is Mme Toscani. She is trustworthy, and by sending her a box containing a piece of cloth [*for a mourning frock coat with buttons*] or other items as though for Mr Craufurd, she will forward it [*without danger*]. She has not mentioned it to Mr C. [Craufurd], because he is so fearful and prudent that he would have hesitated and one would never do anything. It is [*even*] for that reason that he did not wish her to see J., for besides that he has no secrets from her and tells her everything. [*I will explain it all to M. Gog when he passes through, and I will notify you of the dispatch of the biscuits.*]

49. Fersen to Marie-Antoinette, 19 April 1792

AN 440AP/1. Autograph note from Fersen to the Queen sent in code and numbered 4. It is logged in his register to the 'Queen of France'. The code word is froid, from page 166 of the code book. Goguelat has returned from his mission to the King of Hungary (soon to be Emperor Franz II), and he seems to be ready to come to the aid of his aunt Marie-Antoinette. Fersen indicates that Goguelat is returning directly to Paris – 'he is passing through France' – instead of taking a circuitous route through England as he did on his outward journey.

166 No. 4
Cipher to the Queen

19 April 1792

I received your number 4 yesterday, but number 3 is missing. M. Goguelat arrived this morning. He brings good news, but they will mean nothing unless we have more positive tidings from Berlin. It seems that they have finally decided to march, and Baron Thugut told the baron [Breteuil] so yesterday in the greatest confidentiality. I will send you the details on Saturday in a box of biscuits. Send someone to Mr Craufurd's on Tuesday at six in the evening; get them to ask for Mme Toscani. She will hand over the papers. M. Goguelat is leaving tomorrow; he is passing through France.

Gustav III's death was a real loss for Marie-Antoinette and Louis XVI, and they mourned him sincerely. He had desperately wished to help them; but his constant activity and equally constant principles in favour of the Ancien Régime in France had made him a target for the Jacobins, who had rallied disenfranchised Swedish nobles to their cause in order to get rid of him. Baron Taube's letters to Fersen reveal that Sweden would now be reduced to the role of spectator in European affairs, for want of money to continue to participate in the counter-revolution. Fersen also feared he would be recalled to Stockholm, but Taube reassured him that he would remain in his post in the hope of Louis XVI's eventual restoration to power following the war which France had just declared on Austria on 20 April 1791. It was assumed that France would lose, and that the peace negotiations would allow the allies to impose an absolute monarchy – a very risky and ultimately disastrous strategy.

Taube's letter of 10 April also reveals that the Constitutionals had demanded to see the copy of a dispatch Fersen had written. Curiously, the new Swedish regent, Gustav's brother the Duke of Södermanland, was the originator of the idea of a joint declaration by the allies against the *enragés* who were threatening the existence of the Royal Family's – a declaration to be launched in August 1792 as the 'Brunswick Manifesto'.

Extracts of letters from Taube to Fersen

Stockholm, 29 March
at 4 o'clock in the afternoon
Everything is finished for us, my dear Axel. The King breathed his last this morning at five minutes past 11. I am in the greatest distress and my grief can end only with my existence . . . Count no longer, my friend, on Sweden being of any assistance to the unfortunate sovereigns of France.

3 April 1792
The soul of Sweden no longer exists, and that unique astonishing man, master of all, of himself and of destinies, is dead, and with him all our hopes and all our means . . . I have also told him [the Duke Regent] that the late King intended you to be his Ambassador to Their Majesties when he sent them one. I told him that the late King wanted to give you the hussars after Mörner's death.[223]

6 April 1792
If your father writes to get you to return, tell him that you have received orders from the Duke to remain in your post and that he wants you to continue the negotiations you were charged with by the late King.

10 April 1792
That the Queen of France found herself forced to write the memorandum to the Emperor, that the villains had demanded that she give them your dispatch to the King of the 24th, my friend, makes one's hair stand on end, and especially at the present time, when all the most dreadful events seem to conspire together to add to the horror of their situation and to paralyse for some time all rescue from abroad.

The declaration which the Empress has just made to the court of Vienna on the new Polish constitution will stop all efforts and help from the courts of Vienna and Prussia for several months . . . The Duke is very well disposed, but our means our absolutely nil.

1 May 1792

Do you remember, my friend, what I told you a month ago, that the Duke had proposed to the Empress that a common declaration should be made which might stop the rage and the fury of the *enragés* and the *clubistes* who then seemed to be threatening the lives of the Royal Family . . . [224]

50. Marie-Antoinette to Fersen, 19 April 1792

AN 440AP/1. Autograph decrypt by Fersen of the fragment of a letter from the Queen. He records his reply on 15 May, when he logs his first 'Josephine' letter since 24 February 1792 in his register: 'Josephine – No. 6 by Goug[enot].' He therefore considered this letter No. 5 from the Queen to be part of the 'Josephine' correspondence. There are two lines blacked out, the first deletions in any of the letters since 2 March; however, Marie-Antoinette tells Fersen he can get someone else to decipher it.

Received 3 May 1792, cipher from the Queen
Rep. 15 May

No. 5, 19 April 1792

What follows is likewise in the same code, but you can get someone else to decipher it. The baron must say all that on my behalf to M. de Mercy, for I haven't dared to write to him directly, nor by the secretary, since I am horribly spied on at the moment. Perhaps I will no longer even be able to write to you. I shall always try to find ways but [*2 lines deleted*] . . .

The King desires that the King of England alone knows that the letter M. Chauvelin carries which is in is hand is not in the least in his style. Farewell. I will get someone to write to you in a couple of days inside the wrapper of the *Moniteur*.

Tomorrow the ministers and the Jacobins are declaring war in the King's name on the house of Austria, on the pretext that by the treaties she made last year she breached that of the alliance of '56, and that she has not replied categorically to the last dispatch. The ministers hope that this measure will create fear and that they will negotiate in three weeks' time. God willing it is not so and that at last one will be avenged for all the outrages one receives from this country. In what is going to be said, they will complain a great deal about Prussia's proceedings, but it is not being attacked.

Marie-Antoinette to Fersen, 21 April 1792, letter missing

The Queen said in her letter of 19 April: 'I will get someone to write to you in a couple of days inside the wrapper of the *Moniteur*', meaning that news of the declaration of war against Austria would be written by

Goguelat – probably in invisible ink – inside the wrapper of the newspaper *Le Moniteur*.

The final paragraph of Fersen's letter to the Queen on 24 April 1792 hints at a rapprochement between them. There are at last some endearments for Marie-Antoinette, so cruelly absent from his letters since the beginning of March; he sounds once more like the Fersen of old, writing in the same style as he did before his visit to Paris. Doubtless Gustav's death brought home to him how fleeting life could be and how essential it was to give his beloved some signs of affection when she was facing such great danger. Had she felt the same thing on learning of Gustav's tragic end? The tone of her letters must have revived Fersen's 'faint hopes'. He swears his devotion to her; never will he abandon her, he would rather sell all his possessions than return to Sweden, despite pressure from his father and the Duke Regent . . .

In reality, Fersen knew very well that such drastic measures would not be necessary. It was a ploy to appeal to the Queen. He had told Taube on 18 April that he would not leave Brussels: 'I have decided, my friend, not to return to Sweden at present. As I alone hold the thread of affairs, and all those of Their Majesties pass through me, I could not leave without them suffering, or even without them being completely interrupted.'[225] Fersen's diary reveals that there was in fact no danger of a recall to Sweden. On 19 April, five days before he wrote this letter to Marie-Antoinette, he noted: 'Letters from Sweden. I'm being continued in my post. I shall have new credentials. That pleased me.'[226] So much for the diplomatic service. There was also no indication that his father had pressed for his return. But in order to touch Marie-Antoinette's heart he had to make her see the risk of his possible recall to Sweden and his removal from diplomatic affairs – for now it was these affairs alone that obliged them to continue their correspondence. She had to fear she would lose this tenuous bond that still linked them, and then, perhaps, she could be persuaded to become his 'Josephine' once again.

51. FERSEN TO MARIE-ANTOINETTE, 24 APRIL 1792

AN 440AP/1. Autograph copy of a letter from Fersen to Marie-Antoinette, logged in his register to 'the Queen of France, invisible ink in biscuits addressed to Mme Tosc[ani]'. Almost twelve lines have been deleted at the end of the letter. I have succeeded in reading the words printed in bold type.

To the Queen in invisible ink in a case of biscuits

Brussels, 24 April 1792

I am sending you a dispatch from Berlin which is interesting. It will give you an idea of what is going on. In support of this dispatch is the news B[aron] Thugut told the baron [Breteuil], that the King of Hungary had sent word here that he was tired of everything that was happening in France, that he was determined to put a stop to it and to act, that he would make his troops march in concert with the King of Prussia; that if the French attacked it would be necessary to amuse them for six weeks or two months to give the armies time to arrive; that if they did not attack, he was still determined to attack them, and it would be equally necessary to amuse them by the semblance of peace right up to the moment when he could take action. I do not know the reason why M. de Mercy will not admit to this letter; he has not mentioned it.

I received news of the declaration of war yesterday, and I am very glad. It is the best and the only course to take to make the powers make up their minds. The Empress has declared to Vienna her intention to involve herself actively in French affairs, and that she wants the monarchy re-established as it was before the Revolution. It's M. de Mercy who repeated this news. The news from Spain is not good, and it will only act in accordance with the conduct of the King of Hungary and the King of Prussia. The most useful thing she could do and which sits well enough with her projects would be to provide a cordon of 20,000 men on the frontier, to provide weapons and munitions to the Catholics and malcontents in the Mediterranean provinces. It is what has already been asked for and which needs to be insisted on.

I have not yet received news concerning myself, and I do not know if I shall be continued [in my post] or not. My father is pressing me to return and abandon everything. It is what I shall never do, even should I be reduced to penury; I have enough effects to survive some while yet by selling them. But if he should persuade the Duke to have the same desire, I will find myself in difficulty by the loss of my small income. As I am dependent on them for it, they hope to control me that way, and if the Duke doesn't lend himself to this idea, I fear my father may still try. But, **my dear and tender friend**, I'm determined, nothing in the world could make me **move away from you** or abandon everything at this moment. **You are now more than ever everything to me. I've lost a friend, a protector** . . .

[*9 lines deleted and illegible*]

Fersen recorded only one letter to Marie-Antoinette in his letter register for the whole of May 1792 – number 6 addressed to 'Josephine' on 15 May, which is missing. No letters from her to him this month are traceable. The next to be found in the archives is number 8 on 2 June. Fersen's letters numbered 5 and 7 are lost, as well as Marie-Antoinette's replies. Not a single letter from Fersen to the Queen from 2 June contains endearments; the tone is certainly much more amiable than it was in March, but the old tenderness is not there.

All the remaining letters are logged in Fersen's register under the heading 'the Queen of France'. The war made communication even more difficult, not to mention hazardous. Marie-Antoinette charged her secretary François Goguelat to correspond with Fersen, hence the singular content of several letters. Messages were sent either in code or invisible ink in open business letters written by Goguelat and addressed to Fersen under his code name Rignon. Several editors, starting with Klinckowström, have feminized the adjectives and participles in these letters, attributing them exclusively to Marie-Antoinette. It is important to remember that she did not write them herself.

Fersen to Marie-Antoinette, May 1792, letters nos 5, 6 and 7 missing

The very last 'Josephine' letter in Fersen's register on 15 May 1792 was numbered 6. It is missing. Numbers 5 and 7, also missing, are not recorded in the register. The next letter in the series, Number 8, was logged to the 'Queen of France'.

52. FERSEN TO GOGUELAT/MARIE-ANTOINETTE, 2 JUNE 1792

AN 440AP/1. Autograph copy of a letter from Fersen to the Queen's secretary François Goguelat, written in invisible ink. It is logged in the register to 'the Queen of France, invisible ink by Tosc. [Mme Toscani]'. The letter is marked 'to Gog' and Fersen changed the date from 3 to 2 June. In the margin he wrote '49 adroit' indicating not only the code word but also – according to the instructions in his letter of 6 March 1792 – that Goguelat was indeed the intended recipient and the code (of which there is no trace) meant nothing: 'If there is 49, that is, a dash underneath, then the letter will be for him; the code will be meaningless unless there is a full-stop or semi-colon after the number.'

Fersen changed the order of the paragraphs in this letter before sending it. The transcription below reproduces the final order. He asks Goguelat to send him blank powers of attorney signed by Louis XVI in order to authorize himself and the Baron de Breteuil to make agreements in the King's name. The granting of such an authorization confirms that Louis XVI and Marie-Antoinette retained absolute confidence in Breteuil and Fersen to protect their interests in negotiations with the allied armies.

49 adroit
In invisible ink to Gog[uelat] by Mme Tosc[ani]

[3] 2 June 1792, No. 8

Prussia is good; it is the only one you can rely on. Vienna still plans for a partition and to negotiate with the Constitutionals.[227] Spain is no good. I hope that England will not be worse. The Empress is sacrificing your interests for Poland. Our regent is well disposed towards you, but he can do nothing or very little. He is going to expel the man who has been sent to him; that is the reason why he has recalled his chargé d'affaires. He has engaged the Empress to do the same. Try to keep the war going and do not leave Paris. Have you sent me the powers and to which address? Mme Toscani will give you my letters.

The V[icomte] de C[araman] has returned.[228] He brings a positive assurance from the King of Prussia that he will listen to no proposal or accommodation, that he wants the King to be free and thus the master to make whatever constitution he wishes. He desires that the King knows it, that this resolution on his part will not change and that he can count on it. He is providing money for the troops which will pass through.

The commander of the Prussian army arrives on 9 July. All will be in place on 4 August. They will take action around the Moselle and the Meuse; the émigrés from Philippsburg and the Austrians in the Brisgau. The Duke of Brunswick is coming to Coblentz on 5 July. When everything has arrived there, the Duke of Brunswick will advance, cover the strongholds and march straight on Paris with 36,000 elite troops. The Empress is sending 15,000 men, including three thousand cavalrymen. They are disembarking at Wismar and marching through Germany. On the 22nd [May] she sent 30,000 men into Poland.

53. GOGUELAT/MARIE-ANTOINETTE TO FERSEN, 5 JUNE 1792

Stafsund, RA/720807/022/11. This letter in Goguelat's handwriting is kept in the Swedish archives. There are open paragraphs and one in code. The code word is adroit *in all letters. This decrypt is the author's. Goguelat gives worrying news of the Royal Family – 'your friends' – in the final paragraph. In his diary on 10 June Fersen notes: 'letter from the Q., orders to Luckner to attack &&'.*

Rep. the 11th

5 June 1792

[*no code*]

I received your letter No. 7. I immediately took the trouble to withdraw your funds from the Boscaris company. There was no time to lose, for the bankruptcy was declared yesterday, and this morning it was public knowledge in the Bourse. It is said that the creditors will lose a great deal. Here is a statement of the different affairs I have on my books. **49.**

[*in code*]

There are orders for Luckner's army to attack soon; he is opposed to it, but the government wants it. The troops lack everything and are in the greatest disorder.[229]

[*no code*]

Let me know what to do with these funds. If it were up to me, I would place them profitably by acquiring some fine properties belonging to the clergy; it is, whatever they say, the best way to place one's money. You can reply to me the same way as I am writing to you.

Your friends are quite well. The loss they have suffered causes them much sorrow. I am doing what I can to console them. They believe that it will be impossible to re-establish their fortune or, at least, that it is a long way off. If you can, give them some comfort on this subject. They need it; their situation grows more dreadful every day. Farewell. Accept their compliments and the assurance of my entire devotion.

54. GOGUELAT/MARIE-ANTOINETTE TO FERSEN, 7 JUNE 1792

AN 440AP/1. Letter written by Goguelat, partly in code. He mentions his mission to Vienna in March. There is an autograph minute by Fersen of the coded passage. In decoding it to verify the text one uncovers a striking change; Fersen writes 'my Constitutionals' rather than 'the Constitutionals' as actually written by Goguelat. The code word is paroîtra, *from page 141 of the code book.*

In his letter of 2 June Fersen had raised the question of Austria's plan to negotiate with the Constitutionals: the aim being to partition France (in French it is 'the dismemberment') in return for recognizing their Constitution. This would mean that Austria would regain provinces ceded to France after the War of the Austrian Succession. In this letter Goguelat informs Fersen of the imminent arrival in Vienna of a man sent by the Constitutionals to negotiate this act of treason, without the knowledge of the Assembly – in which they had compromised Marie-Antoinette. She is trying through Goguelat to thwart their scheme. When Mercy discussed this letter with Fersen on 16 June he at last showed some emotion, railing against the Constitutionals and saying 'that it was no longer possible to negotiate with any party; they are all scoundrels who only want to seize power; there is nothing left but bayonets'.[230]

Received 15 June
Rep. 21 June

7 June 1792

[*in code*]

141: **The** Constitutionals are sending a man to Vienna. He will pass through Brussels. M. de Mercy must be warned to treat him as though he were announced and recommended by the Queen, to negotiate with him along the lines of the memorandum I gave him. They want him to write to Vienna to announce him; recommend to him that he keeps my journey secret, and say that we are keeping to the plan made by the courts of Vienna and Berlin, but that it is necessary to appear to enter into the Constitutionals' views and to convince, above all, that it is in accordance with the wishes and demands of the Queen. These measures are very necessary. It is not the abbé Louis who goes; I do not know the name of the man who is replacing him. Tell M. de Mercy that one cannot write to him because one is too closely watched.

[*no code*]

Here is the state of your affairs with Boscary and Chol, whose bankruptcy I told you of in my last letter. I am waiting for news from La Rochelle to tell you where you stand with Daniel Farouché and Jacques Guibert. All I know is that their bankruptcy is not too serious. You would have done better had you done as I advised and bought clergy assets than to keep your funds in a bank. If you wish, I will employ those which are due to you next month in that manner.

I have received your numbers 7 and 8.

55. FERSEN TO MARIE-ANTOINETTE, 11 JUNE 1792

AN 440AP/1. Autograph copy of a letter numbered 9 in code from Fersen to Marie-Antoinette, sent via Mme Toscani and Goguelat and logged in his register to 'the Queen of France'. The code word is adroit. *Fersen expresses all his anguish on the Queen's fate without, however, using any endearments.*

Cipher to the Queen by Goguelat to Mme Toscani

No. 9, 11 June 1792

The King of Prussia wishes you to know that the Chevalier de Boufflers[231] is returning to Paris; that he asked him for his orders, but that as he [the King] has a bad opinion of him he told him nothing, and the Chevalier knows nothing at all of his dispositions, and therefore you should put no faith in all he might say to you, since he is charged with nothing. I believe you would do well not to see him at all.

Oh God, how your situation pains me! My soul is keenly and grievously affected. Only try to remain in Paris and rescue will come. The King of Prussia is determined on it and you can count on that. The Empress has asked us [Sweden] for six thousand men, but we need money.

You haven't told me if you sent the powers [of attorney] and how or where.

56. FERSEN TO MARIE-ANTOINETTE, 21 JUNE 1792

AN 440AP/1. Autograph copy of a letter from Fersen to Marie-Antoinette, numbered 10 and logged in the register to 'the Queen of France'. The code word is paroitra. *Fersen asks if he should make use of a power with Louis XVI's signature that he has kept back from the Baron de Breteuil and asks for more. The Austrians are continuing to betray Marie-Antoinette: the price for their help is the partition of France, and if they cannot obtain if from Louis XVI they hope that the Constitutionals will be more inclined to deal with them to safeguard their constitution.*

141: Code and invisible ink to the Queen by Mme Toscani and Goguelat

No. 10, 21 June 1792, Brussels

[*in code*]

That they knew at Coblentz that Goguelat had been sent to Vienna on the very day that he arrived here and that a courier was dispatched to St Petersburg the same day to inform them. Bombelles sends this news from there. There is undoubtedly someone in your household who writes everything to the princes. That if d'Aranda wants to have a direct correspondence with you it should be avoided, because he is bad and wants to negotiate, and then you are ruined. That our regent means well, that he has sent me letters of notification for you with the order to send them to you without passing through your ministers, with whom we have no communication. That I fear that Spain, England and the Emperor want to negotiate, that we are trying to counter it. That the Emperor's plan is for a partition, and that if he does not obtain it from you he will deal with the Constitutionals and obtain it from them, and you will lose even more of your authority without preventing the partition; that it might therefore be better to decide on it if it is inevitable. What is your wish on the subject?

But there is perhaps a way to prevent it: that is to give the King of Prussia a written engagement for the reimbursement [of the costs of the war]. He wishes it, but it requires the King's signature. I still have one blank power left which I haven't mentioned to the baron. Do you wish me to make use of it, should it be useful in order to assure ourselves of the King of Prussia's opposition to any partition? Have you sent me more and how? It would be good if I were to have three more.

[*in invisible ink*]

Buy two pretty hats *à la Charlotte* – mourning hats **but all in white**. Take them to Mlle Binet's and tell her to make them in Mme Sullivan's style. They will then be better made. Take them to Mme Toscani and get her to sew the three papers in the bottom, between the lining, and ask her to send them to Mme Sullivan. She knows how. The name can be written in black or even if necessary in invisible ink. In that case the place where the name is must be marked in pencil. One could even, in either case, write on a merchant's bill, because only the other page is needed. Rest assured [*in code*] that I will only give out the signatures if it is necessary and useful. I have given your message to M. de Mercy. He understood it very well and should already have written to Vienna in consequence.[232]

In the business in which Gouvion[233] was killed, Lafayette lost 400 men [*who were buried by*] according to the peasants; the Austrians, 114 dead or wounded. Reinforcements have reached them, and there is nothing more to fear. I have warned Russia and Berlin about the Constitutionals' mission lest someone be tempted to turn it to ill account.

Paris was growing ever more dangerous; the Jacobins were in charge and their plan was to annihilate the Royal Family. On 20 June 1792, the Tuileries were invaded, Louis XVI himself was threatened with death and forced to wear a revolutionary *bonnet rouge*, while the Queen, her children and Madame Elisabeth, were held captive behind a table for several hours as the mob swarmed through the palace and hurled insults and threats. Fersen received an account of it all three days later, writing in his diary: 'Horrible account of the assassination attempt on the 21st in the palace of the Tuileries; it's attached. The consequences make one shudder.' He also read in an edition of the *Patriote* that all the Jacobin ministers had been replaced by Constitutionals. 'Lafayette is writing a very strong letter against the Jacobins. He wants to march on Paris to deliver the King from the Jacobins; she [Marie-Antoinette] will be denounced.'[234] Once again Lafayette intended to target the Queen.

57. Goguelat/Marie-Antoinette to Fersen, 23 June 1792

Stafsund, RA/720807/022/11. This letter written by Goguelat is in the Swedish archives. The code word is adroit. *In the final paragraph he highlights the extreme danger faced by the Queen ('your friend'), confirming that he has passed the information in Fersen's letters to her ('I have finished all your affairs with him').*

Received 29th, rep. 30th

23 June 1792

[*in code*]

49: Dumouriez is leaving tomorrow for Luckner's army. He has promised to make Brabant rise up. St Huruge is also leaving to attain the same object.[235]

[*no code*]

Here is a statement of the sums I have paid for you. I will send your statement of income when it is complete. I believe I have received all the letters. The last two were 8 and 9. No. 9 was from 11 June – I haven't kept the date of the other.

Your friend is in the greatest danger. His illness is making terrifying progress. The doctors no longer know what to do. If you wish to see him, make haste. Tell his relations of his unhappy situation. I have finished your affairs with him, so have no worries on this matter. I will send you his news regularly.

Fersen to Marie-Antoinette, 25 June 1792, letter missing

Letter No. 11, logged in Fersen's register to on 27 June 1792 to 'the Queen of France, dated 25th, No. 11, in code by Goug[enot] – above all try not to leave Paris and use every means; this must be your only goal, then it will be easy to come to your rescue and it will come.' The letter was sent to Gougenot at 2 rue Lepeletier. Fersen annotated Marie-Antoinette's reply dated 3 July 'cipher from Josephine'.

58. Goguelat/Marie-Antoinette to Fersen, 26 June 1792

Stafsund, RA/720807/022/11. Autograph letter from Goguelat, which is kept in the Swedish archives. The Royal Family's situation is now desperate.

Received 30th

26 [June 1792]

I have just received your letter No. 10. I hasten to acknowledge receipt. You will very shortly receive details relative to the clergy's assets I have acquired on your behalf. Today I will restrict myself to reassuring you on the placement of your assignats. I have few left, and in a few days I hope they will be as well placed as the others.

I am vexed not to be able to reassure you on the situation of your friend. However, for three days now, the malady has made no progress, but its symptoms are no less alarming; the most able physicians despair of it. A prompt crisis is needed to bring him out of this business, and it is not apparent yet. It makes us desperate. Let the people who do business with him know of his situation so they may take their precautions. Time is running out . . . I will be punctual in informing you of whether he gets better or worse. Send rigorously through the post. Farewell. Receive the kind regards and compliments of all who interest you.

All Fersen's hopes now rested on a prompt march on Paris by the Prussian army to liberate the Royal Family. Austria sought to slow down operations, to give the King and Queen's position time to deteriorate yet further so they would be forced to accept a partition of France. Russia was occupied with Polish affairs, while the Prussians demanded the reimbursement of the cost of the war by Louis XVI once he regained his power. It was a perfect example of complete European disunion. Fersen had foreseen all these machinations for a long time and had asked for diplomatic credentials from Baron Taube in order to be able to try to prevent them. Letters sent to him from Stockholm in the summer of 1792 show that he had absolutely no intention of abandoning Marie-Antoinette.

Letters from Baron Taube to Fersen, extracts

22 June 1792

M. de Frank will send you by post next Tuesday the credentials you have requested for the Emperor, the King of Prussia and the Duke of Brunswick.

26 June 1792

In the event that the King of France is at liberty, the Duke wishes you to go at once to join him to assist him with your advice and to prevent as far as is possible the partition of France, and to yield no part of royal omnipotence.

11 July 1792

On my arrival here I learnt of the new atrocities or, rather, their renewal and continuation, which were committed at Paris and in the Tuileries [on 20 June 1792] . . . Despite the horror I felt on reading the recital of it all, I felt complete satisfaction on learning with what dignity and courage the King received and replied to the cannibals and fanatics who surrounded him. It was a firmness and composure worthy of our late master. His soul would have greatly rejoiced, my friend, if he could have known of it, and Louis XVI would already have been freed from these assassins if he had always conducted himself thus. What the Queen did on this occasion no longer surprises; not a single event of her life has ever made her forget that She is a queen and worthy of being one.[236]

Instructions from the Duke Regent of Sweden to Fersen

26 June 1792

Lieutenant-General Baron Taube has communicated to us your letter dated the 13th of this month which he received today, in which you express the desire to know what course you should take in the event that the King and Queen of France, by some fortunate and unexpected event, should be freed; and we consider it of the utmost importance that in this case you should go to Their Most Christian Majesties without the slightest delay to assist them with your wise counsel and to express to them the court of Sweden's alacrity to affirm to them the sincere interest it takes in all that concerns the Royal House of France. You can on this occasion, and without waiting for new orders, present the credentials which have already been sent to you.[237]

59. FERSEN TO MARIE-ANTOINETTE, 30 JUNE 1792

440AP/1. Autograph copy of a letter from Fersen to Marie-Antoinette sent in invisible ink and numbered 12. It is logged in his register to 'the Queen of France' and is a reply to Goguelat's letter of 23 June. Direct correspondence with Marie-Antoinette proving almost impossible, Fersen asks that Goguelat writes a bulletin twice a week to keep him informed. For the first time he mentions the Brunswick Manifesto, the declaration proposed by the Swedish regent to Catherine II in April. Without doubt the dreadful events of 20 June 1792 at the Tuileries had revived this idea.

No. 12
To the Queen in invisible ink by Toscani

30 June 1792

I received your letter of the 23rd yesterday. There is nothing to fear so long as the Austrians are not beaten; a hundred thousand like Dumouriez would not get this country to revolt, even though it be well disposed to do so.

Your position troubles me ceaselessly. Your courage will be admired and the King's firm conduct will have an excellent effect. I have already sent the account of his conversation with Pétion everywhere. It is worthy of Louis XIV. You must continue the same, and, above all, try not to leave Paris – that is the capital point, then it will be easy to reach you, and that is the Duke of Brunswick's plan. His entry will be preceded by a very strong manifesto in the name of the allied powers which will hold the whole of France, and Paris in particular, responsible for royal persons. Then he will march straight on Paris, leaving the combined armies on the frontiers to cover the positions and prevent the troops there from acting elsewhere to oppose his operations. The Empress has deployed 15,000 men. Our regent has granted the 8,000 men she requests; they are ready and will march as soon as we have some money.

The Duke of Brunswick arrives at Coblentz on the 3rd. The first Prussian division arrives there on the 8th. Seven thousand men will straight away be deployed to this country, and will occupy Luxembourg so that the Austrians can increase their forces with the troops which are there. They were stupid not to attack Luckner when he entered; at present he's too well positioned and entrenched, and it

311

would appear that he will be left there until the troops have arrived. They were careless in letting themselves get taken 60 *cleas* before Maubeuge.

A M. Viette passed through here; he told the Vicomte de Caraman that he had been sent by you to Coblentz charged with a message. He showed him a letter addressed to General Schmitt and written, he said, in invisible ink between the lines. Doubtless he will have made the same confidence to various others of his acquaintance.

I wrote No. 11 to you on the 25th by **Goug**[enot]; No. 10 by Mme Tosc[ani] on the 21st. Reply to me about the powers and the partition. You must get Goguelat to write to me every Sunday and Wednesday [*to send me news*] to give me details of what is happening. When he says: *they say, but I do not believe it at all*, I shall know then that the thing is certain. All letters of this nature arrive.

60. MARIE-ANTOINETTE TO FERSEN AND THE
COMTE DE MERCY, 3 JULY 1792

AN 440AP/1. Autograph decrypt by Fersen of a letter from the Queen on which he has written 'cipher from Josephine', doubtless because she had written that she was 'very touched' by his letter of 25 June (which is missing). In his diary Fersen writes:

> *8 July . . . Lasserez arrived with a letter from the Queen for me and Mercy. She wants action and talks as soon as possible; that cannot happen before the forces arrive, because one must not talk except by acting.*[238]

The Queen confirms she will send the blank powers 'as you requested them', that is, sewn into the lining of two hats *à la Charlotte*. The 3 July 1792 was a Tuesday: they would therefore be sent on 5 July.

Received 8th by Mr Lasserez
Rep 10th by Lasserez
Cipher from Josephine

3 July 1792

I have received your letter of the 25th No. 11. I was very touched by it. Our position is dreadful, but don't worry too much. I am taking heart, and I have something inside me that tells me that we will soon be happy and saved. This is the only idea that sustains me. The man I am sending is for M. de Mercy. I am writing to him very strongly, so that finally they decide to talk and act in a manner that will impress them here. It is urgent, and there is no way to wait any longer.

The blank powers will **leave** on **Thursday** as you requested them. Farewell. When will we see each other again in peace?

61. MARIE-ANTOINETTE TO FERSEN, EARLY JULY 1792

AN 440AP/1. Autograph minute by Fersen of a letter from Marie-Antoinette, with two lines replaced by dots at the beginning. Leonard, the Queen's celebrated coiffeur, took the letter to Brussels as Fersen recorded in his diary.

9 July . . . Saw Mercy. He agrees with me, that one must be ready to act when one is going to talk. The Queen asks him that in the manifesto Paris is made responsible for the King and his family. She asks if it would be right to leave Paris. He replies yes, if one is sure of someone to protect the departure, and to go then to Compiègne and call the departments of [?] and Soissons. He speaks well of the manifesto; that to save the King hope should be given to all except to the rebels . . . Leonard arrived from Paris. He is ruined; brought a letter from the Queen for me.[239]

9 July received from Leonard

— —
— — — — — — — — — — — — — — — —Do not torment yourself too much on my account; believe that courage always inspires respect. The decision we have just taken will, I hope, give us time to wait, but six weeks is still a very long time. I dare not write more to you. Farewell. Hasten, if you can, the help which has been promised for our deliverance.

[*in invisible ink*]

I am still alive, but it is a miracle. The 20th was an appalling day. It is no longer me they hate the most; they want even my husband's life. They hide it no longer. He showed a firmness and strength which have impressed for the moment, but the dangers could recur at any time. I hope that you are receiving our news.[240] Farewell. Look after yourself for us, and do not worry about us.

62. Goguelat/Marie-Antoinette to Fersen, 6 July 1792

AN 440AP/1. Autograph decrypt by Fersen of a letter 'from the Queen',
although it appears to be a bulletin from Goguelat rather than a letter
from Marie-Antoinette. The last paragraph shows the difficulties
Goguelat faced in getting the powers to Brussels.

Received 10th
Rep. 18th

6 July [1792]

I was handed your last letter in invisible ink after the handwriting had
been exposed. That is the second time this has happened. Other
measures must be taken so there are no more mistakes; you will easily
understand the importance of this warning.

A terrible catastrophe is expected on the 14th in every corner of
Paris, and at the Jacobin club particularly they are preaching regicide.
There are sinister projects afoot, but as they are known it may perhaps
be possible to foil them. The Jacobins from all the provinces are
arriving here in mobs. There is not a day that passes when the
Queen is not warned to be on her guard; sometimes it is a busybody,
sometimes an intriguer. They do not give her a second's peace.

I have the three blank powers, but I do not know how to send
them to you. The public coaches are no longer running. Tell me of a
safe route other than that.

63. GOGUELAT/MARIE-ANTOINETTE TO FERSEN, 7 JULY 1792

Stafsund, RA/720807/022/11. Letter written by Goguelat and kept in the Swedish archives. The code word is paroîtra. *Goguelat has found someone to take the blank powers to Craufurd. They are signed in invisible ink. This letter took over a fortnight to reach Fersen.*

Received 23rd
Replied 26th

7 July [1792]

141: A few days ago I sent you a statement of your current debts. Here is the supplement I received today from your banker in London.

[*in code*]

The different parties in the National Assembly came together today; this reconciliation cannot be sincere on the part of the Jacobins.[241] They are dissembling to hide some project or other. It might be suspected that one of them would be to demand a ceasefire through the King and to engage him to negotiate the peace. You must send warning that any official measure of that nature will not be the King's wish; that if circumstance were to force him to express such a wish, he will do it through the organ of M. de Breteuil. Mr Craufurd will receive the blank powers tomorrow by an occasion: warn him, so that he opens the parcel with care. They are signed in invisible ink.

[*no code*]

I still think you can do no better than to place your funds here. Peace is returning and all the parties are joining together at the moment to make the constitution work. Give me carte blanche, I am sure to make some fine acquisitions for you and your funds will double in two years. I have just finished the purchase of the house we saw together, rue de l'Université; it will cost me, all fees included, 157,000 *livres*.

Farewell. The whole family is well, sends you a thousand compliments and ardently desires to see you again soon.

64. FERSEN TO MARIE-ANTOINETTE, 10 JULY 1792

*AN 440AP/1. Autograph copy of a letter from Fersen to Marie-Antoinette
written in invisible ink. It is the reply to the 'cipher from Josephine' of 3
July, and Fersen logged it in his register to 'the Queen of France, replied to
the letters by Lasserez and Leonard, in invisible ink by Lasserez'. He
mentions the 'great pleasure' her letters gave him – possibly because the
lines replaced by dots contained some affectionate words or perhaps
simply because they were the first letters actually written by Marie-
Antoinette rather than by Goguelat for a month. Fersen begs the Queen
not to trust Lafayette (one imagines she hardly needed such a warning). It
is clear from his diary that he feared Lafayette would try to take the Royal
Family hostage to guarantee his own security and bargain for the
recognition of the constitution by Austria.*

To the Queen in invisible ink by Lasserez

Brussels, 10 July 1792

M. Lasserez and M. Leonard have arrived and given me your letters. I
have no need to tell you that they gave me great pleasure. Your
courage is admirable and your husband's firmness has had a great
effect. You must use both to resist any attempt to get you out of Paris.
It is most beneficial to stay there; however, I am entirely of M. de
Mercy's opinion on the single eventuality where it might be necessary
to leave. But you must be very sure before attempting it of the courage
and loyalty of those who will protect your departure, because were it
to fail you would be lost without resource and I cannot think of it
without trembling. It is not therefore an attempt to be made lightly or
without being sure of success. If you do it, you should never call on
Lafayette but on the neighbouring departments.

We are hurrying up operations as much as possible. The
Prussians' arrival has already been brought forward a little, and they
can commence at the beginning of August. But to speak strongly at
the moment, without being ready to take action, would be a measure
that would lose its effect; it would not be as imposing and could
endanger you more. From what you tell me about the dispatch of the
blank powers, I assume that you approved of what I told you, and I
will make use of the one I still have according to the greater or lesser
urgency of circumstances.

The conduct of Spain is shameful and is criticized throughout Europe. England is well disposed. Because of Staël's intrigues, our regent no longer wishes to put himself forward. I try to thwart him [Staël] as much as possible. Staël sees a lot of M. Verninac.[242] Care will be taken that the manifesto is the best possible. We are busy with it. In it, Paris will be held accountable for the safety of the King and his family. The horrible scene of the 20th [June 1792] revolted the whole of Europe and has lost the Revolution many supporters.

Luckner and Lafayette seem to be abandoning this frontier to go into the [Trois] Évêchés. If the Austrians had been more active, they could have seized the Duc d'Orléans and Luckner's army at Courtrai. The princes want to create an assembly of *parlements* and peers at Mannheim: it is madness. We are trying to prevent it. It is M. de Luxembourg who is [*arranging*] provoking it all.

65. GOGUELAT/MARIE-ANTOINETTE TO FERSEN, 11 JULY 1792

Stafsund, RA/720807/022/11 and AN 440AP/1. Autograph letter, partly in code, from Goguelat, the Queen's secretary. The original is to be found in Stockholm, while Fersen's decrypt of the paragraphs in code is at Pierrefitte. The code word is once again paroîtra. *The numbering has restarted, which means it was sent by post. Goguelat has adopted the formula recommended by Fersen for sending news, saying that he 'does not believe a word' of the rumour that Louis XVI will confirm the decree of the department to dismiss Pétion; this of course means that the rumour is true. The encrypted paragraph highlights a difference between Louis XVI and Marie-Antoinette over Lafayette's plan to take them to Compiègne. The farewell is far warmer in tone than it was in the letter of 5 June.*

Received 23rd
Rep. 26th

No. 1, 11 July [1792]

I well understand, my dear Rignon, that because of your financial ventures you have a great interest in being kept informed of events. Therefore I shall do everything incumbent upon me to leave you nothing to desire in this regard. However, I must warn you that as my relations are not very extensive and I live in a very narrow circle, I shall be a poor resource to you. But still, even if I cannot be of real use to you, at least I shall demonstrate my zeal and goodwill.

Doubtless you have heard of the rapprochement between the different parties in the Assembly, of the King's measure with regard to this Assembly, of the suspension of Pétion and Manuel by the department, of several small movements by the people to get the mayor reinstated in his function and of the wishes of one part of the Assembly in this matter. This event still occupies Parisians today. It's said that Pétion will be reinstated, because the department's decree is incorrectly worded and that the King will not confirm it. Others say that the King, frightened of the mayor's power, disgusted by his pride and convinced of his evil intentions, will confirm the department's decree, but I do not believe a word of it.

The peace which Lamourette wrought in the National Assembly reigned only for a moment. Brissot has delivered a speech in favour of investigating the King's conduct since the start of the Revolution and of suspending him; in favour of declaring the homeland to be in danger, of making all the ministers responsible and declaring that they don't have the nation's confidence, of issuing a decree of accusation against Chambon, &&. This incident made everyone fall out again **and caused some very lively discussions**. As a result, word was sent to the six ministers, ordering them to give an account within twenty-four hours of the situation within France, on the borders and of the army: they were scolded so much for four hours, and found themselves so overwhelmed by the burden of their responsibility, that yesterday morning they all handed in their resignations, so that today the King has no more ministers. Since they had nothing to fear in obeying the Constitution, their cowardice is generally criticized.

There are worries at the approach of the Federation [14 July]; it is feared that this religious and patriotic festival may serve as the pretext for an insurrection against the Tuileries. The ceremonial has not yet been fixed. The Royal Family must attend this ceremony. The number of delegates expected, especially from the southern provinces is considerably less that was thought. Some are stopped for fear of being sent to the frontiers, others by works in the countryside. The biggest number come from neighbouring departments, and there is every reason to hope that is will all pass off peacefully.

The Duc d'Orléans has left the army in Flanders; he has been at Raincy for the last three or four days. He was so discredited among the troops that he was obliged to flee. I shall give you a summary of the business I have concluded for you since the 1st of this month:
[*in code*]

141: The Constitutionals together with Lafayette want to take the King away to Compiègne the day after the Federation. To this end, the two generals are coming here. The King is disposed to give in to this plan; the Queen is opposing it. One does not know what will be the outcome of this great enterprise, of which I am very far from approving. Luckner is taking the army of the Rhine, Lafayette goes to the one in Flanders, Biron and Dumouriez to the one in the centre.
[*no code*]

Your banker in London is not very prompt in transferring your funds to me. I beg you to drop him a line. Farewell, my dear Rignon, I kiss you with all my heart. In future my letters will be numbered at the top of the page, like this one.

Extract from Fersen's diary

14 July 1792 . . . Received a leaflet from Paris – *The Cry of Pain or the Day of 20th June.* It is by Mercier, very well done and worth keeping.[243]

66. Goguelat/Marie-Antoinette to Fersen, 15 July 1792

Stafsund, RA/720807/022/11. Autograph letter from Goguelat, the Queen's secretary, kept in the Swedish archives. It is one of the regular bulletins requested by Fersen. The packaging for the gloves he mentions would undoubtedly have contained a letter.

Received 23rd
Replied 26th

No. 2, 15 July [1792]

Evil-minded people caused great uneasiness for the period of the Federation. They had announced the arrival of a multitude of brigands who had a criminal enterprise in view. You may be troubled by the same fears, so I hasten to reassure you on the fate of all that interests you here. M. Pétion was recalled to his office by the National Assembly and the will of the people. He is generally trusted, which makes us hope that if anyone, through their personal influence, can keep the peace and usefully oppose the rebels' projects, it is this magistrate, father of the people: this is how he is known to true patriots.

General Luckner arrived here during the night of the 13th to 14th. He will appear tomorrow before the National Assembly. It is claimed that he has just asked for 50,000 more men for his army. Paris is still greatly agitated, a great event is expected, which each party wants to direct to its own advantage but which I cannot explain. A single day can destroy every surmise and change circumstances absolutely. To keep you informed of events it would be necessary to write to you twice a day.

We have five or six thousand delegates here, almost all from the Jacobin club. Some will remain here, the others are going to the camp at Soissons. In the next few days the armies of Marseilles and Bordeaux are expected. The three line regiments who formed the guard in Paris are leaving for the frontier in two or three days, by virtue of a decree from the Assembly. It is largely a question of making the Swiss Guard leave. And this, my dear Rignon, is very much how things are. I will write to you tomorrow on your private affairs; I do not have the time today. Farewell; I am all yours.

Tell me if you received the gloves I sent you.

67. FERSEN TO MARIE-ANTOINETTE, 18 JULY 1792

AN 440AP/1. Autograph copy of a letter from Fersen to Marie-Antoinette written in invisible ink and logged in his register to 'the Queen of France'. Fersen has had the Brunswick Manifesto written by M. de Limon.

To the Queen in invisible ink by Toscani

No. 13, Brussels, 18 July 1791

I have received all your letters and the three blank powers, but the name appears very faint and I'm not sure that we will be able to make use of them. It would be good if you could find a safe way to send me some where it is written in darker ink.

The princes have sent a memorandum to all the powers in which they establish that the King, in agreement with the Constitutionals and deceived by their promises, is going to negotiate to secure a ceasefire, && and to beg them to take no notice of it. They sent this memorandum to the baron and asked for his reply. He was outraged by it and positively denied it. He immediately wrote to tell Count Schulembourg and the Duke of Brunswick that the princes were misleading them, and I have written everywhere about it. In order to give the impression that the baron agreed with this conduct, M. de Calonne said: 'You'll see, the baron won't reply.' He is advising the princes to commit a thousand stupidities. M. de Lambert serves perfectly and tries to stop them, and the Duke of Brunswick keeps them in check, but it gives a great deal of trouble.

The assembly of the *parlements* and peers at Mannheim will no longer take place. All those here refused to go. It was Calonne's idea, promoted by the Duc de Luxembourg. The Austrians wanted to seize a battalion of the National Guard at Orchies; they missed it and only took one canon and a few wagons in the town. Otherwise everything is going well in the exterior; if only I could be reassured about the interior! We wait for the post here every day in mortal dread.

I hope that England will refuse the mediation which M. de Chauvelin has requested. I have received very good instructions from Sweden; we are only waiting for the money to send off our troops. Poland is occupying the Empress more than France; however, I hope she will send forces. The Prince de Nassau, who came and spent a day here, is very dissatisfied with d'Esterhazy. The Comte d'Aranda is as bad as ever; he nevertheless seems to be coming round a little.

We are working on the manifesto. I have had one drawn up by M. de Limon, which he gave to M. de Mercy without knowing it came from me. It's very well [written] and such as can be desired. Nothing is promised to anyone, no party is repelled, one is committed to nothing, and Paris is held responsible for the safety of the King and his family. It is said that operations will commence on 15 August. Send six copies of *The Cry of Pain*; it should be sent everywhere. I wrote to M. Goguelat yesterday.

Goguelat/Marie-Antoinette to Fersen, No. 3, July 1792, letter missing

It is apparent from the numbered letters that survive that a letter from Marie-Antoinette or Goguelat numbered 3 dated between 15 and 21 July is missing.

68. Goguelat/Marie-Antoinette to Fersen, 21 July 1792

Stafsund, RA/720807/022/11. Autograph letter numbered 4 from Goguelat kept in the Swedish archives. He confirms that the Jacobins want to take the Royal Family out of Paris. The Queen is impatient for the publication of the Brunswick Manifesto, because the Marseillais who have arrived in Paris for the Fête de la Federation on 14 July have remained; they have been given free access to the gardens of the Tuileries and a new attempt against the Royal Family is being actively prepared. Despite the impossibility of writing to Fersen directly, Marie-Antoinette charges Goguelat to tell him that she has received his letters with pleasure; the farewell shows how much they touched her. In his diary Fersen notes the arrival of this 'letter from Paris, hardly reassuring'.

Received 24th
Rep. 26th

No. 4, 21 July [1792]

Today I am sending two leaflets to you, two to Mme Sullivan and two to Mr Craufurd. I am very glad you were happy with the gloves I sent you. Doubtless you will also be pleased with the hats.[244]

All the members of the department of Paris have resigned. A large number of deputies on the right will not be slow in doing the same. M. Mathieu **Montmorency** gave his resignation, then left for England.[245] Tomorrow there will be a definitive pronouncement on the fate of M. de Lafayette. It is generally believed that he will be formally accused.

The King, the Queen and Madame Elisabeth cannot appear in the garden without being insulted, despite the precaution taken only to permit entry to the delegates [to the federation] and people with cards for the Household. The latter accuse the delegates, but it's more likely to be an abuse of the cards than abuse by the delegates. In addition, there is a rumour – and I warn you that I do not believe a word of what I am about to tell you[246] – that the Jacobins more than ever have a plan to leave Paris with the King and to go to the southern provinces. For this purpose, it is said, they have summoned from the provinces numerous detachments of national guards from all the Jacobin clubs; tomorrow **500** arrive from Marseilles. It is said that there will be enough of them here in a week to execute this plan. Others say that the

Jacobins in the Assembly are waiting for the manifesto from the foreign powers before taking a decision. It was expected this week. It is not known what has delayed its dispatch. If you have any knowledge of some of the principal articles, I should be pleased to know them. For my part, I shall keep you informed as much as I can of news from this country. Let me know if you have received all my letters.

Everyone who interests you is well. I gave news of you yesterday evening, it was received with pleasure. I was charged to tell you this and to make you promise to send it as often as you can. Farewell, my dear Rignon; I kiss you very tenderly.

Fersen commented in his diary on the news from France.

23 July . . . Received four letters from Paris. Their situation is alarming. They demand the publication of the manifest and the entry of the armies. They believe they will be carried off. The Queen did not want to yield to the proposal by the Constitutionals with Lafayette and Luckner to go to Compiègne, in order not to fall into their hands and provide the powers who are ill-intentioned with a pretext to negotiate.

The missing letter No. 3 must have provided these details (perhaps it was the letter sent with the gloves). On 24 July Fersen recorded: 'My two dogs were poisoned this morning when they went into the courtyard. That hurt me. Immediately thought of the Queen, that she could be [poisoned], too.'[247]

69. Goguelat/Marie-Antoinette to Fersen, 24 July 1792

*AN 440AP/1. Autograph letter partly in code from Goguelat. The code
word is* paroîtra. *In the final paragraph he confirms receipt of Fersen's
letter to Marie-Antoinette of 18 July. He presses for the Brunswick
Manifesto, because 'one day's delay could produce incalculable misfortunes'.*

Received 29th
Rep. 3 August
Cipher from the Queen

No. 5, 24 July [1792]

[*in code*]

141: During the course of this week the Assembly is supposed to
decree the King's suspension and his transfer to Blois. Every day
produces some new scene but always tending towards the destruction
of the King and his family. Petitioners have said, on the stand at the
Assembly, that if he is not deposed they will massacre him; they were
given the honours of the session. Tell M. de Mercy, therefore, that the
lives of the King and Queen are in the gravest danger, that one day's
delay could produce incalculable misfortunes, that the manifesto
must be sent at once, that it is awaited with extreme impatience, that it
will necessarily rally many people to the King and place him in safety;
that otherwise no one can answer for that. The troop of assassins has
been increasing constantly for twenty-four hours.

[*no code*]

I have spent the rest of the funds, herewith an exact statement, in
the purchase of two houses which are almost new and have a good
yield. The first comprises a principal building at the end of the
courtyard, raised one floor above the ground with a panelled loft
roofed in tiles. Another building to the left, serving as stables, carriage
house and with a shop on the street front, with a hay loft above, also
has a tiled roof. This house has its entrance through double doors and
a courtyard paved in sandstone, with wells and conveniences. The
second consists of a main building with its entrance along a drive and
comprises two shops, backrooms, stairs and a rear courtyard, with
conveniences and adjoining well, above which a sluice has been
created to take water to the house. The whole is five storeys tall with

cellars below and panelled servants' quarters in the attic, which has a tiled roof. Each floor is arranged in two small apartments, each composed of two rooms with fireplaces and another with the fireplace on the stairs, with English-style conveniences. These two houses can be let for 9,500 *livres*, so you see that your funds have been invested well.

Let me know if you have received the four previous letters. Two days ago I was handed a letter from you which I delivered to its address. You should have received the six leaflets you asked for.

Fersen continued to hope that a prompt march by the Duke of Brunswick could still save the Queen and the Royal Family, but his fears grew with each post. He intended to join the Royal Family in France as soon as they were free. A letter from Taube dated 25 July 1792 gave him hopes of being soon reunited with Marie-Antoinette: 'In my last meeting with the Duke before my departure, I spoke of you, my friend, and he then told me that he definitely intended you for the embassy in France.'[248]

70. FERSEN TO MARIE-ANTOINETTE, 26 JULY 1792

AN 440AP/1. Autograph copy by Fersen of a letter written in invisible ink and logged in his register to 'the Queen of France'. The Brunswick Manifesto was written. In his diary Fersen noted that it was 'by Limon, except the introduction, which has been suppressed'. It is widely believed that the Brunswick Manifesto, in which the city of Paris was held responsible for the safety of the Royal Family, precipitated the events of 10 August 1792 and the overthrow of the monarchy. The correspondence of Marie-Antoinette and Fersen, which traces the origin of this declaration, proves instead that it was written at the request of the Queen, after a suggestion from the regent of Sweden, in response to the terrifying threats constantly levelled against the Royal Family. 'For a long time now the rebels have taken no trouble to hide their plan to annihilate the Royal Family,' wrote Goguelat on 1 August. The invasion of the Tuileries on 20 June had failed, but a fresh assassination attempt was expected at any moment. In July 1792 there was no doubt that the Jacobins were assembling their forces in order to massacre the Royal Family and declare a republic in France; not having enough troops in Paris, they had called them up from the provinces (in this case, Marseilles). The Brunswick Manifesto was a last desperate effort to prevent the execution of a plan which was already well advanced. In his diary on 26 July Fersen recorded the arrival of the Marseillais at Lyon, where 'they sang horrible songs against the Queen' at the theatre. Breteuil's suggestions for Louis XVI's new cabinet sent to her the same day are decidedly out of place in view of the rapidly deteriorating situation in Paris.

To the Queen in invisible ink by Toscani

No. 14, Brussels, 26 July 1792

I have received your letters, the last number 4 and the one without a number from the 7th. We have already warned that nothing should be trusted unless it comes from the Baron de Breteuil. You did very well not to let yourselves be carried off by Lafayette and the Constitutionals. We have not stopped pressing for the manifesto and for operations – they start on the 2nd or 3rd.

The manifesto is finished, and here is what M. de Bouillé, who has seen it, writes to the baron. 'Your principles and, dare I say it, ours have been followed completely for the manifesto and the general plan, despite the intrigues I have witnessed and which made me laugh, being quite sure from what I knew that they would not prevail.' He is at Mayence and is very well treated by the Duke and the King, the Vicomte de Caraman is, too. He has been made a major in the Prussian service to be [**better**] able to follow the King and the Duke, but he is treated as the minister for France. We insisted that the manifesto was threatening, especially as regards the responsibility for royal persons, and that there was never any question of the constitution or the government. Schulembourg wrote to the baron that the King [of Prussia] will listen to no negotiation and that he wants the King's freedom. They have printed a succinct exposé of their reasons for going to war (which I am sending to you), which is quite well done.

Here is the baron's proposal for the cabinet. He wants it all to be in his hands to avoid contradictions and annoyances. He gives War to La Galissonière, who, he says, has furnished some very good ideas; the Navy to Du Moutier, the Seals to Barentin, Foreign Affairs to Bombelles, Paris to La Porte, and Finance to the Bishop of Pamiers, to avoid all the systems and to have an organized and resolute man there, with a council of finances comprised of six people – Latour, Danecourt, a trader (probably Fouache du Havre) – I cannot remember the others. Let me know as soon as possible what you think of it. He leaves La Vauguyon in Spain and Saint-Priest in Russia.

We have succeeded in excluding La Marck from affairs and have prevented him being sent by the Emperor to reside near the Duke of Brunswick. The King of Prussia did not want M. de Mercy at the conference. He blames him for the slow, weak and duplicitous conduct of Vienna. The émigrés have been separated into three corps to act with the armies, but they will not be in the vanguard as they demanded, and they will not be allowed to take action alone. I emphasized that strongly. The princes remain with the King of Prussia, the Prince de Condé with the Prince Hohenlohe (the Austrian), and M. d'Egmont who commands the 3rd Corps is with General Clairfait. The Maréchal de Castries boasts of having direct communication with the King; he has even let it be known to the baron. By the way, he has a poor head for diplomatic affairs.

71. FERSEN TO MARIE-ANTOINETTE, 28 JULY 1792

AN 440AP/1. Autograph copy of a letter from Fersen sent in invisible ink and logged in his register to the 'Queen of France'. It has not been possible to identify the location of the wine cellar in the Louvre he proposes the Royal Family use as a hiding place.

To the Queen in invisible ink by Toscani

Brussels, 28 July 1792

I have this instant received the Duke of Brunswick's declaration. It is very good. It is the one by M. de Limon, and it is he who sends it to me. To avoid suspicion, I will not send it to you, but Mr Craufurd will send it to the English Ambassador and to Milord Kerry.[249] He will surely give it to Mme de Lamballe. Now is the critical moment, and my soul trembles. God keep you all safe. That is my only prayer.

If it were ever useful for you to hide, I beg you not to hesitate to take this course. It might be necessary to allow enough time to reach you. In this case, there is a cellar in the Louvre adjoining M. de La Porte's apartment. I believe it is little known and secure. You could make use of it. The Duke of Brunswick starts marching today. He will need 8 to 10 days to reach the frontier. It is generally believed that the Austrians will mount an attack against Maubeuge.

Marie-Antoinette/Goguelat to Fersen, number 6, July 1792, letter missing

The numbering of the surviving letters confirms that there was a letter numbered 6 from the Queen or Goguelat between 24 July and 1 August 1792.

On 2 August 1792, Fersen received an addendum to the Brunswick Manifesto, which he considered dangerous for the Royal Family: 'The additional declaration for the Duke of Brunswick has arrived; I disapprove of it – to forbid such a thing gives the idea that it's feasible'[250] (see letter of 3 August 1792).

72. GOGUELAT/MARIE-ANTOINETTE TO FERSEN,
1 AUGUST 1792

Stafsund, RA/720807/022/11. Autograph letter from Goguelat with two pages written in invisible ink, which are virtually illegible because the ink is so faded. The transcription of these pages is therefore taken from Klinckowström's edition of the correspondence. The Royal Family's situation is dire.

Received 6th August
Rep. 7th August

No. 7, 1 August 1792

I received your letter No. 14 of 2 July with a leaflet attached. I therefore concluded the business you mentioned to me; it only remains to send me the necessary funds to meet my obligations, and I believe it should be done so they are sent in cash, because there is much to be gained in the exchange with assignats. I have not yet managed to let your houses. The troubles in Paris cause all the people who could live in them to leave. M. d'Eprémesnil's assassination, the arrival of a great number of very suspect strangers and the fear of pillage in Paris are the principal causes of emigration.[251] Those people who are not leaving France are retiring to Rouen and its environs. The event of the 30th has increased fears, angered part of the National Guard and discouraged the rest. Weak people who have good intentions, and those with probity but uncertain courage are going into hiding.

Only those with evil intentions show themselves brazenly. It needs a crisis to get the capital out of its current state of contraction. Everyone desires it, everyone wants it for his own reasons, but no one dares to calculate the effects for fear of arriving at a result which favours the scoundrels. Whatever happens, the King and all decent people will not allow any attempt against the Constitution, and if it is overthrown they will perish with it.

Your friends are well, they send you a thousand compliments and ardently desire to see you soon.

P.S. The parcel I have sent to you by the stage bears the number 141, and each piece of material has the following letters.

n	m	f	p	x	a	n	m	g	o	q
p	a	r	o	i	t	r	a	p	a	r
i	l	y	a	d	u	b	l	a	n	c

There is invisible ink.

[in invisible ink]

The King's life has clearly been threatened for a long time now, as has the Queen's. The arrival of around 600 Marseillais and a quantity of other deputies from all the Jacobin clubs greatly increases our concerns, which are unfortunately only too well founded. Every kind of precaution is being taken for Their Majesties' security, but murderers roam continually around the palace. The people are being stirred up. One part of the National Guard is ill-intentioned and the other is weak and cowardly. The only resistance which can be made to the villains' plans consists of a few people who have decided to make their bodies a rampart for the Royal Family, and the Swiss Guards. The business which took place on the 30th, following a dinner on the Champs Elysées between 180 elite grenadiers from the National Guard and the deputies from Marseilles, clearly demonstrated the cowardice of the National Guard and the little reliance which can be placed in this troop, which cannot really impress except in numbers. The 180 grenadiers took to their heels; two or three were killed and a score or so injured. The Marseillais police the Palais Royal and the garden of the Tuileries, which the National Assembly has thrown open.

In the midst of so many dangers, it is difficult to concern oneself with the choice of ministers. If one has a moment's peace, I will let you know what is thought of your proposals. At present, one must think about avoiding daggers and trying to thwart the conspirators who swarm around a throne which is about to disappear. For a long time now the rebels have taken no trouble to hide their plan to annihilate the Royal Family. In the last two nocturnal assemblies, they only disagreed on the means to employ. You will have been able to judge by an earlier letter how beneficial it is to gain 24 hours. I shall only repeat it again to you today, adding that if [help] does not arrive only Providence can save the King and his family.

73. FERSEN TO MARIE-ANTOINETTE, 3 AUGUST 1792

AN 440AP/1. Autograph copy by Fersen of a letter logged in his register to the 'Queen of France'. The very disturbing news reaching him from Paris has changed his mind, and he advises Marie-Antoinette to leave Paris before the coalition armies arrive.

To the Queen in invisible ink by Toscani

No. 16, Brussels, 3 August 1792

I have received number 5. You already have the manifesto and you should be happy with it. M. de Limon, who wrote it, deserves praise. He has been wonderfully well treated by the King of Prussia, the Emperor and their ministers; even by the princes. The Comte d'Artois spoke to him perfectly on his intention to obey blindly the King and the ministers he chooses. He told him [Limon] that Calonne was leaving him, that he had made him realize that it was impossible to employ him in anything because the King of Prussia and the Emperor had declared that they did not wish to deal with him and that their ministers did not even wish to see him. Calonne is going to Italy.

The Duke of Brunswick has just made an additional declaration which is very strong and in which he calls on all towns and villages to oppose the passage of the King, the Queen and the family if the rebels attempt to carry them off and holds them responsible for any lack of obedience.[252] You will need money in the first instance: how much do you have in London? Arrange for it to be available from one moment to the next, once it is certain that you are free. Do you consent to your diamonds being given as surety? Believe me that if it is not necessary it will not happen, and I will stop it. You must take the crown jewels with you. The baron tells me that La Balue is an honourable man who is completely devoted to him and by flattering him a little and mentioning the baron he would give two million [*livres*]. See if you can or dare get someone to speak to him. I will see about finding you money in England, perhaps from the King's purse. Reply to me as soon as possible.

When the armies are in France, I shall go for a day to see the King of Prussia and the Duke of Brunswick, the baron will, too. Amid all my sorrows, I've suffered the loss of my two dogs. They were poisoned the same morning and died at the same time. This has been a very keen loss. They were precious to me. If the Duke of Brunswick arrives in Paris, he must be lodged in the palace; that would be better than elsewhere.

If you could find a safe way of leaving Paris, take this course. Tell me if you wish it, and we will find a way. Perhaps it might even be essential.

74. Fersen to Marie-Antoinette, 7 August 1792

AN 440AP/1. Autograph copy of a letter from Fersen logged under the heading the 'Queen of France' in his register.

To the Queen in invisible ink by Toscani

No. 17, Brussels, 7 August 1792

I have received your No. 7. No. 6 is missing. My anxiety is extreme, and the little faith one can place in the National Guard, even the well-disposed part it, makes me desperate. I have always been convinced that one could not count on them any more than one can on well-disposed people in Paris, who are afraid to put themselves forward for fear of getting a scratch and who limit themselves to saying prayers while the villains take action. I have always viewed them the same way, and this certainty has always made me tremble. We are pressing as hard as we can for the operations, and Prussian willingness is perfect. The Emperor's is, too, personally, but he is not so well seconded by his cabinet. Mercy has lost almost all his influence with him, so has the Archduchess, and M. de Metternich, who is coming back from Frankfurt and who means well, has full powers. It is believed that because of that she will leave. La Marck has been kept away from everything by the King of Prussia, as a follower of M. de Mercy.

The Prussian army arrived at Trèves on the 5th. It remains there for a few days to get bread and forage; that will delay its march a little, but the Duke of Brunswick will enter France on the 15th or 16th with all his forces. I tremble for this moment and never stop praying – if only I could do more. A big mistake was made in not sending the declaration officially. Nobody thought of it. I made the observation at once and indicated a means; I hope it will be adopted and that it is done.

Simolin has returned. He says that the 18,000 Russians should be leaving Warsaw and that he believes they are already on the march. He says that Vaudreuil did everything he could in Vienna to blacken the baron and Bombelles and that he succeeded just as Calonne succeeded at St Petersburg; that the Empress is very biased towards the princes, that he brought her round a little. It is the Duc de Bourbon who commands instead of M. d'Egmont, but the émigrés are so lacking in everything that possibly only a quarter will be able to participate in operations. The Duke of Brunswick is already very weary of them. The princes absolutely want to issue a manifesto; we are trying to prevent it, but I do not know if we will succeed.

All this military activity was now useless – slow, bound by diplomatic wrangling and so well announced that the French had ample time to prepare their defences. The only person in Fersen's circle in Brussels who seemed to appreciate the gravity of the situation in which the French Royal Family found themselves was Eléonore Sullivan. In his diary on 7 August 1792 Fersen records a discussion of an initiative to get help from England.

> Very worrying demand made by the municipality of Paris for the overthrow of the King. Mme Sullivan, who is distressed about it all the time, who never ceases to think of it and who is even ill with worry, suggested to me that someone be sent to England to demand some action from the King to save their lives; to make him say that he would not permit an attempt on their lives and that he would exact a resounding vengeance . . . She spoke to Simolin who agreed with her and thought that it could succeed; she got Craufurd to consent to go there, and he hoped for the best. In the evening I spoke to the baron; he was completely opposed to the idea for the same reasons I had had in the morning, adding that he feared Pitt's ill will, which could reveal it all and, by instructing the rebels of this step, endanger the King. That was excessive, and I proved it to the baron, but he persisted in his refusal, adding that in politics a futile effort was always harmful. I put forward the same reason as Mme Sullivan had in the morning and begged him to sleep on it and that I would come back in the morning for his answer. While waiting I agreed with Craufurd that, if he persisted, we would send a man with letters to the Duke of Dorset to try to get him arrange this measure.[253]

The following morning Breteuil had come round to the idea, and the Bishop of Pamiers set off for London with letters for the Duke of Dorset and the British Prime Minister, William Pitt.

Marie-Antoinette/Goguelat to Fersen, early August 1792, letter missing

On 10 August 1792, Fersen received a letter that heightened all his anxieties about the Royal Family. 'The palace is constantly under threat. The King and the Queen take it in turns to sleep; one of them is always up.'[254] The same day he wrote to Marie-Antoinette. She would be a prisoner of the National Assembly before his letter even left Brussels.

75. FERSEN TO MARIE-ANTOINETTE, 10 AUGUST 1792

AN 440AP/1. Autograph copy of a letter from Fersen written in code and invisible ink, dated 10 August 1792 with 11 August in the margin (the date it was sent). For the very last time Fersen recorded a letter to Marie-Antoinette in his register, under the heading the 'Queen of France' – a letter she would not have received. The code word is paroitra.

In this letter, Fersen appears to try to justify himself with regard to Eléonore Sullivan, which reinforces the idea that Marie-Antoinette knew of his liaison with her in February – or possibly from some of the missing letters in May. Fersen could certainly not be sent to London to solicit the intervention of the British government, because he was not French. Moreover, Craufurd had informed the British Prime Minister the preceding year that Fersen was believed to be the father of the Dauphin. His mission would have been severely compromised, for Pitt would have seen only the Queen of France's lover desperate to preserve his own interests. It was all now far too late anyway. The Jacobins had no intention of listening to reason, and the British government in the end made no public statement and simply recalled their Ambassador from Paris once his situation there became untenable.

To the Queen in invisible ink by Toscani

No. 18, Brussels, 10 August [1792]

[*code*]

I've persuaded the baron to make an approach to Mr Pitt to engage the King of England to declare that he will avenge any attempt against your persons in a resounding fashion. The bishop has gone there. The dangers you face made me adopt this measure, perhaps useless, but for such an interesting object everything must be tried.

[*invisible ink*]

It is Mme Sullivan's idea. The baron was opposed to it, considering it to be futile, but he adopted it afterwards when I had set it out to him in detail. M. Craufurd was ready to go, but we felt afterwards that as a compatriot he might perhaps encounter obstacles and that the bishop would have more effect. My plan was to go, but when they told me I could be more useful [here] I gave up this idea which so pleased my heart.

My anxiety for you is extreme. I don't have a moment's peace and my only consolation is to see that my worries are shared by Mr Craufurd, who is occupied only with you and ways to serve you. {And by Mme Sullivan, who never ceases to think of you, to bewail your fate and to pray. Her affection for you is truly touching, and it is what made me love her. We often cry together, and I live only with these good people. It was she who first had the idea and who persuaded Craufurd to go when it was decided that I could not. God willing it succeeds and may be of use to you.}

The Duke of Brunswick is still entering [France] on the 15th. The Prince Hohenlohe has had some successes. It is believed that he is outside Landau and that the position will fall to him. Duke Albert has entered France with all his forces.[255] He is believed to have plans against Condé or Maubeuge. I am very sorry that you have not left Paris.

Extract from Fersen's diary

13 August 1792. Terrible news from Paris. On Thursday morning the palace was attacked, the King and Queen took refuge in the Assembly; at one o'clock they were still fighting in the courtyards and the Carrousel. The blood was flowing; many people killed and hanged, the palace stormed everywhere, eight cannon trained on it and firing ... My God, what horror![256]

Fersen to Countess Sophie Piper, 15 August 1792

You will get details from the Duke of the dreadful day of the 10th. The Royal Family is safe, but one cannot, however, be reassured about their future. God save them – I would give my life to save them. The whole palace was pillaged and ransacked and the family is in prison in the Feuillants. No one dare see them or go near them. Farewell, my dear friend – pity me and love me.[257]

On 19 August 1792, Fersen fell ill. He suffered from an inflamed right testicle and fever that confined him to bed and caused him recurrent health problems for over a year; the symptoms are described at length in his diary and indicate epididymitis. Evidently Eléonore Sullivan had given him more than just a passing pleasure. He suffered difficulties in walking and standing, and his diary was written up later, once his fever had subsided. He relates news from France with remarkable detachment, still believing that the Prussian army would reach the gates of Paris in time to force the Jacobins to negotiate. But the men who had now seized power in France did not share Louis XVI's and Marie-Antoinette's scruples about starting a civil war. Any political opponents who had not fled were rounded up, imprisoned and massacred in an orgy of blood-letting which saw the birth of the French Republic.

Fersen received heartbreaking news every day – friends arrested, tortured, murdered. He mourned them all sincerely. But he was implacable towards the Constitutionals. On 29 August he wrote to Silversparre, Cabinet Secretary for French affairs in Stockholm: 'Barnave and Charles Lameth have been arrested, and I hope they will be executed; nobody deserves it more.'[258] His hatred of the Constitutionals never ceased. In April 1794 he felt a deep repugnance when invited to a dinner with M. Jarry: 'He was a constitutional and I always consider them the cause of all the ills of France and of all my sorrows. I will never forgive them for it.' On 1 September 1792 he learnt of the separation of Louis XVI and Marie-Antoinette. 'This news saddened me. Her separation from the King must have been very painful for the Queen.'[259]

Things were about to get even worse. The government of the Austrian Netherlands was not at all prepared for the successes of the French revolutionary army, and on 6 November 1792 Fersen learnt that Archduchess Marie-Christine and Mercy had given orders to evacuate Brussels. Fersen, who still shared a house with Craufurd, Eléonore Sullivan and Simolin, decided to seek refuge in Germany. Before leaving for Düsseldorf he paid a visit on Mercy to ensure that Marie-Antoinette's diamonds were safe. It is interesting that she has become 'Josephine' again in his diary. The Queen's correspondence was also in danger of destruction.

Extracts from Fersen's diary

6 November . . . I went to see Mercy to ask him if he had taken care of Josephine's diamonds. He had the gall to tell me that he did not know that he had any, that he had certainly received a box but he had given the key to the Archduchess on her arrival; yet it was I who wrote the letter to him at the time and who sent the box . . . I was in despair at having to move and to leave Brussels . . . Sometimes I was tempted to despair altogether and abandon everything.

9 November . . . It was decided that we would get into the carriages. They wanted me to burn the portfolio containing the Queen's papers, but I did no such thing. I placed them with my own in Simolin's carriage. I had resolved the day before to give them to Lord Elgin to be sent to England, but the insurrection at Anvers made me change my mind, or, rather, Mme Sullivan did not hand them over when he sent his courier for them in the night.[260]

Most of Fersen 's correspondence with his sister Sophie for 1791–2 is missing, but on 8 November he entrusted his faithful officer Reutersvärd, who was returning to Sweden, with a letter for her; 'spoke of Eléonore', notes Fersen in his register. On arriving at Düsseldorf he learnt that Louis XVI's trial had started. 'The gazette of the 12th [December] tells of the King's interrogation on the witness stand – what an indignity! He replied perfectly.'[261] The fate of the Royal Family occupied Fersen constantly.

Fersen to Sophie Piper, 1 January 1793

. . . we must always love one another; we need this feeling to console ourselves for all our sorrows. Mine have been dreadful for two years and they renew themselves daily. Only the friendship of my friends can ease them. Always conserve yours for me. It is essential to me.[262]

Extracts from Fersen's diary, January 1793

2 January. The King was in the dock on the 26th. De Sèze read his defence statement, which is a powerful thing. The King added with feeling that what hurt him most was being accused of having wanted to spill the blood of his people, he who since the start of his reign had sought nothing but their happiness.

22 January . . . I was very sad about them, about Sweden and my future and about politics in general. If they perish all is lost for me.

23 January . . . I received the attached statement from the Archbishop of Tours in the evening; I was devastated. It seemed to me that all hope was gone.[263]

Fersen to Sophie Piper, 24 January 1793

Ah, my tender and kind Sophie, it is only with you that I can find some comfort, and now more than ever I feel the need to talk with you and the value of your friendship. Taube will tell you all the details; they make one shudder and my soul is deeply affected. It is torn by all its suffering. We will only get the final verdict tomorrow, but my fears are unimaginable. Poor unfortunate family, poor Queen, why can I not save her with my own blood? It would be the greatest joy for me, the sweetest enjoyment for my soul. Ah, how well I feel at present all that I should feel and all that I have ever felt. Think then how wretched I am and how dreadful my situation is. Yes, my dear Sophie, it is almost unbearable. I would have sacrificed myself for this respectable and too unhappy family and now I can no longer do anything for them. Monsters and villains from the scum of the populace exercise the most dreadful tyranny over them and perhaps are dragging them even now to their agony. The idea is unbearable; it overwhelms me. No, there are no more fine days ahead for me – my happiness is over and I am condemned to eternal sorrows and to drag out a sad and languishing existence. Never will their images leave my memory. I shall mourn them all my life. I shall think of them, their kindness towards me, their confidence. My God, why did I have to know them, or why didn't I die before them and for them? But, my dear friend, I must not afflict you too much. It is telling you too much about my grief. It will be eternal and will poison the rest of my days. Your tender and caring friendship will help me bear the burden but will never be able to efface it.

My dear Sophie, I received yours of the 4th. How kind and sweet you are! Ah, don't fear, it would be impossible for me not to do everything for them, even to sacrifice myself for them. She herself [Eléonore] never stops pushing me, but I have no need of that. I wouldn't have loved her otherwise, but at present I am acutely aware of the difference in this feeling; it cannot even comfort me. No, my Sophie, nothing could have turned me away from the task I was devoted to, I put all my claim to praise in it and my most ardent prayer is to be able to prove it to them still, but, alas – no, I have not the strength to talk about it any more, and I do not know how I support the state I am in. The restraint I am obliged to impose upon myself only increases the horror if it, and yet I cannot hide it, and the few people who encounter me can see it but too well.[264]

The news of Louis XVI's execution came two days later and with it a report that the entire Royal Family had been massacred. The shock finally made Fersen's immense self-control snap, and forgetting the King entirely he poured out all his feelings for Marie-Antoinette.

Extract from Fersen's diary

26 January . . . I spent the whole day in a dreadful state with my uncertainties. El. cried. I was desperate not to be able to be alone with her to cry, but we were never alone. Ah, how much I felt that I loved <u>Her</u> and how much I suffered. At nine o'clock in the evening, Baron Lillien, director of the Imperial Post, came to see me. He told me that a courier had brought the news to M. de Valence that the King had been executed and the whole family massacred.[265]

Fersen to Sophie Piper, 26 January 1793

My tender, kind Sophie. Ah, pity me, pity me! Only you can understand the state I am in. I have now lost everything in the world. You alone and T. [Taube] are left for me – ah, do not abandon me. *She* who was my happiness, she for whom I lived – yes, my tender Sophie, because I have never stopped loving her, no, I could not ever, not for an instant; I have not stopped loving her, and I would have sacrificed absolutely everything for her, and I well feel that at this moment – she whom I loved so much and for whom I would have given a thousand lives is no more. Oh my God, why do you destroy me so? What have I done to deserve your anger? *She* no longer lives! My grief is overwhelming, and I do not know how I stay alive. I do not know how I bear my sorrow; it is extreme, and nothing will ever efface it. She will always be present in my memory, and I shall weep for her for ever. Everything is over for me, my dear friend. Ah, why didn't I die at her side and for her – for them – on 20 June [1791]? I would have been happier than dragging out my miserable existence in eternal sorrows, in sorrows that will end only with my life, because never will her adored image be effaced from my memory, and you insulted me by even imagining for a moment it could be. You do not know me; you do not do justice to my heart. This heart is truly wretched and will be now for as long as it lives. Your own feels too deeply not to pity me. Ah, I have real need now of my friends. They alone support me at the moment, and to crown my horrors at this cruel time I still have the wretched task of writing down these sad and dreadful details. I do not know how I have the strength . . .

27th

It is midnight. We receive the sad certainty of the King's execution. My heart is so torn I have not the strength to tell you more. There is no word of the rest of the family, but my fears are terrible. Ah, my God, save them and have mercy on me![266]

Fersen to Sophie Piper, 1 February 1793

My dear Sophie, I still have a moment and I give it to you, but I do not even know how I still have the strength to occupy myself with anything. My soul is so tormented, so torn by the memory of the loss I have just suffered and my fears for the future that I scarcely have the faculty to think of anything else. The condition of this unhappy family – their pains, their sorrows, their sufferings – never leave my mind. Constantly I imagine them, I see them and what I feel cannot be imagined. Accursed nation of cowards and villains, whom I hate, scorn and despise! It is made solely to be governed by tyrants. This family was too good, too honourable for them. They are a nation of tigers and cannibals – may the curse of Heaven and a just but too tardy vengeance fall on them and avenge the innocent blood they have spilt and which I fear they will still spill. I never stop being afraid of this ultimate horror and villainy. They are capable of everything, and the idea is devastating. It pursues me night and day.[267]

With Louis XVI now dead, Fersen realized that the lives of seven-year-old Louis XVII and Marie-Antoinette were at even greater risk; the new regime in France had no intention of restoring the monarchy, even in a limited constitutional form. Fersen wanted foreign governments to speak as little as possible of Marie-Antoinette, believing that any steps by the Austrians to claim her – especially when accompanied by demands for a slice of French territory – would simply hasten her trial, which had been decreed at the same time as that of Louis XVI. He thought that the English and money would be more effective in securing her release and wrote on the subject to the Comte de Mercy, the Baron de Breteuil and the Duke of Dorset on 3 February 1793.

3 February 1793

... I wrote a long letter to the Comte de Mercy (attached), wrote on the same subject to the Duke of Dorset by courier. Someone sent word to M. Quidor, who is here, that they wanted to declare the Dauphin a bastard, shave the Queen's head and lock her up in the Salpetrière. One dare not think about it, it is so horrific, but everything is possible. Young Bouillé said that the Prince of Wales had a plan with the Duc de Choiseul and others to abduct the King. That made me think of the idea for the rest of the family, but only the English could do it, and I still see a thousand difficulties. However, I am clinging to this idea.[268]

Fersen to the Comte de Mercy, 3 February 1793

Stafsund, SE/RA/720807/005. Autograph copy of a letter from Fersen to the Comte de Mercy on measures to liberate Marie-Antoinette after the death of Louis XVI. His main concern was not to do or say anything that would hasten her trial or lessen her value as a bargaining chip should the allied armies be victorious.

Düsseldorf, 3 February 1793

The letter Your Excellency did me the honour to write me on 31st last was handed to me this evening. I was flattered that Your Excellency approved my reflections on the regency. As for measures to take to save the Queen, it would be very difficult to give a definitive answer on such an important step and it would require a much more exact understanding than I have on the current manner of thinking; but the more I consider everything that has happened, the more I am strengthened in my opinion that the only way to serve her is by doing nothing for her. It is appalling to have to confine one's zeal to inactivity, but, although the effort is painful, the joy will be all the greater if it is crowned with success. A simple proposal by the Emperor, and which had no other object than to demand the Queen, would without contradiction comply with the Emperor's dignity; but if this proposal, far from being useful to the Queen, were harmful to her, would it not be finer, nobler and more generous to sacrifice everything to such a great interest, and would not the Emperor's dignity be covered if a secret explanation justifies his silence in the eyes of the courts of Europe?

The aim of this proposal would be the Queen's departure from the kingdom, but the rebels will never consent to it. The interest the press would take in this princess's misfortunes – they would hope for or demand the details she will be able to give – the intelligence she will be able to suggest, the desire for revenge they think will motivate her; all this opposes such a hope. It remains to consider this step under the single aspect of its effects. It will be either helpful, harmful or neutral. Does not the example of the past and the way in which Spain's demands were ignored and only speeded up the King's death prove the negligible effect to be expected from such proposals, and does it not lead to the unhappy confirmation that force is the only thing that could change the Queen's fate if it has already been decided? But will not a very public proposal start a discussion on the Queen's trial, which was decreed at the same time as the King's but which has not yet been mentioned and which one party wants to allow to be forgotten? Will it not serve as a pretext to hasten the Queen's sentence, as was said at the King's trial, in order to avoid similar proposals from the other powers?

Will not the interest shown by the Emperor for his aunt be an excuse for the rebels and a means they will employ to destroy her, in reviving hatred for the Austrians and painting the Queen as a foreigner complicit in the crimes they attributed to the King? In vain the most just reasonings demonstrate the impossibility of a trial by the absence of any proofs and even in the rebels' own interest; but we have seen that such considerations haven't stopped them, so can one dare to hope that at present they will be wiser and less atrocious? If a proposal of this sort could be absolutely neutral, then the Emperor's honour should commit him to making it, but how can one believe it to be neutral when, on the one hand, it seems certain that it is futile, since it will not achieve its objective, and, on the other, one can perceive the possibility that it would be harmful; and isn't it then a question of not making a proposal?

In my view, a more effective way of helping the Queen would be by using English intelligence agents to win over with money and promises the leaders of the Orléans party such as Laclos, Santerre, Dumouriez, because the Duc d'Orléans should not be approached; he is as useless and incapable as he is villainous and cowardly, and it is only through others that you get to him. Your Excellency is in a better position than I am to know how far this idea is practicable. Judging by the rebels' conduct, I am convinced that they hope that by destroying the Royal Family they will also destroy the powers' interest for the monarchy, and that then the views of the powers being confined to a partition of the kingdom, they will give them up at the moment when they can establish their republic and shield themselves from the punishments they so justly deserve. This is what makes me hope that if the powers behave in a way that lets them keep this hope, they will not want to needlessly charge themselves with a new crime in slaughtering what remains of this unhappy family. My zeal and my affection for the Queen alone have dictated all these reflections, which I submit with confidence to Your Excellency's experience.

Like the Bishop of Pamiers's mission in August 1792, this proposal to use English agents (which was backed by Breteuil and Mercy) also met with a stony silence from William Pitt, despite the efforts of the Queen's English friends. On 13 March 1793 Fersen heard that the Swedish regent had offered him the embassy in London. 'It was a bolt from the blue for me. I saw myself obliged to leave El. [Eleonore] and to move away from *Her* [Marie-Antoinette] and from affairs that put me in a position to serve her and contribute to her deliverance.'[269] He promptly demanded credentials as Ambassador to Louis XVII – and worked to have Marie-Antoinette recognized as regent instead of Monsieur. In his letters to Sophie 'them' always means the Queen and her son. 'I will never be diverted from what I owe them,' he wrote to Sophie. His master, however, was the King of Sweden. Why should he owe his duty to Marie-Antoinette and Louis XVII?

Fersen to Sophie Piper
14 March 1793

Taube will tell you what I am asking for. Work for it on your side, and remember, my tender Sophie, that I cannot nor do I wish to move away from them or abandon them – honour, affection, feeling, all make it a law to me to serve them and I shall never fail in that.

15 March 1793

My resolution is invariable. I will never be diverted from what I owe them nor from what may contribute to their service; as long as they have need of me I will serve them and I would sacrifice everything for that. My feelings and my duty dictate this conduct, and I would have done nothing if I didn't act consistently.[270]

Extracts from Fersen's diary

17 March. Nicolay writes from Paris that on the 26th one section had a debate on the Temple and it was said that Louis Capet [Louis XVII] was born to be a bad man, that it was necessary to make him into a good one and to remove him from two incorrigible women. There is talk of petitions for the Queen's trial. It seems certain that the Orléans party is hard at work; it is believed that they are even profiting from the unrest due to misery and shortages or that they excite them to prove that a sovereign is needed so they can nominate the Duc d'Orléans.

31 March . . . Received a letter from the Duchesse de Polignac, who tells me she has received news of the Queen from a doctor; it must surely be La Caze. Here is the letter.[271]

Unfortunately neither this letter, nor several others from the Duchesse de Polignac to Fersen, are to be found in the archives. At the beginning of April 1793 hope suddenly returned. General Dumouriez, a former Jacobin minister, defected to the Prussians and proposed a march on Paris with his whole army to restore the monarchy. Fersen was like a man reborn; deliriously happy at the thought of a swift return to Paris where he would be reunited with Marie-Antoinette and young Louis XVII, he swung into action; he held discussions with diplomats, wrote everywhere and made his preparations . . . He wrote a 'Note for the Queen' on the regency and the steps she would need to take as soon as she was free. It was exactly as though she were still in the Tuileries, sending letters through Goguelat or Gougenot in invisible ink. But the note remains unfinished, because Dumouriez's army refused to follow him.

76. FERSEN TO MARIE-ANTOINETTE, 8 APRIL 1793

AN 440AP/1. Autograph note by Fersen for Marie-Antoinette on the subject of her regency for Louis XVII, written after the defection of General Dumouriez. Interestingly, Fersen talks of 'the re-establishment of your authority as regent' rather than the 'establishment of your authority', which tends to confirm that Fersen always regarded her as sovereign rather than Louis XVI.

Note for the Queen

8 April 1793

The position you are going to find yourself in will be very awkward. You will owe great obligations to a rogue, who in fact has only yielded to necessity and only wanted to act well when he saw the impossibility of further resistance. That is all his merit towards you. But this man is useful. You must make use of him and forget the past, even seem to believe what he will tell you of his good intentions, act frankly even with him to attain those things you may wish for and the re-establishment of the monarchy in its entirety and such as you wish it to be and such as circumstances allow it to be. With regard to Dumouriez, you run no risk; at the moment his interest is closely tied to yours and the re-establishment of your authority as regent. He must fear a regency under Monsieur and the influence of the princes and the émigrés. But you must try not to commit yourself too much with him, and, above all, keep at a distance all the other intriguers he will want to place and recommend. [**You cannot risk**] His people will be a hindrance, and it will be easy to prove to him that they will be the same for him and could weaken the obligations that you owe him and lessen the recompense that he must expect by impeding what you might be tempted to do for him. He is a vain and greedy man, he will feel the force of this argument, and your own sense will suggest better than I can the things to say to him on the subject.

[**You must, however, prepare yourself to see**] your wishes on the re-establishment of the monarchy obstructed by the influence of the allied powers. There is no longer any doubt that the partial partition of the kingdom has been decided upon. Except for Prussia, Russia and Spain, their interest is to give France a government that will keep her in a feeble state. M. de Mercy cannot and must not advise you except on this basis [*and Dumouriez cannot be far away from it up to a certain point, but you must try*], therefore you must be somewhat wary of what he will say to you on the matter and weigh it up with the advice of wise people, interested like you in the re-establishment of the monarchy and of your authority; an outcome less unfavourable to you can result from this opposition.

[*It would be a good idea to summon the presidents at Moutiers who have stayed in France (because in the beginning you must not call the émigrés); but do not see them as a single body but individually, to be enlightened by them. This proposal does not seem to present any drawbacks and presents the advantage of being able to form an opinion which, compared with the powers' bad intentions, can temper them and yield a result that is less unfavourable for you. This, in general and in brief, is my opinion, which the bishop will explain to you in detail if you wish. It is based on my knowledge of your position abroad; that which you have on things and people within will make you able to judge better than I how far I may be right, not knowing.*]

You cannot be regent without the Chancellor and registration by the *parlements*, and it is important to insist on that point; it is even an excuse to do as little as possible until that time. You will need a regency council; it needs to be convened before you do anything. You must not hesitate to summon the princes to it, even the Prince de Condé – it is a means of rendering him nil. You must try to prevent Dumouriez from wanting to be the president or a member of it and speak to him frankly on the subject if he evinces the slightest wish. In everything, up until the moment when you are recognized as regent and have formed your cabinet, you must do as little as possible and pay everyone in compliments.

I have talked about this a great deal with the bishop and told him of my ideas, and he will explain them to you better than I could in writing. You will be happy with him and his wisdom. He will inform you of everything, and I found him very reasonable and conscious of the need to adapt to circumstances. If it were necessary to have Dumouriez as head of the regency council, or even if you were to appoint Monsieur, it would be a good idea for you to appoint the baron to it if you do not wish to make him head of it. My zeal alone has dictated these insights; circumstances may cause infinite variations, and they are only for consideration.

It will be necessary to write to the Emperor and the Kings of Prussia and England: they have been perfect for you, especially the King of Prussia. You should also write to the Empress, but a simple and dignified letter because I am not pleased with her conduct. She never replied to your letter.

Widowed and imprisoned, Marie-Antoinette was still thinking of 'the most loved and loving of men'. In April 1793 she entrusted the Chevalier de Jarjayes, who was forced to leave France after a failed attempt to extract the Royal Family from the Temple, with a message for Fersen. It was not until 22 July that he received Jarjayes's letter – which gave him 'very great pleasure'. However, Jarjayes did not give details of the Queen's message.

I have searched in vain until now for a means to acquit myself of a message I was charged with for you on my departure from Paris at the end of April last . . . I will wait for your reply before passing on what I have to give you, to be sure that you will receive it safely. The person who gave me this message was in reasonably good health when I left.[272]

Fersen logged a letter to Jarjayes in his register the following day, begging him to 'tell me if has means or can give anything to receive news, that he writes to me'.[273] Doubtless he hoped that a servant in the Temple could possibly serve as an intermediary for communication with the Queen. He was avid for news from Paris – from newspapers and letters from the few people who remained there and were able to get letters out. His diary and his letters to Sophie trace several months of anguish, false hopes and attempts to snatch Marie-Antoinette from the Jacobins' clutches. On 20 April 1793 he returned to Brussels with his friends and the Comte de Mercy when the French retreated from the city. News from Paris now arrived every day.

Extracts from Fersen's diary, 1793

22 May. La Caze went to the Temple. He found the Queen very little changed, Mme Elisabeth so unrecognizable that he recognized her only when the Queen called her 'my sister'. She was in the room in a nightcap, dressed in a very plain muslin gown. Little Madame had

ulcers over her whole body and was threatened by a dissolution of the
blood . . . They write from Paris that the young King had been ill and
that the Commune refused the Queen the doctor she asked for on the
pretext he was aristocratic and sent one of its own persuasion.

3 June. Motion in the Convention to deport the Royal Family. It is
received without mutterings, they pass to the day's business. Roux,
who is opposing it, is a child of Versailles. He used to be in army
headquarters, Mme Campan's lover, and very attached to the Queen
before he became a Jacobin.

Fersen had written to Sweden about this last possibility.

8 June. Letter from Taube, who tells me that the Duke replied <u>Yes</u>,
when he asked him if, in the event that Louis XVII were free and
outside France in a foreign country I should go there immediately.[274]

He would never abandon Marie-Antoinette and her son. The war
seemed to be going the allies' way, and on 9 June 1793 Fersen wrote to
Sophie:

We have good news from everywhere, may it continue the same.
News on the august prisoners is very reassuring and up to now there
have been no motions or agitations against them. That gives me a little
hope of seeing them one day freed from their long captivity. If ever I
could enjoy such a sight, what a moment for my heart![275]

But every sign of interest in the Queen and her son was fatal, because
the Commune of Paris ruled with despotic violence. On 10 July Fersen
heard from a traveller who arrived from Paris 'that people are beginning
to think well of the Royal Family; that the Queen takes the air and she is
applauded when she can be seen; that they even cry "Long live the
Dauphin!"' Two days later he received crushing news.

12 July. The Dauphin separated from the Queen by the [Commune]
and put in another room in the Temple. That looked extremely bad to
me. What dreadful pain for the Queen, unhappy princess![276]

Fersen to Sophie Piper, 21 July 1793

Our news from Paris is not so bad. They write that the Queen sees her son twice a day ... This news has somewhat lessened the dreadful pain this separation caused me. It is one of the things which has caused me the most pain in a long while. What appalling barbarity! Her only consolation was the care of this child, it was her only pleasure, the only thing which could make her support the horror of her situation. I pictured her grief, her anxieties; they would have been dreadful, and my suffering was extreme. How much more do I regret the loss of our dear and unfortunate master [Gustav III]. His death has deprived me of all means of wreaking my vengeance on these villains, for whom the most dreadful tortures are still too gentle, and at present I am reduced to the sad role of spectator who can only pray for them.[277]

In fact Marie-Antoinette was not allowed to see her 'Chou d'Amour' every day. She would never see him again, but she could hear him weeping in his tower room, and his cries of desperation as he was dragged away from her must have echoed in her head constantly. She surely realized what was coming next. On 10 August Fersen received the devastating news.

Appalling news of the Queen in the evening when the Comte de Mercy gave me the gazettes of 2 and 3 August ... They confirm this calamity. My soul was torn. I pictured her condition, her sorrows, her sufferings, and I also felt keenly all I have lost since the arrest at Varennes. Eléonore alone was able to comfort me a little but could not stop me feeling deeply, and the uncertainty over what I should do made my position even more dreadful, for I regard her death as inevitable, and yet I try to hope. It cost me a great deal of pain to hide my terrible grief.[278]

The following day he went to see Mercy with the Comte de La Marck to propose a swift march on Paris by the Austrian army, but Mercy was glacial about this idea.

Fersen to Sophie Piper, 14 August 1793

My dear Sophie, my one and only friend, you doubtless know by now of the dreadful calamity of the Queen's transfer to the prisons of the Conciergerie and the decree by that execrable Convention which delivers her up to the Revolutionary Tribunal to be tried. Since that moment, I no longer live, because it is not living to exist as I do or to suffer all the pain I feel. If I could still do something to free her I think I would suffer less, but to be able to do nothing except through solicitations is dreadful for me. Taube will tell you of the only hope we have left, and which I have demanded – a prompt march on Paris is the only thing left to save her, and I still face the horror of the uncertainty as to whether this plan will be adopted. I am losing, in the space of eighteen months, three sovereigns, my friends, who were dear to me for more than one reason. My sorrows will be eternal, and nothing but death will make me forget them. I cannot occupy myself with anything, I can only think of the miseries of this unfortunate and noble princess. I do not even have the strength to express how I feel. I would give my life to save her and I cannot. My greatest happiness would be to die for her and to save her. I would have this happiness if cowards and villains had not deprived us of the best of masters . . . Pray for her and love your unhappy brother.[279]

On 19 August 1793 Fersen proposed that Mercy send an agent to Paris in order to try to buy Marie-Antoinette's freedom. He proposed a M. Ribbes, who knew Danton; but Austrian duplicity naturally delayed his mission. Fersen wanted the Queen to be ransomed as 'a private individual', the Emperor's aunt. The Austrians wanted to partition France. In addition to Alsace, Lorraine and the French Low Countries, Fersen felt they also intended to take Picardy. Marie-Antoinette counted for nothing in their political equations – indeed, she was an embarrassment, since she was mother to the King of France whose territory they intended to seize. After far too many discussions and Mercy's watering down of his mission, Ribbes at last left Brussels on 29 August. Fersen's letters to his sister depict his feelings better than his diary.

Fersen to Sophie Piper

4 September 1793

We know nothing of the unhappy Queen, and we are forced to rejoice at that. What a dreadful position! I think of it all the time. I often reproach myself even for the air I breathe when I think she is shut up in a dreadful prison. This idea is breaking my heart and poisoning my life, and I am constantly torn between grief and rage.

8 September 1793

My troubles and my anxieties are continual and perpetual. I don't know how to reassure myself about the fate of the Queen and her unfortunate family. Almost everyone seems to me to be reassured. The arguments are very good. I make them myself: this must be thus . . . but how can one expect anything reasonable from madmen and *enragés* such as these scoundrels? And this reflection removes all hope of seeing them follow another course than that of their villainy and their cruelty . . . You asked if there are not enough decent people in Paris to save her. There are a few, perhaps even the majority would like to, but they are governed by fear. They are all cowards. Only the scoundrels are courageous and they govern the majority despotically. It is what I have seen ever since the beginning of the Revolution . . .

Yes, my dear friend, I will have lost everything, but I regret nothing but them. I still have the satisfaction of having done my duty, of having sacrificed everything to them as I should. I would like to be able still to give up my life for them, and I would give it with pleasure to save them. The state the Queen is in, alone in an infamous prison, separated from everything she holds most dear in the world, given over to the full horror of her thoughts – this condition is constantly presented to my imagination and overwhelms me. We have made some moves for her, may they be successful. Taube will be able to tell you about them. Why did I have to lose every means of serving them, and how has Providence permitted so many crimes? May that Providence listen to my vows and my prayers and save them, may I be happy enough to see them again. Without that there will be no more happiness for me in this world and my wretched existence will be filled only with regrets.[280]

Extract from Fersen's diary

13 September. News from Paris that arrived the day before and which is in the little *War Journal* is very bad for the Queen. The intention is clear to start her trial. Ribbes came back. He took the decision to write to Danton in a way that would be unintelligible to anyone but him, and he sent the letter. I fear it will arrive too late. What will M. de Mercy have to reproach himself with then, he who wasted eight days by his stay in the country, and four more after his return, with all the difficulties he made! It is horrible to think about it. God preserve *Her* and give me the satisfaction of seeing *Her* again one day.[281]

Fersen to Sophie Piper, 15 September 1793

Our anxieties about the Queen are always the same, and they have even increased in the past three days. A man called Michonis has been accused of writing to her to try to save her – it chilled me with terror, and I felt all my fears and my pain even more keenly. However, there have been no consequences and I am a little calmer, yet without hoping for more, because I regard this accusation as an excuse to start her trial, for which I am sure there is no evidence, but of what use is that when the villains will fabricate it when they have none.

I only live on worries and fears. They return every day, but don't worry, I have been prepared for everything for a long time, and it seems to me I could receive the most appalling news with equanimity. It is a dreadful state to be in, and I do what I can to bear it.[282]

The catastrophe was hurtling towards them. Ribbes's mission led to nothing. Later Fersen would hear of other attempts to save the Queen – the one organized by Jarjayes, when she was still in the Temple; a plan by Baron Esbeck, who managed to bribe her gaolers in the Conciergerie; the so-called 'carnation plot' organised by M. de Rougeville and M. Michonis, a member of the Paris Commune.[283] In the autumn of 1793 he awaited the arrival of newspapers from Paris with mortal dread. The announcement by the Austrians that they had captured Drouet, the postmaster at Sainte-Menehould who had recognized Louis XVI and galloped on back roads to sound the alarm at Varennes and who later as member of the Convention voted for the King's death, greatly upset Fersen. He went to see him in prison, and all his feelings of rage, impotence and anger at the failure of the Royal Family's escape made him seethe inside, but he managed to remain cool on the outside. However, it made him feel ill. His icy exterior revealed nothing of the man within, a man burning with a furious desire for revenge.

Extracts from Fersen's diary 1793

22 September. I also received quite an interesting letter from [the Duke of] Deux-Ponts on M. d'Esbeck's return; he was abducted by the French. What he says of the plan to hand the Queen over to the mob horrified me. I can't think of it without rage and anguish. What I feel about that can only be felt, and I sometimes think I would be happier if her fate were decided one way or another; but then I feel at the same time that if I lose her I lose everything and I will be almost entirely alone in the world.

26 September. A clerk of Perregaux's arrived; he left [Paris] on 27 August. He has been sent word that the Queen underwent an interrogation at the Revolutionary Tribunal, that they asked her if she were the widow of Louis Capet, that she replied: 'You know that I am the widow of your King.' On a second question, she replied: 'You may be my executioners, my murderers, but you will never be my judges.' Then she had an attack of nerves which meant she had to be taken back to her [cell].

6 October. Drouet arrived at 11 o'clock . . . I went with Col. Hervey to see him in his prison . . . The sight of this infamous villain made me angry, and the effort I made to say nothing to him because of the abbé de Limon and the Comte de Fitzjames, who were with us, made me ill. I would like to have been able to present him with all his infamy and the miseries which are going to follow it. I was vexed to see him so well lodged. I would have liked to see him in a damp, infected dungeon and in constant agonies. It is this infamous villain who is the cause of all the miseries and of the war. I spoke about it in the evening to Mme de Metternich, and I asked her to see that he was very badly treated and to remember all his crimes – the King's death, the Queen's dreadful imprisonment, all the details, the evils of the war && to get her treat him as he deserves. Another officer captured with him said that the Queen was in no danger, that she was very well treated and that she had everything she wanted. The scoundrels, how they lie! An Englishman who has arrived in Switzerland says he paid 25 *louis* to enter the Queen's prison. He carried a jug of water. It's underground, where there is only a poor bed, a table and a chair. He found the Queen seated, her face supported and covered by her hands, her head swathed in two kerchiefs and very badly dressed. She did not even look at him, and he said nothing to her; that was agreed. What horrible circumstances!

10 October. The Queen's trial makes me tremble. If it takes place, this great and unhappy princess is lost; the Convention will never rule against itself to acquit her. The monsters! And God allows them to live! May Almighty God save such a precious head. I will have lost too much if I lose her.

11 October. The gazettes of the 5th say nothing about the Queen, and that makes me quake and makes me fear that her trial is under way. Alas, I believe her loss is certain. Perhaps we now have only to mourn her; the idea is appalling. What is most cruel of all is the constraint to which I am forced.[284]

Fersen's on–off relationship with Eléonore Sullivan continued to give him trouble. On 13 October 1793 she tried to push him into committing to her – but he was incapable of doing so as he still hoped that some miracle would spare Marie-Antoinette . . . The same day in Paris she was appearing before the Revolutionary Tribunal at the beginning of a two-day show trial.

Extracts from Fersen's diary

13 October. El. spoke to me of her position. She is excessively tired of it, she told me she was resolved to end this [way of] life which was insupportable to her. She assured me that she would come with me but that she couldn't go to Sweden because the climate was too cold, and she could finish nothing [with Craufurd] until I had made up my mind. That embarrassed me a great deal. I used to love her, I would have been glad to live with her. Moreover I need someone to look after me. But if *She* lives, I neither want to nor can I abandon *Her*.

19 October. There is an account of the young King's interrogation that makes one shudder and by which it is proved that they want the child to serve as an instrument in his mother's death. My God, are there enough punishments for such villains and will your justice not work in favour of the innocent!

The news of Marie-Antoinette's execution did not reach Brussels until 20 October 1793.

20 October. At 11 o'clock Grandmaison came to tell me that Ackermann, a banker, had received a letter from his correspondent in Paris saying that the Queen's sentence had been pronounced the day before, that it was to be carried out immediately but that circumstances had delayed it; that the people, that is, the paid mob, were beginning to complain; that it was <u>this morning that Marie-Antoinette would appear at the national window</u> [guillotine]. Although I was prepared for it and since her transfer to the Conciergerie I expected it, this certainty overwhelmed me. I did not have the strength to feel a thing. I went out to talk of this calamity with my friends and Mme de Fitzjames and the baron, who I found there. I cried with them, especially with Mme de Fitzjames. The gazette of the 17th speaks of it. It was on the 16th at 11.30 a.m. that this execrable crime was committed, and divine vengeance has not yet struck these monsters![285]

Fersen was numb with shock for several days, tormented by his memories, his grief, his remorse and anguish that perhaps Marie-Antoinette had not realized how much he had loved her. Eléonore could never replace her; he even felt a sudden disgust for her.

20 October. I was astonished myself not to be more deeply affected. I seemed to feel nothing. I was constantly thinking of her, of all the horrible circumstances, of her children; of her unhappy son and his education which will be ruined, of the ill-treatment to which they may subject him, of the Queen's misery at not seeing him in her last moments, of the doubt she may perhaps have been in about me, about my attachment and my interest. This idea devastated me. Then I felt all I had lost in different ways: love, interest, existence, everything was united in her, and all was lost. At last I thought of everything and of nothing. I even had moments of disgust for El. It was not the same love – that delicacy, that solicitude, that tenderness . . . I felt truly wretched, and all seemed to be over for me.[286]

Fersen to Sophie Piper, 20 October 1793

My dear Sophie, I have the ability only to tell you that it is all over for me. Taube will tell you the details. Do not worry; my heart is cruelly broken, but for four years now I have learnt how to suffer. So do not worry, I will withstand it. The hope and the need for revenge sustains me.[287]

Extracts from Fersen's diary

21 October. I could think only of my loss. It was dreadful to have no positive details. That she was alone in her last moments, without comfort, with no one to talk to, to give her last wishes to, is horrifying. The monsters from hell! No, without revenge my heart will never be satisfied.

22 October. My whole day passed in silence without talking; I did not even want to. I could only think aimlessly. I formed thousands and thousands of plans. If my health would have permitted it I would have gone to serve, to avenge her or get myself killed. Ah, I felt myself to be very miserable, and I could not feel otherwise. Here is the act of arraignment with the names of those murderous judges to whom I vow an eternal hatred which can never end.

23 October. My grief, instead of easing, increases as the surprise and shock diminish.

24 October. Here is yet another extract on the too unfortunate Queen. Her image, her sufferings, her death and my love never leave my mind, I can think of nothing else. Oh, my God, why did I have to lose her, and what will become of me? I read those interrogations – it makes one boil with anger to think that the Queen of France was so debased to be placed in front of bandits and villains of that sort. Her replies are fine and good, and there is nothing against her.

26 October. [The Austrians] have lost this campaign. Alas, what I reproach them with most is with having lost the unfortunate Queen;

in marching on Cambrai and Péronne and threatening Paris, she would be saved. Every day I think of it, and every day my grief increases. Every day I feel even more all that I've lost over the last four years. I am very wretched . . . [Mercy] spoke a great deal about his attachment to the unfortunate Queen and his grief at her death but always based on his respect for the memory of Maria-Theresa, because he has always affected to be attached to the Queen only because of her mother, whereas he should have been because of all the kindness and confidence this too unhappy princess showed him.[288]

The Chevalier de Rougeville, who had tried to extract Marie-Antoinette from the Conciergerie, had managed to escape from Paris and arrived in Brussels. Fersen went to see him on 18 November to find out about Rougeville's rescue attempt. He heard some horrible details on the Queen's state of health and her captivity.

Extracts from Fersen's diary

17 November. They say that the fiacre which took the unfortunate Queen from the Temple to the Conciergerie was filled with blood; that the coachman didn't know who he was driving, but he suspected who it was, having waited for a long time; that having arrived at the Conciergerie they stayed a long time without getting out, that the men got out first and the woman afterwards, that she had leant on his arm and that he had found his fiacre full of blood – but all that is not properly confirmed.

18 November . . . Here are the particulars about the Queen. Her room was the third as you enter on the right, opposite that of Custine. It was on the ground floor. The window looked out on the courtyard, which was full the whole day long with prisoners looking through the window and insulting the Queen. The room was small, damp and fetid; it had neither stove nor fireplace. There were three beds – one for the Queen, the other beside hers for the woman who served her, the third for the two gendarmes who never left the room, not even when she had needs or bodily functions to see to. Like the others, the Queen's bed was of wood, with a straw mattress, a mattress and a holed and dirty wool blanket which had been used by the prisoners for a long time. The sheets were of grey canvas like the others. There were no curtains but an old screen.

The Queen was dressed in a black camisole, her hair cut at the front and back. It was completely grey. She was so thin it was difficult to recognize her, and she was so weak she could barely keep upright. She had three rings on her fingers but no stones. The woman who served her was a type of fishwife about whom she greatly complained. The guards told Michonis that Madame wasn't eating and she couldn't go on living like that; they said her food was very bad and brought over a thin chicken which Madame hadn't eaten and which had been served to her for four days. The gendarmes complained about their bed even though it was the same as the Queen's. The Queen always slept fully dressed in black, expecting at any moment to be slaughtered or taken to her execution and wanting to go in mourning. Rougeville said it made Michonis cry with grief. He had confirmed to him that the Queen kept losing blood and said that when he had to go to the Temple to get the black camisole and the linen the Queen needed he was not permitted to go until after a debate in the council.[289]

All these cruel details about the woman he loved tormented Fersen. He bitterly reproached himself for his liaison with Eléonore, born out of the circumstances of the Revolution in 1791. The arrest at Varennes and imprisonment in the Tuileries had forced Marie-Antoinette to sacrifice the 'most loved and loving of men' to her duty, but it is clear from his diary and letters that he had never given up hope that they would one day be reunited.

I want to gather the most minute details on this great and unfortunate princess I shall love all my life; everything of hers is precious to me. Oh, how I reproach myself for my wrongs towards her, and how I know at present how much I loved her. El. will not replace her in my heart. What gentleness, what tenderness, what kindness, what solicitude, what a delicate, loving and feeling heart! The other [Eléonore] hasn't got all that, and yet I love her; I look on her as my only consolation, and without her I would be too wretched, but one has to find the goodness of her character and her feelings through a thousand brusqueries and a thousand ill humours which it pains me to put up with. Oh, how my existence has changed, and how little happiness it promises me after having been the finest in the world and the most worthy of envy.[290]

Fersen to Sophie Piper, 24 November 1793

I will not speak to you, my dear friend, of the state of my soul; it is still the same. Thinking of her and mourning her are my sole occupations; looking for everything I can find of Hers and conserving what I have is my whole care and pleasure; speaking of her my only consolation, and sometimes I have that enjoyment but never as often as I would like. Losing her is for me the grief of my entire life and my sorrows will leave me only when I die. Never have I felt so much the value of all I possessed, and never have I loved her so much. I will not talk to you, my dear Sophie, of my plans; I have none, and I am incapable of making any. This child [Louis XVII] still interests me. His fate increases my pain yet more. And that unfortunate girl [Madame], what will become of her? What horrors, what humiliations will they not put her through? It breaks my heart to think of it.[291]

In 1794, Fersen tried to organize his life, but the difficulty he had in taking a decision with regard to Eléonore Sullivan was intimately bound up with the love he would always feel for Marie-Antoinette.

8 January. Wrote to Taube on my private affairs. I'm still, however, uncertain as to whether I should ask for London or Italy . . . It's El. who is causing this indecision, because we can never have a conversation together and we cannot arrange anything; and yet it seems to me that I would be happy if we stayed together. Ah, I well feel every day how much I lost in *Her* and how perfect she was in everything. Never has there been nor will there be another woman like *Her*.[292]

Fersen was a broken man, who lived only to gather together souvenirs and relics of Marie-Antoinette; but by some miracle comfort arrived. At last he received another letter from the Chevalier de Jarjayes. He had had to write three times before receiving the sublime message that Marie-Antoinette had entrusted to Jarjayes in April 1793. It was a simple scrap of card bearing the message '*Tutto a te mi guida*'.

21 January 1794. M. Bury . . . brought me a letter from M. de Jarjayes, which didn't tell me all I had hoped for. He sent me only the fragment of a letter from the Queen to him. Here's the copy. She wrote it herself.

'. . . When you are in a safe place, I would very much like you to give news of me to my great friend who came to see me last year. I don't know where he is, but either Mr Gog. [Goguelat] or Mr Crawford, who I believe to be in London, will be able to tell you. I dare not write to him, but here is a stamp of my motto. Tell him when you send it that the person to whom it belongs feels that it has never been more true.'

This motto was a seal with the emblem of a flying pigeon and the motto *Tutto a te mi guida*. Her idea at the time had been to take my arms, and they had mistaken the flying fish for a bird. The stamp was on a scrap of card; unfortunately the heat had completely erased the impression. I will nevertheless guard it preciously in my box with the copy of the note and the design of the seal.[293]

It appears that this cryptic message arrived too late for Fersen, who was extremely depressed, to grasp its full meaning. But this scrap of card with this particular motto was the most beautiful declaration of love he could have ever wished for. At last, and for the first time in her life, Marie-Antoinette was free to express her feelings openly; she was no longer bound by duty to her husband. She no longer had to hide. And so she sent Fersen the imprint of their secret seal, the one she used to write to him in their golden days. She wanted to remind him of their past happiness. In this context, '*Tutto a te mi guida*' accompanied by the words that 'never has it been more true' indicates that she saw her future with Fersen. Despite their cruel separation in February 1792 and all they had endured since, she had never stopped loving him. Her heart still belonged to him.

Is it necessary to follow Axel von Fersen's 'sad and languishing existence' for several years after the Queen's death? He never resolved his situation with Eléonore Sullivan, who in the end refused to leave Craufurd for him. Fersen was no longer the dashing Swedish colonel who had risked all to drive the King of France and his family out of Paris on that fatal night of 20 June 1791. He was a shadow man who could only ever give half his heart and who for ever mourned the love of his love, Marie-Antoinette. He returned to Sweden after his father's death, and it was there in 1795 that he received one last word from 'Josephine'.

77. MARIE-ANTOINETTE TO FERSEN, UNDATED, RECEIVED IN MARCH 1795

Stafsund, SE/RA/720807/02/6/II/5. The end of an autograph note from Marie-Antoinette to Fersen. It is glued to his diary on the page for 19 March 1795.

Mme de Korff sent me the end of a note from *Her* to me – here it is – which gave me great pleasure. It seemed to me to be a final farewell, and I was deeply moved. I don't know how it was left in her hands, and I've written to her to find out.[294]

19 March 1795, received from Mme de Korff

Farewell, my heart is all yours.

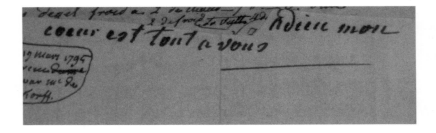

V
THE DISCOVERIES –
METHOD AND EXAMPLES

Method

A good number of letters in this collection have been redacted, sometimes more than once. During the French Revolution Fersen sent a significant proportion of his letters to Marie-Antoinette in code. As a result, we still have his draft letters before encryption. He used to write the code word exactly underneath the words in his clear copy, marking the exact number of letters in each word and separating the words by a vertical line. After having encrypted the letter to be sent to Marie-Antoinette, he immediately crossed through intimate passages in his copy. These deletions were made using the same ink as that used in the original letter. However, many passages were subsequently deleted again, either by Fabian von Fersen or Baron Klinckowström, in a much darker ink. Often entire words are written over the original text.

In the same way, certain passages in Marie-Antoinette's autograph letters as well as in Fersen's decrypts of her letters have been heavily redacted; unfortunately, without the separation of words and letters to be found in the letters prepared for encryption, it is much harder to read beneath the blacked-out lines in these passages, although it is not impossible. After very close examination of high-resolution digital photographs with adjustments in size, contrast and colour balance, I succeeded in reading some of these passages, too, although the bulk of my discoveries come from the letters prepared for encryption.

As there are only four autograph letters from Marie-Antoinette, it made sense to make a detailed analysis of Fersen's handwriting – which in any case I know extremely well, having read thousands of pages of his letters and diaries in Swedish archives. This yielded a very useful checklist to assist with the verification of words discovered in redacted passages. Fersen had elegant and very legible handwriting, with fairly generous spacing between letters and words and some idiosyncratic traits. The letters with loops or bars above and below the line are the most helpful for establishing the 'frame' of the letter, since they give most of the consonants, and the dotted letter *i* is also of great help. A loop at the top of the right stem of the *v* is also crucial for *vous* ('you'). After having recognized one or more letters, and knowing the exact number of letters in a word on account of the code underneath, it is not too difficult to guess the word: '*tendre*' for example throws up a very recognizable *t* and *d*. We know that it is a six-letter word starting with *t* with *d* as the fourth letter and that the other letters do not have bars or loops; it is preceded by a two-letter word and followed by a four-letter word with *i* as the third letter . . . '*Ma tendre amie*' ('my tender friend') is the only combination that makes sense in the context. Several words strung together require certain common conjunctions or prepositions, which then become recognizable in other redacted lines (*c'est, pas, que, ce que, il y a*, etc.). The overall meaning of three or four words combined suggests other words to verify in order to make up the sentence.

Examples

Fersen to Marie-Antoinette, 29 October 1791

This declaration of love was actually not too hard to discover, despite the double deletions. '*à la folie*' (madly) at the end is very easy to guess as the *f, l* and *i* of *folie* are quite recognizable; it is preceded by *à* (the accent is helpful), followed by a two-letter word beginning with *l* – which can only be *la* because *folie* is a feminine noun. This makes '*j'aime*' ('I love') and '*vous*' ('you') something of a necessity, although they, too, are quite easy to see. Fersen's long T bars make *toutte* (his spelling for toute) very recognizable, and it is not difficult to build up the rest of the sentence by looking for standard phrasing ('*adieu, ma tendre amie*') and so on.

Adieu / ma / tendre / amie / je / vous / aime / et / vous / aimerai
toutte / ma / vie / à la / folie

Farewell, my tender friend, I love you and will love you
madly all my life

Marie-Antoinette to Fersen, 4 January 1792

Here is my discovery in a letter from Marie-Antoinette to Fersen. Without the adjustments offered by photo-editing software, it would be very difficult to read beneath these heavily blacked-out words. The ink used to delete the words is much blacker than the ink used by Fersen, so these deletions may well have been made after his death. Note Marie-Antoinette's disconnected letters and the very wide spacing. We are aware of her endearments for Fersen from the notes in code written just after Varennes in 1791 – so it is not too hard to spot '*tendre ami*' in the second line, with a characteristic letters *t* and *d* plus the dot on the *i* for *ami*. This means we must find '*mon*' – however, it is not visible before *tendre*, which is preceded by a *t*, suggesting *et* ('and'). The *d*, *b* and *l* for *adorable* are visible, which mean the *mon* has to be the last word on the first line . . . *mon adorable et tendre ami*.

Je ne vous écris qu'un mot **mon**
adorable et tendre ami, la personne

. . . my adorable and tender friend . . .

NOTES

I: Acknowledgements and Introduction

1. Valérie Nachef and Jacques Patarin, 'Marie-Antoinette, reine . . . de la cryptologie' (*Pour la Science*, No. 382, August 2009) and 'Je vous aimerai jusqu'à la mort: Marie-Antoinette à Axel de Fersen' (*Cryptologia*, Vol. 34, No. 2, 2010, pp. 104–14).

2. Baron R.M.Klinckowström, *Le Comte de Fersen et la Cour de France*, 2 vols (Paris: Firmin-Didot, 1877–8), Vol. I, pp. v–vi. The departure from Paris was on 20 June 1791.

3. Löfstad, SE/VALA/02249/BXXVa/8, Axel von Fersen to Sophie Piper, 17 November 1793.

4. Löfstad, SE/VALA/02249/B XXVa/10, Fabian von Fersen to Sophie Piper, 1810.

5. Ibid., undated, by the content, written in 1811. On 13 March 1809 Gustav IV Adolf, son of Gustav III, was deposed in a coup d'état.

II: Analysis of the Correspondence

1. A. Geoffroy, *Gustave III et la Cour de France*, 2 vols (Paris: Didier, 1867), Vol. I, pp. 360–1.

2. Roger Sorg, 'Fersen, officier français et Marie-Antoinette' (*Mercure de France*, 15 July 1933), pp. 325–7. This article contains a facsimile of Taube's letter. The phrase in Swedish translates as 'when each one takes his own [woman], then I take mine and the others have nothing'.

3. Klinckowström, Vol. I, p. 45.

4. Stafsund, SE/RA/720807/02/5/II/8, 22 May 1782. In the French: *colonel en second*.

5. Ibid., 3 October 1782.

6. Stafsund, SE/RA/720807/02/6/III/10 (1783–1808).

7. Alma Söderhjelm, *Fersen et Marie-Antoinette: correspondance et journal intime inédits du comte Axel de Fersen* (Paris: Editions Kra, 1930).

8. Stafsund, SE/RA/720807/02/6/III/10.

9. Comte Valentin d'Esterhazy, *Mémoires* (Paris: Plon, 1905), pp. xxxiii–v.

In his diary and letters, Fersen refers to Marie-Antoinette as *Elle* ('She'); and in her letters to their mutual friend Valentin d'Esterhazy, the Queen refers to Fersen as *Lui* ('Him').

10. AN 440AP/1.

11. Stafsund, SE/RA/720807/02/6/III/10.

12. Esterhazy, *Mémoires,* pp. xxxiii–iv.

13. Ibid.

14. Duc de Choiseul, *Relation du départ de Louis XVI le 20 juin 1791* (Paris: Baudouin Frères, 1822), p. 39. Claude Antoine Gabriel, Duc de Choiseul-Stainville (1760–1838).

15. AN 440AP/1, 24 December 1791.

16. Stafsund, SE/RA/720807/10/20.

17. AN 440AP/1. The Queen refers to Quintin Craufurd (1743–1819), an expatriate Scot living in Paris who had made a fortune in India. A friend of Fersen and the French Royal Family, he was deeply involved in Marie-Antoinette's secret diplomacy after Varennes.

18. Stafsund, SE/RA/720807/10/20.

19. Ibid.

20. Stafsund, SE/RA/720807/02/6/IV/11.

21. Marie-Antoinette to Mercy, 19 October 1791 in F. Feuillet de Conches (ed.), *Louis XVI, Marie-Antoinette et Madame Élisabeth, lettres et documents inédits,* (Paris: Plon, 1866), 6 vols, Vol. IV, p. 212; MA to Fersen, AN 440AP/1.

22. AN 440AP/1.

23. Ibid.

24. Ibid.

25. Ibid.

26. Ibid.

27. Ibid.

28. Ibid.

29. Ibid.

30. Ibid.

31. Stafsund, SE/RA/720807/02/6/III/10.

32. Florimond, Comte de Mercy-Argenteau, *Correspondance secrète entre Marie-Thérèse et le Comte de Mercy-Argenteau,* 3 vols (Paris: Firmin-Didot, 1874), Vol. II, p. 164.

33. *Journal de l'abbé de Véri,* 2 vols (Paris: Tallandier, 1928 and Plon, 1930), Vol. II, p. 114.

34. AN 440AP/1.

35. Ibid.

36. Löfstad, SE/VALA/02249/BXXVa/8, 25 March 1788.

37. AN 440AP/1.

38. Stafsund, SE/RA/720807/02/6/IV/14, 12 October 1791.

39. Ibid. 18 October 1791.

40. AN 440AP/1. 'The bishop' is the Bishop of Pamiers, aide to the Baron de Breteuil in Louis XVI's secret diplomatic service.

41. Ibid.

42. Ibid.

43. Taube to Fersen, Stafsund, SE/RA/720807/02/6/IV/14; Marie-Antoinette to Fersen, AN 440AP/1.

44. Stafsund, SE/RA/720807/02/6/IV/14, 8 February 1793.

45. *Lettres de Marie-Antoinette*, ed. Rocheterie and Beaucourt, 2 vols (Paris: Alphonse Picard, 1896), Vol. II, p. 223.

46. François Goguelat, *Mémoire . . . sur les événements relatifs au voyage de Louis XVI à Varennes,* (Paris: Baudouin Frères, 1823), p. 12.

47. Feuillet de Conches, Vol. I, p. 351. The letter is addressed to Count Ostermann, Catherine II's Foreign Secretary.

48. Stafsund, SE/RA/720807/02/6/I/3.

49. *Liste générale et très exacte* (Paris, 1793), p. 26.

50. AN 440AP/1.

51. Ibid.

52. Stafsund, SE/RA/720807/02/6/II/5.

53. Quintin Craufurd, *Notice sur Marie-Antoinette*, (Paris: J. Gratiot, 1819), pp. 46–7.

54. Löfstad, SE/VALA/02249/B XXVa/10, Fabian von Fersen to Sophie Piper, 21 September 1810.

55. Ibid., 25 December 1810.

III: The Lost Correspondence

1. Löfstad, SE/VALA/02249/BXXVa/8, 25 March 1782.

2. Ibid., 25 April 1782.

3. Stafsund, SE/RA/720807/02/6/IV/15a.

4. Löfstad, SE/VALA/02249/BXXVa/8, 12 May 1782.

5. Ibid., March 1783.

6. Ibid., 27 June 1783.

7. Marc Marie, Marquis de Bombelles, *Journal 1780–1789,* 2 vols (Geneva: Droz, 1978–82), Vol. I, p. 236. Bombelles (1744–1822) was a diplomat and courtier. His wife Angélique de Mackau was Madame Elisabeth's best friend,

and his mother-in-law was an assistant governess to the royal children. During the Revolution he undertook several missions for Louis XVI as an agent of Breteuil.

8. Evelyn Farr, *Marie-Antoinette and Count Fersen* (London: Peter Owen, 2013), Chapter 6.

9. Löfstad, SE/VALA/02249/BXXVa/8, 31 July 1783.

10. Stafsund, SE/RA/720807/02/6/II/5, 16 October 1794.

11. Stafsund, SE/RA/720807/02/6/II/7, 15 July 1798. One has to wonder at Alma Söderhjelm's reasons in significantly altering these important words of Fersen's. In *Fersen et Marie*-Antoinette, p. 386, she published: '*Je me rappelle de ce jour, quand je suis arrivé de Dun[kerque ?] et que je descendai chez Madame de Matignon et j'allai pour la première fois chez Elle.*' ('I remember this day, when I arrived from Dun[kirk?] and alighted at Mme de Matignon's and went to Her for the first time.' The implication, of course, is that 'Elle' is Mme de Matignon, not Marie-Antoinette. The original text corrects this distortion, since it is clear that, far from arriving chez Matignon, Fersen had in fact left Mme de Matignon's house party at Dangu to go and see 'Elle' – Marie-Antoinette – in private. The diary entry is very clearly written, so a transcription error may be ruled out.

12. Bombelles, Vol. I, p. 244.

13. Adèle Boigne, Comtesse de Boigne, *Récits d'une tante* (Paris: Emile Paule, 1921), Vol. I, pp. 35–6.

14. Bombelles, 2 July 1783, Vol. I, p. 242.

15. Ibid., I, p. 247.

16. Löfstad, SE/VALA/02249/BXXVa/8, 10 August 1783. Germaine Necker, daughter of Louis XVI's Finance Minister Jacques Necker, a Swiss banker, was one of the richest heiresses in Europe; as a Protestant, she would have been considered a highly suitable match by Fersen's father.

17. Ibid., SE/VALA/02249/BXXVa/14.

18. Bombelles, Vol. I, p. 252. The doctor Vermond was the Abbé de Vermond's brother.

19. Ibid.

20. Ibid., Vol. I, p.253.

21. Löfstad, SE/VALA/02249/BXXVa/8, 11 July 1783.

22. Ibid., 20 September 1783 ; Bombelles, Vol. I, p. 263.

23. Löfstad, SE/VALA/02249/BXXVa/14, 26 September 1783.

24. Stafsund, SE/RA/720807/02/6/III/10.

25. Louis Charles Auguste Le Tonnelier, Baron de Breteuil, diplomat and politician (1730–1807) was a friend of Fersen's father. In 1783 he became

Minister of the King's Household and Paris. He emigrated in 1789. Curt von Steding (Stedingk in the modern spelling), Baron then Count (1746–1837), a Swedish soldier and diplomat, served with distinction in the French army during the American War of Independence. He was colonel commandant of the Royal Suédois regiment for several years and became Ambassador to France at the Restoration in 1814. Baron Erik Staël von Holstein (1749–1802), who married the heiress Germaine Necker, was named Swedish Ambassador to France by Gustav III in 1785 on Fersen's recommendation. His friendship with Fersen did not survive the Revolution.

26. Stafsund, SE/RA/720807/02/6/III/10.
27. Rocheterie and Beaucourt, *Lettres*, Vol. II, p. 30. MA to Joseph II, 20 December 1783.
28. Véri, *Journal,* Vol. II, pp. 262 and 264.
29. Lever, *Marie-Antoinette: Correspondance*, p. 394.
30. François Claude Amour, Marquis de Bouillé, *Souvenirs et fragments*, 2 vols (Paris: Picard, 1906), Vol. I, p. 394, p. 190.
31. Stafsund, SE/RA/720807/02/6/I/1, 7 June 1785.
32. Ibid., 20 July 1785.
33. Eléonore Sullivan was the long-term mistress of Quintin Craufurd, and Fersen first got involved with her during preparations for the Royal Family's escape from Paris in 1791. See Part III.
34. Löfstad, SE/VALA/02249/BXXv a/9, 11 April and 2 December 1797.
35. Stafsund, SE/RA/720807/02/6/II/6, 11 March 1795.
36. Chatsworth, CS5/604, Lady Elizabeth Foster to the Duchess of Devonshire, from Naples, 29 February 1784. C. Chapman and J. Dormer, *Elizabeth and Georgiana,* (London: John Murray, 2002), p. 55.
37. Löfstad, SE/VALA/02249/BXXVa/8.
38. Chapman and Dormer, pp. 114–15.
39. Löfstad, SE/VALA/02249/BXXVa/8, letter to Sophie, 7 December 1780. 'For seven months now I haven't known how you are, whether you are thinking of your brother who loves you with all his heart, whether you still live. I left you in a critical state for a feeling heart – my situation is dreadful.'
40. Stafsund, SE/RA/720807/02/6/III/10.
41. Löfstad, SE/VALA/02249/BXXVa/8, 5 May 1784.
42. Florimond, Comte de Mercy-Argenteau, *Correspondance secrète du Comte de Mercy-Argenteau avec l'Empereur Joseph II*, 2 vols (Paris: Imprimerie Nationale, 1889–91), Vol. I, p. 264.
43. Bombelles, Vol. I, p. 304. February 1784.
44. Stafsund, SE/RA/720807/02/5/II/9, 20 June 1784.

45. Gunnar W. Lundberg, *Lavreince: Nicolas Lafrensen, peintre suédois* (Paris: Bibliothèque Nationale, May–June 1949), p. viii.

46. Stafsund, SE/RA/720807/02/6/III/10.

47. Ibid.

48. Ibid.

49. Ibid.

50. The Queen used the pet name *Chou d'Amour* (literally, 'the darling of love' or 'Love's darling') for the Duc de Normandie in her correspondence with her close friend the Duchesse de Polignac, Governess to the royal children. See Farr, *Marie-Antoinette and Count Fersen*, Chapter 7.

51. Louis Nicolardot, *Journal de Louis XVI* (Paris: E. Dentu, 1873), pp. 43–4.

52. Stafsund, SE/RA/720807/02/6/III/10.

53. Ibid., SE/RA/720807/02/6/1, 26 May 1785. The 'Italians' is the theatre the Comédie Italienne.

54. Ibid., SE/RA/720807/02/6/III/10.

55. Ibid., SE/RA/720807/02/6/1/1, 20 July 1785.

56. Mercy, *Joseph II et le Prince de Kaunitz*, Vol. I, p. 437.

57. Stafsund, SE/RA/720807/02/6/I/1, 20 July 1785.

58. Ibid., 9 September 1785. Cardinal de Rohan was administrator of the Quinze Vingts Hospital and had transferred it to its current site in 1779, increasing the number of patients to 800.

59. Löfstad, SE/VALA/02249/BXXVa/8, 24 September 1785.

60. Stafsund, SE/RA/720807/02/6/III/10.

61. Ibid.

62. Ibid.

63. Chatsworth, CS5/703.

64. Ibid., CS5/720.

65. Ibid., CS5/722.

66. Ibid., CS5/724.

67. Ibid., CS5/725.

68. Dorset KHLC, U269/C170. Dispatch to Lord Carmarthen 15 June 1786.

69. Stafsund, SE/RA/720807/02/5/II/9,10 March 1786.

70. Chatsworth, CS5/738.

71. *Correspondance Secrète inédite sur Louis XVI, Marie-Antoinette, la Cour et la Ville*, ed. Maturin de Lescure, 2 vols (Paris: Plon, 1866), Vol. II, p. 54, 4 July 1786.

72. Stafsund, SE/RA/720807/02/6/III/10.

73. Ibid.

74. Chatsworth, CS5/749.

75. Stafsund, SE/RA/720807/02/6/III/10.

76. Ibid.
77. Löfstad, SE/VALA/02249/BXXVa/8, 5 June 1787; Stafsund, SE/RA/720807/02/6/III/10.
78. Stafsund, SE/RA/720807/02/6/III/10.
79. Ibid.
80. Ibid.
81. Ibid.
82. AN, O/1/1802.
83. Löfstad, SE/VALA/02249/BXXVa/8, 15 June 1787.
84. Stafsund, SE/RA/720807/02/6/III/10.
85. Ibid.
86. Löfstad, SE/VALA/02249/BXXVa/8, 3 July 1788.
87. Chatsworth, CS5/871; CS5/872.
88. Löfstad, SE/VALA/02249/BXXVa/8, 4 July 1788.
89. Ibid. Letter probably sent on 10 August 1788, since Fersen wrote to his father the same day, saying 'everything is finished here'.
90. Ibid., 6 November 1788.

IV: The Letters

1. See Part II.
2. Steding, commandant of the Royal Suédois.
3. Gustave III.
4. Staël, the Swedish Ambassador to France.
5. Jean Baptiste Donatien de Vimeur, Comte de Rochambeau (1725–1807), general who commanded the French army in America.
6. These observations are not to be found with the letter.
7. Louis Marie Athanase de Loménie, Comte de Brienne (1730–94), Secretary of State for War.
8. Stafsund, SE/RA/720807/02/6/VI/22. L. s. d. = Livres, sols, deniers.
9. Ibid., SE/RA/720807/02/5/II/9, 8 March 1789.
10. Söderhjelm, p. 132.
11. Stafsund, SE/RA/720807/02/6/III/10. Balthasar is doubtless Fersen's coachman Balthasar Sapel, who took part in the flight to Varennes.
12. Ibid., SE/RA/720807/02/5/II/9, 26 June 1789.
13. Victor François de Broglie, Duc de Broglie (1718–1804), was War Minister for only three days. Louis Pierre de Chastenet, Comte de Puységur (1727–1807), War Minister (30 November 1788–12 July 1789).
14. Stafsund, SE/RA/720807/02/6/III/10. Fersen's maternal aunt Mlle de La

Gardie lived at Versailles.

15. Chapman and Dormer, p. 100. It would be interesting to read what has been edited out of the passage about the Dauphin.

16. Ibid., SE/RA/720807/02/5/II/9, 16 August 1789.

17. Ibid., 3 September 1789.

18. Valentin Ladislas, Comte d'Esterhazy (1740–1805), had been a friend of Marie-Antoinette's since escorting her to Versailles from Vienna in 1770. A professional soldier, he joined the War Council in 1787.

19. Arnail François, Marquis de Jaucourt (1757–1852), Protestant, royalist and a Constitutional. He was elected to the Legislative Assembly in 1791.

20. Stafsund, SE/RA/720807/02/5/II/9, 14 September 1789.

21. Karl, Duke of Södermanland (1748–1818), brother of Gustav III, Regent (1792–6) and King of Sweden as Karl XIII (1809–18). He had two sons by Fersen's cousin, Countess Augusta Löwenhielm.

22. Stafsund, SE/RA/720807/02/5/II/9, 14 September and 30 September 1789.

23. Saint-Priest, *Mémoires* (Paris: Calmann-Levy, 1929), p. 80. François Emmanuel Guignard, Comte de Saint-Priest (1735–1821), diplomat and government minister.

24. Ibid., p. 84.

25. Stafsund, SE/RA/720807/02/5/II/9, 9 October 1789.

26. *Correspondance de Madame Elisabeth,* ed. Feuillet de Conches (Paris: Plon, 1858), p. 120; Gouverneur Morris, *A Diary of the French Revolution,* ed. B.C. Davenport, 2 vols (London: Harrap, 1939), Vol. I, p. 245. The Marquis de Capellis frequented the salon of Morris's mistress, Adèle de Flahaut. Esterhazy gives the same information in his memoirs, as does Lady Elizabeth Foster in her diary. General Gilbert du Motier, Marquis de Lafayette (1757–1834), had drawn France into the American War of Independence. A republican allied to the Duc d'Orléans, sworn enemy of Marie-Antoinette, he was a leader of the Jacobin party at the beginning of the Revolution.

27. Stafsund, SE/RA/720807/02/5/II/9, 22 October 1789.

28. Morris, Vol. I, p. 271. 25 October 1789.

29. Quintin Craufurd to William Pitt and Lord Grenville, 3 August 1791, Hutton, *Selections from the Letters and Correspondence of Sir James Bland Burges* (London: John Murray, 1885), pp. 364–5.

30. AN, 440AP/4.

31. Löfstad, SE/VALA/02249/BXXVa/8, 27 December 1789. 'Our friend' is Baron Evert Taube, Grand Chamberlain to Gustav III and Sophie's lover, wounded in the war against Russia. Hedda, Fersen's older sister, never enjoyed the confidence he gave to Sophie.

32. Marie-Antoinette to Mme de Polignac, AN 440AP/4. Louis XVI to Mme de Polignac, 6 February 1790, Feuillet de Conches, t. 1, p. 307 (letter sold by Sotheby's, 26 November 2013).

33. Stafsund, SE/RA/720807/02/6/I/1, 7 January 1790.

34. See Part I.

35. *Bland Burges,* p. 366.

36. Morris, I, pp. 381–4, 24 January 1790.

37. Chatsworth, CS5/1051, Dorset to Duchess Georgiana, 19 March 1790. Sylvain Bailly (1736–93) was the first mayor of Paris; Lafayette, hero of the American War of Independence, was leader of the Jacobins and commander of the Parisian Garde Nationale; Joseph Francois Foulon (1715–89), appointed Finance Minister by Louis XVI on 12 July 1789 and his son-in-law Louis Bénigne François Berthier de Sauvigny (1737–89), in charge of army provisions, were both brutally massacred by a mob in Paris on 22 July 1789 while Bailly and Lafayette at the head of the Garde Nationale calmly looked on.

38. Löfstad, SE/VALA/02249/BXXVa/8.

39. Stafsund, SE/RA/720807/02/6/III/10. '15 August 1789, Sophie: that she speaks to our friend [Taube] about my plan for an embassy. 12 October 1789, Sophie: spoke about the embassy.'

40. Löfstad, SE/VALA/02249/BXXVa/8.

41. Ibid.

42. Stafsund, SE/RA/720807/02/6/III/10, 24 August 1789. Löfstad, SE/VALA/02249/BXXVa/8.

43. Stafsund, SE/RA/720807/02/5/II/9, 16 July 1790.

44. Löfstad, SE/VALA/02249/B XXV b/8. Unpublished.

45. Ibid., 31 July 1790; 8 August 1790.

46. Saint-Priest, p. 91.

47. Klinckowström, Vol. I, p. 80. Honoré Gabriel Riqueti, Comte de Mirabeau (1749–2 April 1791), orator, writer and confirmed democrat before becoming a monarchist on Louis XVI's payroll. According to Gouverneur Morris, he had sworn to ruin Lafayette.

48. Löfstad, SE/VALA/02249/B XXVa/10, 30 November 1790.

49. La Marck to Mercy, 9 November 1790. A. de Bacourt, *Correspondance entre le Comte de Mirabeau et le Comte de La Marck* (Librairie Veuve Le Normant, 1851), Vol. II, p. 300.

50. See unpublished letter from Lafayette to the Duchess of Devonshire, 18 July 1791, attached to Letter No. 25 from Fersen to Marie-Antoinette.

51. Stafsund, SE/RA/720807/02/6/II/5, Diary, 18 November 1793.

52. Löfstad, SE/VALA/02249/BXXVa/8.

53. Ibid.

54. Ibid. The dates of all these letters have been established using Fersen's letter register.

55. Ibid., 22 [October 1790].

56. Morris, Vol. II, p. 157, 8 April 1791. Armand Marc, Comte de Montmorin de Saint-Herem (1745–92) was in favour of the Court's negotiations with Mirabeau. He was killed in the September Massacres of 1792.

57. Mercy to Kaunitz, 22 January 1791, Feuillet de Conches, Vol. I, p. 452.

58. Hutton (ed.), *Bland Burges*, pp. 365–6. Charles Alexandre de Calonne (1734–1802), former Finance Minister, disgraced in 1787.

59. Marie-Antoinette to Leopold II, 11 July 1790, Feuillet de Conches, Vol. I, p. 345.

60. Marie-Antoinette to Mercy, 11 January 1791, Feuillet de Conches, Vol. I, p. 417.

61. Mercy to Marie-Antoinette, 7 March 1791, Evelyne Lever, *Marie-Antoinette: Correspondance* (Paris: Tallandier, 2005), pp. 523–5.

62. François Claude Amour, Marquis de Bouillé (1739–1800), royalist general who commanded the regions of Alsace and Franche-Comté, where he had put down popular uprisings in 1790. With his son, Comte Louis de Bouillé, the Duc de Choiseul, François Goguelat and Axel von Fersen, he organized the Royal Family's escape in 1791.

63. Armand Maximilien François Joseph Olivier de Saint-Georges, Vicomte, then Marquis de Vérac (1768–1858), secretary and special envoy of the Baron de Breteuil.

64. Balthazar François Barthélemy (1747–1830), secretary at the French embassy in London from 1784. He was created a marquis in 1817.

65. Louis René Quentin de Richebourg de Champcenetz (1759–94), royalist, wit and author; his father was the governor of the Tuileries.

66. This Fonbrune remains an enigma. Bombelles, who met him in 1790, when he claimed to have the complete confidence of Louis XVI and Marie-Antoinette, does not paint a very flattering portrait of him.

67. Jean François de Peyrusse, Baron then Duc d'Escars (1747–1822), soldier and royalist, he joined the émigré princes, who sent him on a mission to Stockholm in 1791. In letters to his sister Sophie, Fabian von Fersen mentions d'Escars's fondness for alcohol and his unsuitability for diplomatic work. Claude Perreney de Grosbois (1756–1840), president of the *parlement* of Besançon and a deputy for the nobility at the States General in 1789. The 'barons de Flacksland' remain untraceable – perhaps it is Fersen's spelling for the Baron de Flaschlanden, who became an agent for the princes.

68. The Comte d'Artois – Charles Philippe de Bourbon (1757–1836), youngest brother of Louis XVI, became Charles X on the death of Louis XVIII

('Monsieur') in 1824. He was deposed in the 1830 Revolution. Louis V Joseph de Bourbon Condé, 8th Prince of Condé (1736–1818), was a leader of the French emigrant army.

69. Wenceslas Antoine von Kaunitz (1711–94), Count von Rietberg and Prince von Kaunitz, diplomat and statesman attached to the house of Habsburg; he was Chancellor of the Empire from 1753 to 1792.

70. Paul François de Quelen de La Vauguyon, Duc de La Vauguyon (1746–1828), diplomat. José Moñino y Redondo, Conde de Floridablanca (1728–1808), was Spanish Prime Minister from 1777. François Joachim de Pierre, Cardinal de Bernis (1715–94), was French envoy to the Holy See from 1774.

71. On 18 April 1791 the King and the Royal Family were forced to return to their apartments in the Tuileries when an aggressive mob prevented them from leaving for Saint-Cloud to celebrate Easter. However, Fersen's letter is dated 2 April – possibly in error, with the correct date being the 20 April.

72. Stafsund, SE/RA/720807/02/6/I/3.

73. Ibid.

74. Stafsund, SE/RA/720807/02/6/II/5.

75. Ibid.

76. *Bland Burges Papers*, pp. 366–7.

77. Chatsworth, CS5/1086. Dorset to Georgiana, 30 June 1791. Lady Elizabeth Foster pencilled a note over the sentence about Louis XVI being drunk: 'I believe this is not true.'

78. Ibid., CS5/1091, 3 July 1791.

79. Löfstad, SE/VALA/02249/BXXv/a/8.

80. Stafsund, SE/RA/720807/10/15.

81. *Bland Burges*, pp. 368–89.

82. Archduchess Marie-Christine, Governor of the Austrian Netherlands.

83. Stafsund, SE/RA/720807/02/6/II/5.

84. Ibid.

85. Louis Hilaire de Conzié, (1736–1804), Bishop of Arras since 1775, agent for the princes.

86. Stafsund, SE/RA/720807/02/6/II/5.

87. Antoine Barnave (1761–93), a lawyer elected to represent the Third Estate at the States General in 1789. He founded the Jacobin club and became president of the National Assembly. He fell under Marie-Antoinette's spell during the return journey from Varennes and attempted to convert her to the constitutional cause. Arrested in 1792, he was guillotined in Paris six weeks after the Queen.

88. 'My brothers' are Louis-Stanislas, Comte de Provence, known as Monsieur and the Comte d'Artois. The king is Gustave III.

89. Esterhazy, *Mémoires*, pp. xxxiii–v.
90. Esterhazy, *Lettres à sa femme* (Paris: Plon, 1907), pp. 331–2. This is an exact quote. Elsewhere in his edition of these letters, Daudet has rather oddly transcribed this code name for Fersen as 'la Chose' ('the Thing'). 'Le Chou' or 'the Darling' makes much more sense and also links to Marie-Antoinette's pet name for the Dauphin. Esterhazy's handwriting may explain why Daudet has sometimes incorrectly transcribed it. 'His detestable handwriting cannot be so easily deciphered as his style, especially with regard to proper names; on several occasions we have had to give up' (pp. vii–iii). The inscription on the ring is: *Lord, Save the King and the Queen.*
91. Klinckowström, I, p. 157.
92. Stafsund, SE/RA/720807/02/6/II/5.
93. Stafsund, SE/RA/720807/02/6/III/10.
94. Stafsund, SE/RA/720807/02/6/II/5.
95. Ibid.
96. Stafsund, SE/RA/720807/02/6/IV/15, Lady Elizabeth Foster to Fersen, 16 September 1791, unpublished and hitherto unidentified letter in French. I succeeded in identifying it by the style, the handwriting, the content and a note in Fersen's diary on 7 October 1791: 'letter from Lady Elizabeth Foster'. On the letter itself he has noted: 'received 7 Oct'.
97. Löfstad, SE/VALA/02249/BXXVa/8, 18 October 1791. Fersen had been afflicted by haemorrhoids and a weak stomach since his youth, and it sometimes prevented him from walking or riding.
98. The Declaration of Pillnitz was signed by Leopold II and Friedrich Wilhelm II of Prussia at the end of August 1791. Marie-Antoinette was quite correct in saying that it would not bring prompt help to the French Royal Family.
99. The Château de l'Hermitage, built for the Prince de Croÿ at the beginning of the Revolution, is situated in the forest of Bonsecours Condé.
100. It would appear from this deleted sentence that Fersen had prepared a memorandum for the Queen, which he did not send after reading her letter to the Comte de Mercy.
101. This letter is referred to by Fersen in his diary on 16 October 1791 – he will write to foreign courts to promote the Queen's demands for a congress.
102. Jean-Philippe de Franquetot, Chevalier de Coigny (1743–1810), soldier. He undertook several missions for Louis XVI and Marie-Antoinette.
103. Stafsund, SE/RA/720807/022/13.
104. Bimbenet, Eugène, *Fuite de Louis XVI à Varennes*, 2nd edn (Paris: Firmin-Didot), pp. 134–5.
105. Stafsund, SE/RA/720807/02/6/II/5; Feuillet de Conches, Vol. IV, p. 214.

106. Elénor François Élie du Moustier (1751–1817), soldier and diplomat. He was French Ambassador to the United States from 1787 to 1789.

107. Louis-Philippe, Comte de Ségur (1753–1830), diplomat. He did not replace Montmorin as Foreign Minister.

108. Stafsund, SE/RA/720807/02/6/II/5.

109. The valet de chambre's wife was Mme Louvet. Fersen noted in his diary on 20 October 1791 that 'Mme Louvet has seen the Queen, who sent for her to discuss my affairs.'

110. Charles Eugène Gabriel de La Croix, Marquis de Castries, Maréchal de France (1727–1801). Former Secretary of State for the Navy (1780–7), he emigrated in 1789 and found a refuge in Switzerland with his old friend and ministerial colleague, Jacques Necker.

111. Anders Fredrik Reutersvärd (1756–1828), soldier and diplomat.

112. Stafsund, SE/RA/720807/016/2.

113. AN 440AP/1.

114. Ibid.

115. Evidently Fersen had sent the Queen a copy of this letter from Monsieur to the Baron de Breteuil. Feuillet de Conches, II, pp. 143–4.

> Brussels, 2 July 1791
>
> Having been informed directly, Monsieur, that the intention of the King, my brother, during his captivity, is that in concert with the Comte d'Artois, I do in his name all that can aid the reestablishment of his liberty and the good of the state by negotiating on this subject with those powers from whom we can hope for succour, I cannot believe that His Majesty desires that any further action should be taken regarding those commissions and powers which he may have previously given. You will therefore kindly regard as finished all such matters which may remain in your hands, and are to employ your zeal in conformity with whatever may be prescribed by us. We remain happy to be apprised by you of any useful means you may feel you can propose to us. In consequence, if you have anything to communicate to us, we invite you to attend us at Coblentz, where we are going without further delay. After this notice, there is no need to tell you that you will be responsible for any undertaking that does not accord with ours.

116. Marie-Antoinette refers to Fersen's letter of 26 October 1791, which is missing.

117. Friedrich Melchior, Baron von Grimm (1723–1807), Bavarian diplomat and man of letters. He returned to Paris to recover his property before establishing himself in Hamburg as the envoy of Catherine II.

118. Antoine Charles du Houx de Vioménil (1728–92), distinguished general. He died from wounds received while trying to defend the Royal Family at the Tuileries on 10 August 1792.

119. Germaine Necker (1766–1817), daughter of Louis XVI's former Finance Minister, Jacques Necker, was married to the Swedish Ambassador to France, the Baron de Staël. Comte Louis de Narbonne Lara (1755–1830), close friend of Lafayette, was her lover.

120. Arnaud de La Porte (1737–92), former Navy Minister, was Minister of the King's Household. He was guillotined on 23 August 1792.

121. Charles Constance César Joseph Mathieu d'Agoult (1747–1824), Bishop of Pamiers from 1787, royalist and politician. He was the Baron de Breteuil's right-hand man and the lover of Breteuil's daughter, Mme de Matignon. He gave up the bishopric of Pamiers on his return to France in 1801. He carried Fersen's memorandum of 26 November 1791 to Marie-Antoinette.

122. Archives of John Sackville, 3rd Duke of Dorset, Kent History and Library Centre (Dorset KHLC), U269/C181, Craufurd to Dorset, 18 November 1791.

123. Klinckowström, Vol. I, pp. 222–5.

124. Dorset KHLC, U269/C181, Craufurd to Dorset, 22 November 1791.

125. Stafsund, SE/RA/720807/02/6/V/17.

126. Dorset KHLC, U269/C181, Craufurd to Dorset, 22 November 1791.

127. Stafsund, SE/RA/720807/02/6/II/5.

128. Hans Rudolf von Bischoffwerder (1741–1803), soldier and Foreign Minister to Friedrich Wilhelm II of Prussia.

129. Werner von der Schulenburg (1736–1810); Ewald Friedrich, Count von Herzberg (1725–95), Prussian statesman.

130. Frederick, Duke of York and Albany (1763–1827), second son of George III, soldier, army reformer – 'the Grand old Duke of York' from the nursery rhyme.

131. Count Nikolai Petrovich Rumyantsev (Romanzoff in French) (1754–1826) became Russian Foreign Minister and Chancellor.

132. William V of Orange-Nassau (1748–1806), last Stadtholder of the United Provinces of Holland (1791–5). He was married to the Duke of Brunswick's niece.

133. On 6 August 1791 the Diet of Ratisbon (Regensburg) pronounced in favour of German princes who held lands in France, who had been stripped of their feudal dues and rights by the National Assembly. These princes rejoined the Holy Roman Empire.

134. Note that Louis XVI still entrusted his secret diplomacy to Breteuil, despite the baron's dismissal by Monsieur in July 1791.

135. On 11 November 1791, Louis XVI vetoed a decree against French émigrés.
136. Charles François Hurault, Vicomte de Vibraye (1739–1828), diplomat. Vérac – see Part IV, note 63.
137. On 31 October 1791 the Assembly ordered all émigrés to return to France by 1 January 1792 or face losing their property.
138. Chatsworth, CS5/971 and Löfstad, SE/VALA/02249/BVIII/a/1–2.
139. Morris, Vol. II, p. 71.
140. Lady Henrietta Frances Spencer (1761–1821), Countess of Bessborough.
141. The letter dated 31 October and 7 November 1791.
142. This entire paragraph was suppressed by Klinckowström.
143. Jérôme Joseph Geoffroy de Limon (1746–99), financial controller to the Duc d'Orléans and a deputy of the Third Estate in 1789; he became a royalist émigré and author of the Brunswick Manifesto published in August 1792.
144. Johann Amadeus Franz, Baron von Thugut (1736–1818), Austrian diplomat, assistant to the Comte de Mercy, Plenipotentiary Minister of the Austrian Netherlands.
145. 'The note' is Louis XVI's memorandum for Breteuil enclosed with Marie-Antoinette's letter of 25 November 1791.
146. Stafsund, SE/RA/720807022/13.
147. The Bishop of Pamiers.
148. Probably Jean Antoine, Comte d'Agoult (1753–1826), deputy for the Nobility at the States General, soldier and émigré in Coblentz. 'The fat baron from Lorraine' is presumably Breteuil. Marie-Antoinette's indignation stems from the fact that Monsieur dismissed Breteuil ten days after Louis XVI's arrest at Varennes.
149. Antoine François de Bertrand de Molleville (1744–1818), Minister for the Navy. He resigned in 1792 but remained loyal to Louis XVI. The Queen is being ironic about Mme de Staël's flagrant amours.
150. The letter dated 4 December 1791.
151. Stafsund, SE/RA/720807/02/6/II/5.
152. Stafsund, SE/RA/720807/22/14. Taube to Fersen, 21 December 1791.
153. Ibid.
154. Baron von Brantzen, Dutch diplomat.
155. Probably François Emmanuel d'Emskerque, Vicomte de Toulongeon (1748–1812); deputy for the nobility at the States General, he was one of the first to join the Third Estate and demand a National Assembly.
156. Karl Wilhelm Ferdinand von Braunschweig-Wolfenbüttel, always known as the Duke of Brunswick (1735–1806), Prussian general.
157. Étienne Narcisse de Durfort (1753–1839), serving in the princes' army.

158. Marie-Antoinette's and Louis XVI's letters for Sweden and Prussia.

159. Renaud Philippe Louis Armand de Custine (1768–94), son of General de Custine, a great admirer of the Prussian army.

160. See the 'note for the Queen', 8 April 1793.

161. Stafsund, SE/RA/720807/02/6/III/10.

162. Archives Nationales and CRCC, press release, November 2015, 'Les passages cachés des lettres de Marie-Antoinette au comte de Fersen livrent leurs premiers secrets.'

163. Stafsund, SE/RA/720807/02/6/II/5.

164. Baron Oxenstierna was Gustav III's envoy to the princes at Coblentz.

165. Stafsund, SE/RA/720807/02/6/II/5. Mr Hodges was an English friend of Quintin Craufurd.

166. Ibid.

167. Ibid. 'Young Vibraye' is doubtless the Vicomte de Vibraye's son.

168. The princes de Lambesc and de Vaudémont were paternal cousins of Marie-Antoinette. Charles Eugène de Lorraine, Prince de Lambesc (1751–1825) and his younger brother Marie Joseph de Lorraine, Prince de Vaudémont (1759–1812) were both officers who had emigrated. They dropped their French titles to become princes of Lorraine attached to the house of Austria.

169. Breteuil only had one daughter, Mme de Matignon, who was a widow. Perhaps he is referring to his granddaughter's husband, the Duc de Montmorency.

170. Stafsund, SE/RA/720807/02/6/II/5.

171. Dorset KHLC, U269/C181, Craufurd to Dorset, 27 January 1792.

172. Feuillet de Conches, Vol. V, pp 167–8.

173. Ibid., Vol. V, pp. 211–13.

174. 'The young archduke' is Franz, eldest son of Emperor Leopold II.

175. Franz Georg Karl, Count von Metternich (1746–1818), Austrian diplomat, father of the celebrated Austrian Chancellor Prince Metternich. Segur's suicide attempt did not succeed.

176. Stafsund, SE/RA/720807/22/14.

177. Klinckowström, Vol. I, pp. 278–9.

178. Fersen's diary, Stafsund, SE/RA/720807/02/6/II/5; letter register, SE/RA/720807/02/6/III/10.

179. Stafsund, SE/RA/720807/02/6/II/5.

180. Craufurd, *Notice sur Marie-Antoinette*, p. 55.

181. SE/RA/720807/02/6/III/10.

182. Stafsund, SE/RA/720807/02/6/II/5.

183. Stafsund, RA/720807/022/13.

184. Feuillet de Conches, Vol. V, p. 337.

185. Stafsund, SE/RA/720807/02/6/II/5.

186. Bimbenet, *Varennes*, Vol. II, p. 140.

187. Stafsund, SE/RA/720807/02/6/II/5.

188. Klinckowström, Vol. II, p. 177.

189. Stafsund, SE/RA/720807/22/14.

190. Ibid.

191. Stafsund, SE/RA/720807/02/6/II/5.

192. Dispatch to Gustav III, Stafsund, SE/RA/720807/02/6/I/1; Diary, SE/RA/720807/02/6/II/5.

193. Feuillet de Conches, Vol. V, pp. 272–3.

194. Ibid., Vol. V, pp. 281–2.

195. SE/RA/720807/02/6/II/5.

196. Feuillet de Conches, Vol. V, p. 293.

197. Leopold II.

198. Klinckowström, Vol. II, pp. 202–3.

199. SE/RA/720807/02/6/II/5.

200. Michel Félix Victor Choiseul d'Aillecourt (1754–96), deputy to the States General, émigré.

201. Letter register, Stafsund, SE/RA/720807/02/6/III/10; Diary, SE/RA/720807/02/6/II/5.

202. Pedro Pablo Abarca de Bolea, Conde d'Aranda (1718–98). He replaced Floridablanca as Spanish Prime Minister on 28 February 1792 but was in turn replaced on 15 November 1792.

203. SE/RA/720807/02/6/II/5.

204. Dorset KHLC, U269/C181, Craufurd to Dorset, 16 March 1792.

205. Chatsworth, CS5/1123.

206. SE/RA/720807/02/6/II/5.

207. Ibid.

208. Klinckowström, Vol. II pp. 215–16.

209. SE/RA/720807/02/6/II/5.

210. Ibid.

211. It is the address of 'Mr Brown', that is, Louis XVI, probably that of Gougenot, the King's steward, at 2 rue Lepeletier, Paris.

212. Charles François du Perrier du Mouriez, known as Dumouriez (1739–1823), general, Foreign Minister from 15 March to 15 June 1792. He ended his days in England, having passed into the service of the British.

213. François Bernard de Chauvelin, Marquis de Grosbois (1766–1832), spent a year in London before his credentials were withdrawn by the British

government after the execution of Louis XVI. In his letter to the Duke of Dorset on 16 March 1792 Quintin Craufurd speaks of 'that boy Chauvelin' being sent to England.

214. Charles Pierre Claret, Comte de Fleurieu (1738–1810), former Navy Minister, explorer, hydrographer and politician.

215. See Part I.

216. Stafsund, SE/RA/720807/02/6/III/10.

217. Klinckowström, II p. 224.

218. M. de Septeuil was Treasurer of Louis XVI's Civil List.

219. Dorset KHLC U269/C190.

220. SE/RA/720807/02/6/II/5.

221. Emmanuel Gabriel, Vicomte de Maulde, Baron de Hosdan (1740–1806), general, Deputy to the States General, revolutionary. He was appointed Ambassador to the Netherlands.

222. 'Servirés' is the eighteenth-century spelling for 'servirez', but the accent is not required for the code.

223. See Fersen's letter to Marie-Antoinette of 10 October 1791, where he says he has refused a regiment of hussars offered to him by Gustav III (words discovered by Evelyn Farr).

224. Stafsund, SE/RA/720807/22/14. By *clubistes* Taube means members of the political clubs in Paris – Jacobins, Feuillants and so on.

225. Stafsund, SE/RA/720807/016/2.

226. Stafsund, SE/RA/720807/02/6/II/5.

227. Austria wanted to reclaim the provinces of Alsace and Lorraine – this is the 'partition' or 'dismemberment' mentioned in several letters.

228. Probably Louis Charles Victor de Riquet de Caraman (1762–1839), diplomat.

229. Nicolas, Baron de Luckner (1722–94), Maréchal de France, of German origin. He was a Constitutional.

230. Stafsund, SE/RA/720807/02/6/II/5.

231. Stanislas de Boufflers (1738–1815), soldier and poet.

232. The message is contained in the letter of 7 June 1792, regarding the sending of a man to Vienna by the Constitutionals.

233. Jean-Baptiste Gouvion (1747–92), revolutionary general, friend of Lafayette, killed by a cannonball on 11 June 1792 near Maubeuge.

234. Stafsund, SE/RA/720807/02/6/II/5.

235. Victor Amédée de La Fage, Marquis de Saint-Huruge (1738–1801), an agitator from the Palais Royal.

236. Stafsund, SE/RA/720807/22/14.

237. Stafsund, SE/RA/720807/02/6/I/1.

238. Stafsund, SE/RA/720807/02/6/II/5.
239. Ibid.
240. These are the bulletins sent twice-weekly by Goguelat.
241. This is the 'baiser Lamourette', encouraged by deputy Antoine Lamourette on 7 July 1792 to reconcile the different factions in the Assembly.
242. Raymond de Verninac Saint-Maur (1761–1822), diplomat, Jacobin and a great friend of Staël.
243. Stafsund, SE/RA/720807/02/6/II/5.
244. The blank powers.
245. Mathieu Jean Felicité de Montmorency, Duc de Montmorency-Laval (1767–1826), who proposed the abolition of titles and feudal dues. He emigrated to England with the help of Mme de Staël.
246. This expression means that Gogulat believes the news to be true.
247. Stafsund, SE/RA/720807/02/6/II/5.
248. Stafsund, SE/RA/720807/22/14.
249. The British Ambassador is George Granville Leveson-Gower, Earl Gower (1758–1833), who succeeded the Duke of Dorset in 1790. 'Milord Kerry' is Francis Thomas-Fitzmaurice, Earl of Kerry (1740–1818).
250. Stafsund, SE/RA/720807/02/6/II/5.
251. Jean-Jacques Duval d'Eprémesnil (1745–94), magistrate, deputy for the nobility to the States General, counter-revolutionary, was lynched in Paris on 17 July 1792; he was rescued by Pétion and thrown into prison. Despite being released and thus escaping the September massacres, he was guillotined in 1794.
252. Fersen 'strongly disapproved' of the declaration added to the Brunswick Manifesto.
253. Stafsund, SE/RA/720807/02/6/II/5.
254. Ibid.
255. Duc Albert de Saxe-Teschen (1738–1822), husband of Marie-Antoinette's older sister, Archduchess Marie-Christine.
256. Stafsund, SE/RA/720807/02/6/II/5.
257. Löfstad, SE/VALA/02249/BXXVa/8. The Feuillants was a former convent on the rue St Honoré, used as a meeting place for the Constitutionals.
258. Stafsund, SE/RA/720807/02/6/I/3.
259. Stafsund, SE/RA/720807/02/6/II/5.
260. Ibid.
261. Ibid.
262. Löfstad, SE/VALA/02249/BXXVa/8.
263. Stafsund, SE/RA/720807/02/6/II/5.

264. Löfstad, SE/VALA/02249/BXXVa/8.
265. Stafsund, SE/RA/720807/02/6/II/5. 'El.' is Eléonore Sullivan, '_Her_' is Marie-Antoinette.
266. Löfstad, SE/VALA/02249/BXXVa/8.
267. Ibid.
268. Stafsund, SE/RA/720807/02/6/II/5. The Salpetrière was a notorious Paris prison for prostitutes and the criminally insane.
269. Ibid.
270. Löfstad, SE/VALA/02249/BXXVa/8.
271. Stafsund, SE/RA/720807/02/6/II/5. The 'two incorrigible women' are Marie-Antoinette and her sister-in-law Madame Elisabeth.
272. Stafsund, SE/RA/720807/022/13.
273. Stafsund, SE/RA/720807/02/6/II/5.
274. Ibid.
275. Löfstad, SE/VALA/02249/BXXVa/8.
276. Stafsund, SE/RA/720807/02/6/II/5.
277. Löfstad, SE/VALA/02249/BXXVa/8.
278. Stafsund, SE/RA/720807/02/6/II/5.
279. Löfstad, SE/VALA/02249/BXXVa/8.
280. Ibid.
281. Stafsund, SE/RA/720807/02/6/II/5.
282. Löfstad, SE/VALA/02249/BXXVa/8. Jean-Baptiste Michonis (1735–94). A member of the Paris Commune and inspector of prisons, he was guillotined for his devotion to Marie-Antoinette.
283. Alexandre Dominique Joseph Gonsse, Chevalier de Rougeville (1761–1814), royalist and counter-revolutionary.
284. Stafsund, SE/RA/720807/02/6/II/5.
285. Ibid.
286. Ibid.
287. Löfstad, SE/VALA/02249/BXXVa/8.
288. Stafsund, SE/RA/720807/02/6/II/5.
289. Ibid.
290. Ibid.
291. Löfstad, SE/VALA/02249/BXXVa/8.
292. Stafsund, SE/RA/720807/02/6/II/5.
293. Ibid.
294. Ibid.

REFERENCES

Manuscript Sources

France

Archives Nationales, Paris

AN 440AP/1: correspondence of Marie-Antoinette and Axel von Fersen – original letters and transcriptions by Baron R.M. Klinckowström.

AN 440AP/4: letters from Marie-Antoinette to the Duchesse de Polignac.

AN O/1/1802: note by Loiseleur regarding the installation of a Swedish stove in Fersen's lodging in the Queen's apartment at Versailles, 1787.

Sweden

Riksarkivet, Stockholm – Stafsund Archive

SE/RA/720807/022/11: eight letters from the Marie-Antoinette–Fersen correspondence written by the Queen's secretary François Goguelat in 1792.

SE/RA/720807/10/20: codes for the Marie-Antoinette–Fersen correspondence.

SE/RA/720807/02/6/III/10: Fersen's letter register.

SE/RA/720807/02/6/II/4 – 9: Fersen's diary.

SE/RA/720807/02/5/II/8 – 9: Fersen's letters to his father.

The Stafsund archive also contains documents relating to the flight to Varennes, diplomatic dispatches, copies of letters sent by Louis XVI and Marie-Antoinette to foreign governments and the Baron de Breteuil, part of Klinckowström's manuscript and notes for his edition of Fersen's papers, as well as Fersen's correspondence with, among others: Gustav III, Countess Sophie Piper, Baron Taube, the Chevalier de Jarjayes and Fredrik Reutersvärd.

Landsarkivet, Vadstena – Löfstad Archive

SE/VALA/02249/B XXv a/8 – 9: Fersen's letters to his sister, Countess Sophie Piper.
SE/VALA/02249/B XXv a/10: Fabian von Fersen's letters to Countess Sophie Piper.
The Löfstad archives also contain documents entrusted to Fersen for safe-keeping by Marie-Antoinette: her correspondence with Barnave, letters from Leopold II, political memoirs and other papers pertaining to the French Revolution.

England

Chatsworth – Archives of the Dukes of Devonshire

Correspondence of Georgiana, 5th Duchess of Devonshire with:
Duke of Dorset, British Ambassador to France
Lady Elizabeth Foster
Marquis de Lafayette
Duchesse de Polignac

KHLC Dorset

Archives of John Sackville, 3rd Duke of Dorset
Kent History and Library Centre, Maidstone, Kent
Correspondence of the Duke of Dorset with:
Quintin Craufurd
the Foreign Secretary (1784–90, copies of his dispatches from Paris)
British diplomats at Brussels (1791–3)

BIBLIOGRAPHY

Archives Nationales and CRCC, 'Les passages cachés des lettres de Marie-Antoinette au comte de Fersen livrent leurs premiers secrets', press release November 2015 ('The Secret Passages in Marie-Antoinette's Letters to Count Fersen Reveal Their First Secrets')

Bacourt, A. de (ed.), *Correspondance entre le Comte de Mirabeau et le Comte de La Marck pendant les années 1789, 1790 et 1791* (Paris: Librairie Veuve Le Normant, 1851)

Bibliothèque Nationale, *Lavreince: Nicolas Lafrensen, peintre suédois, 1737–1807* (Paris: Bibliothèque Nationale, May–June, 1949)

Bimbenet, Eugène (ed.), *Relation fidèle de la fuite du roi Louis XVI et de sa famille à Varennes, extraite des pièces judiciaires et administratives* (Paris: G.A. Dentu, 1844)

Boigne, Adèle, Comtesse de, *Récits d'une tante, mémoires de la Comtesse de Boigne, née d'Osmond* (Paris: Emile-Paule, 1921)

Bombelles, Marc-Marie, Marquis de, *Journal 1780–1789*, ed. J. Grassion and F. Durif, 2 vols (Geneva: Librairie Droz, 1978–82)

Bouillé, Louis Joseph Amour, Marquis de, *Souvenirs et fragments pour servir aux mémoires de ma vie et mon temps*, 2 vols (Paris: Picard, 1906)

Chapman, Caroline and Dormer, Jane, *Elizabeth and Georgiana: The Two Loves of the Duke of Devonshire* (London: John Murray, 2002)

Choiseul, Duc de, *Relation du départ de Louis XVI le 20 juin 1791* (Paris: Baudouin Frères, 1822)

Correspondance Secrète inédite sur Louis XVI, Marie-Antoinette, la Cour et la Ville, ed. M. de Lescure, 2 vols (Paris: Plon, 1866)

Craufurd, Quintin, *Mélanges d'histoire, de littérature* (1809)

_____ *Notice sur Marie-Antoinette, Reine de France* (Paris: J. Gratiot, 1819)

Elisabeth, Fille de France, *Correspondance de Madame Elisabeth*, ed. Feuillet de Conches (Paris: Plon, 1858)

Esterhazy, Valentin, Comte d', *Lettres du Comte Valentin Esterhazy à sa femme 1784–1792*, ed. E. Daudet (Paris: Plon, 1907)

_____ *Mémoires*, ed. Ernest Daudet (Paris: Plon, 1905)

Farr, Evelyn, *Marie-Antoinette and Count Fersen: The Untold Love Story* (London: Peter Owen, 2013)

Feuillet de Conches, F. (ed.), *Louis XVI, Marie-Antoinette et Madame Elisabeth: lettres et documents inédits*, 6 vols (Paris: Plon, 1864)

393

Foreman, Amanda, *Georgiana, Duchess of Devonshire* (London: Harper Collins, 1998)

Geffroy, A., *Gustave III et la Cour de France: suivi d'une étude critique sur Marie-Antoinette et Louis XVI apocryphes*, 2 vols (Paris: Didier, 1867)

Goguelat, François de, *Mémoire de M. le Baron de Goguelat sur les événements relatifs au voyage de Louis XVI à Varennes* (Paris: Baudouin, 1823)

Hutton, James, *Selections from the Letters and Correspondence of Sir James Bland Burges, Bart., Sometime Under-Secretary of State for Foreign Affairs* (London: John Murray, 1885)

Klinckowström, Baron R.M., *Le Comte de Fersen et la Cour de France: extraits des papiers de Grand Maréchal de Suède, Comte Jean Axel de Fersen*, 2 vols (Paris: Firmin-Didot, 1877–8)

Lever, Evelyne, *Marie-Antoinette: Correspondance* (Paris: Tallandier, 2005)

Liste générale et très exacte des noms, âges, qualités et demeures de tous les conspirateurs qui ont été condamnés à mort par le Tribunal Révolutionnaire établi à Paris par la loi du 17 août 1792 & par le second Tribunal établi à Paris par la loi du 10 mars 1793 pour juger tous les ennemis de la patrie (Paris, 1793)

Mercy-Argenteau, Florimond, Comte de, *Correspondance secrète entre Marie-Thérèse et le Comte de Mercy-Argenteau avec les lettres de Marie-Thérèse et de Marie-Antoinette*, ed. Alfred Arneth and A. Geffroy, 3 vols (Paris: Firmin-Didot, 1874)

_____ *Correspondance secrète du Comte de Mercy-Argenteau avec l'Empereur Joseph II et le Prince de Kaunitz*, ed. Alfred Arneth and Jules Flammermont, 2 vols (Paris: Imprimerie Nationale, 1889–91)

Morris, Gouverneur, *A Diary of the French Revolution*, ed. B.C. Davenport, 2 vols (London: Harrap, 1939)

Nachef, Valérie et Patarin, Jacques, 'Marie-Antoinette, reine . . . de la cryptologie' (*Pour la Science*, No. 382, August 2009)

_____ 'Je vous aimerai jusqu'à la mort: Marie-Antoinette à Axel de Fersen' (*Cryptologia*, Vol. 34, No. 2, 2010, pp. 104–14)

Nicolardot, Louis (ed.), *Journal de Louis XVI* (Paris: E. Dentu, 1873)

Rocheterie, M. de and Beaucourt, Marquis de, *Lettres de Marie-Antoinette: recueil des lettres authentiques de la reine*, 2 vols (Paris: Alphonse Picard, 1896)

Saint-Priest, Francis Emmanuel Guignard, Comte de, *Mémoires: règnes de Louis XV et Louis XVI*, ed. Baron de Barente (Paris: Calmann-Lévy, 1929)

Söderhjelm, Alma, *Fersen et Marie-Antoinette: correspondance et journal intime inédits du comte Axel de Fersen* (Paris: Editions Kra, 1930)

Sorg, Roger, 'Fersen, officier français et Marie-Antoinette' (*Mercure de France*, 15 July 1933)

Stuart, Dorothy M., *Dearest Bess: The Life and Times of Lady Elizabeth Foster* (London: Methuen, 1955)

Véri, Joseph Alphonse de, *Journal de l'abbé de Véri*, ed. J. de Witte, 2 vols (Paris: Tallandier, 1928 and Plon, 1930)

INDEX

American War of
Independence, 16, 17, 32, 34, 59

Anckarström, Jacob,
assassinates Gustav III of
Sweden, 22

Angoulême, Marie Thérèse
Charlotte, Duchesse de
('Madame Royale'), daughter of
Marie-Antoinette and Louis
XVI, 16, 138–9, 228, 262,
282–3, 306, 352, 360, 364

Aranda, Comte d', Spanish
prime minister and diplomat,
280–1, 288, 305, 324, 387

Artois, Charles Philippe, Comte
d' (youngest brother of Louis
XVI), 20, 41, 105, 126, 153,
189, 205, 334, 380
and Louis XVI, 124, 141–3,
151–3, 189, 334
and Marie-Antoinette, 153,
160, 169, 177–8, 181, 186, 223,
238, 282
politics, 131–2, 141–3, 148,
151, 160, 169, 178, 181, 186,
205, 230, 238, 268

Barnave, Antoine,
constitutional deputy, 27, 85,
139, 149, 152, 157–8, 165, 175,
191, 214–15, 224, 227, 233,
237, 240, 243, 255, 258–9, 262,
277, 285, 341, 381, 392
Fersen jealous of, 85, 157, 165,
214, 233, 240, 255, 262, 341

Bastille, fall of, 20, 105, 120

Boigne, Comtesse de, on Fersen
and Marie-Antoinette, 62

Bombelles, Marquis de, 41, 62,
129, 131, 208, 235, 305, 336,
373
on Fersen, 61, 64, 73
on Louis XVI, 72
on Marie-Antoinette, 60–3, 65

Bouillé, Comte Louis de, 208,
346
on Fersen and Marie-
Antoinette, 66–7

Bouillé, Marquis de, and escape
to Varennes, 125, 127, 130,
133–7, 139, 172, 220, 235, 329

Brelin, Carl (Fersen's secretary,
1791–2), 51–2, 219, 228, 238

Breteuil, Baron de, 22, 41, 45,

51, 60, 62, 64, 78, 105, 133–5,
150, 159, 337, 345, 348
Louis XVI's and Marie-
Antoinette's confidence in,
124–5, 151, 205, 213, 236, 269,
278, 281, 299
Louis XVI's brothers' hatred
for, 148, 177, 183, 202, 230–1
political role during revolution,
22, 127–32, 143, 164, 174, 184,
186, 188–90, 198, 204, 206,
208, 227, 233–4, 245, 247, 249,
251, 264, 269, 271–2, 274, 279,
286–7, 292, 297, 305, 316,
329–30

Brunswick, Duke of, Prussian
general, 234–5, 240, 275, 300,
309, 311, 323, 328, 330, 334–7,
340

Brunswick Manifesto, 311, 323,
327, 329, 331, 334, 385, 389
suggested by Swedish regent,
293–4

Calonne, Charles Alexandre de,
41, 143, 164–5, 173–4, 185,
230, 323–4, 336, 380
Louis XVI's and Marie-
Antoinette's mistrust of, 124,
148, 179

Campan, Madame, 16, 38, 57,
84, 261, 353

Caraman, Vicomte de, 312, 330,
388

Carlos IV, King of Spain, 41,
117, 125–7, 130–1, 162, 164,
173, 175, 184, 188, 192–3, 199,
203–5, 210–11, 222, 231,
280–1, 297, 299, 305, 318

Castries, Maréchal de, 34, 174,
181, 212, 230, 235, 245, 279,
330

Catherine II, Empress of Russia,
41, 93, 161–2, 164, 173, 179,
184–6, 195–6, 200, 204, 206,
208–9, 213, 220, 223, 233, 236,
248, 250–1, 275, 281, 291, 294,
297, 299–300, 304, 311, 323,
336, 352, 373, 383

Charles X, see Artois, Comte d'

Choiseul-Stainville, Duc de, 38,
136, 219–20, 346

Chou d'Amour, see Louis XVII

Coblentz, French émigré

princes and émigrés there, 164,
173–4, 179, 181–3, 185–6, 205,
207, 212, 218, 220, 226–7, 230,
234, 284, 300, 305, 311–12,
383, 385–6

Coigny, Chevalier de, 45, 164–5,
168, 282, 380, 382

Conciergerie, prison, 23, 355,
360, 362–3

Condé, Prince de, 126, 131–2,
330, 351, 381

Cowper, Miss Emily, 67

Craufurd, Quintin, 41, 55, 57,
124, 136, 141, 148–9, 156, 161,
164, 168–9, 177, 183, 185, 190,
197, 208, 214, 221, 225–6, 228,
234, 238–40, 246, 248, 250,
254–6, 259–60, 263–4, 266–7,
270, 272, 274, 277, 279, 285–8,
291–2, 316, 325, 331, 340–1, 372
and Eléonore Sullivan, 68,
137–8, 265, 287, 337, 359, 365
on Fersen, 112–13, 139
on Lafayette and duc d'Orléans,
282
on Marie-Antoinette, 187,
261–2, 282–3
on paternity of Louis XVII,
113, 339

Creutz, Count (Swedish
Ambassador to France), 60
on Fersen and Marie-
Antoinette, 32

Dauphin, Louis-Charles
(1785–95), *see* Louis XVII

Dauphin, Louis-Joseph
(1781–89), 17, 20, 61, 66, 72,
78, 82, 102

De La Gardie, Mademoiselle
(Fersen's aunt), lodgings at
Versailles, 105, 377–8

Devonshire, Georgiana, 5th
Duchess of, 10, 85, 89, 375, 392
and Lady Elizabeth Foster, 66, 69
correspondence with Lafayette
in support of Marie-
Antoinette, 140, 158–9,
214–17, 225
on Fersen, 88
correspondence with the Duke
of Dorset, 55, 84–7, 118, 283

Diamond Necklace Affair, 18,
81–2

395